IMPERIUM

Much has been said already about this unique and disturbing book, but this much is reasonably certain: A thousand times more is yet to be said.

Imperium is the first sequel the literary world knows to Spengler's monumental *The Decline of the West*.

In fact, the author of *Imperium* does more than even Spengler attempted—he defines and creates the *pathology of Culture* in all of its infinitely urgent importance, including the discipline of *Cultural Vitalism*.

Imperium rejects the Nineteenth Century: the parched fossils of its thought—Marx, Freud and the scientific-technical world outlook; its exhausted political nostrums—the pluralistic state, liberalism, democracy, communism, internationalism; all of which fail to satisfy the organically vital realities of politics.

Imperium presents unique and almost esoteric political, social and historical definitions and explanations which shall become more widely known—indeed, commonly understood—if our West survives.

Imperium is probably the first book to advocate European unification—to dogmatically predict it—in terms other than the crassly materialistic.

Imperium is the first comprehensive and profoundly constructive alternative to the Marxist-liberal degeneracy surrounding us.

Imperium is the creation of a man who believed in his Destiny—and in this book—so thoroughly that he became a martyr to it.

Imperium is written with a dramatic style and flair for expression seldom encountered even in novels.

Yet rising above all else is the simple fact that in *Imperium* a creative genius has given the world something new: A fourth dimension of intellect and a new concept of spirituality. *Imperium* heralds the dawn of a new day of Faith.

Among all books, therefore, *Imperium* has a distinct status. Hardly a man alive will agree with all it contains, yet will not find his personal horizons extended by the reading of it.

The original two volumes are here combined, unabridged, into one, with a brilliant Introduction by W.A. Carto.

IMPERIUM

THE PHILOSOPHY OF HISTORY AND POLITICS

ULICK VARANGE

(Francis Parker Yockey)

THE NOONTIDE PRESS

Copyright©1962 by

The Noontide Press
1822½ Newport Blvd., Suite 183
Costa Mesa, CA 92627 USA

Library of Congress
Catalog card number: 62-53156
Call number: CD 425 V42i

ISBN: 0-911038-10-8

Manufactured in the United States of America

First published, 1948.

First Noontide edition, 1962.
First hardback printing, November 1962.
Second printing, May 1963.

First Noontide paperback printing, May 1969.
Second paperback printing, April 1983.
Third paperback printing, February 1991.

To the hero of the Second World War

Was mich nicht umbringt, macht mich stärker

NIETZSCHE

Introduction

DIMLY, I could make out the form of this man—this strange and lonely man—through the thick wire netting. Inwardly, I cursed these heavy screens that prevented our confrontation. For even though our mutual host was the San Francisco County Jail, and even though the man upon whom I was calling was locked in equality with petty thieves and criminals, I knew that I was in the presence of a great force, and I could feel History standing aside me.

Yesterday, the headlines had exploded their sensational discovery. "MYSTERY MAN WITH THREE PASSPORTS JAILED HERE," they screamed. A man of mystery—of wickedness—had been captured. A man given to dark deeds and—much worse— forbidden thoughts, too, the journalists squealed. A man who had roamed the earth on mysterious missions and who was found to be so dangerous that his bail was set at $50,000—a figure ten or twenty times the normal bail for passport fraud. The excitement of the newspapers and the mystery of it all seemed to indicate that this desperado was an international gangster, or a top communist agent.

At least, this is what the papers hinted. But I know now that it erred in many ways, this "free press" of ours.

I know now that the only real crime of Francis Parker Yockey was to write a book, and for this he had to die.

* * *

It is always impossible, of course, to come to grips with the essence of greatness. There are the known facts of a great life, but facts are dead and almost mute when we seek the essential reality of a creative personality. But let us review some of the facts we know of a life which is at once significant, fascinating and tragic.

Francis Parker Yockey was born in Chicago in 1917. He attended American universities, taking a B.A. degree in 1938 and, three years later, a degree in law from Notre Dame, where he was graduated *cum laude*.

From earliest childhood, Yockey was recognized for his prodigious abilities, and resented for them by many. History may reveal that the combination of originality and high intelligence in rare individuals is essential for human progress, but we mortals find these qualities more admired in biographies than in classmates, friends and underlings.

Yockey was a concert-level pianist; he was a gifted writer. He studied languages and became a linguist. As a lawyer, he never lost a case. He had an extraordinary grasp of the world of finance —and this is surprising, for we learn that in his philosophy economics is relegated to a relatively unimportant position. And it is as the Philosopher that Yockey reached the summit; it is this for which he will be remembered; he was a man of incredible vision. Even so, his personality was spiced by the precious gift of a sense of humor.

Like the great majority of Americans, Yockey opposed American intervention in the Second World War. Nevertheless, he joined the army and served until 1942 when he received a medical discharge (honorable). The next few years were spent in the practice of law, first in Illinois and subsequently in Detroit, where he was appointed Assistant County Attorney for Wayne County, Michigan.

In 1946, Yockey was offered a job with the war crimes tribunal and went to Europe. He was assigned to Wiesbaden, where the "second string" Nazis were lined up for trial and punishment. The Europe of 1946 was a war-ravaged continent, not the prosperous land we know today. Viewing the carnage, and seeing with his own eyes the visible effects of the unspeakable Morgenthau Plan which had as its purpose the starvation of 30 million Germans, and which was being put into effect at that time, he no doubt found ample reinforcement for his conviction that American involvement in the war had been a ghastly mistake. And feeling the might of the sinister power in the East, he might well have wondered whose interests were being served by such a "victory."

As Senator Robert A. Taft and many other responsible and thinking men of the day who had the courage to state their convictions, Yockey concluded that the entire procedure of the "war crimes trials" was serving the interests—*and was meant to serve the interests*—of international communism The use of torture, doctored evidence and *ex-post-facto* law before a court which was judge, jury, prosecutor and defense were merely part of the preposterous juridical aspects. Of even more importance was the reversion to barbarism which was inherent in the spectacle—a reversion so pointedly explored later by Britisher F. J. P. Veale in *Advance to Barbarism.*

For eleven months, Yockey's duty in Wiesbaden was to prepare reports on the various cases. Having a long view of history, he tried to do an objective job. Finally, in Washington, someone complained, and his superior called him on the carpet. "We don't want this type of report," he was told. "This has entirely the wrong slant. You'll have to rewrite these reports to conform with the official viewpoint."

Yockey felt that the time had come to take a stand, even if it meant to break with conformity and plunge into the lonely waters of social ostracism. "I am a lawyer, not a journalist," he said, "you'll have to write your own propaganda"; and he quit on the spot.

After Wiesbaden, he returned to America for five months. But following this taste of *weltpolitik* he was unable to settle down. He could not ignore an insistent feeling that he must immolate himself in the flames of controversy. And this conviction so destroyed his peace of mind that he knew he had no choice.

It was late 1947 when Yockey returned to Europe. He sought out a quiet inn at Brittas Bay, Ireland. Isolated, he struggled to begin. Finally, he started to write, and in six months—working entirely without notes—Francis Parker Yockey completed *Imperium*.

The formidable task of publishing it was the next step. Here, also, Yockey ran into serious problems, for no publisher would touch the book, it being too "controversial." Hungry publishers of our advanced day know that any pile of trash, filth, sex, sadism, perversion and sickness will sell when wrapped between two gaudy covers and called a book, but under no circumstances may they allow readers to come into contact with a serious work unless it contains the standard obeisances to the catchwords of equality, democracy and universal brotherhood.

Finally, however, Yockey was able to secure the necessary financing, and production began.

The first edition of *Imperium* was issued in two volumes. Volume I has 405 pages and three chapters. Volume II has 280 pages and also three chapters. Both were published in 1948 in the name of Westropa Press. Volume I was printed by C. A. Brooks & Co., Ltd. and Volume II by Jones & Dale—both of London. Both volumes measure 5 x 7¼ inches in dimensions and have a red dust jacket with the title in black script on a white field. The cover of Volume I is tan and that of Volume II is black.

It is known that 1000 copies of Volume I, but only 200 copies of Volume II, were finished. The discrepancy in quantity and the change in printers point to the difficulty in financing the job. Copies of the first edition are, of course, virtually unobtainable today.

The rarest combination in man is that of the philosopher and man of action. When Yockey tried his hand at political organization he proved that he was no exception to the rule—or was it that the times then were too out of joint with the future for a constructive movement to be started? Organizing the European Liberation Front in 1949, he and friends issued a manifesto called *The Proclamation of London.* But outside of getting beaten up in Hyde Park, nothing much happened. And here again he encountered the old trouble. Even among the forward-looking intellectuals and individualists who were his co-workers, his brilliance shone through. He was resented, and the effort soon collapsed.

His money and immediate hopes gone, Yockey procured a job with the Red Cross. He resigned in 1951 and travelled throughout Europe.

In 1952 the State Department refused to renew his passport. Repeatedly, he applied; each time he was rejected. A game then developed between the FBI and Yockey, for the FBI had received orders to keep him under surveillance at all times. This is a pattern which has since become obvious to vigorous anti-communists in all parts of the United States, especially in the South. When Yockey's whereabouts was known, the FBI would watch him night and day. When he dropped temporarily from sight, as he did frequently, his friends and relatives and contacts were constantly interrogated by agents who—they kept repeating—"just want to talk to him."

And this was undoubtedly the truth. This is all they wanted to do. They just wanted to know where he was, what he was doing, whom he was seeing, what he was saying and where he was going next.

Why, you ask? Why all the interest in Francis Parker Yockey, author? He himself gave the answer to a friend. "My enemies have evaluated me better than my friends," he said, and it was true.

* * *

And as I peered through the thick screens in the San Francisco Jail, and made out the indefinite shape on the other side, that tenth day of June, 1960, I knew that I would have to help the prisoner as best I could. I could do nothing else.

I have read your book, I said to the shadow, and I want to help you. What can I do?

Wait, he said. Wait, and do as your conscience tells you.

The following week was full of news of Yockey's appearance before Rabbi Joseph Karesh, the U.S. Commissioner.

Twice, I attended the hearings, and each time was fascinated by this man, Yockey. In stature he was about five feet, ten inches. He was light of weight, perhaps 145 pounds, and quick on his feet. His hair was dark, and starting to grey. The expression on his face—pensive, sensitive, magnetic—this was the unforgettable thing. It was his eyes, I think. Dark, with a quick and knowing intelligence. His eyes bespoke great secrets and knowledge and such terrible sadness. As he turned to leave, one time, those eyes quickly searched the room, darting from face to face with a sort of desperation, though the expression on his face of a determined resignation never wavered. What was he looking for? In that lions' den, what else but a friendly countenance? As his gaze swept across, and then to me, he stopped and for the space of a fractional second, spoke to me with his eyes. In that instant we understood that I would not desert him.

Friday morning, June 17, I arose as usual. I heard the radio announcer pronounce words that stunned me.

June 17

Yockey was dead.

"I'll sleep through 'til morning" was the cryptic message he gave his cellmate, last night. Was the morning he anticipated the dawn of a new age?

A garbled note was found. The coroner declared it suicide and said the poison was potassium cyanide. No one knew where he had gotten it. The case was closed.

As Americans, we have been taught from infancy to believe that we live in a free country. But times change, and America has become transformed in many ways. Often, the old formalities are observed, but the meaning and inner reality of America has changed, and no one saw this more clearly than Francis Parker Yockey. How the press, for example, loves to brag to its victims—its readers—about its freedom. Yes, the press may be free to lie and distort and suppress and deceive and malign, but is it free to tell the truth?

The spectacle of a man being persecuted, framed and driven to his death simply because he wrote a book is not one we would expect to see in the Twentieth Century in the land of the free and the home of the brave.

But are we free when an American citizen whose only crime was to write a book is denied a passport by the State Department —a privilege which is given to all but the most notorious degenerates and criminals? It was not until April 24, 1962, that the State Department finally got around to beginning hearings to deny passports to the most important communists—but the "free press" somehow forgot to report at the time that no report of a confidential nature from the FBI or any other source would be used against a communist unless he was given the "right" of confrontation with his accuser. And, of course, the right of appeal would be scrupulously honored, even then.

Are we free when a citizen can be arrested without a warrant and held in jail without charges, but with the fantastic bail of $50,000 levied against him? Are we free when the vultures of the

"fress press" can swoop down upon the victim to heap calumny
and scorn upon his head and accuse him of doing things he never
did and saying things he never said in an effort to build up
"public opinion" against him? Is America a free country when a
sensitive genius can be held in the filthiest of jails with Negro
and White criminals and is denied even clean clothes and a bath?
Are we free when such a "criminal" is not allowed to see his
sisters in private, and when a group which has supposedly been
set up to defend the constitutional rights of citizens—the American Civil Liberties Union—would rather defend the "rights" of
homosexuals, traitors, murderers and pornographers than a sin-
cere patriot like Francis Parker Yockey, whose every thought
and effort was in behalf of his fellow man? Are we free, I ask,
when a judge can rule that a prisoner is not to have a "speedy and
public trial by an impartial jury . . . ," as guaranteed in the Bill
of Rights, but, instead, must have a mental examination for the
obvious purpose of eliminating a jury trial altogether? And
finally, are we free when another group—vastly more powerful
than the ACLU or the government itself—so powerful, indeed,
that men dare not speak its name above a whisper, unless in terms
of the most groveling praise—are we free when this group is able
to dictate to the government the exact procedure which is to be
used in disposing of troublemakers like Francis Parker Yockey?

If such things as I have enumerated can happen—and they did
—then our vaunted "freedom" is a fake thing; an empty word
given to us by our watchful masters to keep us amused and quiet
—as a parent gives a shiny bauble to a child.

It is enlightening to review the standard means whereby our
masters combat positive ideas and movements. There is a pattern
in such tactics which constructive forces will do well to study. The
first tactic is suppression and determined non-recognition of the
rebel and his works. The press will unanimously give the well-
known "silent treatment." Even at this early stage, if the movement gives promise of becoming significant, assassination is con-

sidered and carried out if possible. The murder of young Newton Armstrong, Jr., in San Diego, on the night of March 31, 1962, is a case in point. Quoting from Che Guevara's book on guerilla warfare and the question of when to resort to assassination:

> *It is generally against the policy of the Communist Party to resort to assassination . . . However, it requires two criteria and a high-level policy decision . . . The criteria for the individual in question are that he must be highly effective and it must serve some sort of example—some sort of a highly effective example.*

The next tactic is the Smear through libel, distortion, misrepresentation and the sowing of confusion wherever possible. This may be a negative smear with the purpose of destroying the effectiveness of an enemy or a positive smear for the purpose of building a haze around the truth to enable a disintegrative movement to develop. The falsification of the truth about Castro which was indulged in by virtually all of the press and, of course, the State Department, is a classic example of this. The Smear is usually started as an underground whispering campaign that viciously builds up to an outright and overt campaign, with the "free press" called into play. The object is to isolate enemies of the present regime and discredit them. The third tactic is infiltration into the movement and/or the building up of false leadership in order to sabotage the movement at the optimum time, meanwhile diverting patriot energies into harmless or controlled activities. The fourth and final stage is called upon only as a last resort, after the movement or philosophy has become institutionalized and is immune to grosser tactics. This is to "interpret" it so as to bring it as closely as possible into conformity with approved patterns. (Characteristically, the conflicting philosophies of both Jesus Christ and Friedrich Nietzsche have suffered this deadening interpretation.) Two or more of the above maneuvers are usually used simultaneously. For instance, in addition to the suppression of his *Imperium*, Yockey was also victimized by the Smear; and he was also in danger of assassination—and his enigmatic end settled the problem. Now it is with no gift of prophecy that one may predict that this present republication of his work will call forth the same sequence.

I tell you that the injustice of it all is enough to drive one mad. How can a man stomach the cynical or ignorant drivel of the liberals as they whine for "freedom of speech" and "right to dissent" and shake their bony fists at "conformity" and all the rest of their legerdemain when one knows that these moral cripples and ethical perverts demand their peculiar freedoms only for those who are working to destroy the West? We have seen their reaction when one committed to saving the West is in need of some of their medicine.

It was like a certain wise, old reporter whispered to one of Yockey's sisters as she slumped tearfully and quietly in her solitude. "Your brother is a martyr—the first of a long line of them —if we are to take back our country from those who have stolen it from us."

A surprising word on the Yockey affair came some weeks after his death, and was provided by the tight-lipped silence of the man who had been charged with railroading him to the insane asylum, the United States Attorney. Suddenly, inexplicably, he resigned his job, left his wife and children and joined a monastery.

Let us assume that at least one devoted servant of the Democracy has a conscience, even if displayed a little late.

* * *

Please allow me to expose to you my prejudice so that there will be no misunderstanding. *I favor the survival of our Western cultural organism.* I love those who fight for the integrity of the

West, whoever they may be. And, as much as I fear and mistrust the outer enemies of the West, I despise our inner enemies and the cowards who support them far more—and I hate their putrid doctrine that calls our continuing degradation "inevitable."

Further, I believe that the West *can* survive. It all hinges on *faith:* faith in our future; faith in our superiority and survival. Skepticism, sophistication, cosmopolitanism, cynicism has destroyed the old faith, and it has not been replaced by a new one. But faith is and will always remain the essential ingredient in every historical force. Only a unifying faith can provide the common motivation for survival—the just and deep conviction of our right to live—and spark the single-minded and intolerant power which can clean and redeem our fast-decaying, rotting milieu. Very simply: the imperative of inspiring that faith is the central problem of our time.

And when I say, "survive," I mean nothing more. For we are so far gone; our philosophies, liberties and cultural patterns are so perverted or eroded that bare survival is all that is possible. I mean to say that those who are to save the West must realize at the outset that only part of it can be saved; that much must be sacrificed and that the resulting structure will be different from the past. Those who have gone before have allowed the dank "winds of change" to corrode the old life, and many weeds have sprung up which cannot entirely be eliminated. It is one thing to fight for an attainable ideal, but another to sacrifice for a lost cause. In determining what is attainable and what is forever lost a philosophy of history is needed.

And although our job is to *rebuild* we must not lose sight of the reality, for we cannot rebuild until we have *captured.* Political power is the essential criterion, not wishes or windbags, and to the goal of political power all else must be temporarily sacrificed. To say less is to insure defeat. He who is on board a sinking ship in a storm may be required to throw all his possessions overboard if this is necessary for common survival. Or, to use another image:

Those who would guide the West back across the Styx and out of the dark must travel first through the gates of Hell.

The practical problem of the recapture of political power divides itself into other questions. For one, is it possible to formulate an ethic and faith which, in itself, offers at least as much popular attractiveness as the painted lie of Marx? For another, how can those who would naturally lead such a movement compete with the highly-developed Leninistic operational diabolism in the perpetually savage and untamable jungle of political warfare—or is it necessary to do so? After all, the conspiracy we face is the hideous monster spawned of four millenniums of experience in guile and deception; so much so, in fact, that its main ally always has been the obtuse blindness of those on whom it feeds. "Struggle" to a man of the West means bullets, armies, and aircraft carriers. But to our enemy, international wars are of little meaning; "struggle" to him means not war but politics, and accordingly he has perfected his weapons in this most decisive of areas. Soldiers have never made good politicians, and, by the nature of their respective crafts, the soldier must always lose to the man of politics.

Finally comes the main consideration in formulating such a doctrine: *will it certainly eradicate the politico-social evils and diseases of our day and lead mankind toward a better world?*

It is by this standard and no other that you will, if you are wise, judge the work of Francis Parker Yockey.

To quit the search for such an ethic is to abandon history like the intellectual and spiritual nihilists—the liberals and beatniks. To quit the search is to turn over to the inner enemy *carte blanche* control over our lives, souls and fate.

The failure to provide this philosophy is not alone the fault of the saprophytes among us, however. Nor is it only the fault of the chameleon-like inner enemy of the West (the Culture Distorter, to use Yockey's apt term) which mercilessly persecutes and smashes all who dare to cry out against our rapid decline and degeneration; in all truth, it is mainly the fault of the many thousands who fully know the issues at stake yet have not the moral courage to identify and fight the Culture Distorter; or—worse yet —who have, by diligent self-persuasion, convinced themselves that the battle for survival against an enemy that demands nothing less than total surrender can be fought and won with tax-deductible corporations, measured, "moderate" words and avoidance of "extremists." These dainty combatants swarm over every anti-communist movement like ants on sugar. By shrilly demonstrating their anti-communism they bribe their consciences to give them peace and often go so far as to join in the crucifixion of those few with moral courage lest they, too, be adjudged "guilty" by association. America has too many of such anti-communists and too few real patriots.

There is much in *Imperium* which can be easily misinterpreted. There is something for everyone to agree with. And there is something for everyone to disagree with. This is a distinguishing characteristic of every truly vital and revolutionary departure.

Yockey's criticism of Darwinism is an example of the first possibility, and it should be borne in mind that he is speaking of *journalistic Darwinism*, not the theory of evolution. A related point is his usage of the word, *race*. It would have added to clarity if another word, such as *nobility*, was used to describe those who feel the Imperative of the Age, for the genetic interpretation of race is a necessary, useful and valid one if we are to see all of our problems clearly and accurately. Also, Yockey cites some tests of doubtful validity when he asserts that children of immigrants into America are quite different in anthropological measurements than their parents. There is no doubt some truth to this; there are bodily differences caused by food and climate, but such conclusions can be carried into the realm of Lysenkoism unless great caution is used. Troyfim Lysenko is the Russian communist quack and high priest who "proved" through his hocus-pocus that environment and not heredity creates the man. Such a theory is the basic fallacy upon which the entire communist theory of man rests, though few people realize this. But heredity is a matter of genes and genes never change except through mutation unless genes of one type (race) are mixed with genes of another type (race). One of the best books on the subject to appear recently is Dr. Conway Zirkle's *Evolution, Marxian Biology and the Social Scene.* Evolution, biology and genetic inheritance must be treated as matters of life-facts, and any theory for the future has to accept them.

Yockey's usage of the word *authority* may be a source of misinterpretation. It should be remembered that the individual enjoyed far more liberty in Europe under the monarchs than in America, today. Doubters should familiarize themselves with Edmund Burke, Thomas Carlyle, Herbert Spencer, and the more recent work of Otto von Habsburg, *The Social Order of Tomorrow.* It is sure that by the use of this word, he does not mean Marxist-type collectivization.

Some readers have raised the question of Yockey's apparent anti-Russianism, and a clarifying word is necessary here. In later writings, Yockey made his views on Russia more clear; in fact, certain of his captors called him "anti-American and pro-Russian," during his San Francisco ordeal. Although this libel was of course vomited for the benefit of gullible newspaper readers, it shows that some of his later writings could have been misinterpreted as being pro-Russian, just as *Imperium* indicates an anti-Russian attitude. Of course, Yockey was neither pro- nor anti-Russian; he was concerned with the health and continuity of the West, and his view of the rest of the world was at all times subjective to what he considered in the best interests of the West *at that time.*

Accusations of "anti-Semitism," unless the imprecation is meant as simply having an open mind on the Jewish question, should be interpreted on the same level. The fact that he was captured in the home of a Jewish friend—even though that friend subsequently repudiated him—is instructive to the truth here.

Comment could be made on dozens of the brilliant thoughts and concepts presented in *Imperium,* such as, for one example, his relegating economics to its proper level—organically, the alimentary tract. His advocacy of European unification, long before this idea had gained any headway, is another case in point. This is perhaps a proof of his assertion that things that are considered "extreme" today are the dogmas of tomorrow; the genius lives in the future, as he says, and whereas he used to be considered merely a little "odd" by his contemporaries, and avoided or tolerantly humored (unless, that is, he incurred the righteous wrath of the Church, in which case things could be made very hot for him) he is today declared by modern Freudianism to be mentally ill and unfit for the ancient protections of law; and this is surely indicative of the "progress" we have made in a thousand years.

The significance of the pseudonym Yockey chose as author of *Imperium,* Ulick Varange, should be noted. Ulick is an Irish given name, derived from Danish, and means "reward of the mind." Varange, of course, refers to the Varangians, that far-roving band of Norse heroes led by Rurik who, upon invitation from the Slavs, came to civilize Russia in the 9th Century, built the Russian Imperial State and formed the gifted and handsome Russian aristocracy until they were butchered by the Bolsheviks—along with some 20 million other Christians and Moslems—in that bloody terror. The name, therefore, drawn as it is from the Eastern and Western antipodes of Europe, signifies a Europe united "from the rocky promontories of Galway to the Urals," as he, himself, exhorts. Finally, the surname, Varange, by itself signifies the Western origin of historic Russia.

Imperium throughout is—again as the author says—not a book in the sense that it presents *argument.* It is *prophetic;* the work of an intuitive seer. You will find no bibliography or footnotes in *Imperium* for this reason in spite of the vast reading that the author has obviously done. And it is prophetic not only in the large historical sense, for could Yockey have been thinking of him-

self and predicting his own violent end when he stresses that the
prophets of a new age often come to unnatural deaths? Twice this
thought is brought out—once in the chapter THE ARTICULA-
TION OF A CULTURE, and again, GENIUS.

Another interesting and mysterious fact about the manuscript
he completed at Brittas Bay and that you now hold in your hand is
that it is "keyed" so that, if the secret code can be discovered, the
author's name is spelled. Thus, the question of authenticity which
is always raised about a great work after the author dies cannot
ever be a problem with *Imperium*.

* * *

It is important to seek the origins of Yockey's philosophy, for all
are compelled to build on the backs of those who have gone before
and to see the past clearly is to understand more fully. With more
exaggeration than accuracy, Yockey states, "There is nothing original in the content of this book."

A grounding in Oswald Spengler is fundamental to understanding Yockey; in fact, it can be said that *Imperium* is really a sequel
to Spengler's monumental *The Decline of the West*. Spengler, of
course, is *persona non grata* to prevailing "intellects" for reasons
that become very clear to any reader of *Decline,* so this revival of
his influence—an inevitable revival, I'll add—will be a great
shock to the tender minds of the beatniks, liberals and communists who have sucked at the dry pap of historical conformity for
so long. These intellectual infants are always very eager to assure
us that Spengler is "repudiated," a favorite semantic weapon of
theirs, used regularly whenever they wish to avoid discussing issues
and facts.

But Oswald Spengler—"the philosopher of the Twentieth Century," as Yockey calls him—along with Gregor Mendel, Thomas
Malthus and Charles Darwin—has shown us the pattern of the
world of yesterday and the outline of it in the future, for better or

for worse. Each of these giants is primary in his own field of study, and to study history while rejecting Spengler is quite as foolish as studying disease and rejecting the germ theory, or studying mathematics and rejecting numbers. The pathetic intellectual nihilists, materialists, equalists and do-gooders may yap, yap at the heels of Spengler until they are hoarse, but History cannot hear them.

"In this book is attempted for the first time the venture of pre-determining history . . ." Spengler opens *Decline,* and follows it with two thick volumes of delightful and profound excursions into world history, war, philosophy, poetry, music, art, politics, religion, even mathematics.

Perhaps the best synopsis of Spengler—if there can be such a thing—has been done by Egon Friedell in his *A Cultural History of the Modern Age,* a three-volume work of which, incidentally, Yockey was very fond. Says Friedell in listing significant thinkers:

Lastly, and with deep admiration, we come to the name of Oswald Spengler, perhaps the most powerful and vivid thinker to appear on German soil since Nietzsche. One has to climb very high in the world's literature to find works of such scintillating and exuberant intellect, such triumphant psychological vision and such a personal and suggestive, rhythmic cadence as his *Decline of the West.* What Spengler gives us in his two volumes is the "outlines of a morphology of history." He sees, in place of the "monotonous picture of linear world-history" the "phenomenon of a plurality of mighty Cultures." "Each Culture has its own new possibilities of self-expression, which arise, ripen, decay and never return. There is not *one* sculpture, *one* painting, *one* mathematic, *one* physics, but many, each in its deepest essence different from the others, each limited in duration and self-contained, just as each species of plant has its peculiar blossom or fruit, its special type of growth and decline. These Cultures, sublimated life-essences, grow with the same superb aimlessness as the flowers of the field." Cultures are

organisms, and cultural history is their biography. Spengler
establishes nine such Cultures, the Babylonian, the Egyptian, the
Indian, the Chinese, the Classical, the Arabian, the Mexican,
the Western and the Russian, and he throws light upon each in
turn, naturally not an equally bright and full light in every case,
as, of course, our information concerning them is very unequal.
But in the evolutionary course of these Cultures certain paral-
lelisms rule, and this leads Spengler to introduce the conception
of "contemporary" phenomena, by which he understands historical facts that, "each in its own Culture, occur in the same—
relative—positions and, therefore, have an exactly corresponding significance." "Contemporary," for example, are the rise of
the Ionic and that of the Baroque; Polygnotus and Rembrandt,
Polycletus and Bach, Socrates and Voltaire are "contemporaries." But within the individual Culture itself, too, there is naturally complete congruence of all its life-expressions at each of
its stages of evolution. So, for instance, there is a deep connection of form between the Classical Polis and the Euclidean ge-
ometry, between the space-perspective of the Western oil-painting and the conquest of space by railways, telephones, and
long-range weapons. By means of these and like guiding principles, now Spengler arrives at the most interesting and surprising discoveries. The "Protestant brown" of the Dutch and the
atheistic *plein air* of the Manet school, the "Way" as prime
symbol of the Egyptian Soul, and the "Plain" as the leitmotiv
of the Russian world-outlook, the "Magian" Culture of the
Arabs and the "Faustian" Culture of the West, the "second
religiousness" in which late Cultures revive the images of their
youth, and the "fellahdom" in which man becomes again historyless—these, and many more like them, are unforgettable
glimpses of genius that light up for a moment vast tracts of
night, incomparable discoveries and hints of an intellect that
possesses a truly creative eye for analogies. That the Cimmeri-
ans of learning have opposed to such a work nothing but stolid-

ity and a deaf incomprehension of what his questions and answers are about is not surprising to anyone who knows the customs and mentality of the republic of scholarship.

Spengler published *Decline* in July, 1918, and we are still being washed in the very first breakwaters of that titanic event. For *The Decline of the West* was fully as revolutionary to the study of history in 1918 as Copernicus' theory of heliocentricity was to the study of astronomy in 1543.

What, we may ask, is the main cause of resistance to accepting Spengler aside from the fact that he is a massive roadblock to the total victory of the marxist-liberal "intellectual"? The main difficulties, I think, are two: the necessity of acknowledging the essentially alien nature of every cultural soul, and the apparent necessity to reconcile ourselves to the dismal fact that our own Western organism must, too, die as have all those which have passed before.

Paradoxically, the fundamental problem of the second difficulty lies in the very Faustian Soul of the West which Spengler himself defined: *"The Faustian Soul—whose prime symbol is pure and limitless space,"* he said; and it is true, for we need, in our innermost being, the perpetual reach to infinity. The idea of unlimited *progress* flows from this spiritual reality; this is a concept which is deeply and inextricably imbedded in every man of the West. Thus, the thought of inevitable death draws a fundamental rejection and is called pessimism.

As for the first specific difficulty, the acknowledgment of the essentially alien nature of each cultural soul, it follows that if every culture has its own inner vitality, it will be uninfluenced by the spirit of any other. This also runs against the very deepest grain of Western man who, for five hundred years and more, has been proselyting men all over the world in the vain hope of making them over into his own beloved image.

This psychological block runs deep in the West—so deep that

it is an error which is apparent in all philosophical strata, certainly not only the leftist variety. Name any philosopher, economist or religious adept of Western history, except Hegel * (yes, even including Spengler) and you are virtually certain to find a man who sought to lay *universal* laws of human behavior; who, in other words, saw no essential difference between races. This error is so fundamental it is usually unconscious. (What would Lord Keynes, for example, do with his "universal" theory of *oversaving* if he were to try to apply it to Ghana or Haiti?) The Roman Catholic Church is a case in point. Tradition-minded Westerners rightly speak of the Church as being a bulwark of the West, but sometimes go so far as to identify the Church *as* the West. Unfortunately, the compliment is not returned. The Holy Roman Church is a *universal* Church—one Church for all men—which sees all people, wherever they are and whoever they be, as equal human souls whose bodies are to be brought to the holy embrace of Vatican City. It is the first to reject the impious suggestion that it owes a primary loyalty to the West. Scientific and philosophical demonstrations that men and cultures are, nevertheless, different in many fundamental respects and that it is unhealthy—*unethical*—to mix

* Extracts from the interesting Introduction to Georg Wilhelm Friedrich Hegel's *Philosophy of History:*

"The peculiarly African character is difficult to comprehend, for the very reason that in reference to it we must quite give up the principle which accompanies all our ideas—the category of Universality. . . . Another characteristic fact in reference to the Negro is slavery. . . . Bad as this may be, their lot in their own land is even worse, since a slavery there quite as absolute exists; for it is the essential principle of slavery, that man has not yet attained to a consciousness of his own freedom, and consequently sinks down to a mere Thing—an object of no value. Among the Negro moral sentiments are quite weak, or more strictly speaking, non-existent. Parents sell their children and conversely children their parents, as either has the opportunity . . . the polygamy of the Negroes has frequently for its object the having of many children, to be sold, every one of them, into slavery . . . From these various traits it is manifest that want of self-control distinguishes the character of the Negroes. This condition is capable of no development or culture, and as we see them at this day, such have they always been. . . . At this point we leave Africa, not to mention it again. For it is no historical part of the World; it has no movement or development to exhibit."

them are sure to meet with the same inhospitable reception that the Church earlier gave to Copernicus and Galileo. In April of 1962 three Catholics in New Orleans were excommunicated for daring to stand on this heretical Verity.*

A central point when thinking about this subject is the growth and now the total supremacy of the Western idea of technics. The entire world of science is a reflection of Western man and no other, and we have seen Western technics conquer the world. We see our science being appropriated to varying degrees and in varying manners by every simian Culture on the planet which has advanced beyond the arboreal stage. The stone age Negro denizens of Africa, Haiti, New Guinea and the southern Philippines are fascinated by clocks, radios and even sails. When an American city wants to get rid of its old street cars, it sells them to Amerindian Mexico. The Semitic Arabs ride their Cadillacs and use rifles

---

* In his final work, *History of the People of Israel,* Ernest Renan said, "Socialism may bring back by the complicity of Catholicism a new Middle Age." And there are, indeed, some rather horrifying straws in the wind as regards the Church's traditional hostility toward communism. March 7, 1963 witnessed the Pope grasping the hand of Alexi Adzheubi, an official representative of the same Bolshevism which so far has murdered at least 50 million patriots in Russia, China and elsewhere. What are millions to think—Catholic and non-Catholic—who have heretofore looked upon Rome as a bulwark against this unspeakably degenerate conspiracy? (Decent Catholics should not be too surprised or chagrined; Protestant sects by and large were captured by the Culture Distorter years ago.) But should the two equalitarian religions converge, compromise is required on the part of the Communist Party, too; being totally bankrupt intellectually, this is not too great a price. An anonymous letter supposedly written by a CP member was reprinted in the May, 1963 *Truth Seeker,* a strongly anti-communist free-thought periodical. It bears repetition:

". . . The Party has soft-pedaled atheism for years and now we are dropping it completely. Atheism divides the masses and offends all the good religious people in the Party and who work closely with us. Fanatical atheists who insist on preaching their views are thrown out . . . confusing the political problems we have with religious matters is asinine. By far the most progress the Party is making today is being made through the churches. . . . I expect to see a complete convergence of the Catholic Church and the Party within the next fifty years. . . . The shadow of this is clearly foreshown in Poland. Perhaps you have heard of Pax? This is a Catholic lay organization run by communist priests . . . tolerated by both the Party and the Church. . . . You may yet live to see the day when the dictatorship of the proletariat will be proclaimed by the Pope!"

made in Belgium; both of which are bought with the gold of oil royalties from Wall Street, Dallas or London. The Oriental Chinese have learned well, and are expected to explode an atomic bomb at any moment. And even the half-Western Russians, from the days of Peter the Great, or even Rurik, have constructed their ships, cannon and rockets with European engineers. But does this mass appropriation of Western technics have the slightest effect on the inner and distinctive soul of the culture which appropriates? The answer is no, and we should not allow our foolish pride to think otherwise.

The other cause of rejecting Spengler lies in the difficulty of reconciling ourselves to the apparent necessity of the death of the West as a cultural organism.

But it is not necessary, in my opinion, to make this reconciliation. For although a Culture is an organism, it is a peculiar one; and, by accepting the analogy in the first place, we are able to intelligently seek for the possibility of extending or renewing its life.

Yockey rejects this hypothesis and, as a thorough Spenglerian, foresees the end of the West. But it can be argued that the very introduction of the organic concept into historical philosophizing and theorizing plus the unparalleled mastery over Nature which the West has attained—and the infinite possibilities of this for the future—hold out the conception that the organism of the West need not suffer the same Destiny as cultures which have gone before and which had none of this knowledge. In other words, we now have the *proper concept,* thanks to Spengler, and have, for the first time in all history, identified the pathology of Culture, thanks to Yockey. And, in addition, Western technics have created the equally unique physical means to apply to the problem.

To carry this examination further, the Western Culture excels all others in history in these areas:

(1) The obsession with fact-history.

(2) The development of the organic concept of Culture, and recognition of its pathology.

(3) The development of science and master technics. Nearing-subjection of the microcosm and time, and the macrocosm and space.

Let us now turn to the so-far final and, according to Spengler, the "inevitable" phase of a Culture—the imperialistic. First of all, it is in this area that the Spenglerian theory, as applied to "the venture of predetermining history," appears to falter because the West appears to be behind on the timetable. Yockey comments on this and attributes it to the retarding influence of Money. This is probably true. The question is, if Money can disturb the cycle, cannot other things, too?

Here may be mentioned another unique fact as regards the Western situation. The condition of overproduction has become a fact of life that almost all sectors of political opinion are loath to recognize. Nevertheless, this is a fundamental departure for men, with widespread implications. Until now, slavery was necessary to support a high standard of living. (And, of course, slavery has always been sanctioned by religion and law when it is economically desirable.) So were foreign conquests for exploitation. *This is no longer the case.* The main economic problem for the West is to dispose of its surplus production, not to feed and clothe its masses. (This elemental truth is known by every so-called "laboring man" but it has escaped the notice of theorists and economists of both Right and Left.) Overproduction and technics, then, appear to have destroyed the economic imperative for imperialism. Finally, the atomic bomb and its far more terroristic descendants have infinitely diminished the use of war as an instrument of national policy. From these points of view, imperialism as a policy of gain is as dead as the slave trade and the battleship. And if imperialism is not to be undertaken as a deliberate policy of gain, from what standpoint is it to be undertaken? Religious fervor? Popular enthusiasm for capitalism? No, the day of the Crusades is also past for the West. We shall not see the West march to conquer the world in any other fashion but that of Wall Street's and the Peace

Corps'—unless the need to dump our products finally can be resolved only in "war, the coward's solution for the problems of
peace."

Now if one were to object that the above considerations smack
of the causal view of history—against which Yockey inveighs—
and assert that the final phase of our Culture is subject to purely
spiritual phenomena, I should be bold to suggest the possibility of
a miscalculation by Spengler which could have been based on a
misinterpretation of his own data and his own theory which, if
seen in a slightly different perspective, not only clears up the
meaning of the theory in the light of present developments, but
also validates it completely. Space permits only the barest of outlines here, at the risk of unintelligibility to all but those initiated
in the mysteries of Spenglerism.

Spengler's method was to show the correlation of all aspects of
the history of a cultural organism. As the Friedell quotation earlier
suggests, Spengler drew analogies between apparently diverse elements within a Culture, all of which are given shape and meaning
by the *zeitgeist* (spirit of the age) which is the creation of the cultural soul in its singular Destiny. Hence, in the search of the past
he saw as the culminating stage that which expresses itself spiritually as universalism. In the realm of religion, it becomes a "second
religiosity," starting as a conglomeration of many sects and cults
which no one takes seriously but everyone concerns himself with.
(This is what we have today. It is called the "social gospel" and
appears in a thousand forms, profane as well as sacred. It is not
true religion at all but cultism.) Finally this anarchy stabilizes into
the form of a generally-accepted and genuine religion—and we
are about 200 years away from this. In the realm of the economic,
there is "big business" and the growing power of Money, which,
however, is finally broken by the force of politics. In art, the zeitgeist expresses itself as the importation of exotic art forms, and
inane experimentation which has no significance whatsoever except

as natural degeneracy of the native form. Finally, in foreign outlook, there is imperialism, military expansion.

We can plainly see all of the above running true to form and right on schedule except for the latter. Why? Simply because the subjection of technics to the service of the West and the mastery of economics over the West has sublimated this stage of spiritual universalism from militaristic imperialism to other forms of expansion. Verily, never before has there been such an aggressive army of gun-shy expansionists and pacifist imperialists. World government fanatics literally swarm over the West. They and others staunchly support the United Nations—an anachronism which cannot possibly be effective toward its alleged purposes— yet support for this harmful fossil is a matter of personal morality with millions. The zeitgeist is always reflected in definitions, so it is the height of insult for a White man today to be labeled an "isolationist" or "nationalist." White folks must all be "free traders," "internationalists" and "cosmopolitan" in our outlook, and how we admire the "citizen of the world," whatever that is. Our view is intently focused away from our marches; it is far easier, we have discovered, to solve the problems of total strangers than to solve our own. Non-Western peoples are not so enlightened as we, and it is eagerly excused, utilizing a newly-discovered Christian double standard which is a mark of modern moral superiority, like belonging to the Classics Book Club or contributing to the Negro College Fund. What, asks Nietzsche, has caused more suffering than the follies of the compassionate? It is *good* for colored peoples to be nationalistic; we encourage it, in fact, and snap up Israel Bonds with a warm feeling of self-righteousness. We are joyful when colored peoples and Jews exhibit "race pride," the cardinal sin and taboo of our own puritanical environment. (Incidentally, why is it that every subject except one can be discussed in our enlightened age? Atheism is now a dull subject. Marxism is even duller, after one hundred years of popularity. A step further has taken us past plain sex to sadism and perversion;

the Marquis de Sade is even becoming jaded. What racy topic is left to discuss since the equalists have brought democracy's blessings? Only one thing cannot be discussed in polite company: race.)

The heroes of Wall Street reap the most from this type of "imperialism," and today investors big and little interest themselves in foreign investments which are actually given tax advantages over domestic investments (Tax favoritism: the final criterion of status in our democracy)—or they support "foreign aid"—remembering to stipulate, naturally, that a portion of this neat gimmick to dispose of our surplus production be allotted to their own products. The ultimate expression of this militant water-pistol imperialism is the hilarious yet deeply symbolic "Peace Corpse," the true expression of the zeitgeist. Created out of the typically American combination of abysmal do-good stupidity and inability to gauge the feelings of others, and enlightened greed, this is the perfect symbol for today.

No, we do not need imperialism so long as we have leaders like Mennen Williams and Adlai Stevenson; savants like Eleanor Roosevelt and Arnold Toynbee and altruists like Herbert Lehman, James Warburg, and Douglas Dillon to solve our problems for us.

To further pursue this inquiry into the applicability of Spengler today it is important to bring out a certain point of view which is heard most infrequently, thanks to the purveyors of intellectual freedom and democracy. Neo-Spenglerians who are attuned to the racial view of history (call them "racists" for convenience) hold that the "final" phase of a Culture—the imperialistic stage—is final *only* because the cultural organism destroys its body and kills its soul by this process.

Obviously, if we are to draw analogies between cultures and organisms we must agree that the soul of the organism dies only because of the death of the body. The soul can sicken—the soul of the West is now diseased and perhaps mortally ill—but it cannot die unless the organism itself dies. And this, point out the racists, is precisely what has happened to all previous cultures; death of the organism being the natural result of the suicidal process of imperialism.

A word on the racial view of history before proceeding further. Today, of course, history is written from the marxist standpoint of economics, linear progress and class warfare—and Yockey explains this triple error well. Previous to the first World War history was written largely from the racial point of view. History was seen as the dramatic story of the movements, struggles and developments of races, which it is. Suppression of the racist point of view reached its apex about 1960. (It is no coincidence that the power of the Culture Distorter in every other field, including the political, gave signs—however faint—of wavering at that time, too.)

Perhaps the biggest reason for a growing tendency of White folks to look at the races objectively is, paradoxically, precisely because they have been forced to look at them subjectively! It is no problem to maintain a myth in ignorance. Negro equality or even supremacy, for example, is easier to believe in if there are no Negroes around to destroy the concept. In a word, internationalism in practice quickly metamorphoses into racism.

To turn from experience to academic matters, how many Americans or Britons are acquainted with the stupendously elemental fact that they are—in the historical sense—Germans; that they are, like it or not, a part of that great Teutonic-Celtic family which—millenniums before the dawn of Rome or even Greece—was one tribe, with one language? How many otherwise enlightened and well-meaning people who have heretofore judged their patriotism according to the degree of hatred they have had for their continental brothers know that the ancestors of the great Teutonic-Celtic family were the same Aryans who subjected India and civilized it, speaking the Sanskrit language and creating the caste system which, incidentally, was nothing originally but a system of racial segregation endowed with a religious significance in order to maintain it? Or that, before this, there were the Sumerians and the Persians, and that the modern name for Persia—Iran—is merely a corruption of Aryan?

Greece and Rome, also, were created by this great, far-roving, culture-bearing race of conquerors. In whatever part of the world it went, a different civilization was created, each of which was distinctive because it developed in tune with the environmental conditions in whatever location its history began, yet bearing unmistakable traces of its Aryan origin.

There are some civilizations about which we know little, as far as the racial elements are concerned. All we know for certain about the Egyptians is that they were Caucasian, and that they, like all slavemasters, mingled their blood with that of their Negro slaves. As for the so-called Amerindian civilizations, we now know without doubt that civilization was superimposed upon Indian savages by a White racial stock. In his popular books, *Kon-Tiki* and *Aku-Aku,* Thor Heyerdahl cleverly reveals the forbidden racist view, in spite of the fact that a million people who are familiar with the adventure described in the books are totally ignorant of the deep racial message he wrote into them. (It is a sad commentary indeed when a gifted scientist, in order to reveal a simple truth, must risk his life and then write an adventure story in code which, when interpreted, shows a forbidden fact.)

In *Kon-Tiki,* Heyerdahl writes, "*. . . . There is not a trace of gradual development in the high civilizations which once stretched from Mexico to Peru. The deeper the archeologists dig, the higher the culture, until a definite point is reached at which the old civilizations have clearly arisen without any foundation in the midst of primitive cultures.*" All of the wonders in South and Central America before the arrival of the Spaniards had been brought about suddenly by a race of White conquerors and that, as they melted their blood slowly into that of their subject native population, the civilization dwindled. The very reason Cortez conquered the Aztecs so easily was because Montezuma believed that the Spaniards were the "fair-skinned, bearded men coming from the

East" which, Quetzalcotl's prophecy foretold, would *return;* and the Incas in Peru had the very same legend. The name, Inca, by the way, is the name only of the aristocracy of the Peruvians. The Incas were White and the princesses were quite beautiful; so much so that many of the Spanish officers married them and took them back to Spain. A glance at the present "Incas" in Peru shows at once that these were not the creators of the great Peruvian Culture.

Some of the very best writing on this subject and, for that matter, on the fascinating subject of world prehistory generally is found in Paul Hermann's *Conquest By Man,* an extremely valuable book which, strangely enough, is now in print (Harper)!

An even cloudier origin must be ascribed to the Chinese civilization. Suffice it to say that there is abundant indication of early White movements to North China and there is much similarity between early Chinese culture and Babylonian. Genghis Khan, a Mongol, came from a tribe called "the gray-eyed men," according to biographer Harold Lamb, and he had red hair and green eyes. The Chinese have shown that they have the ability to *maintain* a civilization but we cannot prove that they have ever created one.

The intensive suppression, misrepresentation, condemnation and opposition to the racial view of history has had its effect. We still not only have much to learn (the surface of prehistory has barely been scratched and will never be more than scratched if the scientists persist in spending their time in well-financed projects in the so-called "cradle of civilization" in the Middle East) but the results of historical perversion have been satisfyingly abundant in the social area. This has allowed the Distorter to convince Europe that all that Europe has it owes to the Greeks, the Romans and an obscure tribe of vagabonds which some religious crackpots refer to as "God's Chosen People." * In *The Testimony of the Spade,* however, Geoffrey Bibby relates some results of his straying off the

---

* Or, as Samuel Hoffenstein put it in his earthquaking couplet:
> *How odd of God*
> *To choose the Jews.*

beaten archeological track and looking for the origins of Europe
in Europe instead of the alien Orient; results which will be surprising to persons brought up to believe that their ancestors were
bearskin-clad savages, civilized only when forced to acknowledge
the superiority of Rome. In truth, virtually *everything* the West
has it owes to itself, including holidays like Christmas and Easter
(originally Teutonic celebrations of the Winter Solstice and the
coming of Spring, with the latter celebration dedicated to the Goddess Eostre), to law, ethics and single-breasted jackets. The world
wears leather shoes and trousers, not sandals and togas. Wearing
apparel very similar to items sold at Sears, Roebuck today have
been discovered in Europe dating back some three thousand years.

*The Western Culture had its birth many millenniums ago. It be-
gan autochthonously and developed to the present point, when it
now stands upon the verge of physical and spiritual annihilation
only because it has ceased to believe in itself.* This is the lesson we
glean.

Further, there is a correlation too perfect to be a coincidence in
that in every case on record of the death or stagnation of a Culture
there has been simultaneously an abortive attempt to digest large
numbers of cultural and racial aliens into the organism. In the
case of Rome and Greece death came about through imperialism
and the resulting, inevitable backwash of conquered peoples and
races into the heartland as slaves, bringing exotic religions, different philosophies; in a word, cultural sophistication first, then cultural anarchy. In the case of Persia, India and the Amerindian
civilizations, a race of conquerors superimposed their civilization
upon a mass of indigenous people; the area flourished for awhile,
then the Culture vanished or, in the case of America, was on the
verge of vanishing, as the descendants of the conquerors became
soft, fat and liberal and took on more and more of the accoutre-
ments and blood of the subject population. In the case of Egypt,
the alien blood was brought in over the course of many centuries

by the importation of Negro slaves. The inevitable racial mongrelization followed, creating the Egypt we know today.

We thus see the real reason underlying the "inevitable" decline and destruction of a cultural organism. It is because, at a certain stage, a Culture develops a bad case of universalism. Speaking pathologically, unless this is sublimated to harmless channels by proper treatment, it will inevitably kill the organism through the absorption of a resulting flood of alien microbes.

It is, therefore, the natural by-product of universalism which kills the organism; the death of the organism itself is neither natural nor necessary!

This conclusion comes by a synthesis of the Spenglerian and the racial point of view. Each tempers the other; together a comprehensive and hopeful theory of history can be developed which holds a deep meaning to Westerners of this day. At all costs, the imperialistic phase of our development must be avoided, and we must guard against the digestion of alien matter we have already partially absorbed. The West need not die if it learns to sublimate the present "universal" stage of the West from the orthodox to something more constructive which will not only satisfy the "inevitable" yearning that the West now displays for expansion and universalism but, at the same time, will provide a basis for the West to continue its development. What can that be?

Faintly shining above the wreckage of seven Cultures we can now detect a dim ray of hope which gives to us, as men of the West, reason to believe that the Destiny of our Culture can work itself out through a completely new path. This ray of hope shines from the same developments which have brought the West to its position of unqualified superiority to every other Culture. For the West has already embarked upon the greatest adventure in all history—*the attempt to conquer Space—the attempt to bring the very Universe under the control of the race!* This imperative needs no justification other than the one Sir Edmund Hillary gave when he was asked why he wanted to climb Mount Everest: "Because it's there." This is the pristine reality of the Faustian Soul of the West, and it is beyond the logic of the rationalists.

Could any goal be at once so totally challenging, so impudent and impossible as this—and also so metaphysically necessary to the spiritual need of our Culture? And more—could any goal be so perfectly adapted to the physical situation in which we find ourselves?

The fates have provided the West well with the means of survival. At this point in history, our technics, industrial overproduction and the "population explosion" become all-important, for we see that finally the West has the means to turn the poetic imperative of the Faustian drive for the Infinite to *reality;* indeed, the inescapable need to do so.

For it is true that, regardless of all arguments to the contrary, Western man is bound to conquer Space or to die in the attempt. No longer is the drive toward infinity and largeness held back by earthly boundaries. Now, in fact, we have infinity at our elbow.

What I am suggesting is that at last the White man has burst the ties to Earth. I am stating the simple fact that, barring calamity caused by universal physical or biological destruction, we are now headed for the stars, and there is no power in heaven or earth to stop us. Coming days will see the present drive for Space magnified a thousandfold—a millionfold. All limits to the possibility of expansion have disappeared. Geographical expansion on Earth is senseless—and worse than senseless—it is suicide. The Frontier has come back—a Frontier that can never be dissipated. And with that Frontier comes literally limitless opportunities not only for physical expansion but for economic exploitation—and for the Soul of Faustian man to find its true expression.

Of course, man cannot conquer the heavens. Man cannot move the solar system, change planets in their orbits, add billions of square miles of dirt to the surface of the Earth, move other planets closer to the life-giving Sun to adapt them for colonization, refuel the Sun when it starts to fade and, most noble impossibility

of all, actually upgrade the human species through deliberate biological mechanics *; for, in the attempt to conquer Nature, we
must fail; this is the eternal tragedy of the Faustian Soul, says
Spengler in *Man and Technics.* But—and this is the important
thing—we can try. *And we will.* The final end does not matter;
time has no end; only the goal matters.

At the same time there is the grave danger that we will, with
our attention fixed on the nearing stars, succumb to the subtle
urging of the Culture Distorter and ignore the problems at home.
The Infinite Challenge is of unspeakable excitement, but the mun-
dane problem of the quality of men and their earthy environment
is of more importance. Our venture to Infinity will be very short-
lived if we come home to an earth peopled with a rapidly-degen-
erating human species; to nights that crawl with the prowlings of
depraved, raceless savages, with only barred doors keeping the
jungle out of the laboratory and the boudoir until day breaks; to
a tyranny over our government that is exercised by organized and
predatory minorities; to impossible taxes to support degenerative
"welfare" schemes that are deliberately designed to proliferate the
unfit and inferior at the expense of the productive and creative; to
an organized filth that calls itself literature; to the ethical syphilis
of Hollywood; to systematic lies that masquerade as scholarship;
to purposeful journalistic and official propaganda that has as its
sole aim the perpetuation of cultural decline; to thralldom to an
economic system dedicated to extirpating individual excellence and
personal responsibility; to a liberal philosophy and a sick religion—
perfect for slaves—which ferociously combats all creative efforts of
noble souls, revealing its own loftiest aspiration to be the implanta-
tion of a subconscious death wish in our people; to a cowardly
hypocrisy that makes it impossible to speak of our real problems—

---

* In *Nature and Man's Fate,* biologist Garrett Hardin of the University of California has done what too few academicians can do: created a book of both beauty
and far-seeing scope. But alas, words are only words; politics alone, let us ever
remember, is the art of the possible.

and all of this for the purpose of stabilizing the total supremacy of the Culture Distorter, which feeds and fattens on these conditions.

Oswald Spengler, then, can be seen not as the prophet of inevitable doom, but as a *challenger*, as a seer who was—in common with all great creators—unable to see the final consequences of his creation. Hence, the importance of Spengler becomes the size of the future, and all men who are free from the grip of the destroyers must, as a categorical imperative, accept his basic teaching. What we do with it—whether or not we have the courage to build on the structure he built—this is up to us. We must hope that more men like Yockey will come to add a little more onto the concept he created, for the development of the Western cultural organism is not coming to an end, it is just beginning.

* * *

What is the significance of *Imperium*? Simply this. That now, for the first time, those soldiers who enlist in the service of the West have a profound theory to inspire and guide them. *Imperium,* after conquering all attempts to suppress it and destroy it—as have all constructive advances in the past of man—is seen as the only foundation which can be used to overthrow the inner enemies, re-conquer the Soul of the West and pave the way to the future.

In spite of the difference of opinion which *Imperium* will stir, this much is certain: here is a book which is basically different from other books, precisely as the author states on the first page. Whether it does, indeed, signal a turning-point in history such as the author describes, or not, it contains a vast amount of pregnant thinking and new concepts which any fair-minded person will welcome. It breaks through the straitjacket of present sterile intellectualism which affronts us from a thousand futile towers of "higher learning" and will undoubtedly endow every reader with possessions of thought which will enrich him and, in time, our Culture. Whether the apocalyptic prophecies are borne out, or whether an alternative and more constructive course can be imposed upon history—or whether the West and the world will come to its finality not with a bang but with a whimper, only the unfoldment of time can tell; but no intelligent man will ignore *Imperium*.

In one respect, *Imperium* is akin to *Das Kapital*, for Karl Marx gave to the conspiratorial Culture Distorter the necessary ideological mask to hide its mission of ruthless, total destruction. He provided an ugly and invalid theory of man, cloaked in putrifying equality, mewling hypocrisy, the disease of undiscriminating altruism and the "science" of economics. By so doing, he thrilled the rationalists with a totally specious verity, something their stunted, guilty souls desperately needed after they killed God.

Francis Parker Yockey has done the same thing for those who are constructive-minded and who have the intellectual and moral courage to face reality and seek and speak truth.

This is why, although Yockey's plan for the West may not be perfect, it contains atomic power. If only one man reading this book is influenced to lead, and if others are made to see the world a little more clearly than they do now—and if they are thereby enabled to discriminate between their true friends and their real enemies, and to recognize the need for leadership and coordinated action—then Yockey's life of suffering and persecution and his monumental accomplishment in spite of all has not been in vain.

And whatever course Destiny may take from this day forth, I shall always be baffled by two questions.

For one, is the republication of this book, in itself, concrete evidence that its prophecy is being worked out?

And lastly—now you must accept this at my word and question me no further—it is most strange that two men—neither of whom can bring themselves to believe in either "Destiny" nor "Eternal Justice"—that these two heathens and bitter realists—these two rationalists, if you will—were the only ones with faith enough to take it upon themselves to see that *Imperium* is not forgotten but is made available for you, dear reader.

—W. A. CARTO

Foreword

THIS BOOK is different from other books. First of all, it is only in *form* a book at all. In reality, it is a part of the life of *action*. It is a turning-point in European history, a late turning-point, but a real one. There is nothing original in the content of this book, the book itself only is original. The craze for originality is a manifestation of decadence, and the decadence of Europe is the ascendancy of the Barbarian.

This is the first of a line of works—the political literature of Europe. Heretofore all political works on the imperative side have been addressed to one nation of Europe alone. Among other things, this book marks the end of Rationalism. It does not bring it about—not books but only the advance of History can accomplish anything of that sort—it merely rings its *funeral* knell. Thus the imperative side of Life returns to its pristine source, the will-to-power. Henceforth there will be no discussion of action in terms of abstract thought.

This is addressed to all Europe, and in particular to the culture-bearing stratum of Europe. It summons Europe to a world-
historical struggle of two centuries' duration. Europe will par-
take in this struggle either as a participant, or as the booty for
marauding powers from without. If it is to *act*, and not merely
to *suffer* in this series of gigantic wars, it must be integrated,
and there is *only one way* this can occur. The Western Culture
is suffering from disease, and the prolongation of this disease is
the prolonging of Chinese conditions in Europe.

The word Europe changes its meaning: from now on it means
the Western Civilization, the organic unity which created as
phases of its life the nation-ideas of Spain, Italy, France, England and Germany. These former nations are all dead; the era
of political nationalism has passed. This has not happened
through *logical* necessity, but through the organic advance of
the History of the West. It is this *organic* necessity which is the
source of our imperative, and of the integration of Europe. The
significance of the organic is that its alternatives are either to do
the necessary or to sicken and die.

The present chaos—1948—is directly traceable to the attempt
to prevent the integration of Europe. As a result, Europe is in a
swamp, and extra-European forces dispose of former European nations as their colonies.

In this book are the precise, organic foundations of the Western soul, and in particular, its Imperative at this present stage.
Either Europe will become totally integrated, or it will pass
entirely out of history, its peoples will be dispersed, its efforts
and brains will be at the disposal forever of extra-European
forces. This is shown herein, not by abstract formulae and intellectualized theories, but organically and historically. The conclusions therefore are not arbitrary, not a subject for choosing
or rejecting, but *absolutely compelling* to minds which wish to

take part in affairs. The real author is the Spirit of the Age, and its commands do not admit of argumentation, and their sanction is the crushing might of History, bringing defeat, humiliation, death and chaos.

I condemn here at the outset the miserable plans of retarded souls to "unite" Europe as an economic area for purposes of exploitation by and defense of the Imperialism of extra-European forces. The integration of Europe is not a subject for *plans,* but for expression. It needs but to be recognized, and the perpetuation of nineteenth century economic thinking is entirely incapable here. Not trade and banking, not importing and exporting, but Heroism alone can liberate that integrated soul of Europe which lies under the financial trickery of retarders, the petty-stateism of party-politicians, and the occupying armies of extra-European forces.

The imperative integration of Europe takes the form of unity of People, Race, Nation, State, Society, Will—and naturally also—economy. The spiritual unity of Europe is there, its liberation will automatically allow the full blooming of the other phases of the organic unity, which all flow from the spiritual.

And thus, this book is a renewal of a war-declaration. It asks the traitors to Europe, the miserable party-politicians whose tenure of office is dependent upon their continued serviceability to extra-European forces, "Did you think it was over? Do you think that your misery and shame will remain securely forever on a world-stage which has seen true heroes upon it? In the war which you let loose, you taught men how to die, and thereby you have freed a spirit which will engulf you next, the Spirit of Heroism and Discipline. There is no currency that can buy this spirit, but it can overcome any currency."

Lastly, this book is itself the first blow in the gigantic war for the liberation of Europe. The prime enemy is the traitor within

Europe, who alone makes possible the starving and looting of Europe by the outer forces. He is the symbol of Chaos and Death. Between him and the spirit of the twentieth century is unremitting war.

ULICK VARANGE

Brittas Bay, January 30, 1948

CONTENTS

CULTURAL VITALISM.
(A) CULTURE HEALTH

CULTURAL VITALISM.
(B) CULTURE PATHOLOGY

AMERICA

THE WORLD SITUATION

THE 20th CENTURY
HISTORICAL
OUTLOOK

"Thus, as we do nothing but enact history, we say little but recite it: nay, rather, in that widest sense, our whole spiritual life is built thereon. For, strictly considered, what is all knowledge too but recorded experience, and a product of history; of which, therefore, reasoning and belief, no less than action and passion, are essential materials?"

CARLYLE

"The individual's life is of importance to none besides himself: the point is whether he wishes to escape from history or give his life for it. History recks nothing of human logic."

SPENGLER

Perspective

FAR OUT in exterior darkness where no breath stirs, no light shines, and no sound is heard, one can glance toward this spinning earth-ball. In the astral regions, illumination is of the soul, hence all is dark but this certain star, and only a part of it is aglow. From such a distance, one can obtain an utterly untrammeled view of what is transpiring on this earth-ball. Drawing somewhat closer, continents are visible; closer yet, population-streams. One focal point exists whence the light goes forth in all directions. It is the crooked peninsula of Europe. On this tiny pendant of the great land-mass of the earth-ball, the greatest intensity of movement exists. One can see—for out here the soul and its emanations are visible—a concentration of ideas, energy, ambition, purpose, expansiveness, will-to-form. Hovering above Europe we can see what never before was so clearly visible—the presence of a *purely spiritual organism*. A close look reveals that the light stream is not flowing from the surface of Europe *upward* into the night sky, but *downward* from the hitherto invisible organism. This is a discovery of profound and revolutionary importance, which was only vouchsafed to us by reason of our complete detachment from terrestrial events in the outer void, where spirit is visible and matter visible, only by reason of the light from the spirit.

More discoveries follow: on the other side are two islands, small in comparison with the land-mass. The pale glow diffused over isolated parts of these two islands is seen at once to be a reflection from the other side.

What is this supra-terrestrial phenomenon? Why does it hover over Europe in particular? What is the relationship between it and the human material under it? The latter is shaped up into intricately formed pyramidal structures. Ranks are formed. Movements proceed along channels of labyrinthine complexity. Persons stand to one another in defined relationships of command and obedience. Apart from this tiny peninsula, the human currents are horizontal, swirling, eddying like the water in the streams, the currents in the ocean, the herds on the vast plains. It is, then, the spirit-organism which forms and impresses the population of the peninsula into their intricate organic shapes.

With what can we compare this being, which could not be seen by us while we were earth-bound? It is alone at present.

But out here we have the freedom of time as well as the freedom of space. We are allowed to look upon a hundred generations as the earth-bound look upon the life-span of a fruit-fly. In our search for something similar to the spirit-organism we have seen, we go back two hundred generations. The ball is the same, but is in almost complete darkness. Things are almost indistinguishable; matter has not passed through the alembic of spirit, and is not apprehensible. A glance backward reveals a continuation of the void. We let a few generations pass in a moment, and spirit begins to make itself felt. A feeble, but promising, glow appears in northeast Africa. Then another, a thousand miles to the northeast, in Mesopotamia. They take names, Egypt, Babylonia. The time is around 3000 B.C. They increase in intensity and the first thing clear in each case is armies marching against the outer populations, who are felt as *the barbarian*. These spiritual organisms do not mix—their higher frontiers are sharp and clear; each being has its own hue, which adheres to it. Each organism seizes the human material in its landscape and impresses them into its service. First it gives them a common World-Idea, then it refines this into *nations*, each nation embodying a separate idea of the higher organism. A nobility and priesthood arise to embody different aspects of the idea. The populations are stratified and specialized, and the human beings live out their lives and destinies in a way entirely subordinate to the higher organism. The latter compels these humans with *ideas*. Only a small spiritual stratum of each human population is adapted to this kind of compulsion, but those who belong to it remain in the service of the idea, once it is felt. They will live and die for it, and in the process they determine the destinies of the population whence they spring. These *ideas*—not mere abstractions, strings of concepts, but living, pulsating, wordless necessities of being and thinking—are the technic by which these higher beings utilize human beings for their purposes. Religions of high complexity of feeling and rationale, forms of architecture, conceived in the spirit of that religion and put into its service, lyric poetry, pictorial art, sculpture, music, orders of nobility, orders of priesthood, stylized dwellings, stylized manners and dress, rigid training of the young up to these developments to perpetuate them, systems of philosophy, of mathematics, of knowledge, of nature, prodigious technical methods, giant battles, huge armies, prolonged wars, energetic economics to support this whole multifarious structure, intricately organized governments to infuse order into the nations created by the higher being acting on the different types of human material—these are some of the floraison of forms which appear in these two areas. Each form is different in Egypt from the corresponding form in Babylonia. If an idea is taken over, it is only apparently adopted; actually it is misunderstood, re-formed, and adapted to the proper soul.

But the higher being approaches a crisis. It has expended itself in this earth-transforming process. It shudders, it apparently weakens, it palpitates—chaos and anarchy threaten its terrestrial actualizations—forces outside gather to strike it down and wipe out its grand creations. But it rouses itself, it puts forward its greatest effort of all—no longer in the creation of inward things, arts, philosophy, theories of life, but in the formation of the purely external apparatus of power: strict governments, giant armies, industry to support them, fleets of ships for war, legal systems to organize and order the conquests. It expands across areas never before investigated or even known, it unifies all of its proper nations into one, which gives its name to the rest and leads them on to the last great expansive effort.

The same great rhythm is observable in each of them. As one watches, the two lights die down from their splendid hues to an ever-paler earth-light. They go out slowly, leaving a glow of memory and legend in the minds of men, and with their last great creations lying in the widened landscape—Imperium.

Outside these two areas, the rest of the earth has remained unchanged. The human bands are distinguishable from the herding-animals only by a primitive culture, and a more intricate economy. Otherwise their existence-forms are devoid of significance. The primitive cultures are the sole thing existing above the plane of economics, in that they attribute symbolic significance to natural occurrences and human conduct. But there is nothing in these movements resembling the High Cultures which transformed the entire appearance of the Egyptian and Babylonian landscapes for almost forty generations from their first beginning until the last sinking.

Physical time flows on and centuries pass in darkness. Then, precisely as in Egypt and Babylonia, but again of a different hue, and to different music, a light appears over the Punjab. It becomes bright and firm. The same wealth of forms and significant happenings work themselves out as in the earlier two organisms. Its creations are all in the highest degree *individual*, as different from its two predecessors as they were *vis-a-vis* one another, but they follow the same grand rhythms. The same multi-colored pageant of nobles and priests, temples and schools, nations and cities, arts and philosophies, armies and sciences, letters and wars, passes before the eye.

II

Before this high culture was well on its way, another had started to actualize itself in the Hwang-Ho valley in China. And then a few centuries later, about 1100 B.C. in our way of reckoning, the Classical Culture begins on the shores of the Aegean. Both of these cultures have the stamp of individuality, their own way of coloring and influencing their terrestrial creations, but both are subject to the same morphology as the others observed.

As this Classical Culture draws to its close, around the time of Christ, another one appears in a landscape subjugated by the Classical in its last expansive phase—Arabia. The fact of its appearance precisely here makes its course an unusual one. Its forms are inwardly as pure as those of all the other Cultures, inwardly it borrows nothing any more than they did—but it was inevitable that the material contiguity of landscape, temporal succession, and contact with the civilized populations of the older organism would influence the new soul to take over the wealth of classical creations. It was subjugated to them only in a superficial way however, for into these old bottles it poured its new wine. Through selection, reinterpretation, or ignoring, it expressed its own soul despite the alien forms. In its later, expansive phase, this culture embraced European Spain as the Western Caliphate. Its life span, its end form, its last great crisis—all followed the same organic regularity as the others.

Some five centuries later the now familiar manifestations of another High Culture begin in the remote landscapes of Mexico and Peru. It is to have the most tragic destiny of any we have yet seen. Around 1000 A.D. the European Culture is meanwhile born, and at its very birth shows itself to be distinguished from the others by the extraordinary intensity of its self-expression, by its pushing into every distance both in the spiritual realm, and in the physical. Its original landscape was even of an extent many times the size of its predecessors, and from this base, in its middle life, it enters upon an Age of Discovery, in which it finds for itself the very frontiers of the earth-ball, and converts the world into the object of its politics. Its Spanish representatives in the two warrior bands of Cortez and Pizarro discovered the Civilization of Mexico and Peru, then in its very last stage of refinement of the material life. The two grand Empires of Mexico and Peru, with social forms, economico-political organization, transportation, communication, city life, all developed to the utmost limits for this particular soul made the invading Spaniards seem like mere naive barbarians. But the technical disinterestedness of these empires left them helpless before the few cannon and horses of the invaders. The last act of this Culture-drama is its obliteration in a few years by the invaders from another world. This consummation is instructive as to the attention that the World-Spirit pays to human values and feelings. What soothsayer would have dared to tell the last Aztec Emperor, surrounded with the pomp of world-historical significance, clothed with the power of the world, that in a short time the jungle would reconquer his cities and palaces, that his armies and systems of control of his world-Empire would vanish before the onslaught of a few hundred barbarians?

Each Culture-soul is stamped with individuality; from the others it takes nothing, and to them it gives nothing. Whatever is on its frontiers is the enemy, whether primitive or Culture-populations. They all are barbarians, heathens, to the proper culture, and no understanding passes between them. We saw the Western peoples prove the lifeworthiness of the European culture by their crusades against the highly civilized Saracens, Moors, and Turks. We saw the Germanic populations in the East and their Visigothic brothers in the South push the barbarian Slavs and the civilized Moors continually back during the centuries. We saw Western ships and Western armies make the whole world into the object of booty for the West. These were the relations of the West to that and those outside.

Within the Culture arose Gothic Christianity, the transcendent symbols of Empire and Papacy, the Gothic cathedrals, the unlocking of the secrets of the world of the soul and the world of nature in monastery cells. The Culture-soul shaped for its own expression the nations of the West. To each it gave individuality, and at the last, each thought it was a Culture in itself, instead of being a mere organ of a Culture. Cities grew out of the hamlets of Gothic times, and from the cities grew intellect. The old problem of the relation of Reason and Faith, the central problem of early Scholastic, is apparently being slowly decided in these cities in favor of the Supremacy of Reason.

The nobility of Gothic times, the masters of the earth who had no superior unless they voluntarily recognized him, become subject to an idea—the *State*. Life slowly externalizes: political problems move into the center; new economic resources are developed to support the political contests; the old agricultural economy metamorphoses into an industrial economy. At the end of this path stands a ghostly and terrifying Idea: *Money*.

Other Cultures also had seen this phenomenon appear at the same stage and grow to similar dimensions. Its slow growth in importance proceeds *pari passu* with the gradual self-assertion of Reason against Faith. It reaches its highest point with the Age of Nationalism, when the parts of the Culture tear one another to bits, even as outer dangers loom threateningly. At its highest point, Money, allied with Rationalism, contests for the supremacy over the life of the Culture with the forces of State and Tradition, Society and Religion. In our brief visit to interstellar space, we found the position of detachment whence we could see this grand life-drama unfold itself seven times in seven High Cultures, and we saw each of the seven surmount the last great crisis of two centuries' duration. The Mexican-Peruvian Civilization overcame the inner crisis only to fall before marauders appearing out of the blue sea.

The great crisis of the West set in forcefully with the French Revolution and its consequent phenomena. Napoleon was the symbol of the transition of Culture into Civilization—Civilization, the life of the material, the external, of power, giant economies, armies, and fleets, of great numbers and colossal technics, over Culture, the inner life of religion, philosophy, arts, domination of the external life of politics and economics by strict form and symbolism, strict restraint of the beast-of-prey in man, feeling of cultural unity. It is the victory of Rationalism, Money and the great city over the traditions of religion and authority, of Intellect over Instinct.

We had seen all this in the previous high cultures as they approached their final life-phase. In each case the crisis had been resolved by the resurgence of the old forces of Religion and Authority, their victory over Rationalism and Money, and the final union of the nations into an Imperium. The two-century-long crisis in the life of the great organism expressed itself in gigantic wars and revolutions. All the Cultural energy that had previously gone into inner creations of thought, religion, philosophy, science, art-forms, great literature, now goes into the outer life of economics, war, technics, politics. The symbolism of power succeeds to the highest place in this last phase.

But at this point, we are suddenly back on the surface of the earth. No longer detached, we must participate in the great Culture-drama, whether we will or no. Our only choice is to participate as subject or as object. The wisdom that comes from the knowledge of the organic nature of a High Culture gives us the key to the events transpiring before our eyes. It can be applied by us, and our action can thereby become *significant,* as distinguished from the opportunistic and old-fashioned policy of stupidity which would try to turn the Western Civilization back in its course because stupid heads are incapable of adjusting themselves to new prevailing ideas.

III

With the knowledge of the *organic nature of a High Culture,* we have achieved an unparalleled liberation from the dross of materialism which hindered hitherto the glimpse into History's riddle. This knowledge is simple, but profound, and is therefore shut off from the inward appreciation of all but the few. In its train flow all the consequences of the necessary historical outlook of the coming times. Since a Culture is organic, it has an individuality, and a soul. Thus it cannot be influenced in its depths from any outside force whatever. It has a destiny, like all organisms. It has a period of gestation, and a birth-time. It has a growth, a maturity, fulfillment, a down-going, a death. Because it has a soul, all of its manifestations will be impressed by the same spiritual stamp, just as each man's life is the creation of his own individuality. Because it has a soul, this particular culture can never come again after it has passed. Like the nations it creates to express phases of its own life, it exists only once. There will never be another Indian culture, Aztec-Mayan Culture, Classical Culture, or Western Culture, any more than there will be a second Spartan nation, Roman nation, French or English nation. Since a Culture is *organic*, it has a life-span. We observed this life span: it is about thirty-five generations at highest potential, or about forty-five generations from its first stirrings in the landscape until its final subsiding. Like the life span of organisms, it is no rigid thing. Man has a life span of seventy years, but this term is not rigid.

The High Cultures belong at the peak of the organic hierarchy: plant, animal, man. They differ from the other organisms in that they are invisible, or in other words, they have no light-quality. In this they resemble the human soul. The body of a High Culture is made up of the population streams in its landscape. They furnish it with the material through which it actualizes its possibilities. The spirit which animates these populations shows the life-phase of the Culture, whether youthful, mature, or at the last fulfillment. Like each man, a Culture has ages, which succeed one another with rhythmic inevitability. They are laid down for it by its own organic law, just as the senility of a man is laid down at his conception. This quality of *direction* we call Destiny. Destiny is the hallmark of everything living. Destiny-thinking is the type of thought which understands the living, and it is the only kind which does. The other method of human thought is that of *Causality*. This method is inwardly compulsory in dealing with *inorganic* problems of technics, mechanics, engineering, systematic natural philosophy. It finds the limits of its efficacy there, however, and is grotesque when applied to Life. It would tell us that youth is the *cause* of maturity, maturity of old age, that the bud is the *cause* of the full-blown flower, the caterpillar the *cause* of the butterfly.

The Destiny-Idea is the central motive of organic thinking. If anyone thinks it is merely an invisible causality, he understands it not. The idea of Causality is the central motive of systematic, or inorganic thinking. The latter is scientific thinking. It aims at *subjugation* of things to understanding; it wishes to name everything, to make outlines distinct, and then to link phenomena together by classification and causal linkage. Kant is the height of this type of thinking, and to this side of Western philosophy belong also Hume, Bacon, Schopenhauer, Hamilton, Spencer, Mill, Bentham, Locke, Holbach, Descartes. To the organic side belong Macchiavelli, Vico, Montaigne, Leibnitz, Lichtenberg, Pascal, Hobbes, Goethe, Hegel, Carlyle, Nietzsche and Spengler, the philosopher of the twentieth and twenty-first centuries.

Scientific thinking is at the height of its power in the realm of matter, that which possesses *extension*, but no *direction*. Material happenings can be controlled, are reversible, produce identical results under identical conditions, are recurrent, can be classified, can be successfully comprehended as though they are subject to an *a priori*, mechanical, necessity, in other words, to *Causality*.

Scientific thinking is powerless in the domain of Life, for its happenings are uncontrollable, irreversible, never-recurring, unique, cannot be classified, are unamenable to rational treatment, and possessed of no external, mechanical necessity. Every organism is something never seen before, that follows an *inner* necessity, that passes away, never to reappear. Every organism is a set of possibilities within a certain framework, and its life is the process of actualization of these possibilities. The technique of Destiny-thinking is simply *living into* other organisms to understand their life-conditions and necessities. One can then apprehend what *must* happen.

The word *Fate* is an inorganic word. It is an attempt to sub-jugate Life to an external necessity; it is of religious provenance, and religion comes from the causal type of thinking. There is no science without a precedent religion. Science merely makes the sacred causality of religion into a profane, mechanical necessity.

Fate is *not* synonymous with destiny, but the opposite to it. Fate attributes necessity to the *incidents* of a life, but Destiny is the *inner* necessity of the organism. An incident can wipe out a life, and thus terminate its destiny, but this event came from *outside* the organism, and was thus apart from its destiny.

Every fact is an incident, unforeseeable and incalculable, but the inner progression of a life is destined, and works itself out through the facts, is helped or hindered by them, overcomes them, or succumbs to them. It is the destiny of every child that is born ultimately to become senile; incident may intervene in the form of disease or accident, and this destiny may be frus-trated. These outer incidents—that may elevate a man to the heights despite his blunders, or cast him into defeat despite his efficiency and mastery of the idea of his time—are without meaning for Destiny-thinking.

Destiny inheres in the organism, forces it to express its pos-sibilities. Incident is *outside* the organism, is blind, uninformed by necessity, but may nevertheless play a great role in the actualization of an organism, by smoothing its way, or imposing great obstacles to it. What is called Luck, Doom, Fate, Providence, express the bafflement and awe of men in the presence of this mystery, forever unknowable.

Destiny-thinking and Causality-thinking are related to one another, however, through their common provenance: both are products of Life. Even the most inorganic thinker or scientifico, the crassest materialist or mechanist, is subject to his own destiny, his own soul, his own character, his own life span, and outside this framework of destiny his free, unbound flight of causal fancy cannot deliver him. Destiny is Life, but Causality is merely a thought-method by which a certain form of Life, namely Culture-man, attempts to subjugate all around him to his understanding. Thus there is an order of rank between them: Destiny-thinking is unconditionally prior, for all Life is subject to it, while Causality-thinking is only an expression of a part of Life's possibilities.

Their differences may also be expressed in this way: Causality-thought is able to understand because its non-living material opposes no resistance, but submits to any conditions imposed upon it, having no inner compulsion of its own. When, however, Causality attempts to subjugate Life, the material itself is active, moving independently, will not stand still and be classified or systematized. Destiny-thinking can understand because each one of us is himself moved by Destiny, has an inner compulsion to be himself, and can thus, by transference of inwardly-experienced feelings, live himself into other forms of life, other individuations. Destiny-thinking moves along with its subject-matter; Causality stands still, and can only reach satisfactory conclusions with subject-matter that is also standing still.

Just as even the most highly developed systematizers are subject to Destiny, so do they—all unwittingly—apply Destiny-thinking in their daily lives and relationships with other human beings. The most rabid reflexologist unconsciously applies some of the psychological wisdom of the Abbe Galiani or Rochefoucauld, even though he has never heard of these seers of the soul.

The Two Aspects of History

THE TOTAL DIFFERENCE between the methods of human thinking represented by the central-ideas of Destiny on the one hand, and Causality on the other, was sharply accented for the reason that only one of them is adapted to the understanding of History. History is the record of fulfilled destinies—of Cultures, nations, religions, philosophies, sciences, mathematics, art-forms, great men. Only the feeling of *empathy* can understand these once-living souls from the bare records left. Causality is helpless here, for at every second a new fact is cast into the pool of Life, and from its point of impact, ever-widening circles of changes spread out. The subterranean facts are never written down, but every fact changes the course of the history of facts. The true understanding of any organism, whether a High Culture, a nation, or a man, is to see—*behind* and *underneath* the facts of that existence—the soul which is expressing itself by means of, and often in opposition to, the external happenings. Only so can one separate what is significant from what is unimportant.

Significant thus is seen to mean: having a Destiny-quality. Incidental means: without relationship to Destiny. It was Destiny for Napoleon that Carnot was Minister of War, for another man would probably not have seen Napoleon's project for an invasion of Italy through the Ligurian Hills, buried as it was in the files of the Ministry. It was a Destiny for France that the author of the plan was a man of action as well as a theoretician. It is thus obvious that the feeling for what is Destiny and what is Incident have a high subjective content, and that a deeper insight can make out Destiny where the more superficial sees only Incident.

Men are thus differentiated also with regard to their capacity for understanding History. There is an *historical* sense, which can see behind the surface of history to the soul that is the determinant of this history. History, seen through the historical sense of a human being, has thus a *subjective aspect*. This is the first aspect of History.

The other, the objective, aspect of History, is equally incapable of rigid establishment, even though at first glance it might seem to be. The writing of purely *objective* history is the aim of the so-called reference, or narrative, method of presenting history. Nevertheless, it inevitably *selects* and *orders* the facts, and in this process the poetic intuition, historical sense, and flair of the author come into play. If these are totally excluded, the product is not history-writing, but a book of dates, and this, again, cannot be free from selection.

Nor is it history. The genetic method of writing history attempts to set forth the *developments* with complete impartiality. It is the narrative method with some type of causal, evolutionary, or organic philosophy superimposed to trace the growth of the subsequent out of the precedent. This fails to attain objectivity because the facts that survive may be either too few or too numerous, and in either case artistry must be employed in filling gaps or selecting. Nor is impartiality possible. It is the historical sense which decides *importance* of past developments, past ideas, past great men. For centuries, Brutus and Pompey were held to be greater than Caesar. Around 1800, Vulpius was considered a greater poet than Goethe. Mengs, whom we have forgotten, was ranked in his day as one of the great painters of the world. Shakespeare, until more than a century after his death, was considered inferior as a playwright to more than one of his contemporaries. El Greco was unnoticed 75 years ago. Cicero and Cato were both held, until after the First World War, to be great men, rather than Culture-retarding weaklings. Joan of Arc was not included in Chastellain's list, drawn up on the death of Charles VII, of all the army commanders who fought against England. Lastly, for the benefit of readers of 2050, I may say that the Hero and the Philosopher of the period 1900–1950 were both invisible to their contemporaries in the historical dimensions in which you see them.

The Classical Culture looked one way to Wincklemann's time, another way to Nietzsche's time, yet another way to the 20th and 21st centuries. Similarly, Elizabethan England was satisfied with Shakespeare's dramatization of Plutarch's Caesar, whereas *fin-de-siécle* England required Shaw to dramatize Mommsen's Caesar, Wilhelm Tell, Maria Stuart, Götz von Berlichingen, Florian Geyer, all would have to be written differently today, for we see these historical periods from a different angle.

What then, is History? *History is the relationship between the Past and the Present.* Because the Present is constantly changing, so is History. Each Age has its own History, which the Spirit of the Age creates to fit its own soul. With the passing of that Age, never to return, that particular History picture has passed. Seen from this standpoint, any attempt to write History "as it really happened" is historical immaturity, and the belief in objective standards of history-presentation is self-deception, for what will come forth will be the Spirit of the Age. The general agreement of contemporaries with a certain outlook on History does not make that outlook *objective,* but only gives it rank—the highest possible rank it can have—as an accurate expression of the Spirit of the Age, true for this time and this soul. A higher degree of truth cannot be attained, this side of divinity. Anyone who prates of being "modern" must remember that he would have felt just as modern in the Europe of Charles V, and that he is doomed to become just as "old-fashioned" to the men of 2050 as are the men of 1850 to him. A journalistic view of History stamps its possessor as lacking in the historical sense. He should therefore refrain from talking of historical matters, whether past or in the process of becoming.

The Relativity of History

HISTORY must always have its subjective aspect, and its objective aspect. But the determining thing is always neither the one, nor the other, but simply the *relationship* between the two. Each of the first two aspects can be arbitrary, but the relationship is *not* arbitrary, but is the expression of the Spirit of the Age, and is therefore *true,* historically speaking.

Each of the eight Cultures which passed in brilliant review before us had its own relationship to History generally, and this relationship developed in a certain direction through the life-course of the Culture. It is only necessary to mention the Classical in this connection. Tacitus, Plutarch, Livy, Suetonius were regarded as historical thinkers by the Romans. To us they are simply story-tellers, totally lacking in the historical sense. This could not be a reflection on them, but only tells us something about ourselves. Our view of History is as intense, fierce, probing and extensive, as the whole cast of our Western soul generally. If there were ten millennia of history instead of five, we would find it necessary to orient ourselves to the whole ten instead of to the mere five.

Not only are the Cultures differentiated from one another also in their historical sense, but the various Ages within the Culture's development are so distinguished. Although all tendencies exist in all the Ages, it is nevertheless correct to say that one certain Life-tendency dominates any one Age. Thus in all Cultures, the *religious* feeling is uppermost in the first great Life-phase, lasting some five centuries, and is then superseded by the *critical* spirituality, lasting somewhat less long, to be succeeded by the *historical* outlook, which gradually merges again into the final rebirth of religion. The three Life-tendencies are, successively, sacred, profane, and skeptical.

They parallel the political phases of Feudalism, corresponding to religion; Absolute State, and Democracy, corresponding to early and late Critical philosophy; and Resurgence of Authority and Caesarism, the counterparts of skepsis and rebirth of religion.

The intra-Cultural development of the idea of Science, or Natural Philosophy, is from *Theology* through, in succession, *physical sciences and biology,* to pure, untheoretical, *Nature-manipulation,* the scientific counterpart of skepsis and resurgent authority.

The Age which succeeds to the Age of Democracy can only see its predecessors under their purely *historical* aspect. This is the only way it can feel itself as related to them. This too, however, as will be apparent, has its imperative side. Culture-man is always a *unity,* and the mere fact that one Life-tendency is uppermost cannot destroy this organic unity.

In all Ages, the individuals therein are separated from one another also by their varying development of the historical sense. Think of the different historical horizon of Frederick II and one of his Sicilian courtiers, of Cesare Borgia and one of his captains, of Napoleon and Nelson, of Mussolini and his assassin. A political unit in the custody of a man with no historical horizon, an opportunist, must pay with its wasted blood for his lack.

Just as the Western Culture has the most intensely historic soul, so does it develop men with the greatest historical sense. It is a Culture which has always been *conscious* of its own history. At each turning-point there were many who knew the significance of the moment. Both sides, in any Western opposition, have felt themselves as clothed with and determining the Future.

Therefore Western men have been under the necessity of having a History-picture in which to think and act. The fact that the Culture was continually changing meant that History was continually changing. *History is the continuous reinterpretation of the Past.* History is thus continually "true," because, in each Age, the ruling historical outlook and values are the expression of the proper soul. The alternatives for History are not *true* or *false,* but *effective* or *ineffective.* Truth in the religio-philosophical-mathematical sense, meaning timelessly, eternally valid, dissociated from the conditions of Life, does not pertain to History. History that is true is History that is effective in the minds of significant men.

The highly refined historical sense is the characteristic of two groups: history-writers and history-makers. Between these two groups also there is an order of rank. History-writing has the task of setting forth for the Age its necessary picture of the Past. This picture, clear and articulate, then becomes effective in the thoughts and actions of the leading history-makers of the Age.

This age, like others, has its own appropriate History-picture, and it cannot choose one of a number of pictures. The determining thing in our outlook on History is the Spirit of our Age.

Ours is an external, factual, skeptical, historical, Age. It is not moved by great religious or critical feelings. That which to our Cultural forebears was the object of joy, sorrow, passion, necessity, is to us the object of respect and knowledge. The center of gravity of our Age is in Politics. Pure historical thinking is the close relative of political thinking. Historical thinking always seeks to know what *was,* and not to prove something. Political thinking has the first task of ascertaining the facts and the possibilities, and then of changing them through action. Both are undissociated *realism.* Neither begins with a program, which it desires to prove.

Ours is the first age in Western history in which an absolute submission to facts has triumphed over all other spiritual attitudes. It is the natural corollary of an historical Age, when critical methods have exhausted their possibilities. In the realm of Thought, historical thinking triumphs; in the realm of action, Politics occupies the center of the stage. We follow the facts no matter where they lead, even though we must give up dearly cherished schemes, ideologies, soul-fancies, prejudices. Previous ages in Western history formed their History to fit their souls; we do the same, but our view has no precedent ethical or critical equipment in it. On the contrary—*our ethical imperative is derived from our historical outlook and not vice versa.*

Our outlook on History is no more arbitrary than that of any other age of the West. It is *compulsory for us;* each man will have this outlook, and his level of significance will depend on the focus in these matters which he can attain and hold. Insofar as a man is an effective representative of this time, he has this particular History-picture and no other. It is not a question of whether he *should* have it; so to read is completely to misunderstand. He *will* have it, in his feelings and unconscious valuation of events, even if not in his articulate, verbal, ideas.

The Meaning of Facts

WHETHER OR NOT a man's History-outlook is also intellectually formulated as well as effective in his unconscious doing, thinking, and valuing is merely a function of his general personality. Some men have a greater inner need to think abstractly than others.

It must not be supposed that the sense for facts, the historical sense, dispenses with creative thinking. The development of fact-sense is primarily the seeing what is there without ethical or critical preconceptions of what should or should not be there, might or might not.

Life-facts are the data of History. *A Life-fact is something which has happened.* It does not matter to its status as a fact that no one may know of it, that it has vanished without trace. Obviously creative thinking enters into the process of interpreting the data of History, and a moment's reflection shows also that the process of assessing the *data* of History is a creative one.

Physical facts, like resistance, sourness, redness, are accessible to everyone. Life-facts are not accessible to a man who has a rigid view of History, and who *knows* that the *purpose* of all previous happening was to make this age possible, who *knows* that History has the sole meaning of "Progress." Remnants of social ethics, preconceived historical notions, utility dogmas—all shut out their victims from inner participation in the life of the 20th and 21st centuries.

To this century the new vista now opens of assembling the *lost facts* in previous ages and previous Cultures. Not tiny incidental data, but the broad outline of necessary organic developments that *must* have taken place. From our knowledge of past Cultures and their structures, we can fill in missing developments in some from what has survived in others. Most important to us now alive—we can fill in what remains to the fulfillment of our own Culture. This can be done in the way that a palaeontologist can reconstruct in broad outlines an entire organism from a single skull-fragment. The process is legitimate and trustworthy in both cases, for Life has patterns in which it actualizes its unique individuals. From an anonymous work of literature remaining, a creative thinker can reconstruct a general picture of the unknown author. Can one not draw quite accurately the soul-portrait of the unknown author of *Das Büchlein vom vollkommenen Leben*? So also can the "Crusades" period of a Culture be reconstructed if one has knowledge of its "Reformation" stage, or its "Enlightenment" phase.

The realm of Thought is interested in the missing stages of past Cultures, and the future of our own, but Action is interested in the Past only as the key to effective performance. Thus the higher importance of history-writing and history-thinking is that they serve effective action.

The fact-sense is only operative when dogma, socio-ethical ideas, and critical trappings are put aside. To the fact-sense, it is important that hundreds of millions of people in a certain area believe in the truth of Confucian doctrines. To the fact-sense, it is *meaningless* whether or not these doctrines are true—even though to religion, Progress-ideologies, and journalism, the truth or falsehood of Confucianism is important.

To a 21st century history-writer, the most important thing about the cells, ether-waves, bacillae, electrons, and cosmic rays of our times will be that we believed in them. All of these notions, which the age considers *facts,* will vanish into the one fact for the 21st century that once upon a time this was a world-picture of a certain kind of Culture-man. So do we look upon the nature-theories of Aristarchus and Democritus in the Classical Culture.

And thus *facts* too have their subjective and objective content. And again, it is the relationship between the man and the phenomenon that determines the form of the fact. Each Culture has in this way its own *facts,* which arise out of its own *problems.* What the fact is, depends on what man is experiencing the phenomenon: whether he belongs to a High Culture, to which Culture, to which age thereof, to which nation, to which spiritual stratum, to which social stratum.

The facts of the Second World War are one thing in this year 1948, in the brains of the Culture-bearing stratum of Europe, and something *totally* different in the minds of the newspaper-reading herds. By 2000 the view of the present Culture-bearing stratum will have become also the view of the many, and by that time, more facts will be known to the independent thinkers about the same War than are now known to the few. For one of the characteristics of Life-facts is that distance—particularly temporal distance—shows up their lineaments more clearly. We know more of Imperial history than Tacitus knew, more of Napoleonic history than Napoleon knew, vastly more of the First World War than its creators and participants knew, and Western men in 2050 will know our times in a way that we can never know them. To Brutus his mythological ancestry was a fact, but to us a more important fact is that he believed it.

Thus the fact-sense, the prerequisite of the historical outlook of the 20th century, emerges as a form of the *poetry* of Life. It is the very opposite of the prosaic, drab insistence of the materialistic outlook that facts had to submit to a "progress" ideology in order to be cognized as significant. This view absolutely excluded its victims from any insight into the beauty and power of the facts of history, as well as from any understanding of their significance. The 21st century—whose men will be born into a time when this historical outlook is self-evident —will find it fantastic, if it ever takes notice of it, that in an earlier time men believed that all previous history was merely tending toward them. And yet that was the outlook of the 19th century: whole Cultures, equal by birth and spirituality to our own in every way, lived and died merely that the philistinism of the "progress"-ideologists could chalk up their "achievements" on the wall, meaning a few notions or technical devices.

The Demise of the Linear View of History

LIFE is a continuous battle between Young and Old, Old and New, Innovation and Tradition. Ask Galileo, Bruno, Servetus, Copernicus, Gauss. All of them represented the Future, yet all were overcome, in one way or another, during their own lives, by the enthroned Past. Copernicus was afraid to publish during his lifetime, lest he be burned as heretic. Gauss only revealed his liberating discovery of non-Euclidean geometries after his death, for fear of the clamor of the Boeotians. It is therefore not surprising when the materialists persecute, by maligning, by conspiracy of silence, cutting off from access to publicity, or by driving to suicide, as in the case of Haushofer, those who think in 20th century terms and specifically reject the methods and conclusions of 19th century materialism.

The 20th century view of History has to make its way over the ruins of the linear scheme which insisted on seeing History as a progression from an "Ancient" through a "Mediaeval" to a "Modern." I say ruins, for the scheme collapsed decades ago, but they are heavily defended ruins. Hidden in them are the materialists, the posthumous inhabitants of the 19th century, the "Progress" philistines, the social-ethicians, the superannuated devotees of critical philosophy, the ideologists of every description whatever.

Common to them all is *Rationalism*. They assume as a tenet of faith that History is *reasonable*, that they themselves are *reasonable*, and that therefore History has done, and will do, what they think it should. The origin of the three-stage view of History is found in St. Joachim of Floris, a Gothic religionist who put forward the three stages as a *mystical* progression. It was left for the increasing coarseness of intellect devoid of soul to make the progression a *materialistic-utilitarian one*. For two centuries now, each generation has regarded itself as the peak of all the previous striving of the world. This shows that Materialism is also a Faith, a crude caricature of the precedent religion. It is supplanted now, not because it is wrong—for a Faith can never be injured by refutation—but because the Spirit of the Age is devoid of materialism.

The linear scheme was more or less satisfactory to Western man as long as he knew nothing of history outside the Bible, Classic authors, and Western chronicles. Even then, it would not have held up if the philosophy of history had not been a neglected field of endeavor. However, a little over a century ago began a spate of archaeological investigation, including excavations and deciphering of original inscriptions in Egypt, Babylonia, Greece, Crete, China and India. It continues today and now includes also Mexico and Peru. The result of these investigations was to show the historically-minded Western Civilization that it was by no means unique in its historical grandeur, but that it belonged to a group of High Cultures, of similar structure, and of equal elaboration and splendor. The Western Culture is the first to have had both the intense historical impetus as well as the geographic situation to develop a thorough archaeology, which includes now within its purview the whole historical world, just as Western politics at one time embraced the whole surface of the earth.

The results of this profound archaeological science broke down the old-fashioned linear scheme of regarding History. It was utterly unable to fit in the new wealth of facts. Since there was some *geographic,* even though no *historical,* community between the Egyptian, Babylonian, Classical, and Western Cultures, it had been able to distort them somehow into a picture that could convince those who already believed. But with the opening up of the history of the Cultures that were fulfilled in India, China, Arabia, Mexico, Peru—this view could no longer convince even believers.

Furthermore, the materialistic spirit, which had posited the "influence" of preceding Cultures on subsequent ones, meanwhile died out, and the new, *psychological* outlook on Life recognized the primacy of the soul, the inner purity of the soul, and the superficiality of the process of borrowing of *externalia.*

The new feeling about History was actually coeval with the tremendous outburst of archaeological activity which broke down the old linear scheme. The new outlook became a soul-necessity of Western Civilization at the same time that the history-seeking activity did, even though it was to remain half-articulate until the First World War. This intense outburst of probing of the Past was an expression of a superpersonal feeling that the riddle of History was *not* touched with the old linear device, that it *had to be* unlocked, that the totality of facts *must be* surveyed. As the new facts accumulated, the higher-ranking historians took a wider view, but not until the latter part of the 19th century did any historian or philosopher actually treat Cultures as separate organisms, with parallel existence, independence, and spiritual equality. The idea of "cultural history" itself was a forerunner of this view, and was a prerequisite to the development of the 20th century outlook on History. The rejection of the idea that History was merely the record of reigns and battles, treaties and dates, marked an epoch. The feeling spread that "universal history" was wanted, the combination of the history of politics, law, religion, manners, society, commerce, art, philosophy, warfare, erotic, literature, into one great synthesis. Schiller was one of the first to articulate this general need, although both Voltaire and Winckelmann had written specific histories along these lines.

Hegel, on a spiritual basis, and Comte and Buckle, materialistically, developed further the idea of *total* history, i.e., *cultural* history. Burckhardt not only produced a quite perfect example of a cultural history in his Italian Renaissance book, but developed a philosophy of history-writing pointing toward the 20th century outlook. Taine, Lamprecht, Breysig, Nietzsche, Meray, all are milestones in the development away from the linear view of history. In their times, only Nietzsche, and to a lesser extent, Burckhardt and Bachofen, understood the 20th century idea of the unity of a Culture. But two generations later the idea of the unity of a High Culture is general in the highest spiritual stratum of Europe, and has become a prerequisite to both historical and political thinking.

What was this linear view of History? It was either a mere arbitrary breaking-up of historical materials for handling and reference, without any claim to philosophical significance, or else it was an attempt at a philosophy of history. Its pretensions to the latter could not very well hold up in view of the fact that for generations the starting-point of the "Modern" age has been shifted around from century to century with complete freedom. Each writer has formulated the significance and dates of the three stages differently and the various formulations exclude one another. But if they are not the same view, why the same terminology?

Thus it was no philosophy of history, but a mere set of three *names* which were retained because of a sort of magic which was supposed to inhere in them. Nor was it a satisfactory method of breaking up the historical facts for reference purposes, since it left no place for China and India, and since it treated the Babylonian and Egyptian, in every way the historical equals of the Classical and our own, as though they were mere episodes, together constituting a *prelude* to the Classical. For this grotesque History-outlook, a millennium in Egypt was a footnote, while ten years in our own century were a volume.

II

The basis of the linear view was *Cultural egocentricity,* or in other words the unconscious assumption that the Western Culture was the focus of the whole meaning of all human history, that previous Cultures had importance only insofar as they "contributed" something to us, but that in themselves they had no importance whatever. This is why the Cultures which lived in areas remote from Western Europe are hardly even mentioned. These famous "contributions"—what was meant was a few technical devices from the Egyptian and Babylonian Cultures, and the Cultural remains generally of the Classical. The Arabian, again, was almost totally ignored, for geographic reasons. And yet Western architecture, religion, philosophy, science, music, lyric, manners, erotic, politics, finance, economics all are totally independent of the corresponding Classical forms. It is the archaeological cast of the Western soul, its intensely historical nature, that prompt it to reverence what mere geography might indicate is a spiritual ancestor.

And yet—who believes, or ever did *actually* believe, that the

Rome of Hildebrand, of Alexander VI, of Charles V, or of Mussolini, had any continuity whatever with the Rome of Flaminius, Sulla, Caesar? This whole Classicistic yearning of the West, with its two high points in the Italian Renaissance and above all, in Winckelmann's movement, was actually nothing but a literary-Romantic pose. If we had known less of Rome and more of Mecca, Napoleon's title might have been Caliph instead of First Consul, but nothing would have inwardly altered. The endowing of words and names with magic significance is quite necessary and legitimate in religion, philosophy, science, and criticism, but is out of place in an outlook on History.

Even in the Italian Renaissance, Francesco Pico wrote against the mania for the Classical: "Who will be afraid to confront Plato with Augustine, or Aristotle with Thomas, Albert, and Scotus?" Savonarola's movement also had cultural, as well as religious, significance: into the bonfires went the Classical works. The whole Classicist tendency of the Italian Renaissance has been too heavily drawn: it was *literary, academic,* the possession of a few small circles, and those not the leading ones in thought or action.

And yet this movement has been put forward as the "link" between two Cultures that have nothing in common in order to create a picture of History as a straight line instead of as the spiritually parallel, pure, independent, development of High Cultures.

To the religious outlook, with its branches, philosophy and criticism, "Progress-philistinism," and social ethics, facts figure only as *proof,* and lack any other interest. To the historical outlook, facts are the material sought after, and even doctrines, dogmas, and truths, are treated as simply facts. Previous Western ages were thus satisfied by the linear scheme, despite its complete independence of the facts of history. To the 20th century, however, with its center of gravity in politics, History is not a mere instrument of proving or illustrating any dogma, or socio-ethical "Progress" theory, but the *source* of our effective world-outlook.

And so, in implicit obedience to the Spirit of the Age, the leading minds of the 20th century reject the old-fashioned, anti-factual, linear theory of History. In its place the Spirit of the Age has shown the actual structure of human history, the history of eight High Cultures, each an organism with its own individuality and destiny. The older type of philosophy of history forced the facts to prove some religious, ethical, or critical theory; the 20th century outlook takes its philosophy of history *from* the facts.

The 20th century outlook is none the less subjective because it starts from facts; it is merely obeying the inner imperative of its own historical soul in seeing its History-picture thus. Our view is none the less peculiarly *ours* because it gives priority to facts; other types of men, outside the Western Culture, or beneath it, will never be able to understand it, any more than they can understand higher Western mathematics, Western technics, physics, or chemistry, Gothic architecture or the art of the fugue. This picture of History, absolutely compulsory as it is for the leading men of thought of action in the Western Civilization, is no compulsion for the masses that throng in the streets of the Western capitals. Historical relativity is, like physical relativity, the possession of a few leading minds. History is not experienced, nor made, in the streets, but on the heights. The number of men in the Western Civilization who were aware of the *actual meaning* of the Second World War is countable in thousands. Western philosophy, from the days of Anselm, has always been esoteric. No less so is the 20th century outlook, and correspondingly small is the number of those for whom it is a soul-necessity. But the number for whom the decisions of these few will be decisive is not numbered in hundreds, but in hundreds of millions.

To the 20th century, the regarding of all previous human happening as merely introductory to, and preparatory to our own Western history, is simply immense naïvete. Evolutions that required just as long as our millennium of Western history are contracted into mere casual events; the men in these other Cultures are treated as though they were children, dimly trying to attain to one or another of our specifically Western ideas. But in each of these previous Cultures, the stage was reached and passed that we attained to in the 19th and 20th centuries: free science, social ethics, democracy, materialism, atheism, rationalism, class war, money, nationalism, annihilation-wars. Highly artificial living conditions, megalopolitan sophistication, social disintegration, divorce, degeneration of the old arts to mere formlessness—they exhibited all these familiar symptoms.

The vast amount of historical knowledge of which the 20th century must take account—knowledge unearthed by the historical age which succeeded to the age of Criticism—can tolerate no arbitrary forcing of the facts of history into a preconceived scheme with three magical stages, which must remain three even though no one can agree where one begins and the other leaves off, and of which the third stage has been prolonged indefinitely since Professor Horn of Leyden announced in 1667 his discovery of "the Middle Ages."

The first formulation of the 20th century outlook on History only came with the First World War. Previously, only Breysig had definitely broken with the linear scheme, but his earlier work covered only a part of human history. It was left to

Spengler, the philosopher of the age, to set forth the full outline of the structure of History. He himself was the first to recognize the superpersonal nature of his work, when he said that an historically essential idea is only in a limited sense the property of him to whose lot it falls to parent it. It was for him to *articulate* that at which everyone was groping. The view of others was limited by one or another specialist horizon, and their projects were consequently incomplete, one-sided, top-heavy. Like all products of genius, Spengler's work seems perfectly obvious to those who come afterwards, and again, it was directed to those to come and not to contemporaries. Genius is always directed toward the Future; this is in its nature, and this is the explanation of the usual fate of all works of genius, political and economic, as well as artistic and philosophical, that they are understood in their grandeur and simplicity only by the after-world of their creators.

The Structure of History

ONE OF THE UNCONSCIOUS ASSUMPTIONS of the linear scheme was the idea of the *singularity of civilization.* The concept "civilization" was used as though all highly symbolic Life, wherever and whenever it appeared, was really a manifestation of the same thing—"civilization." "Civilization" outside of the West was imperfect, striving to be Western, stammering and fumbling. This "civilization" was something that previous ages had stupidly allowed to slip away, but somehow it was always found again, hidden in a book somewhere, and "passed on" to the Future.

Again this was Rationalism: it assumed that men made their own history, and whatever happened was traceable to human excellence or to human mistakes.

But, to the pinnacle of historical insight and self-conscious grand historical creativeness of deeds that is the 20th century, History is the record of the lives of eight High Cultures, each an *organism,* impressed with the principle of individuality, each thus a member of a Life-form. The type *High Culture* is a Life-form at the peak of the organic hierarchy of which plants, animals, and man are the lower members. Each of the Cultures that we have seen is a member of this higher genus, an individual. Belonging as they do to one genus, they have common characteristics in their general habitus, their life-necessities, their technic of self-expression, their relation to landscape and population-streams, and their life span.

The differences among the Cultures are in their souls, their individualities, and thus, despite their similar structure, their *creations* are in the highest degree dissimilar. In the organic hierarchy, the principle of individuality is manifested at an increasing level of concentration from plants, through animals, to man. Cultures are even more highly individual than men, and their creations are correspondingly less capable of any inward assimilation by other Cultures.

With the passing of the Age of Materialism, the West knows once more that the development of an organism is the unfolding of a soul. The matter is the mere envelope, the vehicle of the expression of the spirit. It is this ancient and universal wisdom that is the primary source of the liberation of our History-outlook from the darkness and oppressiveness of Mechanism. The events of a human life are the expressions of the soul of that human at its successive stages of unfolding. The identical outward occurrence is a different *experience* for each human being: *an experience is a relationship between a soul and an outer event*. Thus no two persons can have the same experience, because the identical event is quite different to each different soul.

Similarly the reactions of each Culture-soul to externals of landscape, population-streams, and events and movements outside the Culture-area, are *individual* to each Culture. The religious experiences of each Culture are unique: each Culture has its own non-transferable way of experiencing and depicting the

Godhead, and this religious style continues right through the life span of the Culture, and determines completely the philosophy, science, and also the anti-religious phenomena of the Culture. Each Culture has its own kind of atheism, as unique as its religion. The philosophy and science of each Culture never become independent of the religious style of the Culture; even Materialism is only a profane caricature of the basic religious feeling of the Culture.

The choice of art-forms, and the content of the art-forms, are individual to each Culture. Thus the Western is the first to invent oil-painting, and the first to give primacy to music. The number-feeling of the Culture develops in each its own mathematics, which describes its own number-world, which again is inwardly non-transferable, even though external developments may be partially taken over, and then inwardly transformed by other Cultures. The State-idea is likewise individual, as are the Nation-idea, and the style of the final Imperium, the last political creation of the Culture.

Each Culture has its own style in technics—weak and crude in the Classical and Mexican-Peruvian, colossal and earth-shaking in our own—its own war-style, its own relation to economics, its own history-style, or organic *tempo*.

Each Culture has a different basic Morale, which influences its social structure, feelings, and manners, its intensity of inner imperative, and thus the ethical style of its great men. This basic morale determines the style of public life during the last great phase of the life of the Culture—the Civilization.

Not only are the Cultures differentiated from one another by their highly developed representation of the principle of individuality, but each age of each Culture has its own stamp, which sets it off from its preceding age, and from the succeeding. These differences loom larger to the humans within a Culture than the difference between one Culture and another. This is the optical illusion of greater size produced by nearness. To us the difference between 1850 and 1950 seems vast—to the history of 2150 it will be much less so. We have the feeling before we study history that 1300 and 1400 were spiritually much the same, but in fact, in that century there were spiritual developments as far-reaching as those between 1850 and 1950.

Here again, the linear scheme distorted History utterly: it said "Ancient" and thought that thereby it was describing *one* thing, one general spirtuality. But Egypt and Babylonia both had their own corresponding phenomena to our Crusades, Gothic religion, Holy Roman Empire, Papacy, Feudalism, Scholasticism, Reformation, Absolute State, Enlightenment, Democracy, Materialism, Class War, Nationalism, and annihilation wars. So did the others—the Chinese, Indian, Arabian, Classical, and Mexican. The extent of information available is quite different with regard to the various Cultures, but enough remains to show the structure of History. Between one age of Egyptian history and the next, there was as much difference as between 1700, the period of our Spanish Succession Wars, and 1800, our Napoleonic Wars. This illusion about distance finds an analogy in the spatial world; a distant mountain range looks smooth; nearer, it is rocky.

The idea that "civilization" was one certain thing, rather than an organic life-phase of a Culture, was a part of the "Progress" ideology. This profane religion, its own peculiar mixture of Reason and Faith, satisfied a certain inner demand of the 19th century. Further research will probably discover it in other Cultures. It seems to be an organic necessity of Rationalism to feel that "things are getting better all the time." Thus "progress" was a continuous moral improvement of "humanity," a movement toward more and better "civilization." The ideology was formulated slightly differently by each materialist, but it was not allowed to dispute that "Progress" occurred. To do so marked one as a "pessimist." The ideal toward which there was continual "progress" was necessarily unattainable, for if it could be attained, "progress" would cease, and this was unthinkable.

Such a picture fitted the Age of Criticism, but in an historical Age this picture becomes just one more object of interest, as being the expression of one certain life-stage of a certain Culture. It is on a par with the world-picture of imminent catastrophe of mid-14th century, the witch obsession of the 16th century, the Reason-worship of the 18th century. All these outlooks possess now only historical significance. What interests us is that once they were believed. But as for trying to force the old-fashioned "progress" ideology on the 20th century, such an attempt is ludicrous; whoever would try stamps himself as an anachronistic mediocrity.

II

The word history has been employed to cover all human events, those manifesting the development of a Culture, and those outside of any Culture. But the two classes of events have nothing in common. *Man as a species is one Life-form,* Culture-man is another. The word history therefore designates separate things in the two cases.

In what is man as a species distinct from other Life-forms, such as plants and animals? Simply in his possession of a human soul. This soul shapes for man a different world from the world of other forms of life. Man's world is a world of *symbols.* Things that for animals contain no meaning, and no mystery, have for man a symbolic significance. Outside of a High

Culture, this symbolizing-necessity shows itself in the formation of primitive culture. Such cultures have an animistic religion, an ethic of tabu and totem, and social-political forms on the same level. Such cultures are not a unity, i.e., no single *prime symbol* is actualized in all the forms of the culture. These cultures are mere *sums,* collections of motives and tendencies.

Nowhere is primitive man without some primitive culture of this type. Man as a *pure* animal does not exist. All animals have a purely economic-reproductive existence: their whole individual lives consist in the process of nourishing and reproducing themselves, their lives have no spiritual superstructure above this plane.

Nevertheless, man's life in primitivity, and in an area where a High Culture is fulfilling itself, are two incommensurable things. The difference is so vast as to constitute one of kind, and not of mere degree. *Vis-a-vis* the history of Culture-man, primitive man seems merely zoological. The history that Stanley found in progress on his African explorations was of the one kind, and Stanley himself represented the other kind. Similarly zoological is the history of the lake-dwellers in Switzerland, the Chinese today, the Arabs, Bushmen, Indians, Amerindians, Lapps, Mongols, and the countless other tribes, races, and peoples outside our Western Civilization.

The animal is solely concerned with economics, primitive man sees hidden meanings in the world—but Culture-man regards his high symbols as the content of Life. A High Culture re-shapes entirely the economic practice of the populations upon whom it sets its grip; it reduces economics to the bottom of the pyramid of life. To a High Culture, economics has the same significance that the function of eating has to an individual. Above economics are all the manifestations of the High Culture's life: architecture, religion, philosophy, art, science, technics, education, politics, erotic, city-building, imperialism, society. The significance an individual has is the reflex of his personal connection with the symbols of the Culture. This valuation itself is produced by the Culture—to an *anti-cultural* outlook such as the curious "materialistic interpretation of history," any proletaire is worth more than Calderon, for Calderon was not a manual laborer, and therefore accomplished nothing in a world whose entire significance is economic.

The difference between the history of man as a species and the history of man in the service of High Culture is that the first is devoid of grand meaning, and that only the second is the vessel of high significance. In high history, men risk all and die for an *Idea;* in primitivity there are no superpersonal ideas of this force, but only personal strivings, crude lust for booty or formless power. Consequently it would be an error to regard the difference as merely quantitative. The example of Genghis Khan shows this: the events he let loose were considerable in size, but in the cultural sense they have no significance whatever. There was no *Idea* in this sweeping descent of the followers of an adventurer. His conquests were fatal to hundreds of thousands, the empire he erected lasted generations beyond him, but it was simply *there*—it stood for nothing, represented nothing beyond itself. Napoleon's empire on the other hand, brief though it was, was laden with symbolic meaning that is still at work in the minds of Western men, and that is, as we shall see, pregnant with the Future of the West. High Cultures create the greatest wars, but their significance is not merely that they open rivers of blood, but that these men fall in a struggle of ideas.

After a High Culture has fulfilled itself, the populations in its former area return to the condition of primitivity, as the examples of India, China, Islam, and Egypt tell us. The world-cities empty themselves, the outer barbarians plunder them bare, and the men that are left are once more clans, tribes, nomads. When outer events do not destroy the remains utterly, the caste system of the last stage remains indefinitely, as in India and China, but it is the mere skeletal remains of the former Culture, which, like everything living, passes away, never to return. The memory of the Culture remains, but the attitude of the remaining populations toward its products is once more entirely primitive, unchanging, purely personal.

The abandoned world-cities return once more to the landscapes which they once dominated. World-cities that were once as proud as Berlin, London, and New York disappeared under jungle vegetation or the sands of the plain. This was the fate of Luxor, Thebes, Babylon, Pataliputra, Samarra, Uxmal, Tezcuco, Tenochtitlan. In the latter cases, even the names of the great cities have perished, and we call them after nearby villages. But it is an unimportant detail whether the city lies dead upon the surface, inhabited by a few clans who farm in the open spaces, fight in the streets, and shelter in the abandoned structures, or whether the sands shift over the crumbling remains.

Pessimism

It was a remarkably curious phenomenon that when the organically necessary *historical* outlook on History, replacing the religious and critical-philosophical outlooks of previous Western ages, appeared early in the 20th century, it was greeted by the day-before-yesterday thinkers with a cry of "Pessimism." By this word it was apparently thought possible to conjure away the spirit of the coming age, and summon to new life the dead spirit of an age that had passed away. To abstract inorganic thought this feat did not seem considerable, since it regarded History as the field wherein one could do whatever he wanted to make the Past dance to his own tune.

The word pessimism was a polemical word—it described an attitude of general despair, which was supposed to color opinions and assessments of facts. Any person who seriously used this word showed thereby that he was willing to treat a world-historical philosophy in an electioneering fashion. Obviously an asserted fact should be examined entirely independently of the attitude of him asserting it. The whole pessimism cry is thus an *ad hominem* argument, and worthless. Facts are not pessimistic or optimistic, sane or insane—an optimist may assert a fact, a madman may, a pessimist may. Describing the man who uttered the fact still leaves entirely open the correctness or incorrectness of the fact. Its purely *ad hominem* nature was the first weakness in the "Pessimism" view of the 20th century outlook on History.

Pessimism only describes an *attitude,* and not facts, and hence is entirely *subjective.* The attitude toward life that Nietzsche continually belabored as "Pessimism" in its turn described Nietzsche as a pessimist, and both were undoubtedly correct. If someone else thinks my plans are doomed, I consider him a pessimist, from my standpoint. Similarly, if I think his aspirations will come to naught, he thinks me a pessimist. We are both correct.

The "Progress" ideologists, smug in their secure mental armor, insulated from all contact with Reality, naturally felt it to be insulting in the extreme when it was suggested that their particular Faith also had a life span, was also, like all previous world-pictures, merely a description of a particular soul of a certain age, and thus was destined to pass away. To say that the "Progress" religion would come to an end with the Age whose inner demands it satisfied was to deny the truth of this religion, since it claimed to be a universal description of all human history. What was worse was that the 20th century outlook on History was formulated in such a strict factual way as to be *compelling* to the 20th century mind. This meant that catchwords had to be employed against it, since no other form of disputation would avail. With the single word "Pessimism," it was hoped to strangle the 20th century outlook on History.

It would be mistaken to put this down to the malice of the "Progress" religionists. No age submits quietly to the Spirit of the coming age.

The witchcraft religionists certainly did not agree with the first materialists who denied the very existence of witches. The

conflict between the Established and the Becoming goes on continually, and the Becoming always prevails. It does so, not because it is true, and the Established was false, but because both
were the lifestage of an organism, a Culture. Truth and falsehood have as little to do with this process as they do with the
transformation of the boy into a youth, the youth into a man,
the man into a dotard. The grandson is no more *true* than the
grandfather, yet he will prevail, because of the *organic* advantage he has. Similarly does the historical attitude of the 20th
century supplant the 19th century religion of Materialism.
Materialism, Rationalism, "Progress," are all worn out, but the
historical attitude of the 20th century is full of vigor and promise, eagerness to set itself to its great *factual* tasks, to create
its great deeds. This *organic* necessity alone gives it its compelling quality. No one in this gigantic age when nations are
world powers in one decade, and colonies in the next, can con-
scientiously maintain even before himself any shallow and in-
fantile pretense that underneath all these cataclysms there is the
meaning of a steady "moral improvement" of "humanity."

Some men have been rational for short periods—this is the
sum total of the appearance of Reason in History. But such men
have never made History, for it is irrational. The pretense of
Reason being the meaning of History was itself irrational, since
it was a product of History.

When the worship of Reason was instituted in Revolutionary
France as a religion—a Faith—a *fille de joie* was crowned as the
Goddess of Reason. Even Rationalism bears the stamp of Life—
it is irrational.

The meaning of the word pessimism must be further laid
bare. As we have seen, the word is subjective, and thus describes
everybody, if he has a conviction that something is doomed.
Suppose I say—Imperial Rome inwardly decayed, and within a

few centuries the Roman idea was completely dead. Is this pessimism? My grandfather is dead—am I a pessimist to say so?
Someday I shall die—pessimism? Everything living must die—
pessimism? To Life belongs Death—pessimism? Is there any
example of an individual which has moved completely outside
the organic sequence of that Life-form to which he belongs, and
remained constantly at one life-stage for such long time-periods
as to justify the conclusion that it was a case of Life without
Death? An example would be a man who lived for—not 100
years, for we all believe such a man will eventually die—but
two or three hundred years, and continually at one life stage,
say the biological age of 65 years.

We know no such man, no such life-form. The criers of "pessimism" will call this pessimism, no doubt. We should keep up
the pretense before ourselves all of our individual lives that we
shall not die, for to admit mortality is pessimism.

History discloses seven precedent High Cultures to us. Their
gestation-periods were morphologically identical, as were their
birth-pangs, their first life-activities, their growth, their mature
stages, their great Civilization-crises, their final life-forms, the
gradual relaxing, the coming to each of a time when one had to
say, looking at the landscape where the mighty being had fulfilled itself, that it was no longer, that it had died. This realization gives extreme pain to the "Pessimism" wailers, and I know
of no remedy for their pain. These seven Cultures are dead—
it would have been much more remarkable if they had gone
on forever.

II

But our Civilization is itself a stage of a High Culture, the
Culture of the West. Its millennium of history shows that it is
an individual organism belonging to the Life-form High Cul-

ture. Can fact-thinkers pretend that it belongs to the Life-form but has no Life-span?

The question can now be formulated: exactly how is it "Pessimism" to say that since seven High Cultures fulfilled themselves that an eighth will also? If this is "Pessimism," then anyone admitting his own mortality is inevitably a "Pessimist." The alternative to pessimism thus becomes idiocy.

However pessimism is an attitude, and if someone says that to admit the fact that Life is fulfilled in Death is pessimism, he shows something about *himself*. He shows his own cowardly fear of death, his entire lack of heroism, of respect for the mysteries of Being and Becoming, his shallow materialism. One must never forget that these same people are the ones who write and read, in their book and magazine press, a literature on indefinitely prolonging the life-span of the human species. Again, this shows something about *them*. How they delight in juggling insurance statistics in such a way as to make them think they are living *longer*! This is their valuation of life: the longest life is the best. To this mentality, a short and heroic life is *sad*, not inspiring. Heroism generally is thus merely foolish, since indefinitely prolonged life is the aim of "Progress."

In the Gothic religious times, the Western form of the idea of immortality of the soul was formed and developed. With the age of Materialism, this became caricatured into the immortality of the *body*. The doctor of medicine became the priest of the new religion, and a whole literature glorified him as the ultimate human type, since he was *saving life*. And yet, shocking though it is to these people, Death continues to accompany Life. 20th century wars take more lives than 19th century wars. The generations continue their procession to the grave, and even the most cowardly materialist, who can never admit that anything living will ever *die*, goes the way of the materialists in the other eight Cultures.

To people who live in a nameless terror of personal death, naturally the idea of the passing away of a superpersonal soul is also horrible and frightening. Materialists have never been respecters of *facts*—whatever was not measurable by their ruler did not exist. Historical facts are *per se* uninteresting to a rationalist outlook, which begins with a critical principle, and not with facts, and it was hardly to be expected that a view of history resting on five millennia of history rather than on a simple philosophical platitude would take them along with it.

It is curious that the Pessimism-wailers, who denied the Culture would ever *die,* also denied the organic nature of a Culture. In other words, they also denied it *lives.* Their materialism compelled them to the last, their cowardice to the first. Most important about all their attitudes was that they *did not understand* the central idea of the 20th century outlook. The hundreds of volumes that they wrote against it—each one echoing the magic word "Pessimism"—show that distressingly clearly. On every page is a fundamental misunderstanding of the great thesis. By their lack of comprehension, they provided another proof of the accuracy of the outlook, for the view of one age only reflects the soul of that age, and the 20th century outlook was definitely not adapted to their 19th century outlook.

One great historical fact could have given them consolation: the passing of this Culture, which was not alive, and also would never die, according to them, would mean little to them in particular. In the first place, a Culture is not born, nor does it die in a few years; these processes are measured in generations and centuries. Thus no man could ever see a Culture appear or disappear, and no materialist would ever be obliged to undergo the painful experience of watching it die. More important, the lives of the ordinary people, on the everyday plane of life, are little affected by the presence of the Culture or the Civilization, during and after its passing, the life of the ordinary people, in its stark fundamentals, is simply life. The great numbers vanish, since they were only there to perform the last great life-tasks of the Civilization; the artificial living-conditions go, the great wars cease, the great demands, the great deeds. Pacifism—organic pacifism, not ideological pacifism, which stirs up wars —is the end-condition of a Culture.

Now then, the materialists are exclusively among the ordinary people—what concern have they with great things like heroism, great wars, and imperialism? Therefore the end of a Culture should beckon to them. Actually, however, their whole terror rested on an illusion. It would be as foolish for someone now to worry about the events of 2300 A.D. as it would have been for Frederick the Great to worry about the conditions of 1900. He could not have *imagined* those exact conditions, hence he could not have planned for them, hence it would have been foolish for him to *dread* them. They were to be the concern of other people. The day's demands, as Goethe said, constitute one's immediate duty. We living in Europe today have a certain task imposed upon us by the situation, the times, and our own inner imperative. The most we can do about forming the remote Future is to do our utmost in giving to this age the strong and manly form it demands. The generation after the next will have its task also, and the only way we can make ourselves effective in their age will be so to conduct ourselves now that our deeds and example will live after us.

To a materialist, this is pessimism.

III

There are many intellectuals who stop at the title of leading works of an historical age: these gathered the basis for their charge of pessimism against the 20th century world-outlook from the title of the first book fully to outline it: The Decline of the West. *Decline* had a definitely pessimistic sound to these gentlemen; they needed no more. In his essay *Pessimism?* (1921), Spengler mentioned that some people had confused the sinking of a Culture with the sinking of a steamship, whereas, as applied to a Culture, the idea of a catastrophe was not contained in the word. He explains further that this title was decided upon in 1911, when, in his words, "the shallow optimism of the Darwinistic age lay over the West-European-American world." He prepared the book, in which he set forth the thesis of an age of annihilation-wars for the immediate future, for the coming age, and chose the title to contradict the prevailing optimism. In 1921, he wrote, he would choose a title that would contradict the equally shallow pessimism then prevailing.

If pessimism be defined as seeing nothing more to be done, it does not touch a philosophy which sets forth task after task remaining to the Western Civilization. Apart from the political and economic, to which this work is devoted, Western physics, chemistry and technics all have their peaks before them, as have also archaeology and historical philosophy. The formulation of a legal system freed from philology and conceptualizing is also a need. National economy needs to be approached and organized thoroughly in the 20th century spirit, and above all, an education must be created, in the grand sense of consciously training the coming generations, in the full light of the historic necessity of our Future, for the great life-tasks of the Civilization.

The cry of "Pessimism" is dying down—the 20th century outlook on History surveys from its historical peak and to its own unique, vast, historical horizons, the life-courses of eight High Cultures accomplished, and even looks boldly and confidently into its own Culture's future, yet to be accomplished. Readers in 1950 have forgotten, and readers in 2050 will possibly have no way of finding out, that before the 20th century outlook on History appeared, unrealized history was regarded as a blank tablet on which man might write whatever he wished. This was of course the instinctive attitude of no single man of action— they have to know better in order to accomplish the veriest trifle, but even they had to maintain the pretense that the Future was *carte blanche.*

No one thinks in this fashion during the second half of the 20th century; the bleating of the rationalists and the whimpering of the materialists are growing fainter. Even they are now talking about History, instead of about their old platitudes. Even their press now fits out its herd of readers with a history-outlook. History begins in 1870, and it ends after the next war; each war is portrayed as the last. This History-picture did service for more than a generation, and its very existence in materialistic journalism is a sign of the increasingly historical attitude of the age. After the First World War, a "League of Nations" was established to bring about "World Peace," and there was a considerable number of persons in the Western Civilization who took it seriously. Within the short space of one generation, however, a second "League" was founded after a Second World War, but this time, owing to the inner victory in the West of the 20th century world-outlook which had occurred meanwhile, almost no one looked upon the "League" as anything other than a localization of diplomatic war-preparations between the two remaining powers. We have come a long way from the old "Progress" days.

The tables are turned on the wailers of "Pessimism." Actually they are merely the representatives of the Spirit of an Age that has gone forever. Thus they are anachronistic in this Age, and to the extent that they try to intervene in its Life, they must fight against its every expression-tendency. They can only negate the Future with their hopeless attempt to revive the Past. Does not this make *them* pessimists?

The definitive word can now be said about pessimism, and about optimism, for the two are inseparable as concepts. If pessimism is despair, optimism is cowardice and stupidity. Is there any need to choose between them? They are twin soul-diseases. Between them lies realism, which wants to know what *is,* what *must* be done, how it *can* be done. Realism is historical thinking, and it is also political thinking. Realism does not approach the world with a preconceived principle to which things *ought* to submit—it is this prime stupidity which begets both pessimism and optimism. If it looks as though things will not fit, so to declare is pessimism. Optimism continues to pretend that they do, despite the entire course of History, to the contrary. Of the two diseases, optimism is more dangerous to the soul, for it is more blind. Pessimism, by not being afraid to affirm the unpleasing, is at least capable of seeing, and may yield to a flaring-up of healthy instincts.

Every captain must prepare for both victory and defeat, and tactically, the latter part of his plan is more important, and no captain would refrain from taking measures to apply in defeat because someone said to him that this was pessimism. Let us go further—a hundred odd Americans were surrounded in 1836 in the Alamo by Mexican armies numbering thousands. Was it pessimistic for them to realize that their position was hopeless? But there happened something which the materialists—the real pessimists—can never understand. The members of the tiny garrison did not allow the obvious hopelessness of the situation to affect their personal *conduct*—every man chose to fight on rather than surrender. They thought rather of what was *left to do* than of the ultimate annihilation.

This was also the attitude of the Kamikaze pilots who in the

Second World War drove their explosive-laden airplanes on to enemy ships of war. Not only is this attitude entirely outside any stupid optimism-pessimism scheme, but it is the essence of heroism itself. Fear of death does not prevent the hero from doing what has to be done. The 20th century has this heroic attitude once more, and it thinks of its task, and not of the ultimate end of all Life in Death. Least of all does it fear death so much, both individual death and the fulfillment of the Civilization within which we must actualize our possibilities, that it attempts to deny Death in any way. It wants to live Life, not cringe before Death. Optimism and pessimism are for cowards, weaklings, fools, and stupid persons, incapable of appreciating the mystery, power, and beauty of Life. They shrink from sternness and renunciation, and escape from the brutality of facts into dreams of immortality of the body, and indefinite perpetuation of the world-outlook of the 19th century.

As I write—1948—these cowardly pessimists lord it over the submerged Western Civilization, propped up by extra-European forces. They pretend that all is well, now that Europe is the spoils for powers from without, sunk to the level of India and China. The 20th century spirit, however, which they hate because it is young and full of Life, intends to sweep them one day soon into History's dust-bin, whither they were long since consigned. Theirs is the attitude—Do nothing. And yet they have the temerity to brand the representatives of the 20th century spirit with the positive attitude of accomplishment as "Pessimists." The materialists and Liberals talk of "return" to better conditions—always *return*. The new spirit commands: Forward to our greatest Age of all.

This age and its spirit would not shrink from entering upon its task of building the Empire of the West even if it were told that the outer forces are too strong, that they will never succeed.

It prefers to die on its feet rather than live on its knees, like the materialists and other cowards who now make themselves serviceable to the outsiders in their great task of looting and destroying the Western Civilization.

The great ethical imperative of this age is *individual truth-to-self*, both for the Civilization and its leading persons. To this imperative, an unfavorable situation could never bring about an adaptation of one's self to the demands of the outsider, merely in order to live in slavish peace. One asserts himself, determined on personal victory, against whatever odds exist. The promise of success is with the man who is determined to die proudly if it is no longer possible to live proudly.

The Civilization-Crisis

ALL THE CULTURES arrived at the point in their development when their possibilities for culture—in the narrower sense—were fulfilled. The Life-directions of religion, philosophy, and the arts of form, were fully expressed and formed definitively. The Counter-Reformation was the period of the definitive shaping of Western religious formative potentialities, and thenceforward religion was on the defensive against profane tendencies, which gradually increased and finally, with the turn of the 19th century, gained the upper hand. Kant is the high point of Western possibilities in inorganic philosophy, as was his contemporary Goethe for organic philosophy. Mozart is the high point of music, the art that the Western Culture chose as its most perfect for its own soul.

Naturally the Culture had always had both an inner and outer life; politics and war had always continued, since they are inseparable from the life of Culture-man. But in the first centuries of the Culture—say until 1400—Religion had dominated the total Cultural life. Gothic architecture, Gothic sculpture, glass-painting and fresco—all these arts had served religious expression, and these centuries may be called the Age of Religion. This period yielded to new tendencies, less inward, reflected also in the greater development of trade and economic production. The new tendencies are more urban; they contain more adaptation to the external world, but they are still primarily inward. The arts pass into the custody of "Great Masters," and become emancipated from religion. The maturity of the Culture shows itself in its development at this time of its greatest and most refined art. In the West, this was music; in the Classical, it was sculpture.

The Reformation and Counter-Reformation are both steps away from the Age of Religion. Philosophy becomes independent of theology, and natural science challenges dogmas of Faith. The basic attitude toward the world is still sacred, but the illuminated foreground widens constantly. This period is the Baroque in our Culture, lasting from 1500 to 1800, the Ionic in the Classical.

During these centuries, the politics reflected the strict formative stage of the Culture. The struggle for political power was strictly within the bounds imposed by the Culture-soul. Armies were small, professional; war was the possession of the nobility; peace treaties were arrived at by negotiation and compromise; honor was present at every decision of politics or war.

The later Baroque produced the Age of "Enlightenment." Reason was now felt as all-powerful, and to challenge its almightiness became as unthinkable as it would have been to challenge God in Gothic times. The English philosophers from Locke onward, and the French Encyclopedists who adopted their ideas, were the custodians of the spirit of this age.

By 1800, the externalizing tendency has prevailed completely over the old inwardness of the strict Culture. "Nature" and

"Reason" are the new gods; the outer world is regarded as primary. From having examined his own soul, and having expressed its formative possibilities to the limit in the inner world of religion, philosophy, and art, Culture-man now finds his imperative directed to subjecting the outer world to himself.

The great symbol of this transition in our Culture is Napoleon, in the Classical, Alexander. They represented the victory of Civilization over Culture.

Civilization is in one way a denial of the Culture, in another way it is the sequel. It is organically necessary, and all the Cultures went through this stage. This present work is concerned throughout with the problems of Civilization in general, and of our immediate problem for the period 1950–2000 in particular. Therefore it is not necessary to do more than present in this place a bare outline of the significance to the organism of the Civilization-phase.

With the triumph of Reason comes an immense *liberating* effect on the Culture-populations. The feelings that were formerly expressed only in strict forms, whether in art, war, cabinet-politics, or philosophy, are now given free rein, increasingly independent of Culture-bounds. Rousseau for instance, advocated the doing away with all Culture, and the descent of Culture-man to the purely animal plane of economics and reproduction. Art develops increasingly away from strict form, from Beethoven to our day. The ideal of the Beautiful yields finally to the ideal of the Ugly. Philosophy becomes pure social-ethics, when it is not a coarse and crude metaphysics of materialism. Economics, formerly merely the foundation of the great structure, now becomes the focus of immense energy. It too succumbs to Reason, and in this field, Reason formulates the quantitative measure of value, Money.

Reason applied to politics produced Democracy; applied to

war, it produced the mass army to replace the professional one, and the dictate instead of the treaty. The authority and dignity of the Absolute State are felt as tyranny by the new life-tendencies, and in heavy battles, the forces of Money, Economics, and Democracy overcome the State. For its responsible, public, leadership, is substituted the irresponsible, private, rule of anonymous groups, classes, and individuals, whose interests the parliaments serve. The psychology of monarchs is replaced by the psychology of crowds and mobs, the new base for power of the man of ambition.

Production, technics, trade, public power, and—above all—*population-numbers* increase fantastically. These numbers are produced by the enormous final life-task of the Culture, namely *the subjection of its known world to its domination.* In an area where formerly there were 80 millions there are now 260 millions.

The great common denominator of the Civilization ideas is *mobilization.* The masses of the Culture-populations, and the masses whom they conquer, the earth itself, and the power of intellectual ideals—all are mobilized.

II

From the standpoint of the whole life of the organism this stage is a *crisis,* for the whole idea of the Culture itself is attacked, and the custodians of the Culture must wage a battle of more than two centuries against inner attacks, in class war. Down beneath the Culture, the idea awakens in the minds of intellectuals that this Culture is a thing that must be done away with, that man is an animal and is corrupted by development of his soul. Philosophies appear, denying the existence of anything but matter; life is defined as a physico-chemical process; its twin-urges are economic and reproductive; anything above this level is sinful. Both from the economic leaders and from the class-warriors comes the doctrine that all life is nothing but economics. From self-styled "psychologists" comes the doctrine that life is nothing but reproduction.

But the strength of the organism, even in crisis, is too great for a few intellectuals and their mobs to destroy it, and it goes its way. In the Western Civilization, the expansive tendency reached the point where by 1900, 18/20 of the surface of the earth was controlled politically from Western capitals. And this development merely brought an aggravation of the crisis, for this power-will of the West gradually awakened the slumbering masses of the outer world to political activity.

Before the inner war of classes had been liquidated, the outer war of races had begun. Annihilation-wars and World Wars, continuous internal strain in the form of unrelenting class-war, which regards outer war merely as a means of increasing its demands, the revolt of the colored races against the Western Civilization—these are the forms which this terrible crisis takes in the 20th century.

The peak of this long crisis exists now, in the period 1950–2000, and possibly in these very years will be decided forever the question whether the West is to fulfill its last life-phase. The proud Civilization which in 1900 was master of 18/20 of the earth's surface, arrived at the point in 1945, after the suicidal Second World War, where it controlled no part whatever of the earth. World power for all great questions was decided in two outer capitals, Washington and Moscow. The smaller questions of provincial administration were left to the nations-become-colonies of the West, but in power-questions, the regimes based in Russia and America decided all. Where formal control was left with Europe, as in Palestine, actual control was retained in Washington. The food-rations, trade-union policy, leaders, and tasks of the former Western nations were decided upon outside of Europe.

In 1900, the State-system of Europe reacted as a unit when the negative will of Asia thought, by the Boxer rebellion, to drive out the Imperialism of the West from China. Western armies from the leading States moved in, and smashed the revolt. Less than half a century later, extra-European armies are moving freely about Europe, armies containing Negroes, Mongols, Turkestani, Kirghizians, Americans, Armenians, colonials and Asiatics of all areas. How did this happen?

Quite obviously, through the inner division of the West. This division was not material—material cannot divide men if their minds agree. No, it was *spiritual* division that brought Europe into the dust. Half of Europe had a completely different attitude toward Life, a different valuation of Life, from the other half. The two attitudes were respectively the 19th century outlook, and the 20th century outlook. The division continues, and the amount of food a man in the Western Civilization can eat is dependent on the decision of someone in Moscow or Washington. When the spiritual division of Europe comes to an end the extra-European powers will be unable to hold down the strong-willed populations of Europe.

The first step in *action* is thus the liquidation of the spiritual division of Europe. There is only *one* basis on which this can be done; *there is only one Future, the organic Future.* The only changes that can be brought about in a Culture are those which its life-stage necessitates. The 20th century outlook is synonymous with the Future of the West, the perpetuation of the 19th century outlook means the continuation of the domination of the West by Culture-distorters and barbarians. The task of the present work is the presentation of all the fundamentals of the

20th century outlook necessary as the framework for compre-
hending and thorough *action*. First is the *Idea*—not an ideal
which can be summed up in a catchword, or one which can be
explained to an alien, but a living, breathing, wordless feeling, which already exists in all Westerners, articulate in a very
few, inchoate in most. This *Idea*, in its wordless grandeur, its
irresistible imperative, must be *felt*, and thus only men of the
West can assimilate it. The alien will understand it as little as
he has always understood Western creations and Western
codes. In his victory parade in Moscow in 1945, the barbarian
exhibited his Western captive slaves to the jeering crowds of his
cities, and made them drag their national flags behind them in
the dust. If any Westerner thinks that the barbarian makes nice
distinctions between the former nations of the West, he is incapable of understanding the feelings of populations outside
a High Culture toward that Culture. Tomorrow the captive
slaves offered up to the annihilation-instincts of the Moscow
mobs may be drawn from Paris, London, Madrid, as well as
from Berlin. A continuation of the spiritual division of the
West makes this not only possible but *absolutely inevitable*.
Both the outer forces are working for the continued division of
the West; within they are helped by the least worthy elements
in Europe. This is addressed however to the only people that
matter—the Westerners who can feel the Imperative of the
Future working within them.

It is necessary that their world-outlook be the same in all its
fundamentals, and we know in this historical age that the prevailing spirituality of an age is a function of its soul, and that
comparatively little latitude is allowed in its necessary formulation. Therefore, the present work contains not arguments, but
commands of the Spirit of the Age. These thoughts and values
are *necessary for us*. They are not personal, but super-personal

and compulsory for men who intend to do something with their lives.

Our action-task is dictated for us by the fact that the soil of our Civilization is occupied by the outsider. Our inner imperative and outlook on Life is determined for us by the Age. A part of the outlook of any age is simply the *negation* of the outlook of the previous age. Each age has to assert its new spirit *against* its predecessor, which would continue, even in the stage of *rigor mortis,* to dominate the spiritual landscape of the Culture. In establishing itself, the new spirit must deny the hostile old one. In a substantial part, therefore, our 20th century outlook is the negative of the 19th century materialism. Having destroyed this dank ruin, it erects over it its own, appropriate, view of the world and Life.

Since this is written for those whose world-view is researched to its very foundations, the preliminary, negative, aspect must be equally thorough. The world view of the millions is the task of journalism, but those who think independently have an inner necessity for a comprehensive picture. The great foundations of the old outlook were Rationalism and Materialism. They will be completely examined in this work, but here it is proposed to treat only three thought-systems, Darwinism, Marxism, Freudianism, products of materialistic thought, all of which were the focus of great spiritual energy in the 19th century, and which, continuing to have a vogue in the early 20th century, contributed greatly to lead Europe into its present abyss.

Darwinism

ONE OF THE MOST fruitful discoveries of the 20th century was the metaphysics of *nations*. The unveiling of the Riddle of History showed that nations are different manifestations of the soul of the High Cultures. They exist only in Cultures, they have their life span for political purposes, and possess—*vis-a-vis* the other nations of the Culture—individuality. Each great nation is given an Idea, a life-mission, and the history of the nation is the actualizing of this Idea. This Idea, again, must be *felt,* and cannot be directly defined. Each Idea, to actualize which a given nation was chosen by the Culture, is also a stage of the development of the Culture. Thus Western History presents during the recent centuries, a Spanish period, a French period, an English period. They correspond to Baroque, Rococo, and early Civilization. These nations owed their spiritual and political supremacy during these years solely to the fact that they were the custodians of the Spirit of the Age. With the passing of the Age, these custodians of its Spirit lost their spiritually dominating position in the Culture.

The early Civilization was the English period of the West, and all the thought and activity of the whole Civilization was on the English model. All nations embarked upon economic imperialism of the English type. All thinkers became Anglicized intellectually. English thought-systems ruled the West, systems which reflected the English soul, English life-conditions, and English material conditions. Prime among these systems was Darwinism, which became popular, and thus politically effective.

Darwin himself was a follower of Malthus, and his system implies Malthusianism as a foundation. Malthus taught that population increase tends to outrun increase of food supply, that this represented an economic *danger,* and that "checks" on this population increase alone can prevent it from destroying a nation, such as epidemics and wars, unhealthy living conditions and poverty. Malthusianism expressly regards care for the poor, the aged, and orphans, as a mistake.

A word on this curious philosophy; first it has no correspondence whatever to facts, and therefore is not valid for the 20th century. Statistically it has no basis, spiritually it shows complete incomprehension of the prime fact of Destiny, Man, and History—namely that the soul is primary, and that matter is governed by soul-conditions. Every man is the poet of his own History, and every nation of its History. A rising population shows the presence of a life-task, a declining population points to insignificance. This philosophy would legitimate a man's existence by whether or not he is born into an adequate food-area! His gifts, his life task, his Destiny, his soul, are put at naught. It is one example of the great philosophic tendency of materialism: *the animalization of Culture-man.*

Malthusianism taught that the food-population ratio imposed a continuous struggle for existence among men. This "struggle for existence" became a leading-idea for Darwinism. The other leading ideas of Darwinism are found in Schopenhauer, Erasmus Darwin, Henry Bates, and Herbert Spencer. Schopenhauer in 1835 set forth a Nature-picture containing the struggle for self-preservation, human intellect as a weapon in the struggle, and sexual love as unconscious selection according to the interest of the species. In the 18th century, Erasmus Darwin had postulated adaptation, heredity, struggle, and self-protection as principles of evolution. Bates formulated before Darwin the theory of Mimicry, Spencer the theory of descent, and the powerful tautological catchword "survival of the fittest" to describe the results of the "struggle."

This is only the foreground, for actually the road from Darwin back to Calvin is quite clear: Calvinism is a religious interpretation of the "survival of the fittest" idea, and it calls the fit the "elected." Darwinism makes this election-process mechanical-profane instead of theological-religious: selection by Nature instead of election by God. It remains purely English in the process, for the national religion of England was an adaptation of Calvinism.

The basic idea of Darwinism—evolution—is as little novel as the particular theories of the system. Evolution is the great central idea of the philosophy of the 19th century. It dominates every leading thinker and every system: Schopenhauer, Proudhon, Marx, Wagner, Nietzsche, Mill, Ibsen, Shaw. These thinkers differ in their explanation of the purpose and technique of evolution; none of them question the central idea itself. With some of them it is organic, with most purely mechanical.

Darwin's system has two aspects, of which only one is treated here, for only one was effective. This was Darwinism as a *popular philosophy*. As a scientific arrangement it had considerable qualifications, and no one paid any attention to these when converting it to a journalistic world-outlook. As the latter, it had a sweeping vogue, and was effective as a part of the world-picture of the age.

The system shows its provenance as a product of the Age of Criticism in its *teleological* assumptions. Evolution has *purpose* —the purpose of producing man, civilized man, English man— in the last analysis, Darwinians. It is anthropomorphic—the "aim of evolution" is not to produce bacilli, but humanity. It is free trade capitalism, in that this struggle is economic, every man for himself, and competition decides which life-forms are best. It is gradual and parliamentary, for continual "progress" and adaptation, exclude revolutions and catastrophes. It is utilitarian, in that every change in a species is one that has a material use. The human soul itself—known as the "brain" in the 19th century—is only a tool by which a certain type of monkey advanced himself to man ahead of his fellow-monkeys. Teleology again: man became man in order that he might be man. It is orderly; natural selection proceeds according to the rules of artificial breeding in practice on English farms.

II

As a world view, Darwinism cannot of course be refuted, since Faith is, always has been, and always will be, stronger than facts. Nor is it important to refute it as a picture of the world, since as such it no longer influences any but day-before-yesterday thinkers. However, as a picture of the facts, it is grotesque, from its first assumptions to its last conclusions.

In the first place, there is no "Struggle for existence" in nature; this old Malthusian idea merely projected Capitalism on to the animal world. Such struggles for existence as do occur are the exception; the rule in Nature is abundance. There are plenty of plants for the herbivores to eat, and there are plenty of herbivores for the carnivores to eat. Between the latter there can hardly be said to be "struggle," since only the carnivore is spiritually equipped for war. A lion making a meal of a zebra portrays no "struggle" between two species, unless one is determined so to regard it. Even so, he must concede that it is not *physically, mechanically,* necessary for the carnivores to kill other animals. They could as well eat plants—it is the demand of their animal souls however to live in this fashion, and thus, even if one were to call their lives struggles, it would not be imposed by "Nature" but by the soul. It becomes thus, not a "struggle for existence," but a spiritual necessity of being one's self.

The capitalistic mentality, engaged in a competition to get rich, quite naturally pictured the animal-world also as engaged in an intensive economic contest. Both Malthusianism and Darwinism are thus *capitalistic* outlooks, in that they place economics in the center of Life, and regard it as the meaning of Life.

Natural selection was the name given to the process by which the "unfit" died out to give place to the "fit." Adaptation was the name given to the process by which a species gradually changed in order to be more fit for the struggle. Heredity was the means by which these adaptations were saved for the species.

As a factual picture, this is easier to refute than it is to prove, and factual biological thinkers, both Mechanists and Vitalists, like Louis Agassiz, Du Bois-Reymond, Reinke, and Driesch rejected it from its appearance. The easiest refutation is the palaeontological. Fossil deposits—found in various parts of the earth—must represent the possibilities generally. Yet they disclose only stable specie-forms, and disclose no transitional types, which show a species "evolving" into something else. And then, in a new fossil hoard, a new species appears, in its definitive form, which remains stable. The species that we know today, and for past centuries, are all stable, and no case has ever been observed of a species "adapting" itself to change its anatomy or physiology, which "adaptation" then resulted in more "fitness" for the "struggle for existence," and was passed on by heredity, with the result of a new species.

Darwinians cannot get over these facts by bringing in great spaces of time, for palaeontology has never discovered any intermediate types, but only distinct species. Nor are the fossil animals which have died out any simpler than present-day forms, although the course of evolution was supposed to be from simple to complex Life-forms. This was crude anthropomorphism—man is complex, other animals are simple, they must be tending toward him, since he is "higher" biologically.

Calling Culture-man a "higher" animal still treats him as an animal. Culture-man is a different world spiritually from all animals, and is not to be understood by referring him to any artificial materialistic scheme.

If this picture of the facts were correct, species ought to be fluid at the present time. They should be turning into one another. This is, of course, not so. There should actually be no species, but only a surging mass of individuals, engaged in a race to reach—man. But the "struggle," again, is quite inconclusive. The "lower" forms, simpler—less fit?—have not died out, have not yielded to the principle of Darwinian evolution. They remain in the same form they have had for—as the Darwinians would say—millions of years. Why do they not "evolve" into something "higher"?

The Darwinian analogy between artificial selection and natural selection is also in opposition to the facts. The products of artificial selection such as barnyard fowls, racing dogs, race horses, ornamental cats, and song-canaries, would certainly be at a disadvantage against natural varieties. Thus artificial selection has only been able to produce less fit life-forms.

Nor is Darwinian sexual selection in accordance with facts. The female does not by any means always choose the finest and strongest individual for a mate, in the human species, or in any other.

The utilitarian aspect of the picture is also quite subjective— i.e., English, capitalistic, parliamentarian—for the utility of an organ is relative to the use sought to be made of it. A species without hands has no need of hands. A hand that slowly evolved would be a positive disadvantage over the "millions of years" necessary to perfect the hand. Furthermore, how did this process *start*? For an organ to be utile, it must be ready; while it is being prepared, it is inutile. But if it is inutile, it is not Darwinian, for Darwinism says evolution is utilitarian.

Actually all the technics of Darwinian evolution are simply tautological. Thus, within the species it is individuals which have a predisposition to adapt themselves that do so. Adaptation presupposes adaptation.

The process of selection affects those specimens with definite aptitudes which make them worthy of selection, in other words, they have already been selected. Selection presupposes selection.

The problem of descent in the Darwinian picture is treated as finding the interrelations of the species. Having assumed their interrelationship, it then finds they are interrelated, and proves the interrelationship thus. Descent presupposes descent.

The utility of an organ is a way of saying it works for this species. Utility thus presupposes the existence of the very species which has the organ, but lacking that organ. The facts however, have never shown a species to pick up a certain missing organ, which seemed necessary. A Life-form needs a certain organ because it needs it. The organ is utile because it is utile.

The naive, tautological, doctrine of utility never asked "Utility for *what?*" That which serves duration might not serve strength. Utility is not a *simple* thing, but entirely relative to what already exists. Thus it is the inner demands of a life-form which determine what it would like to have, what would be useful to it. The soul of the lion and his power go together. The hand of man and his brain go together. No one can say that the strength of the lion causes him to live the way he does, nor that the hand of man is responsible for his technical achievements. It is the soul in each case which is primary.

This primacy of the spiritual inverts the Darwinian materialism on the doctrine of utility. A *lack* can be utile: the lack of one sense develops others; physical weakness develops intelligence. In man and in animals alike, the absence of one organ stimulates others to compensatory activity—this is often observed in endocrinology in particular.

III

The whole grotesquerie of Darwinism, and of the materialism of the entire 19th century generally, is a product of one fundamental idea—an idea which happens also to be nonfactual to this century, even though it was a prime fact a century ago. This one idea was that Life is formed by the outer. This generated the sociology of "environment" as determining the human soul. Later it generated the doctrine of "heredity" as doing the same. And yet, *in a purely factual sense,* what is Life? Life is the actualizing of the possible. The possible turns into the actual in the midst of outer facts, which affect only the pre-

cise way in which the possible becomes actual, but cannot touch
the inner force which is expressing itself through, and, if necessary, in opposition to, the outer facts.

Neither "heredity" nor "environment" determine these inner
possibilities. They affect only the framework within which
something *entirely new,* an individual, a unique soul, will express itself.

The word evolution describes to the 20th century the process
of the ripening and fulfilling of an organism or of a species.
This process is not at all the operation of mechanical-utility
"causes" on plastic, formless, protoplasmic material, with
purely accidental results. His work with plants led de Vries to
develop his Mutation theory of the origin of species, and the
facts of palaeontology reinforce it to the extent of showing the
sudden appearance of new species. The 20th century finds it
quite unnecessary to formulate mythologies, either in cosmogony or biology. Origins are forever hidden from us, and a
historical viewpoint is interested in the *development* of the
process, not in the mysterious *beginning* of the process. This
beginning, as set forth by scientific mythology, and by religious
mythology, has only an historical interest to our age. What we
note is that once these world-pictures were actual and living.

What is the actual History of Life, as this age sees it? Various species of Life exist, ranked, according to increasing
spiritual content, from plants and animals, through man, to
Culture-man, and High Cultures. Some of the varieties, as
shown by fossils, existed in former earth-ages in their present
form, while other species appeared and disappeared.

A species appears *suddenly,* both in fossil-finds, and in the
experimental laboratory. Mutation is a legitimate description
of the process, if the idea is free from any mechanical-utility
causes, for these latter are only imagined, whereas mutations

are a fact. Each species has also a Destiny, and a given Life-energy, so to speak. Some are stable and firm; others have been weak, tending to split off into many different varieties, and lose their unity. They have also a life span, for many have disappeared. This whole process is not at all independent of geological ages, nor of astral phenomena. Some species, however, outlast one earth-age into the next, just as some 19th century thinkers have survived into the 20th century.

Darwinians offered also an explanation of the metaphysics of their evolution. Roux, for instance, holds that the "fit for the purpose" survive, while the "unfit for the purpose" die. The process is purely mechanical, however, and is thus fitness for purpose without purpose. Nägeli taught that an organism perfects itself because it contains within it the "principle of perfection," just as Moliere's doctor explained that the sleeping potion worked because of a dormitive virtue inherent in it. Weismann denied the heredity of acquired characteristics, but instead of using it to destroy Darwinism, as it obviously does— if every individual has to start anew, how can the species "evolve"?—he props up the Darwinian picture with it by saying that the germ-plasm contains latent tendencies toward useful qualities. But this is no longer Darwinism, for the species does not evolve if it is only doing what it tends to do.

These tautological explanations only convinced people because they believed already. The age was evolutionary, and materialistic. Darwinism combined these two qualities into a biologico-religious doctrine which satisfied the capitalistic imperative of that age. Any experiments, any new facts, only proved Darwinism; they would not have been allowed to do otherwise.

The 20th century does not see Life as an accident, a playground for external causes. It sees the fact that Life-forms be-

gin suddenly, and that the subsequent development, or evolution, is only the actualizing of that which is already possible.
Life is the unfolding of a Soul, an individuality. Whatever
explanation one gives of how Life started only reveals the
structure of his own soul. A materialistic explanation reveals a
materialist. Similarly the imputing of any "purpose" to Life as
a whole transcends knowledge and enters the realm of Faith.
Life as a whole, each great Life-form, each species, each variety,
each individual, has however a *Destiny,* an inner direction, a
wordless imperative. This Destiny is the primary fact of History. History is the record of fulfilled (or thwarted) destinies.

Any attempt to make man into an animal, and the animals
into automata, is merely materialism, and thus a product of a
certain type of soul, of a certain age. The 20th century is not
such an age, and looks upon the inner reality of the human
soul as being the determinant of human history, and the inner
reality of the Soul of the High Culture as being the determinant of the history of that Culture. The soul *exploits* outer
circumstances—they do not form it.

Nor does the 20th century, not being capitalistic, see any
struggle for existence going on in the world, either of men or
animals. It sees a struggle for *power,* a struggle that has no
connection with cheap economic *reasons.* It is a struggle for
domination of the world that the 20th and 21st centuries see. It
is not because there is a shortage of food for the human populations of the world—there is plenty of food. The question is
power, and in the decision of that question, food, human lives,
material, and everything else that the participants can dispose
of, will come into play as *weapons,* and not as *stakes.* Nor will
it ever be decided, in the sense that a lawsuit can be decided.
Readers living in 2050 will smile when told that there was once
a rather widespread belief in the Western Civilization that the

First World War was the "last war." The Second World War was also so regarded, all during the preparations for the Third. It was a case of wish-thinking pacifist idealism being stronger than facts.

Darwinism was the animalization of Culture-man by means of biology; the human soul was interpreted as a mere superior technique of fighting with other animals. We come now to Marxism, the animalization of man through economics, the human soul as a mere reflex of food, clothing and shelter.

Marxism

ALTHOUGH ENGLAND was the nation which actualized the ideas of the early Civilization phase of the West—the period 1750–1900—namely, Rationalism, Materialism, Capitalism, yet these ideas would have been actualized otherwise, even if England had been destroyed by some outer catastrophe. Nevertheless, for England these ideas were *instinctive*. They were wordless, beyond definition, self-evident. For the other nations of Europe, they were things to which one had to adapt oneself.

Capitalism is not an economic system, but a *world-outlook,* or rather, a part of a whole world-outlook. It is a way of thinking and feeling and living, and not a mere technique of economic planning which anyone can understand. It is primarily *ethical* and *social* and only secondarily economic. The economics of a nation is a reflection of the national soul, just as the way a man makes his living is a subordinate expression of his personality.

Capitalism is an expression of *Individualism* as a principle of Life, the idea of every man for himself. It must be realized that this feeling is not universal-human, but only a certain stage of a certain Culture, a stage that in all essentials passed away with the First World War, 1914–1919.

Socialism is also an *ethical-social* principle, and *not an economic program* of some kind. It is antithetical to the Individualism which produced Capitalism. Its self-evident, instinctive idea is: each man for all.

To Individualism as a Life-principle, it was obvious that each man in pursuing his own interests, was working for the good of all. To Socialism as a Life-principle, it is equally obvious that a man working for himself alone is *ipso facto* working against the good of all.

The 19th century was the age of Individualism; the 20th and 21st are the ages of Socialism. No one has understood if he thinks this is an *ideological* conflict. Ideology itself means: the rationalizing of the world of action. This was the preoccupation of the early phase of the Western Civilization, 1750–1900, but no longer engages the serious attention of ambitious men. Programs are mere *ideals;* they are inorganic, rationalized, anyone can understand them. This age however is one of a struggle for power. Each participant wants the power in order to actualize himself, his inner *idea,* his soul. 1900 could not understand what Goethe meant when he said, "In Life, it is Life itself that is important, and not a result of Life." The time has passed away in which men would die for an abstract program of "improving" the world. Men will always be willing to die however, in order to be themselves. This is the distinction between an ideal and an idea.

Marxism is an ideal. It does not take account of living ideas, but regards the world as a thing that can be planned on paper and then set up in actuality. Marx understood neither Socialism nor Capitalism as *ethical* world-outlooks. His understanding of both was purely *economic,* and thus a misunderstanding.

The explanation Marxism offered of the significance of History was ludicrously simple, and in this very simplicity lay its charm, and its strength. *The whole history of the world was merely the record of the struggle of classes.* Religion, philosophy, science, technics, music, painting, poetry, nobility, priesthood, Emperor and Pope State, war, and politics—all are simply reflections of *economics.* Not economics generally, but the "struggle" of "classes." The most·amazing thing about this iedological picture is that it was ever put forward seriously, or taken seriously.

The 20th century finds it unnecessary to contradict this History-picture as a world-outlook. It has been supplanted, and has joined Rousseau. The foundations of Marxism must however be shown, since the whole tendency which produced it is one that this age is impelled to deny as a premiss of its own existence.

Being inwardly alien to Western philosophy, Marx could not assimilate the ruling philosopher of his time, Hegel, and borrowed Hegel's *method* to formulate his own picture. He applied this method to capitalism as a form of economy, in order to bring about a picture of the Future corresponding to his own feelings and instincts. These instincts were negative toward the whole Western Civilization. He belonged with the class-warriors, who appear at a corresponding stage of every Culture, as a protest against it. The driving-force of class-war is the will to annihilation of Culture.

The ethical and social foundations of Marxism are capitalistic. It is the old Malthusian "struggle" again. Whereas to Hegel, the State was an Idea, an organism with harmony in its parts, to Malthus and Marx there was no State, but only a mass of self-interested individuals, groups, and classes. Capitalistically, all is economics. Self-interest means: economics. Marx differed on this plane in no way from the non-class-war theoreticians of capitalism—Mill, Ricardo, Paley, Spencer, Smith. To them all, Life was economics, not Culture. To them all, it was the war of group against group, class against class, individual against individual, whether they say so expressly or not. All believe in Free Trade, and want no "state interference" in economic matters. None of them regard society or State as an organism. Capitalistic thinkers found no ethical fault with destruction of groups and individuals by other groups and individuals, so long as the criminal law was not infringed. This was looked upon as, in a higher way, serving the good of all. Marxism is also capitalistic in this. Its ethics have superadded the Mosaic law of revenge, and the idea that the competitor is *evil* morally, as well as economically injurious.

The competitor of the "working-class" was the "bourgeoisie," and since the "victory of the working-class" was the sole aim of the entire history of the world, naturally Marxism, being a philosophy of "Progress," ranged itself with the "good" worker against the "evil" bourgeois. The necessity for thinking things are getting better all the time—a spiritual phenomenon which accompanies every materialism—was as indispensable to Marxism as it was to Darwinism and 19th century philistinism generally.

Fourier, Cabet, Saint-Simon, Comte, Proudhon, Owen, all designed Utopias like Marxism, but they neglected to make them *inevitable,* and they forgot to make Hate the center of the system. They used Reason, but Marxism is one more proof that Hate is more effective. Even then, one of the older Utopias (that of Marx was the last in Europe, being followed only by Edward Bellamy's in America) might have played the Marxian role, but they came from countries with lower industrial potential, and thus Marx had a "capitalistic" superiority over them.

II

In the Marxian scheme, History got almost nowhere until the Western Culture appeared, and its tempo accelerated infinitely precisely with the appearance of Marxism. The class-war of 5,000 years was ready to be finally wound up, and History was to come to an end. The "victory" of the "proletariat" was to abolish classes, but it was also to dictate. A dictatorship of the proletariat implies someone to receive the dictate, but this is one of the mysteries of Marxism, which kept the conversation of disciples from flagging.

By the time Marxism appeared, there were, says the theory, only two "classes" left, proletariat and bourgeoisie. Naturally, they had to carry on war to the death, since the bourgeois was taking nearly all the proceeds of the economic system, and were entitled to nothing. *Au contraire,* it was precisely the proletaire who was getting nothing who was entitled to everything. This reduction of classes to two was *inevitable*—all History had only existed in order to bring about this dichotomy which would finally be liquidated by the dictate of the proletariat. Capitalism was the name given to the economic system whereby the wrong people were taking everything, leaving nothing for the right people. Capitalism created the proletariat by mechanical necessity, and equally mechanically, the proletariat was fated to swallow up its creator. What the form of the Future was to be was not included in the system. The two catchwords "Expropriation of the Expropriators" and "Dictatorship of the Proletariat" are supposed to contain it.

Actually it was, of course, not even in theory a plan for the Future, but simply and solely a theoretical foundation for class war, giving it an historical, ethical and economic-political rationale. This is shown by the fact that in the preface to the second Russian edition of the *Communist Manifesto* a theory was put forth by Marx and Engels according to which Communism could come directly from Russian peasantry to Proletariat-dictate without the long period of bourgeois-domination which had been absolutely necessary in Europe.

The important part of Marxism was its demand for active, constant, practical, class-war. The factory-workers were selected as the instruments for this struggle for obvious reasons: they were concentrated, they were being mistreated, they could thus be agitated and organized into a revolutionary movement to realize the completely negative aims of the coterie of Marx.

For this *practical* reason, Hate finds its way into a picture of History and Life, and for this reason, the "bourgeois"—simply mechanical parts of a mechanical evolution, according to Marx —are endowed with malice and evil. Hatred is useful in fomenting a war which does not seem to be occurring of itself, and to the end of increasing hatred, Marx welcomed *lost* strikes, which created more hatred than successful ones.

Only to serve this purpose of *action* are the absurd propositions about labor and value put forth. Marx understood journalism, and had no scruple whatever about saying that the manual laborer is the *only* person who works, who creates economic value. To this theory, the inventor, the discoverer, the manager are economic parasites. The fact is, of course, that the manual type of labor is merely a *function* of the value-creating, precedent, prerequisite labor of organizer, intrepreneur, administrator, inventor. Great theoretical importance was attached to the fact that a strike could stop an enterprise. However, as the philosopher said, even a sheep could do that if it fell into the machinery. Marxism, in the interests of simplification, denied even a subsidiary value to the work of the creators. It had *no*

value—only manual labor had value. Marx understood propaganda long before Lord Northcliffe was heard of. Effective
mass-propaganda cannot be too simple, and in the application
of this rule, Marx should have received some sort of prize: all
History is class-war; all Life is class-war; they have the wealth,
let us take it.

Marxism imputed Capitalistic instincts to the upper classes,
and Socialistic instincts to the lower classes. This was entirely
gratuitous, for Marxism made an appeal to the capitalistic instincts of the lower classes. The upper classes are treated as the
competitor who has cornered all the wealth, and the lower
classes are invited to take it away from them. This is capitalism.
Trade unions are purely capitalistic, distinguished from employers only by the different commodity they purvey. Instead of
an article, they sell human labor. Trade-unionism is simply a
development of capitalistic economy, but it has nothing to do
with Socialism, for it is simply self-interest. It pits the economic
interest of the manual laborers against the economic interest of
the employer and manager. It is simply Malthus in new company. It is still the old "struggle for existence," man against
man, group against group, class against class, everyone against
the State.

The instinct of Socialism however absolutely precludes any
struggle between the component parts of the organism. It is as
hostile to the mistreatment of manual laborers by employers as
it is to the sabotage of society by class-warriors. Capitalism con-
vinces itself that a "Struggle for Existence" is organically necessary. Socialism knows that any such "struggle" is unnecessary
and pathological.

Between Capitalism and Socialism there is no relationship of
true and false. Both are instincts, and have the same historical
rank, but one of them belongs to the Past, and one to the

Future. Capitalism is a product of Rationalism and Materialism, and was the ruling force of the 19th century. Socialism is the form of an age of *political* Imperialism, of Authority, of historical philosophy, of superpersonal political imperative.

It is not at all a matter of terminology or ideals, but a matter of feeling and instinct. The minute we begin to think that a "class" has responsibilities to another class, we are beginning to think Socialistically, no matter what we call our thinking. We may call it Buddhism, for all History cares, but we *will* think that way. If we use the terminology of Capitalism and the practice of Socialism, no harm is done, for practice and action are what matter in Life, not words and names. The only distinction between types of Socialism is between efficient and inefficient, weak and strong, timid and bold. A strong, bold, and efficient Socialist feeling will, however, hardly use a terminology deriving from an antithetical type of thought, since strong, ascendant, full Life is consonant in word and deed.

III

Marxism showed its Capitalistic provenance in its idea of "classes," its idea toward work, and its obsession with economics. Marx was a Jew, and had thus imbibed from his youth the Old Testament idea that work was a *curse* laid upon man as a result of sin. Free Capitalism placed this same value on work, regarding it as something from which to be delivered as a prerequisite to the enjoyment of Life. In England, the classic land of Capitalism, the ideas of work and wealth were the central ideas of social valuation. The rich had not to work; the "middle classes" had to work, but were not poor; the poor had to work to exist from one week to the next. Thorstein Veblen, in his "Theory of the Leisure Class," showed the wide ramifications in the life of 19th century nations of this attitude toward work.

The whole atmosphere of the Marxian Utopia is that the necessity for the proletariat to work will vanish with its "victory." After the "Expropriation," the proletariat can retire, and even have *ci-devant* employers for servants.

This attitude toward work is not universal-human, but a thing tied to the existence of English Capitalism. Never before in the Western Culture was there a prevailing feeling that work should be despised; in fact, after the Reformation, the leading theologians all adopted a positive attitude toward work as a high, if not the highest, value. From this period comes the idea that to work is to pray. This spirit is once again uppermost, and Socialistic instinct regards a man's work, not as a curse laid upon him, a hated thing from which money can free him, but as the content of his Life, the earthly side of his mission in the world. Marxism has the opposite valuation of work from Socialism.

Similarly, the Marxian concept of "class" has nothing to do with Socialism. The articulation of society in Western Culture was at first into *Estates*. Estates were primarily *spiritual*. As Freidank said in Gothic times

God hath shapen lives three,
Boor and knight and priest they be.

These are not *classes,* but organic ranks. After the French Revolution came the idea that the articulation of society was a reflection of the situation of money-hoards. The term class was used to describe an *economic* layer of society. This term was final for Marx, since Life to him was simply economics, saturated as he was with the Capitalistic world-outlook.

But to Socialism, money-possession is not the determinant of rank in society any more than it is in an Army. Social rank in Socialism does not follow Money, but Authority. Thus Socialism knows no "classes" in the Marxian-Capitalistic sense. It sees the center of Life in politics, and has thus a definite military spirit in it. Instead of "classes," the expressions of wealth, it has *rank,* the concomitant of authority.

Marxism is equally obsessed with economics as its contemporary English environment. It begins and ends with economics, focusing its gaze on the tiny European peninsula, ignoring the past and present of the rest of the world. It simply wanted to frustrate the course of Western history, and chose class-war as a technique for doing it.

There had been class-war before Marxism, but this "philosophy" gave it a theory which said there was nothing else in the world. There had been jealousy in the lower orders before Marxism, but now this jealousy was given an ethical basis which made it alone good, and everything above evil. Wealth was branded as immoral and criminal, its possessors as the arch-criminals. Class-war was a competition, and something more—it was a battle of good against evil, and thus more brutal and unlimited than mere war. Western thinkers like Sorel could not adopt this attempt to make the class-war exceed any limitations of honor and conscience; Sorel conceived of class-war as similar to international war, with protection of non-combatants, rules of warfare, honorable treatment of prisoners. Marxism regarded the opponent as a class-war criminal. The opponent could not be assimilated into a new system; he was to be exterminated, enslaved, starved, persecuted.

The Marxist class-war concept thus far exceeded politics. Politics is simply power-activity, not revenge-activity, jealousy, hatred, or "justice." Again, it has no connection with Socialism, which is political through and through, and regards a defeated opponent as a member of the new, larger organism, with the same rights and opportunities as those already in it.

This was one more connection of Marxism with Capitalism,

for the latter had a tendency to moralize politics, making the opponent into a *wicked* person.

Lastly, Marxism differs from Socialism in being a religion, whereas Socialism is an instinctive organizatory-political principle. Marxism had its bible, its saints, its apostles, its heresy-tribunals, orthodoxy and heterodoxy, its dogmas and exegesis, sacred writings and schisms. Socialism dispenses with all this; it is interested in procuring cooperation of men with the same instincts. Ideology has even now little importance to Socialism, and in the coming decades it will have ever less.

As Socialism creates the form of the Future, Marxism slips into the Past with the other remnants of Materialism. The mission of Western man is not to become rich through class-war; it is to actualize his inner ethico-politico-Cultural imperative.

Freudianism

As WAS THE CASE with Darwinism and Marxism, Freudianism has no Cultural, but only anti-Cultural significance. All three are products of the *negative* side of the Civilization-crisis, the side which destroys the old spiritual, social, ethical, philosophical values, and substitutes for them a crude Materialism. The principle of Criticism was the new god to whom all the old values of the Western Culture were offered up. The spirit of the 19th century is one of *iconoclasm*. The outstanding thinkers nearly all had their center of gravity on the side of nihilism: Schopenhauer, Hebbel, Proudhon, Engels, Marx, Wagner, Darwin, Dühring, Strauss, Ibsen, Nietzsche, Strindberg, Shaw. Some of these were also, on the other side of their beings, heralds of the Future, the spirit of the 20th century. The leading tendency was however, materialistic, biological, economic, scientific—against the soul of Culture-man and the hitherto acknowledged meaning of his life.

Not on a par with them, but in their tradition, is the system of Freudianism. The soul of Culture-man is attacked by it, not from an oblique direction of economics or biology, but from the front. The "science" of psychology is chosen as the vehicle to deny all the higher impulses of the soul. On the part of the creator of psychoanalysis, this assault was conscious. He spoke of Copernicus, Darwin, and himself as the three great insulters of mankind. Nor was his doctrine free from the fact of his Jewishness, and in his essay on *The Resistance to Psychoanalysis*, he says that it is no accident that a Jew created this system, and that Jews are readily "converted" to it, since they know the fate of isolation in opposition. *Vis-a-vis* the Western Civilization Freud was spiritually isolated, and had no recourse but to oppose.

Freudianism is one more product of Rationalism. It turns rationalism on the soul, and finds that it is purely mechanical. It can be understood, and spiritual phenomena are all manifestations of the sexual-impulse. This was another one of those marvelous and grandiose simplifications which guarantee popularity for any doctrine in an age of mass-journalism. Darwinism was the popular outlook that the meaning of the life of the world was that everything else was trying to become man-animal, and man was trying to become Darwinian. Marxism: the meaning of all human life is that the lowest must become the highest. Freudianism: the meaning of human life is sexuality, actual, optative, conative, or otherwise. All three are nihilistic. Culture-man is the spiritual enemy. He must be eliminated by animalizing him, biologizing him, making him economic, sexualizing him, diabolizing him.

To Darwinism, a Gothic cathedral is a product of mechanical evolution, to Marx it is an attempt of the bourgeois to trick the proletariat, to Freud it is a piece of frozen sexuality.

It is both needless and impossible to refute Freudianism. If everything is sex, a refutation of Freudianism would also be sexual in significance. The 20th century does not approach phenomena that have become historical by asking whether they are true or false. To its *historical* way of thinking, a Gothic cathedral is an expression of the intensely religious, newly awakening young Western Culture, which shadows forth the striving nature of this Culture-soul. In its necessity for self-expression, however, this new outlook must reject the materialistic tyranny of the older, immediately preceding outlook. It must free itself also from Freudianism.

This last great attempt to animalize man also uses critical-rationalistic methods. The soul is *mechanical:* it consists of one simple impulse, the sexual instinct. The whole life of the soul is the process of this instinct getting misdirected, twisted, turned upon itself. For it is elemental to this "science" that this instinct cannot go correctly. To describe the mechanical functions of the soul is to describe *diseases.* The various processes are neurosis, inversion, complexes, repression, sublimation, transference, perversion. All are *abnormal,* unhealthy, misdirected, unnatural. As one of its abecedarian truths, the system states that every person is a neurotic, and every neurotic is a pervert or invert. This applies not only to Culture-man, but to primitive man as well.

Here Freud surpasses Rousseau, who at the beginning of the early Civilization phase of the West, affirmed the purity, simplicity, and soul-healthiness of the savage, in contrast to the wickedness and perversion of Culture-man. Freud has widened the attack—the whole human species is the enemy. Even if one did not know from all the other phenomena that the early Civilization-phase of Materialism and Rationalism had closed, one would know from this system alone, for such complete nihilism is obviously not to be surpassed, expressing as it does anti-Cultural feeling to its uttermost limits.

As a psychology it must be called a patho-psychology, for its whole arsenal of terms describe only aberrations of the sexual instinct. The notion of health is completely dissociated from the soul-life. Freudianism is the Black Mass of Western Science.

Part of the structure of the system is the interpretation of dreams. The purely mechanical workings of the "mind" (for there is no soul) are shown by dreams. Not clearly shown, however, for an elaborate ritual is needed to arrive at the real meaning. "Conscience censorship"—the new name for Kant's "moral reason"—"symbolism," "repetition-compulsion"—these and many more Kabbalistic numina have to be invoked. The original form of the doctrine was that all dreams were wishes.

To dream of the death of a loved person was explained by psychoanalysis as latent parent-hatred, the symptom of the almost universal Oedipus-complex. The dogma was rigid: thus if the dream was of the death of a pet dog or cat, the animal was the focus of the Oedipus-complex. If the actor dreams of not knowing his part, it shows that he wishes he might sometime be so embarrassed. In order to attract more converts, including those of weaker faith, the doctrine was slightly changed, and other dream-interpretations were admitted, such as the "repetition-compulsion," when the same fear-dream recurs regularly.

The dream-world of course reflected the universal sexuality of the soul. Every conceivable object in a dream was capable of being a sexual symbol. "Repressed" sexual instinct appeared in dreams, symbolizing, transferring, sublimating, inverting, and running the whole gamut of mechanical terminology.

Every person is a neurotic in his mature life, and it is no accident, for he became so in his childhood. Experiences in infancy determine—quite mechanically, since the whole process is non-spiritual—which particular neuroses will accompany the person through his life. There is really nothing that can be done about it, except to deliver oneself into the care of a Freudian adept. One of these announced that 98 per cent of all persons should be under the treatment of psychiatrists. This was later in the development of the system; at first it would have been 100 per cent, but, as with Mormonism, the original purity of the doctrine was compromised by the Elders for reasons of expediency.

The average man who is doing his work presents a great illusion to the eye of an observer—it looks as though he is doing what he is doing. Actually, however, Freudianism shows that he is only apparently doing it, for in actuality he is quietly thinking about sexual matters, and all that one can see is the results of his sexual fantasy sifted through mechanical filters of conscience-censorship, sublimation, transference, and the like. If you hope, fear, wish, dream, think abstractly, investigate, feel inspired, have ambition, dread, repugnance, reverence —you are merely expressing your sexual instinct. Art is obviously sex, as are religion, economics, abstract thought, technics, war, State and politics.

II

Freud earned thus, together with his cousin Marx, the Order of Simplicity. It was the coveted Decoration of the age of Mass. With the demise of the Age of Criticism, it has fallen into the discard, for the new outlook is interested, not in cramming all the data of knowledge, experience, and intuition, into a prefabricated mold, but in seeing what was, what is, what must be. Over the portal of the new outlook is Leibnitz's aphorism: "The Present is loaded with the Past, and pregnant with the Future." The child is father to the man—this is ancient wisdom, and describes the unfolding of the human organism from infancy to maturity, every stage being related backwards and forwards because one and the same soul speaks at every moment. Freudianism caricatures this deep organic vision with a mechanical device whereby childhood *determines* the form of maturity, and makes the whole organic unfolding into a causal *process,* and what is more a diabolical, diseased one.

Insofar as it is Western at all, Freudianism is subject to the prevailing spirituality of the West. Its mechanism and materialism reflect the 19th century outlook. Its talk of the unconscious, of instinct, impulse, and the like, reflects the fact that Freudianism appeared at the transition point in the Western Civilization when Rationalism was fulfilled and the Irrational emerged again as such. It was not at all in the terminology or the treatment of the new, irrational elements in the doctrine that Freudianism presages the new spirit, but simply and solely in the fact that irrational elements *appear.* Only in this one thing does this structure anticipate; in every other way, it belongs to the Malthusian-Darwinian-Marxian past. It was merely an ideology, a part of the general Rationalistic-Materialistic assault on Culture-man.

The irrational elements that the system recognizes are subordinated strictly to the higher rationalism of the adept, who can unravel them and lead the suffering neurotic into the light of day. They are, if possible, even more diseased than the rest of the mind-complex. They may be irrational, but they have a rational explanation, treatment, and cure.

Freudianism appears thus as the last of the materialistic religions. Psychoanalysis, like Marxism, is a sect. It has auricular confession, dogmas, and symbols, esoteric and exoteric versions of the doctrine, converts and apostates, priests and scholastics, a whole ritual of exorcism, and a liturgy of mantic. Schisms appear, resulting in the foundation of new sects, each of which claims to be the bearer of the true doctrine. It is occult and pagan, with its dream-interpretation, demonological with its sex-worship. Its world-picture is that of a neurotic humanity, twisted and perverted in its strait jacket of Western Civilization, toward whom the new priest of psychoanalysis stretches out the hand of deliverance through the anti-Western Freudian Gospel.

The Hatred that formed the core of Marxism is present in the newer religion also. In both cases it is the hate of the outsider for his totally alien surroundings, which he cannot change, and must therefore destroy.

The attitude of the 20th century toward the subject-matter of Freudianism is inherent in the spirit of this age. Its center is in action—external tasks call to Western soul. The best will hear this call, leaving those to busy themselves with drawing soul-pictures who have no souls.

Scientific psychology was always thus—it has never attracted the best minds in any Culture. It all rests on the assumption that it is possible by thought to establish the form of what thinks, an extremely dubious proposition. If it were possible to describe the Soul in rational terms—a prequisite to a science of psychology—there would be no need for such a science. The Reason is a part, or better, a partial function, of the Soul. Every soul-picture describes only the soul of him who draws it, and those like him. A diabolist sees things Freud-wise, but he cannot understand those who see things otherwise. This explains the vileness of the Freudianistic attempts to diabolize, sexualize, mechanize, and destroy all the great men of the West. Greatness they could not understand, not having inward experience of it.

Soul cannot be defined—it is the Element of Elements. Any picture of it, any psychological system, is a mere product of it, and gets no further than self-portrayal. How well we understand now that *Life* is more important than the *results* of Life.

Psychology-systems use the terminology—in all Civilizations —of the material sciences of physics and mechanics. They reflect thus the spirit of natural science, and take rank therewith as a product of the age. To the higher rank to which they aspired, namely the systematization of the Soul, they do not attain. No sooner was Freudianism well-established as the new psychoanalytic Church than the onward development of the Western Civilization made it old-fashioned.

The psychology of the 20th century is one adapted to a life of action. To this age psychology must be practical or it is worthless. The psychology of crowds, of armies, of leadership, of obedience, of loyalty—these are valuable to this age. They are not to be arrived at by "psychometric" methods and abstruse terminology, but by human experience—one's own, and that of others. The 20th century regards Montaigne as a psychologist, but Freud as merely the 19th century representative of the witch-obsession of the Western Culture in its younger days, which was also a disguised form of sex-worship.

Human psychology is learned in living and acting, not in timing reactions or observing dogs and mice. The memoirs of a man of action, adventurer, explorer, soldier, statesman, contain psychology of the type that interests this age, both in and between the lines. Every newspaper is a compendious instruction in the psychology of mass-propaganda, and better than any treatise on the subject. There is a psychology of nations, of professions, of Cultures, of the successive ages of a Culture, from youth to senility. Psychology is one aspect of the art of the possible, and as such is a favorite study of the age.

The greatest repository of psychology of all is History. It contains no *models* for us, since Life is never-recurring, once-happening, but it shows by example how we can fulfill our potentialities by being true to ourselves, by never compromising with that which is utterly alien.

To this view of psychology, any materialism could not possibly be psychology. Here Rousseau, Darwin, Marx, and Freud meet. They may have understood other things, but the human soul, and in particular the soul of Culture-man, they did not understand. Systems like theirs are only historical curiosities to the 20th century, unless they happen to claim to be appropriate descriptions of Reality. Anyone who "believes in" these antiquated fantasies stamps himself as ludicrous, posthumous, ineffective, and superfluous. No leading men of the coming decades will be Darwinians, Marxians or Freudians.

The Scientific-Technical World-Outlook

Science is the seeking after exact knowledge of phenomena. In discovering interrelations between phenomena, that is, observing the conditions of their appearance, it feels it has *explained* them. This type of mentality appears in a High Culture after the completion of creative religious thought, and the beginning of externalizing. In our Culture, this type of thinking only began to feel sure of itself with the middle of the 17th century, in the Classical, in the 5th century B.C. The leading characteristic of early scientific thinking, from the historical standpoint, is that it dispenses with theological and philosophical equipment, only using them to fill in the background, in which it is not interested. It is thus materialistic, in its essence, in that its sole attention is turned to phenomena, and not to ultimate realities. To a religious age, phenomena are unimportant compared with the great spiritual truths, to a scientific age, the opposite is true.

Technics is the utilization of the macrocosm. It always accompanies a science in its full blooming, but this is not to say that every science is accompanied by technical activity, for the sciences of the Classical Culture, and the Mexican Culture had nothing at all which we would call technical proficiency. In the early Civilization stage, Science predominates, and precedes technics in all its attempts, but with the turn of the 20th century, technical thinking began to emancipate itself from this dependence, and in our day, science serves technics, and no longer vice versa.

In an Age of Materialism, which is to say, an antimetaphysical age, it was but natural that an antimetaphysical type of thinking like science would become a popular religion. Religion is a necessity for Culture-man, and he will build his religion on economics, biology, or nature, if the Spirit of the Age excludes true religion. Science was the prevalent religion of the 18th and 19th centuries. While one was permitted to doubt the truths of the Christian sects, one was not allowed to doubt Newton, Leibnitz, and Descartes. When the great Goethe challenged the Newtonian light-theory, he was put down as a crank, and a heretic.

Science was the supreme religion of the 19th century, and all other religions, like Darwinism and Marxism, referred to its great parent-dogmas as the basis for their own truths. "Unscientific" became the term of damnation.

From its timid beginnings, science finally took the step of holding out its results, not as a mere arrangement and classification, but as the true *explanations* of Nature and Life. With this step, it became a world-outlook, that is a comprehensive philosophy, with metaphysics, logic and ethics for believers.

Every science is a profane restatement of the preceding dogmas of the religious period. It is the same Cultural soul which formed the great religions that in the next age reshapes its world, and this continuity is thus absolutely inevitable. West-

ern Science as a world-outlook is merely Western religion represented as profane, not sacred, natural, not supernatural, dis-
coverable, not revealed.

Like Western religion, science was definitely priestly. The
savant is the priest, the instructor is the lay brother, and a great
systematizer is canonized, like Newton and Planck. Every Western thought-form is esoteric, and its scientific doctrines were
no exception. The populace were kept in touch with "the advance of science" through a popular literature at which the
high-priests of science smiled.

In the 19th century, science accreted the "Progress" idea, and
gave its own particular stamp to it. The content of "Progress"
was to be *technical*. "Progress" was to consist in faster motion,
further sound, wider exploitation of the material world *ad
infinitum*. This showed already the coming predominance of
technics over science. "Progress" was not to be primarily more
knowledge, but more *technique*. Every Western world-view
strives after universality, and so this one declared that the solution of social problems was not to be found in politics and
economics, but in—science. Inventions were promised which
would make war too horrible for men to engage in, and they
would therefore cease warring. This naivete was a natural
product of an age which was strong in natural science, but weak
in psychology. The solution of the problem of poverty was
machinery, and more machinery. The horrible conditions that
had arisen out of a machine-Civilization were to be alleviated
by more machines. The problem of old age was to be overcome by "rejuvenation." Death was pronounced to be only a
product of pathology, not of senility. If all diseases were done
away with, there would be nothing left to die from.

Racial problems were to be solved by "eugenics." The birth
of individuals was to be no longer left to Fate. Scientific priests

would decide things like parentage and birth. No outer events would be allowed in the new theocracy, nothing uncontrolled. The weather was to be "harnessed," all natural forces brought under absolute control. There would be no occasion for wars, everyone would be striving to be scientific, not seeking power. International problems would vanish, since the world would become one huge scientific unit.

The picture was complete, and to the materialistic 19th century, awe-inspiring: all Life, all Death, all Nature, reduced to absolute order, in the custody of scientific theocrats. Everything would go on this planet just as it went in the picture of the heavens that the scientific astronomers had sketched out for themselves; serene regularity would reign—but—this order would be purely mechanical, utterly purposeless. Man would be scientific only in order to be scientific.

II

Something happened, however, to disturb the picture, and to show that it, too, bore the hall-mark of Life. Before the First World War, the disintegration of the psychical foundations of the great structure had already set in. The World War marks, in the realm of science, as in every other sphere of Western life, a caesura. A new world arose from that war—the spirit of the 20th century stood forth as the successor to the whole mechanistic view of the universe, and to the whole concept of the meaning of Life, as being the acquisition of wealth.

With truly amazing rapidity, considering the decades of its power and supremacy, the mechanistic view paled, and the leading minds, even within its disciplines, dropped away from the old, self-evident articles of materialistic faith.

As is the usual case with historical movements, expressions

of a super-personal soul, the point of highest power, of the greatest victories, is also the beginning of the rapid down-going. Shallow persons always mistake the end of a movement for the beginning of its absolute dominance. Thus Wagner was looked upon by many as the beginning of a new music, whereas, the next generation knew that he had been the last Western musician. The passing away of any expression of Culture is a gradual process—nevertheless there are turning points, and the rapid decline of science *as a world-outlook* set in with the First World War.

The down-going of science *as a mental discipline* had long preceded the World War. With the theory of Entropy (1850), and the introduction of the idea of irreversibility into its picture, science was on the road which was to culminate in physical relativity and frank admission of the subjectivity of physical concepts. From Entropy came the introduction of statistical methods into systematic science, the beginning of spiritual abdication. Statistics described Life and the living; the strict tradition of Western science had insisted on *exactitude* in mathematical description of reality, and had hence despised that which was not susceptible of exact description, such as biology. The entrance of probabilities into formerly exact science is the sign that the observer is beginning to study himself, his own form as conditioning the order and describability of phenomena.

The next step was the Theory of Radioactivity, which again contains strong subjective elements and requires the Calculus of Probabilities to describe its results. The scientific picture of the world became ever more refined, and ever more subjective. The formerly separate disciplines drew slowly together, mathematics, physics, chemistry, epistemology, logic. Organic ideas intruded showing once more that the observer has reached the point where he is studying the form of his own Reason. A chemical element now has a *lifetime,* and the precise events of its life are unpredictable, indeterminate.

The very unit of physical happening itself, the "atom," which was still believed in as a reality by the 19th century, became in the 20th century a mere concept, the description of whose properties was constantly changed to meet and prop up technical developments. Formerly, every experiment merely showed the "truth" of the ruling theories. That was in the days of the supremacy of science as a discipline over technics, its adopted child. But, before the middle of the 20th century, every new experiment brought about a new hypothesis of "atomic structure." What was important in the process was not the hypothetical house of cards which was erected afterwards, but the experiment which had gone before.

No compunction was felt about having two theories, irreconcilable with one another, to describe the "structure" of the "atom," or the nature of light. The subject-matter of all the separate sciences could no longer be kept mathematically clear. Old concepts like mass, energy, electricity, heat, radiation, merged into one another, and it became ever more clear that what was really under study was the human reason, in its epistemological aspect, and the Western soul in its scientific aspect.

Scientific theories reached the point where they signified nothing less than the complete collapse of science as a mental discipline. The picture was projected of the Milky Way as consisting of more than a million fixed stars, among which are many with a diameter of more than 93,000,000 miles; this again as not a stationary cosmic center, but itself in motion toward Nowhere at a speed of more than 600 kilometers a second. The cosmos is finite, but unlimited; boundless, but bounded. This demands of the true believer the old Gothic faith again:

credo quia absurdum, but mechanical purposelessness cannot evoke this kind of faith, and the high priests have apostatized. In the other direction, the "atom" has equally fantastic dimensions—a ten-millionth of a millimeter is its diameter, and the mass of a hydrogen atom stands to the mass of a gram of water as the mass of a post card stands to the mass of the earth. But this atom consists of "electrons," the whole making up a sort of solar system, in which the distances between the planets is as great, in proportion to their mass, as in our solar system. The diameter of an electron is one three-billionth of a millimeter. But the closer it is studied, the more spiritual it becomes, for the nucleus of the atom is a mere charge of electricity, having neither weight, volume, inertia nor any other classic properties of matter.

In its last great saga, science dissolved its own psychical foundations, and moved outside the world of the senses into the world of the soul. Absolute time was dissolved, and time became a function of position. Mass became spiritualized into energy. The idea of simultaneity was discarded, motion became relative, parallels cut one another, two distances could no longer be said absolutely to equal one another. Everything which had once been described by, or had itself described, the word Reality, dissolved in the last act of the drama of science as a mental discipline.

The custodians of science as a mental discipline, one after another, abandoned the old materialistic positions. In the last act, they came to see that the science of a given Culture has as its real object the description, in scientific terms, of the world of that Culture, a world which again is the projection of the soul of that Culture. The profound knowledge was realized through the very study of matter itself that matter is only the envelope of the soul. To describe matter is to describe oneself, even though the mathematical equations drape the process with an apparent objectivity. Mathematics itself has succumbed as a description of Reality: its proud equations are only *tautology.* An equation is an *identity,* a repetition, and its "truth" is a reflection of the paper-logic of the identity-principle. But this is only a form of our thinking.

The transition from 19th century materialism to the new spirituality of the 20th century was thus not a battle, but an inevitable development. This keen, ice-cold, mental discipline turned the knife on itself because of an inner imperative to think in a new way, an anti-materialistic way. Matter cannot be explained materialistically. Its whole significance derives from the soul.

III

Materialism from this standpoint appears as a great *negative.* It was a great spiritual effort to deny the spirit, and this denial of the spirit was in itself an expression of a crisis in the spirit. It was the Civilization-crisis, the denial of Culture by Culture.

For the animals, that which appears—matter—is Reality. The world of sensation is *the* world. But for primitive man, and *a fortiori* for Culture-man, the world separates out into Appearance and Reality. Everything visible and tangible is felt as a *symbol* of something higher and unseen. This symbolizing activity is what distinguishes the human soul from the less complicated Life-forms. Man possesses a *metaphysical sense* as the hall-mark of his humanity. But it is precisely the higher reality, the world of symbols, of meaning and purpose, that Materialism denied in toto. What was it then, but the great attempt to animalize man by equating the world of matter with Reality, and merging him into it? Materialism was not overcome because it was false; it simply died of old age. It is not false even now—it merely falls on deaf ears. It is old-fashioned, and has become the world view of country cousins.

With the collapse of its Reality, Western science as a mental discipline has accomplished its mission. Its by-product, science as a world-outlook now belongs to yesterday. But as one of the results of the Second World War, there appeared a new stupidity—technics-worship as a philosophy of Life and the world.

Technics has in its essence nothing to do with science as a mental discipline. It has one aim: the extraction of physical power from the outer world. It is, so to speak, Nature-politics, as distinguished from human politics. The fact that technics proceeds on one hypothesis today, and on another tomorrow, shows that its task is not the formation of a knowledge-system, but the subjecting of the outer world to the will of Western man. The hypotheses that it proceeds on have no real connection with its results, but merely afford points of departure for the imagination of technicians to think along new lines for new experiments to extract ever more power. Some hypotheses are of course necessary; precisely *what* they are is secondary.

Technics is even less capable than science, then, of satisfying the need for a world-outlook to this age. Physical power—for what?

The age itself supplies the answer: physical power for political purposes. Science has passed into the role of furnishing the terminology and ideation for technics. Technics in turn is the servant of politics. Ever since 1911, the idea of "atomic energy" has been in the air, but it was the spirit of war which first gave this theory a concrete form, with the invention, in 1945, by an unknown Westerner of a new high explosive which depends for its effect on the instability of "atoms."

Technics is practical; politics is sublimely practical. It has not the slightest interest in whether a new explosive is referred to "atoms," "electrons," "cosmic rays," or to saints and devils. The historical way of thinking which informs the true statesman cannot take today's terminology too seriously when he remembers how quickly yesterday's was dropped. A projectile which can destroy a city of 200,000 persons in a second—that however is a reality, and affects the sphere of political possibilities.

It is the spirit of politics which determines the form of war, and the form of war then influences the conduct of politics. Weapons, tactics, strategy, the exploitation of victory—all these are determined by the political imperative of the age. Each age forms the entirety of its expressions for itself. Thus to the form-rich 18th century, warfare also was a strict form, a sequence of position and development, like the contemporary musical form of variations on a theme.

An odd aberration occurred in the Western world after the first employment of a new high-explosive in 1945. Essentially, it was referrable to remnants of materialistic thinking, but there were also perennially old mythological ideas in it. The idea arose that this new explosive would blow up the whole planet. In the middle of the 19th century, when the railway idea was projected, the medical doctors said that such swift motion would generate cerebral troubles, and that even the sight of a train rushing past might do so; furthermore the sudden change of air-pressure in tunnels might cause strokes.

The idea of the planet blowing up was just another form of the old idea, found in many mythologies, Western and non-Western, of the End of the World, Ragnarök, Götterdämmerung. Cataclysm. Science also picked up this idea, and wrapped it up as the Second Law of Thermodynamics. The technics-worshipers fancied many things about the new explosive. They did not realize that it was no end of a process, but the beginning.

We stand at the beginning of the Age of Absolute Politics, and one of its demands is naturally for powerful weapons. Therefore, technics is ordered to strain after *absolute weapons.* It will never attain them, however, and any belief that it will stamps its possessor as simply a materialist, which is to say, in the 20th century, a provincial.

Technics-worship is completely inappropriate to the soul of Europe. The formative impulse of human Life does not come from matter now any more than it ever did. On the contrary, the very way of experiencing matter, and the way of utilizing it, are expressions of the soul. The naive belief of technics-worship that an explosive is going to remake the Western Civilization from its foundations is a last dying gasp of Materialism. This Civilization made this explosive, and it will make others—they did not make it, nor will they ever make or unmake the Western Civilization. No more than matter created the Western Culture can it ever destroy it.

It is still materialism to confuse a civilization with factories, homes, and the collectivity of installations. Civilization is a higher reality, manifesting itself through human populations, and within these, through a certain spiritual stratum, which embodies at highest potential the living Idea of the Culture. This Culture creates religions, forms of architecture, arts, States, Nations, Races, Peoples, armies, wars, poems, philosophies, sciences, weapons and inner imperatives. All of them are mere expressions of the higher Reality, and none of them can destroy it.

The attitude of the 20th century toward science and technics is clear. It does not ask them to furnish a world-outlook—this it derives elsewhere—and it positively rejects any attempt to make a religion or a philosophy out of materialism or atom-worship. It does however have use for them, in the service of its unlimited will-to-power. The Idea is primary, and in actualizing it, superiority in weapons is essential in order to compensate for the immense numerical superiority of the enemies of the West.

The Imperative of Our Age

BY SURVEYING the entire previous happening of the world, Western man understands himself in his 20th century phase. He sees where he stands, he sees also why it was that he was impelled to orient himself *historically*. His inner instinct forbade that he distort History in the materialistic fashion by subjecting it to an ideology of some kind. He sees the ages of previous Cultures to which his present phase is related: the "Period of the Contending States" in the Chinese, the transition to Caesarism in the Roman, the "Hyksos" era in the Egyptian. None of them are ages of the flowering of art or philosophy, all have their center of gravity in politics and action. They are the periods of large-space thinking, of the greatest deeds, of external creativeness of the highest possible magnitude. Philosophers and ideologists, world-improvers and art-traders, slip down to the street-level in these ages, when the imperative is directed to action and not to abstract thought.

Because of his historical position, in a Civilization at the beginning of its second phase, his soul has a certain organic predisposition, and the custodians of the Idea of this time will of necessity think and feel thus, and not otherwise. It can be definitively stated what this relationship is to the various forms of human and Cultural thought and action.

To religion, this age is once more affirmative, the very opposite of the negative atheism of Materialism. Every man of action is in constant contact with the unforseeable, the Imponderable, the mystery of Life, and this precludes the laboratory attitude on his part. An age of action lives side by side with Death, and values Life by its attitude toward Death. The old Gothic religious idea is still with us—it is at his last moment that a man shows what is in him in its purity. Though he may have lived a wastrel, he may die a hero, and it is this last act of his life that creates the image of him that will survive in the minds of his descendants. We cannot possibly value a life according to its length, as Materialism did, or believe in any doctrine of immortality of the body.

Between his earthly task and his relationship to God, there is no conflict for Western man. At the beginning of a battle, it is the custom of soldiers to pray. The battle is the foreground, that toward which the prayer is directed is the transcendent, is God. Our metaphysical imperative has to be fulfilled within a certain Life-framework. We have been born into a certain Culture, at a certain phase of its organic development, we have certain gifts. These condition the earthly task which we must perform. The metaphysical task is beyond any conditioning, for it would have been the same in any age anywhere. The earthly task is merely the form of the higher task, its organic vehicle.

To philosophy, the Spirit of the Age has its own attitude, different from all previous centuries. Its great organizing principle is the morphological significance of systems and events. It rests upon no critical method, for all these critical methods merely reflected the prevalent spirit, and its spirit has outgrown criticism. The center of its thought-life is in History. By History we orient ourselves, we see the significance of the previous centuries of our own Culture, we understand beyond any system or ideology the nature of what we have to do, we see the significance of our own inmost feelings and imperative.

For systems of world-improvement, products of a type of thinking which has become old-fashioned, this age has no use. It is interested solely in what *must* be done, and what *can* be done, and not at all in what *ought* to be done. The world of action has its own organic rhythms, and ideologies belong to the world of thought. Living ideas interest us, stillborn ideals do not.

To art, the Age can have only one attitude. At best, our artistic tasks are secondary, at worst, art has degenerated to frightfulness and chaos. Mass clangor is not music, pictorial nightmares are not even draughtsmanship, let alone the art of painting. Obscenity and ugliness are not literature, materialistic propaganda is not drama, disconnected words thrown formlessly on to paper are not lyric poetry. Whatever art-tasks the age has to fulfill will be carried out by individuals acting quietly within old Western traditions, not noising themselves about with journalistic art-theories.

In an age of action and organization, legal thought reaches a new development. Western law will not stand outside the age of politics, with its accompanying thought-forms of history and psychology. It will be entirely renewed with these ideas, and its old materialism, in public law, commercial, and in particular, in criminal law, will be thrown into the discard.

Technics, and its handmaid, science, are of high importance to the Western Civilization in its present phase. Technics must provide Western politics with a strong fist for the coming struggles.

Into the social structure of the Western Civilization there will be infused the principle of authority, supplanting the principle of wealth. This view is not at all hostile to private property or private management—that belongs to the negative feeling of hatred and jealousy which inform class war. The 20th century Idea liquidates class war, as it does the idea of economics being the determining force in our life.

Economics occupies the position in the new edifice of the *foundation* and its spiritual importance is indicated thereby. The foundation is not the important thing in a structure, but strictly secondary. But in an age of action, economic strength is indispensable to political units. Economics can be a source of political strength, can serve sometimes as a weapon in the power-struggle. For these reasons, the 20th century will not neglect the development of the economic side of life, but will provide it with a new impetus from the now dominant idea of politics. Instead of economics being the sphere wherein individuals battled one another for private spoils, it becomes now a strong and important side of the political organism which is the custodian of the Destiny of all.

The view of the 20th century toward the various directions of thought and action is not arbitrary, any more than that of previous ages was. Most of the best minds of the 19th century were nihilistic in tendency, sensualistic, rationalistic, materialistic—because the age was one of crisis in the Culture-Life, and these ideas were the Spirit of the Age. Similarly, the idea of *political nationalism* was self-evident to that age, but that too was a product of the great crisis, thus a form of *disease* as destructive as it was necessary.

Every juncture of organic happening presents a choice and an alternative. The choice is to do the necessary, the alternative is chaos. This has nothing to do with school-book logic; that logic is just one of the numberless products of Life, and Life will always invent as many logics as it has need for, but Life will always obey *one* logic, *organic logic.* This is not describable by any system, but can be comprehended by Destiny-thinking, the only form of thought serviceable to action. Life goes forward, or it goes nowhere. Opposition to the Spirit of the Age is the will-to-nothingness.

In the realm of *theory,* this age has as many alternatives as it has ideologists to dream them up. In the realm of *fact,* it has only one choice—and that is delineated for it by the Life-phase of the Civilization, and the outer circumstances in which we find ourselves at the moment.

We know that the transition of one age into the next is gradual, and we know that even as it has fulfilled itself in some directions, it thinks it is just beginning in others. Thus while science as a mental discipline has achieved its goal, science as a popular outlook for fools and uncreative persons continues to exist. Materialism no longer claims any of the best minds, but the best minds are not in control at this moment. The West is dominated by the outer world, in the control of barbarians and distorters, and they find the least valuable minds of Europe most serviceable to them. Materialism serves the great cause of destroying Europe, and that is why it is forced on the populations of Europe by the extra-European forces.

There are two ways in which we are sensible of our great task, our ethical imperative which claims our lives. First from our inward feeling, which impels us to look at things this way and no other. Secondly from our knowledge of the history of seven previous High Cultures, each of which went through this same crisis, and each of which liquidated the long Civilization-crisis in precisely the way that our instincts tell us ours is to be resolved.

I I

Our momentary situation takes the form of a great battle—a battle which may take more than one war to resolve it, or which may be resolved by a sudden cataclysmic happening, entirely unforeseeable to us now. On the surface of history it is the unforeseen that happens. The most human beings can do is to be prepared inwardly. In complete contradiction to our instinct, feelings, and ideas, the 19th century sits leering upon the throne of Europe, wrapped in the cerements of the grave, and propped up by the extra-European forces. This means that the age in which we find ourselves takes the form of a deep and fundamental conflict. These ideas can never live again—their supremacy merely means the strangulation of the young, living tendencies of the New Europe. Their supremacy simply consists in forced lip-service to them. They do not affect the action-thinking, the organic-rhythms of the age, they are merely instruments of thwarting the will of Europe by holding it in subjection to the least valuable elements in Europe, who are maintained in power by extra-European bayonets.

The conflict is far-reaching; it affects every sphere of Life. Two ideas are opposed—not concepts or abstractions, but Ideas which were in the blood of men before they were formulated by the minds of men. The Resurgence of Authority stands opposed to the Rule of Money; Order to Social Chaos, Hierarchy to Equality, socio-economico-political Stability to constant Flux; glad assumption of Duties to whining for Rights; Socialism to Capitalism, ethically, economically, politically; the Rebirth of Religion to Materialism; Fertility to Sterility; the spirit of Heroism to the spirit of Trade; the principle of Responsibility to Parliamentarism; the idea of Polarity of Man and Woman to

Feminism; the idea of the individual task to the ideal of "happiness"; Discipline to Propaganda-compulsion; the higher unities of family, society, State to social atomism; Marriage to the Communistic ideal of free love; economic self-sufficiency to senseless trade as an end in itself; the inner imperative to Rationalism.

But the greatest opposition of all has not yet been named, the conflict which will take up all the others into itself. This is the battle of the Idea of the Unity of the West against the nationalism of the 19th century. Here stand opposed the ideas of Empire and petty-stateism, large-space thinking and political provincialism. Here find themselves opposed the miserable collection of yesterday-patriots and the custodians of the Future. The yesterday-nationalists are nothing but the puppets of the extra-European forces who conquer Europe by dividing it. To the enemies of Europe, there must be no rapprochement, no understanding, no union of the old units of Europe into a new unit, capable of carrying on 20th century politics.

In the previous seven High Cultures, the period of the nationalistic disease was liquidated by the spread of one feeling over the whole Civilization. It was not unaccompanied by wars, for the Past has always, and will always, fight against the Future. Life is war, and to wish to create is to bring about the opposition of the great Nay-sayers, those whose existence is tied to the Past, is sunk into the Past. The division of the Civilization was in each case resolved by the reunion of the Civilization, the reassertion of its old, original, exclusiveness and unity. In each case, from petty-stateism came Empire. The Empire Idea was so strong that no inner force could oppose it with hope of success.

Nationalism itself in Europe transformed itself into the new Empire-Idea after the First World War, the beginning of our age. In each Western country, the "Nationalists" were those who were opposed to another European War, and who desired a general political understanding in Europe to prevent its sinking into the dust where it now struggles. They were thus not nationalistic at all, but Western-Imperial. Similarly the self-styled "internationalists" were the ones who wished to stir up wars among the European states of yesterday, in order to sabotage the creation of the Empire of the West. They hated it because they were alien to it in one way or another, some because they were completely outside the Western Culture, others because they were incurably possessed by some ideology or other which hated the new, vital, masculine, form of the Future, and preferred the old conception of Life as money-chasing, money-spending, hatred of strong, ascendant Life, and love of weakness, sterility, and stupidity.

And thus, the extra-European forces, together with the traitorous inner elements in Europe, were able to bring about a Second World War which defeated on the surface the powerful development of Western Empire. But the defeat was, and had to be, *only* on the surface, since the decisive impulse, as this century knows once more, comes always from within, from the Inner Imperative, from the Soul. To defeat on the surface the actualization of an Idea that is Historically essential is to strengthen it. Its energy, that would have been diffusing itself outward in self-expression turns inward and is concentrated onto the primary task of spiritual liberation. The materialists do not know that what does not destroy, makes stronger, and destroy this Idea they cannot. It uses men, but they cannot use it, touch it, injure it.

This whole work is nothing but an outline of the Idea of this Age, a presentation of its foundations and universality, and every spiritual root of it will be traced to its origins and necessity. But in this place, it should be mentioned that the idea of a universal Europe, an Empire of the West, is not new, but is the prime form of our Culture, as of every other. For the first five centuries of our Culture, there was a *universal* Western people, in which the local differences counted but slightly. There was a universal king-emperor, who might have been often defied, but was not denied. There was a universal style, Gothic, which inspired and formed all art from furniture to the cathedral. There was a universal code of conduct, Western chivalry, with its honor-imperative for every situation. There was a universal religion and a universal Church. There was a universal language, Latin, and a universal law, Roman law.

The disintegration of this unity was slowly progressive from 1250 onward, but was not entirely accomplished, even for political purposes, until the age of political nationalism, beginning c. 1750, when Westerners for the first time allowed themselves to use the barbarian against other Western nations.

And now, as we enter upon the late Civilization-phase, the idea of a universal Europe, an Empire of the West in the 20th century style emerges once more as the single, great, formative Idea of the age. The form in which the task presents itself is *political*. It is a *power* question whether this Empire will be established, for strong extra-European forces oppose it, and these forces have divided the soil of our Culture between them.

III

The Empire of the West is a development that no inner European force could possibly oppose with more than token resistance, but its establishment is now crossed by the decisive intervention of outer forces in the life of the West. The struggle is thus spiritual-political, and its motive force derives from the Idea of Western unity. At this moment, the existence of the West in freedom for self-development is a function of the distribution of *power* in the world.

The age is political in a sense that no previous Western age has been so. This is the Age of Absolute Politics, for the whole form of our life is now a function of *power*.

Action, to be effective, must be within a spiritual framework. As Goethe said, "Unlimited activity, of whatever kind, leads at last to bankruptcy." Our action must not be blind. Our ideational equipment must be of a kind which can turn everything to its own account. It frees itself therefore from every kind of ideology, economic, biological, moralistic. It springs directly from the fact-sense which this age takes as its point of departure.

In the universities and in most of the books, outmoded methods of looking at the field of politics are presented. The doctrine is still taught that there are various "forms of government" which can be moved about from one political unit to another. There is republicanism, there is democracy, monarchy, and so on, and so on. Some of these "forms" are held out as "good"; others as "bad." It is better to have Europe occupied by the barbarian than to have a Western Empire under a "bad" "form of government." It is better to eat the rations that Moscow and Washington allow than it is to have a proud and free Europe with a "bad" government.

This is the very height of stupidity. Asininity on this level can only be reached by ideologists without soul and without intellect.

This sort of thing is book-politics, and is traceable to the fact that the word politics has two meanings: it means human power-activity, and it also has the dictionary meaning of a branch of philosophy. Now, if by politics, one means a branch of philosophy, very well. It can then turn into whatever one wishes. *Carte blanche* reigns in the world of philosophy. But— the *real* meaning of the word politics is *power-activity,* and in this sense, acting Life is itself politics. In this sense, *facts* rule politics, and the making of facts is the task of politics. This is the only possible meaning of the word to the 20th century, and this most serious moment of our Cultural life demands the utmost clarity of the minds of active men in order that they may be entirely free from any trace of ideology, whether derived from logic, philosophy, or morality.

And thus we stand before the view of politics which answers the inner demand of the Age of Absolute Politics.

THE 20TH CENTURY POLITICAL OUTLOOK

"Men are tired to disgust of money-economy. They hope for salvation from somewhere or other, for some real thing of honor and chivalry, of inward nobility, of unselfishness and duty."

SPENGLER

"The time for petty politics is past; the next century will bring the struggle for the dominion of the world—the *compulsion* to great politics."

NIETZSCHE, 1885

Introduction

THE DISTRIBUTION of powers in the first two World Wars was grotesque—the way it was occasioned is examined elsewhere. The results of these two wars were consequently grotesque. In both of them the outlook of the nineteenth century was apparently victorious. Superficially it was indeed, but actually such a thing is impossible. Owing to the organic nature of a Culture, as well as of the nations it creates, the Past cannot triumph over the Future—the alternatives are always only *two* in organic life: either forward development, or sickness and extinction.

The Western Civilization was not extinguished by these fearful conflicts, even though its existence was brought to the lowest possible point politically.

The First of the series of World Wars created a new world. The old ideas of history, politics, war, nations, economics, society, culture, art, education, ethics, were swept away. The new ideas of these things however were possessed only by the best brains of Europe, the small Culture-bearing stratum. Unfortunately the political leaders in Europe immediately after the First World War—save one—did not belong to this stratum.

The Second in the series arose from the fact that all Europe had not yet come under the impress of the new idea, the 20th century world-outlook. Half of Europe continued to play the old-fashioned, fatal game of petty-stateism. The leaders responsible for this represent what Goethe had in mind when he said: "The most terrible thing in the world is ignorance in action." Europe has not yet paid the full price for the malice and stupidity of these leaders. Nietzsche had wished to see such an increase in the threatening attitude of Russia that Europe would be *forced* to unite, to abandon the miserable game of political nationalism, petty-stateism. Not only did this happen *politically,* it happened *culturally*—Russia seceded totally from Europe and returned to Asia, whence Peter the Great had dragged it. But Europe continued to luxuriate in the repulsive game of frontiers and customs, little plans, little projects, little secrets—even after it had looked on at the spectacle of the Bolshevik revolution. Nietzsche had *assumed* in his thought that brains would be present at the helm in Europe—he forgot to *wish* that.

Readers in the year 2000 will find it hard to believe that in *1947* a French aspirant for power based himself on a program for making France secure from *Germany,* or that in *1947* England and France signed at Dünkirchen a treaty of alliance against Germany. Both America and Russia allowed these two political powers of yesterday to sign this harmless treaty—it could not in any way conflict with the plans of the extra-Europeans in Moscow and Washington, for it looked not to the future, or even to the present, but solely to the Past. Is it possible that the people who prepared and signed this treaty were under a collective hallucination that the year was 1750, 1850, or in any other century? When politicians become subjects of confusion, their countries must suffer.

Such things could not happen—Europe could not have reached such a low—if the new outlook on politics, the organically necessary outlook, had been clearly present in the ruling stratum in every European land. This new outlook—which becomes automatically the view of anyone who understands it —is now formulated here for the first time in its entirety.

The word politics itself has been subject in recent history— say, since 1850—to a deep misunderstanding. Two things are responsible: first the economic obsession of the nations of our Civilization during the 19th century, second the culture-distorting influence of America on certain European areas. The economic obsession gradually developed into the view that politics was something outmoded, that it only reflected preceding economic realities, that ultimately it would pass away. Thus *war* came to be regarded as an anachronism.

In America, because of the special conditions which prevailed there, unique in Western history, the word politics came to mean adherence to a group or an idea from a chicane motive. American politicians continually accused one another of engaging in "politics." This meant that politics was regarded as something unnecessary, something dishonest, something that could and should be done away with. This was in very truth their understanding of the word.

This deep misunderstanding of the nature of politics in Europe grew because of the extraordinarily long period of peace among the European nations between 1871 and 1914. This seemed to prove that war and politics were gone. The idea was so deeply fixed that 1914 only seemed to be the exception that proved the rule. There was also a mental necessity on the part of weak heads in Europe and America to regard the 1914 war as the last war. Nor did 1939 change this. Again there was a last war. People with this viewpoint are not embarrassed by the necessity of regarding every war as the last war. To an ideologist, his theory is normative—it is the facts which go askew.

The time has come when persistence in this sort of mental legerdemain must cease. Politics is not a subject for logical exercises, but a field for action in the Spirit of the Age.

The Nature of Politics

FIRST, what is politics? That is, politics as a *fact*. *Politics is activity in relation to power.*

Politics is a domain of its own—the domain of power. Thus it is not morality, it is not esthetics, it is not economics. Politics is a way of thinking, just as these others are. Each of these forms of thought isolates part of the totality of the world and claims it for its own. Morality distinguishes between *good* and *evil;* esthetics between *beautiful* and *ugly;* economics between *utile* and *inutile* (in its later purely trading phase these are identical with *profitable* and *unprofitable*). The way politics divides the world is into *friend* and *enemy.* These express for it the highest possible degree of connection, and the highest possible degree of separation.

Political thought is as separate from these other forms of thought as they are from each other. It can exist without them, they without it. The enemy can be good, he can be beautiful, he may be economically utile, business with him may be profitable—but if his power activity converges on mine, he is my enemy. He is that one with whom *existential* conflicts are possible. But esthetics, economics, morality are not concerned with *existence*, but only with norms of activity and thinking within an assured existence.

While as a matter of *psychological* fact, the enemy is easily represented as ugly, injurious, and evil, nevertheless this is subsidiary to politics, and does not destroy the independence of political thinking and activity. The political disjunction, concerned as it is with *existence*, is the deepest of all disjunctions and thus, has a tendency to seek every type of persuasion, compulsion, and justification in order to carry its activity forward. The extent to which this occurs is in direct ratio to the purity of political thinking in the leaders. The more their outlooks contain of moral, economic or other ways of thinking, the more they will use propaganda along such lines to further their political aims. It may even happen that they are not conscious that their activity is political. There is every indication that Cromwell regarded himself as a religionist and not as a politician. A variation was provided by the French journal which fanned the war spirit of its readers in 1870 with the expectation that the poilus would bring car-loads of blonde women back from Prussia.

On the other side, Japanese propaganda for the home populace during the Second World War, accented almost entirely the *existential*, i.e., purely political nature of the struggle. Another may be ugly, evil and injurious and yet not be an enemy; or he may be good, beautiful, and useful, and yet be an enemy.

Friend and enemy are *concrete* realities. They are not figurative. They are unmixed with moral, esthetic or economic elements. They do *not* describe a private relationship of antipathy. Antipathy is no necessary part of the political disjunction of friend and enemy. Hatred is a private phenomenon. If politicians inoculate their populations with hatred against the enemy, it is only to give them a personal interest in the public struggle which they would otherwise not have. Between superpersonal organisms there is no hatred, although there may be existential struggles. The disjunction love-hatred is not political and does not intersect at any point the political one of friend-enemy. Alliance does not mean love, any more than war means hate. Clear thinking in the realm of politics demands at the outset a strong power of dissociation of ideas.

The world-outlook of Liberalism, here as always completely emancipated from reality, said that the concept enemy described either an economic competitor, or else an ideational opponent. But in economics there are no enemies, but only competitors; in a world which was purely moralized (i.e., one in which only moral contrasts existed) there could be no enemies, but only ideational opponents. Liberalism, strengthened by the unique long peace, 1871–1914, pronounced politics to be atavistic, the grouping of friend-enemy to be retrograde. This of course belongs to politics as a branch of philosophy. In that realm no misstatement is possible; no accumulation of facts can prove a theory wrong, for over these theories are supreme, History is not the arbiter in matters of political outlook, Reason decides all, and everyone decides for himself what is reasonable. This is concerned however only with *facts*, and the only objection made here to such an outlook in the last analysis is that it is not factual.

Enemy, then, does not mean competitor. Nor does it mean opponent in general. Least of all does it describe a person whom one hates from feelings of personal antipathy. Latin possessed two words: hostis for the public enemy, inimicus for a private enemy. Our Western languages unfortunately do not make this important distinction. Greek however did possess it, and had further a deep distinction between two types of wars: those against other Greeks, and those against outsiders of the Culture, barbarians. The former were "agons" and only the latter were true wars. An agon was originally a contest for a prize at the public games, and the opponent was the "antagonist." This distinction has value for us because in comparison with wars in this age, intra-European wars of the preceding 800 years were agonal. As nationalistic politics assumed the ascendancy within the Classical Culture, with the Peloponnesian Wars, the distinction passed out of Greek usage. 17th and 18th century wars in West-Europe were in the nature of contests for a prize—the prize being a strip of territory, a throne, a title. The participants were dynasties, not peoples. The idea of destroying the opposing dynasty was not present, and only in the exceptional case was there even the possibility of such a thing happening. Enemy in the political sense means thus *public enemy*. It is unlimited, and it is thus distinguished from private enmity. The distinction public-private can only arise when there is a super-personal unit present. When there is, it determines who is friend and enemy, and thus no private person can make such a determination. He may hate those who oppose him or who are distasteful to him, or who compete with him, but he may not treat them as enemies in the unlimited sense.

The lack of two words to distinguish public and private enemy also has contributed to confusion in the interpretation of the well-known Biblical passage (Matthew 5:44; Luke 6:27) "Love your enemies." The Greek and Latin versions use the words referring to a *private* enemy. And this is indeed to what the passage refers. It is obviously an adjuration to put aside hatred and malice, but there is no necessity whatever that one hate the public enemy. Hatred is not contained in political thinking. Any hatred worked up against the public enemy is non-political, and always shows some weakness in the internal political situation. This Biblical passage does not adjure one to love the public enemy, and during the wars against Saracen and Turk no Pope, saint, or philosopher so construed it. It certainly does not counsel treason out of love for the public enemy.

II

Every non-political human grouping of whatever kind, legal, social, religious, economic or other becomes at last political if it creates an opposition deep enough to range men against one another as enemies. The State as a political unit excludes by its nature opposition of such types as these. If however a disjunction occurs in the population of a State which is so deep and strong that it divides them into friends and enemies, it shows that the State, at least temporarily, does not exist in fact. It is no longer a political unit, since all political decisions are no longer concentrated in it. All States whatever keep a monopoly of *political* decision. This is another way of saying they maintain inner peace. If some group or idea becomes so strong that it can effect a friend-enemy grouping, it is a political unit; and if forces are generated which the State cannot manage peaceably, it has disappeared for the time at least. If the State has to resort to force, this in itself shows that there are *two* political units, in other words, two States instead of the one originally there.

This raises the question of the significance of internal politics. Within a State, we speak of social-politics, judicial-politics, religious-politics, party-politics and the like. Obviously they

represent another meaning of the word, since they do not contain the possibility of a friend-enemy disjunction. They occur
within a pacified unit. They can only be called "secondary." The
essence of the State is that within its realm it excludes the
possibility of a friend-enemy grouping. Thus conflicts occurring within a State are by their nature limited, whereas the truly
political conflict is unlimited. Every one of these internal
limited struggles of course may become the focus of a true
political disjunction, if the idea opposing the State is strong
enough, and the leaders of the State have lost their sureness. If
it does—again, the State is gone. An organism either follows its
own law, or it becomes ill. This is organic logic and governs all
organisms, plant, animal, man, High Culture. They are either
themselves, or they sicken and die. Not for them is the rational
and logical view which says that whatever can be cogently
written down into a system can then be foisted on to an organism. Rational thinking is merely one of the multifarious creations of organic life, and it cannot, being subsidiary, include
the whole within its contemplation. It is limited and can only
work in a certain way, and on material which is adapted to such
treatment. The organism is the whole, however, and does not
yield its secrets to a method which it develops out of its own
adaptive ability to cope with non-organic problems it has to
overcome.

Secondary politics often can distort primary politics. For instance the female politics of petty jealousy and personal hatred
that was effective in the court of Louis XV was instrumental
in devoting much of French political energy to the less important struggle against Frederick, and little French political
energy to the more important struggle against England in
Canada and India and on the seas. Frederick the Great was not
beloved by the Pompadour, and France paid an empire to chas-

tise him. When private hostility exerts such an effect on public decision, it is proper to speak of political distortion, and of such a policy as a distorted one. When an organism consults or is in the grip of any force outside of its own developmental law, its life is distorted. The relation between a private enmity and a public politics it is circumstanced to distort is the same as that between European petty-Stateism and the Western Civilization. The collectively suicidal game of nationalistic politics distorted the whole destiny of the West after 1900 to the advantage of the extra-European forces.

III

The *concrete* nature of politics is shown by certain linguistic facts which appear in all Western languages. Invariably the concepts, ideas, and vocabulary of a political group are polemical, propagandistic. This is true throughout all higher history. The words State, class, King, society—all have their polemical content, and they have an entirely different meaning to partisans from what they have to opponents. Dictatorship, government of laws, proletariat, bourgeoisie—these words have no meaning other than their polemical one, and one does not know what they are intended to convey unless one knows also who is using them and against whom. During the Second World War, for instance, freedom and democracy were used as terms to describe all members of the coalition against Europe, with an entire disregard of semantics. The word "dictatorship" was used by the extra-European coalition to describe not only Europe, but any country which refused to join the coalition.

Similarly, the word "fascist" was used purely as a term of abuse, without any descriptive basis whatever, just as the word democracy was a word of praise but not of description. In the

American press, for example, both during the 1914 war and the 1939 war, Russia was always described as a "democracy." The House of Romanov and the Bolshevik regime were equally democratic. This was necessary to preserve the homogeneous picture of these wars which this press had painted for its readers: the war was one of democracy against dictatorship; Europe was dictatorship, ergo, anything fighting Europe was democracy. In the same way, Machiavelli described any State that was not a monarchy as a republic, a polemical definition that has remained to this day. To Jack Cade the word nobility was a term of damnation, to those who put down his rebellion, it was everything good. In a legal treatise, the class-warrior Karl Renner described rent paid by tenant to landlord as "tribute." In the same way, Ortega y Gasset calls the resurgence of State authority, of the ideas of order, hierarchy and discipline, a revolt of the masses. And to a real class warrior, any navvy is socially valuable, but an officer is a "parasite."

During the period when Liberalism ruled in the Western Civilization, and the State was reduced, theoretically, to the role of "night-watchman," the very word "politics" changed its fundamental meaning. From having described the power activities of the State, it now described the efforts of private individuals and their organizations to secure positions in the government as a means of livelihood, in other words politics came to mean party-politics. Readers in 2050 will have difficulty in understanding these relationships, for the age of parties will be as forgotten then as the Opium War is now.

All State organisms were distorted, sick, in crisis, and this introspection was one great symptom of it. Supposedly internal politics was primary.

If internal politics was actually primary, it must have meant that friend-enemy groupings could arise on an internal political question. If this did happen, in the extreme case civil war was the result, but *unless* a civil war occurred, internal politics was still *in fact* secondary, limited, private, and not public. The very contention that inner politics was primary was polemical: what was meant was that it *should* be. The Liberals and class-warriors, then as now, spoke of their wishes and hope as facts, near-facts, or potential facts. The sole result of focusing energy onto inner problems was to weaken the State, in its dealings with other States. The law of every organism allows only two alternatives: either the organism must be true to itself, or it goes down into sickness or death. *The nature, the essence* of the State is inner peace and outer struggle. If the inner peace is disturbed or broken, the outer struggle is damaged.

The organic and the inorganic ways of thinking do not intersect: ordinary class-room logic, the logic of philosophy textbooks tells us that there is no reason why State, politics and war need even exist. There is no logical reason why *humanity* could not be organized as a *society,* or as a purely economic enterprise, or as a vast book-club. *But* the higher organisms of States, and the highest organisms, the High Cultures, do not ask logicians for permission to exist—the very existence of this type of rationalist, the man emancipated from reality, is only a symptom of a crisis in the High Culture, and when the crisis passes, the rationalists pass away with it. The fact that the rationalists are not in touch with the invisible, organic forces of History is shown by their predictions of events. Before 1914, they universally asserted that a general European war was impossible. Two different types of rationalists gave their two different reasons. The class-warriors of the Internationale, said that international class-war socialism would make it impossible to mobilize "the workers" of one country against "the workers" in another country. The other type—also with its center of gravity in economics, since rationalism and materialism are indissolubly wedded—said no general war was possible because mobilization would bring about such a dislocation of the economic life of the countries that a breakdown would come in a few weeks.

The War-Politics Symbiosis

WE COME to the relation of war to politics. It is not proposed to treat of the metaphysics of war, but to develop a practical outlook of the possibilities and necessities of war to serve as a basis for action.

First, a definition: war is an armed struggle between organized political units. It is not a question of the method of fighting, for weapons are merely a way of killing. Nor of military organization—these things determine nothing about the inner nature of war. War is the highest possible expression of the friend-enemy disjunction. It confers the practical meaning on the word enemy. The enemy is he upon whom one is preparing to make or upon whom one is making war. If there is no question of war he is not an enemy. He may be a mere opponent in a contest for a prize, he may be a mere heathen, a mere ideological opponent, a competitor, a hateful thing for reasons of antipathy. The minute he becomes an enemy, the possibility or actuality of armed struggle, war, enters. War is not an agon, and thus the armed struggles among the States of the Western

Culture up to the middle of the 18th century were not wars in
the 20th century meaning of the word. They were limited in
their object and scope, and *vis-a-vis* the opponent they were not
existential. Thus they were not political in the 20th century
meaning of the word—they were not fought against *enemies*
in our sense of the term. Unfortunately our Western languages
lack the precision which Greek had in this respect to distinguish
between intra-Hellenic struggles, agons, with the opponent the
"antagonist," on the one hand, and wars against the non-Culture member, on the other hand, in which the opponent, e.g.,
the Persian, was the *enemy.* The Crusades were thus war in the
full unlimited sense of the word: the deep spiritual objective
was the assertion of the Cultural superiority, and of the true
Faith against the heathen. The opponent—though one naturally extended *personal* magnanimity to his soldiers because
of the inner imperative of chivalrous honor—was an enemy,
not to be allowed to continue in his unity if it could be destroyed.

Honor in the Crusades forbade personal meanness, but did
not exclude total destruction of the enemy organized unit.
Honor in intra-European struggles did forbid imposing too
harsh a treaty upon the defeated opponent, and it entered no
one's mind to deny the opponent the right to existence as an
organized unit.

During the history of our Culture, from Pope Gregory VII
to Napoleon, the struggle against a member of the Culture was
limited, but that against the heathen, the non-member of the
Culture was true, unlimited war.

Wars before, after and outside a Culture are unlimited. They
are a more pure expression of the barbarian in man, in that they
are not highly symbolic. They are spiritual, for everything
human is spiritual. The spirit is primary with man, the material

is the vehicle of the spiritual development. Man sees symbolic significance in that around him—his experiencing of these symbols and his acting and organizing in accordance are *what* make him man, even though he carry within him also the animal instincts. His soul of course, with its transforming symbolism, completely changes the expression of these instincts. They pass into the service of the soul and its symbolism. Man does not kill, like a tiger, for food to eat—he kills because of *spiritual* necessity. Not even wars entirely outside a High Culture are *purely* animal, *entirely* devoid of symbolic content. With man that would be impossible—only something spiritual can bring masses on to a battlefield. But the symbolism of a High Culture is a *grand* symbolism—it links past, present and future and the totality of things, dissolving them all into a magnificent performance of which it is later realized that that, too, was a symbol. It is only in comparison with these grand meanings, this grand super-personal destiny, that extra-Cultural human phenomena seem merely zoological. Thus, because of their lower symbolic content, lower spiritual potential, these wars can never approach the intensity, scale, or duration of wars connected with High Culture. Defeat is acknowledged much more easily, for it is only the souls of those engaged that are affected. In Cultural wars however, the soul of the Culture is at work, lending its invisible, but invincible strength to those in its service, and a struggle can be maintained for years against fearful odds. A few defeats, and all would have been up with Genghis Khan. Not so with Friedrich der Grosse, or George Washington, for they felt themselves to be the vehicle of an Idea, of the Future.

There can not be said to exist an enmity unless the possibility of war is present. A possibility in *fact,* not a mere conceivability. Nor need the possibility be daily and imminent. Nor need the door be closed on negotiations before the possibility of war, and therefore true enmity can be said to exist.

Not even among warlike States is life a daily blood-shed. War is the highest possible intensification of politics, but there must also be something less intense, the period of recuperating, negotiating, steering, preparing. Without the fact of peace, we would not have the word war, and—what the pacifists have never thought of—without war, we could not have peace, in the blissful, dreamy, saccharine, way they use the word. All the fierce energy that war devotes to super-personal struggles would go into domestic discord of one sort or another, and the casuality list would hardly be less.

The relation of war to politics is clear. Clausewitz, in the usually misquoted passage, called war "the continuation of political intercourse by other means." Usually misquoted, because it does not mean that the military fighting is the continuation of politics, for this it is not. Fighting has its own strategic and tactical grammar. It has its own organic rules and imperatives. War does *not* have however a *motivation* of its own— this is supplied by politics. As is the intensity of the political struggle, i.e., of the enmity, so is the war.

It was insight into this interrelationship that prompted an English diplomat to say that a politician was better trained for fighting than the soldier, for he fights continually and the soldier only occasionally. It is also observable that professional soldiers would turn a war into an agon before political soldiers would. The phrase political soldier is only *ad hoc*, to designate anyone fighting from conviction, rather than from profession.

Clausewitz expressed in the same chapter a description of this relationship between politics and war that has validity in this century: "As war belongs to politics, so does it take on its character. When politics becomes grand and powerful, so does the war, which can ascend to the height where it attains to its absolute form."

War presupposes politics, just as politics presupposes war. Politics determines the enemy, and the time of opening the war. These are not problems for the soldier. Armies must be prepared to fight any political unit.

War and politics cannot be defined in terms of mutual aim, or purpose. It makes no organic sense to say that war is the aim of politics, or politics of war. It could not be, in either case. Each is the prerequisite of the other, neither could exist without the other. A given policy could aim at a *certain* war, naturally, but no politics could possibly aim at war in general.

It is the eventuality of war which gives to political thinking its hall-mark that makes it a different form of thinking from, say, economic thinking, moral, scientific, or esthetic thinking.

II

The disjunction of friend-enemy being the essence of political thinking and acting, is this to say that there is nothing between? No, for neutrality exists as a fact. It has its own rules and conditions of existence. The Western Culture developed as a part of its international law a law governing neutrality. The very formulation of these rules for neutrals shows that the decisive thing is the conflict, the friend-enemy disjunction. The problem for a neutral is how to keep out; it is not the problem of the others in the usual case how to keep the neutral out. The whole practice of the law of neutrality was dependent upon who was at war. If the Great Powers were at war, neutrals had as a matter of practice, few rights. If small powers were engaged in a war, and the Great Powers were neutral, neutrals had many rights.

But the essential thing is that neutrality as a policy stands in the shade of the practical possibility of war and active politics. For a country to become neutral as a form of existence would be to cease to exist as a political unit. It might continue to exist economically, socially, culturally, but *politically* it could not exist if it were neutral. To renounce war is to renounce the right to an enemy. As long as a power is committed to war in any one given eventuality, it has not adopted total neutrality. Thus, Belgium's neutrality during the 19th century was only a word, and not a fact, for it maintained an army, diplomatic representation abroad, and it entered into military understandings with France and England against Germany. As long as a country maintains an army it cannot say its basic national policy is neutrality. An army is an instrument of politics, even if only a politics of self-defense. Politics and neutrality exclude one another, as do neutrality and continued existence. Here again, another instance of the polemical nature of all political language: Neutrality was turned into a polemical word by certain small countries of Europe. Actually by their very existence they were serving the political purposes of one half of Europe against the other half. This position, of being committed by their very existence to one side of a struggle, they called "neutrality." They knew their politics would involve them in war, they knew on which side they would be, and when the war did come, they cried aloud that their "neutrality" had been violated.

To renounce politics—which is what total neutrality means —is to renounce existence as a unit. In many cases it is the part of wisdom and the dictates of Culture to amalgamate with another power, to renounce an empty existence as a unit, an existence without a meaning or a future.

In addition to neutrality as a precarious fact, during war, and neutrality as a polemical fraud, there is neutrality which arises from the hopelessness of carrying on a war successfully. This is closer to true neutrality, for what it means is that powers reduced to such a case have disappeared from the calculations of the other powers, unless of course the land in question is attractive as spoils or as a battlefield. In this case, it must choose for itself to which of the powers still in the struggle it will surrender its independence. If it fails to do this, the choice will be made for it. A power which by its economic weakness, small size, or age, cannot possibly carry on a war has in effect renounced war and become neutral. Whether it is allowed to continue a posthumous existence depends entirely on how attractive its domains are. For purposes of high politics, it is not a political, but a neutral factor.

From the development of colossal war technics came the fact that few powers can support or wage a war. This led the rationalists and Liberals, ever bright with a new wish-informed thought, to announce that the world was becoming pacified. No more war or politics—"power-politics" is their word, just as one could talk of beauty-esthetics, utile-economics, good-morality, piety-religion, legal-law—the world is become neutral, the occasions of war are going, political powers can no longer afford wars, and the like. It is not war or politics which is disappearing, it is only that the number of contestants has grown less.

A pacified world would be one in which there was no politics. It would thus be one where no human difference could possibly arise which could range men against one another as enemies. In a purely economic world men could be opposed, but only as competitors. If morality was also there the proponents of different theories could oppose one another, but only in discussion. Religionists could oppose one another, but only with the propaganda of their respective faiths. It would have to be a world in which there was no one who would kill, or better yet, such a languid, colorless and boring world that no one could possibly take anything seriously enough to kill or risk his life about it.

The only conclusion to be drawn is that a rationalist, Liberal, or pacifist who believes that it is possible for war to vanish simply does not understand what the word war means, its reciprocal existence with politics or the nature of politics as the ranging of men against one another as enemies. In other words, and in the kindliest words possible, these people do not know what they are talking about. They wish to abolish war by politics, or even by war. If war were gone and politics remained, they would then abolish politics by war, or perhaps by politics. They confuse verbal virtuosity with political thinking, logic with soul-necessities, accident with history. As for superpersonal forces, they do not exist, because they cannot be seen, weighed and measured.

III

Since the symbiosis of war and politics forms its own thought-category, independent of other ways of thinking, it follows that a war could not be carried on from a purely nonpolitical motive. If a religious difference, an economic contrast, an ideological disjunction, were to reach the degree of intensity of feeling at which it would range men against one another as *enemies,* it would thereby become *political,* and such units as formed would be political units and would be guided by a political way of manoeuvring, thinking, and valuing, and not by a religious, economic or other way of thinking. *Pure* economics could not possibly wage a war, for war does not pay economically. *Pure* religion could not wage a war, nor *pure* ideology, because war cannot spread religion, cannot convert, but can only result in an accretion or diminution of power. Motives other than strictly political ones can indeed actuate a war—but the war takes them up into itself, and they vanish into it. Western Christianity has motivated wars, such as the Crusades, but these wars did not let loose the forces upon which Christianity places a positive value. Economics has motivated wars, but the immediate result of a war has never been a profit.

For this reason the Liberals and rationalists comfortably convinced themselves before 1914 that war had vanished because it did not show a profit. They were moving in their private world of abstraction, where economics was the sole motive of human conduct, and where invisible superpersonal forces did not exist. And 1914 did not cause them to change their theory —no, where the facts and theory conflict, it is the facts which need revision. 1914 caused them to re-implement their theory: The First World War was all the more proof of their viewpoint, for it showed that it was *economically* necessary that war disappear. These people did not know that economic necessity of human beings is never taken into account by superpersonal forces. Could they get no clue from the statement of one of the most immediate participants in the feverish flurry of negotiations of July, 1914, that all of the statesmen concerned merely drifted into the war? A strictly factual view shows that superpersonal organisms have no economics in our sense of the word, for they are purely spiritual. When Culture populations nourish themselves—and that is what economics is—they are nourishing the higher organism, for the populations are its cells. Its cells are to the superpersonal soul as the cells of a human body are to the human soul.

A war from *purely* religious, economic, or other, motives would be senseless as well as impossible. From religious contrasts arise the thought-categories of believer and non-believer, from economics those of co-worker and competitor, from ideological those of agreer and disagreer. Only from political contrasts come friend-enemy groupings, and only from enmity can come war. The enmity can start elsewhere—the personal distaste of the mistress of a ruler has brought about an enmity grouping among Western States—but when it comes to enmity, it is politics. Although the enmity may have started on a religious contrast, when it comes to war, one will fight against believers, or accept the help of non-believers. Only the Thirty Years War need be mentioned in this connection. Though economics be the beginning of the enmity, once it rises to the intensity of enmity, one fights without regard to the economic consequences of his fighting, but only to the political consequences.

Other thought-categories claim they should have a monopoly of thinking, that the political should be subject to them. The 20th century outlook on politics merely observes that they do not as a matter of fact. From an esthetic standpoint, war and politics may be ugly, from an economic, wasteful, from the moral, wicked, from the religious, sinful. These viewpoints, however, are *neutral* from the political standpoint, which tries first, to assess the facts, and second to change them, but never tries to value them according to a non-political scheme of values. Some politicians do this, it is true. English politicians in particular, after Cromwell, felt an inner compulsion to present every one of their wars as somehow directly involving Christianity, even a war which planted the Hammer and Sickle in the heart of Europe was a war for Christianity. But this does not affect what I am saying here, as this sort of thing only affects vocabulary, but does not touch facts, or action. Using a non-political terminology or propaganda cannot depoliticize politics, any more than using a pacifist terminology can debellicize war.

Politicians are usually not pure in their thinking any more than other men. Even a saint commits sins, even a scientist has his private superstitions, even a divine may have his little taint of mechanism, even a Liberal may have his minuscule trace of animal instinct which if released may cause a sanguinary war, after the conclusion of which he may try to exterminate the human beings comprising the population of the former enemy.

Just as a war *cannot,* as a matter of fact, be purely economic, religious, or moral, it follows that a war *need not* qualify under any other category in order to be *justifiable from the political standpoint.* The Scholastic philosophers set forth the ethico-religious prerequisites of a just war. St. Thomas Aquinas formulated them in a fashion which is final for ethico-religious thought. From the political standpoint however, the test of the justification is quite different. It is of course obvious that the word justification is inadequate, since this word belongs originally to moral thinking and not to political thinking. It must therefore not be interpreted as an invasion of the field of morality if the word justification is used in this connection, for what is meant is appropriateness, desirability, advantageousness, and indeed these are contained in the secondary meaning of the word justification. Now, in this *practical, political* sense, what wars are justified? Politics is activity in regard to power. Units engaged in politics may gain or lose power. Instinct and understanding direct them to seek to increase power. War is the most intense method of trying to increase power. Thus a war which has no practically foreseeable possibility of increasing power is not politically justifiable. A war which promises an increase in power is politically justifiable. This is what the word success means in this connection, i.e., that increased power is the result of the war. When diminished power is the result of the war, the war was unsuccessful.

IV

The words *defeat* and *victory* thus divide into two sharply and precisely defined sets of meanings: the military and the political. Although the armies in the field may be on the winning side, nevertheless the unit to which they supposedly belong may emerge from the war with less power than it entered upon it. I say *supposedly belong* for the reason that when a political unit is in the situation where even military victory means political defeat, *it is not in political reality an independent unit.* Thus: if there were only two powers in the world, the one gaining the military victory in a war would of necessity gain the political victory. There is no second possibility. But if there were more than two powers engaged in a war, and a military victory was gained, one or more powers must have gained the political victory, i.e., must have increased in power. Thus if any power, despite the fact that it was on the winning side in a military sense, nevertheless emerged with less power, it was in fact fighting for the political victory of another power. In other words it was not actually an independent unit, but was in the service of another unit.

To be specific instead of general: after the First World War, England, although on the side of the victorious in a military sense, was weaker in the political sense, i.e., it had less power afterwards than before the War. In the War of the Spanish Succession, France emerged from the War weaker than it had entered, despite the fact that it had gained the military victory.

But between these two sets of meanings of the words victory and defeat, there is an order of rank: the political meaning is primary, for war itself is subsidiary to politics. Any politician would prefer a military defeat coupled with political victory to the converse. Despite the military defeat of France in the Napoleonic Wars, Talleyrand negotiated a political victory for France out of the Congress of Vienna. To say that a unit gained a military victory and also suffered a political defeat is only another way of saying that the military opponent was not a real enemy. A real enemy is he whom one can strike down and thereby increase one's own power.

It is for the politician to determine whom to fight, and if he selects as the enemy a unit at whose expense no power can possibly be gained even in a militarily successful war, that politician was incapable. He may be merely stupid, he may be carrying on a private parasite-politics, using the lives of his countrymen to implement his personal antipathies, like Graf Brühl in the Seven Years War, he may be a distorter, representing an outer force not belonging to the Nation, or even to the Culture.

Such a politician may also be a traitor who sells himself for a private economic consideration, like the Poles who disappeared upon the outbreak of war in 1939 and were never heard of again.

But regardless of why a politician chooses for an enemy a unit which was not a real enemy, the fact remains that in so doing he is abdicating the sovereignty of his State and placing it therewith in the service of another State.

The classic example of this in recent history is, of course, England's participation in the Second World War. England was on the victorious side in the military sense, but sustained a total defeat in the political sense. Already during the war a member of the English Parliament was able to announce that apparently England was a dependency of America. At the conclusion of that War, England's power and prestige had sunk so low that it had to abandon the Empire. Extra-European forces were the victors. England had fought in the Second World War and had given lives and position for the political victory of others. It was not the first time in history, nor will it be the last, but because of its magnitude, it will always remain the classic example.

A tiny island of some 242,000 quadrate kilometers, with only 40,000,000 population, nevertheless, England controlled in 1900 17/20 of the surface of the earth. This includes all the seas, on which England was supreme in the sense that it could deny them to any other power. In less than 25 years, or after the First World War, 1914–1918, England found this sea supremacy gone as well as its commercial primacy, and its position of arbiter of Europe in the sense that it could prevent any power taking first place. In less than 50 years, or after the Second World War, 1939–1945, all was gone, the Empire and also the independence of the homeland. The lesson of course is that a structure built through centuries of war, bloodshed, and high political tradition of choosing always for an enemy him whose defeat would increase the Empire of England—that this can be lost through one or two wars against a power not a real enemy.

In 1939 even there could be no difference of opinion among political thinkers that England could not have an enemy in Europe, since the extra-European forces, Japan, Russia and America had become decisive in world-politics. But in 1946 there could be no difference of opinion on this subject among human beings anywhere in the world, regardless of their ability or inability to think politically. Always excepting the Liberals, of course, who move among theories, and not among facts. Indeed, even after this disastrous War, Liberals, distorters and stupid persons in England continued to glory in the "victory" of England. From the political standpoint, the most hopeful fact for England's future in the period after the War was that the extra-European occupation forces were withdrawn from England.

Thus we have seen again the existential nature of organic alternatives: a unit can either fight a real enemy, or it must lose. And again, a unit not fighting a real enemy is in the service of another power—there is no middle ground. If a unit is not fighting for itself, it is fighting against itself. The broadest formulation of this fundament is: an organism must be true to its own inner law of existence, or it will sicken and die. It is the inner law of a political organism that it must increase its own power; this is the only way it can behave toward power. If it tries to confer power on another organism, it injures itself. If it tries merely to prevent another organism from attaining power, it injures itself; if it gives up its complete existence to blocking another organism, quite regardless of its success in this negative aim, it will destroy itself.

France from 1871 onward is an example of the latter. The whole idea of the existence of France as a State was to block and frustrate a neighboring State. The inspiriting slogan of this idea was *Revanche*. The idea was pursued for decades, and in the process, French power was destroyed. The policy could not of course have arisen in a healthy organism.

The Laws of Totality and Sovereignty

THE ORGANIC Laws of Sovereignty and Totality refer to all political units whatever. They describe any unit, whatever its provenance, that reaches the degree of intensity of expression at which it participates in a friend-enemy disjunction. Totality refers both to *issues* within the organism and to *persons* within the organism. Any issue within the organism is subject to political determination, because every issue is potentially political. Any person in the organism is existentially embraced in the organism. Sovereignty places the decision in every important juncture with the organism. Both of these laws are existential, like all organic conditions: either the organism is true to them, or it is faced with sickness and death. Both laws will be explained.

First the Law of Totality: Any contrast, opposition, or hostility whatever existing within groups among the organism may become political in its nature, if it reaches the point where a group or a unit feels another group, class or stratum to be a real enemy. For such a unit to arise within an organism is for the possibility of civil war to be present, or a severe crisis in the organism, which renders the organism liable to damage or extinction from without. *Therefore, every organism, by its very existence, has the characteristic that it assumes power over the determination of all issues.* This does *not* mean that it *plans* the total life of the population—economic, social, religious, educational, legal, technical, recreational. It means merely that all of these things are subject to political determination. Many of these things are neutral to some States, but objects of interest to others. But all organisms will intervene when an inner grouping may possibly become a focus of a friend-enemy disjunction. This describes all political units whatever, entirely independently of how they formulate their written constitutions, if they have any.

The Law of Totality affects individuals by embracing them existentially in the life of the organism. Politics places the life of every man within the political unit in the balance. It demands, *by its very existence,* the readiness of all individuals in the service of its fulfillment to risk their lives. Other groups may demand dues, periodical attendance at meetings, investment of time in group projects. If they demand however—so fundamental is this organic law of totality—that the member plight his life to the group, they become therewith *political.* The French public law professor Haurion designated it as the hall-mark of a political unit that it embraced the individual *entirely,* whereas non-political groups embrace him only partially.

This is the Law of Totality in other words. It is thus a touchstone of a group for this purpose whether it demands an existential oath.

If a group extracts such an oath from members, the group is political. This Law of Totality, it is hardly necessary to add, is not at all derived from conscription for military service. Conscription exists only for a few centuries within a High Culture, whereas the Law of Totality describes the Culture itself when it is itself constituted as a political organism, and, during the period of concentration of politics in Culture-States, it describes every individual State. Like all organic laws it is existential: if any inner force can challenge it, the organism is sick; if the challenge is attended with success, the organism is in severe crisis and may be annihilated. In any case, its unity will be temporarily in abeyance, with the possibility of partitioning by outer powers.

The Law of Sovereignty is the inner necessity of organic existence which places the decision in every important juncture with the organism, as opposed to allowing any group within to make the decision. An important juncture is any one which affects the organism as a whole, its steering in the world, its choice of allies and enemies, the decision of war and peace, its inner peace, its unchallenged inner right to decide controversies. If any of these can be called into question, it is a sign that the organism is sick. In the healthy organism, this sovereignty is absolutely undisputed, and may continue so for centuries. But a new age with new interests may raise contrasts which the rulers do not grasp; they may blunder, and find themselves on the defensive in a civil war. The challenge of the sovereignty of the organism was the first symptom of crisis. If the organism survives the crisis, the new rulers of the same organism will be the focus of the same sovereignty.

An important fact has been touched upon with this: it is not the rulers who are sovereign within the meaning of this law. Their powers *in fact* are derived from their symbolic-representative position. If a stratum represents and acts in the Spirit of the Age, revolution against it is impossible. An organism true to itself cannot be sick or in crisis.

The Law of Sovereignty does not mean that every aspect of group life within the organism is dominated at all times by the political, nor that everything is organized, or that a centralized system of government necessarily reaches out always and destroys every organization of whatever kind. The outlook developed here is purely *factual,* and the Law of Sovereignty describes *all* political organisms; it is a formulation in words of a quintessential characteristic of a political organism.

Totality of organization—the "Total State"—is a phase of political organizations at certain times and under certain conditions. Some States are neutral in religious matters, others promulgate an official religion. Some States during the 19th century were more or less neutral economically, others intervened in the economic life. In the 20th century *all* States intervene in economic affairs. Different terminology is used to describe this intervention in different States, and the degree of intervention depends on the necessity of the organism. Thus an organism with relatively abundant economic resources will intervene to a lesser degree than one which must make every particle of work and material count. But this does not alter the fact that all States intervene in economics in the 20th century.

The Law of Sovereignty is independent of the fact that in a given organism some internal force, say, religion or economics, may be stronger than the government. Such a thing can, and often does, exist. If this internal force is not yet strong enough to hinder the government, it is not yet political; if it is strong enough only to stalemate the government, but not yet strong enough to create war, then there is no political unit present. If no one can make a determination of enmity, or of war, there is no politics. This means that other units which preserve their political character can either ignore the sick unit in making their own combinations, or can attack it with good initial advantage.

The Law of Sovereignty is thus also existential. It describes a healthy organism, on its path to fulfillment. Where this law does not obtain, the organism is—*vis-a-vis* other organisms of the same kind—in abeyance, and if this condition persists, the political organism will disappear. The best example of a case where the Law of Sovereignty showed its existential character is that of 18th century anarchic Poland. The weakness and sickness of the organism led to its repeated partitioning.

The Pluralistic State

IN THE 19TH CENTURY Western Civilization, the comparative neutrality of the various States, and therefore the apparent weakness of the States *vis-a-vis* internal economics units and their tactics, e.g., trade unions with their strikes, led the Liberals and intellectuals to announce, a bit prematurely as it turned out, that the State was dead.

"This colossal thing is dead," announced the French and Italian syndicalists. They were heard by other rationalists, and Otto von Gierke came out with his doctrine of "the essential equality of all human groups." This was, of course, a way of denying the primacy of the State, and was thus polemical and not factual. The intellectuals *wanted* the State to be dead, and so they announced its passing as a fact. This theory came to be known as the doctrine of "the pluralistic State." It took its philosophical foundation and its political theology from pragmatism, a philosophy of materialization of the spiritual evolved in America. Pragmatism branded the seeking for a last unity, in whatever realm, even in that of nature-study, as a superstition, a remnant of Scholastic. Thus no more Cosmos, and naturally no more State. This outlook was peculiarly adapted to the members of the Second Internationale, which was liberal in tendency. Its two poles of thought were the individual, at one extreme, and humanity, at the other. It saw the "individual" as living in "society" as a member of many organizations, an economic enterprise, a home, a church, a Turnverein, a trade-union, a nation, a State, but none of these organizations had any sovereignty whatever over the others, and all were politically neutral. The fighting proletariat of the Communists became in such a pluralistic State also a politically neutral trade-union or party. All the organizations would have their claim on the individual, who would be bound to a "plurality of obligations and loyalties." The organizations would have relations and mutual interests, but no subjection to the State, which would be merely an organization among organizations, not even *primus inter pares.*

Such a pluralistic State is of course not a political organism. If an external danger were to threaten such a State, it would either succumb at once, or else fight, in which case, it would become at once a political organism, and the "pluralism" would vanish. Such a pluralistic thing is not politically viable. There is always the possibility of an external danger, an internal natural catastrophe, such as a drought, famine or earthquake, which would force centralization, or the arising of a group with political instincts which aims at total power over other groups, and which does not have enough intellect to understand the refined theory of the "pluralistic" State. America, before 1914, was more or less such a thing, and from 1921 to 1933 it resumed its pluralism. This "pluralistic State" came to an end in 1933, when a group arose which seized for itself a totality of power.

Political theories, like "pluralistic State," "dictatorship of proletariat," "*Rechtstaat*," "check and balance," all have political significance, provided they attain to a certain vogue. This significance is dual: first, all such theories are imperative and polemical, and, by demanding a change in the internal form of the State, show by their very existence at least that the State against which they are complaining is sick; secondly, they are a technic for weakening the State further, by working up *real* contrasts and finally rising to the intensity of a friend-enemy disjunction, i.e., Civil War.

The 19th century was the heyday of using theories as political technics. It will be as difficult for the 21st century to understand the idea of "dictatorship of the proletariat" as it is for us to understand how Rousseau's theories could have been the focus of so much political passion. The frightful crisis that occurs in all High Cultures when they enter upon their last great phase, Civilization, the externalization of the Culture-soul, is also the birth-time of Rationalism. As Napoleon said, "Intellect runs about the pavements in France." Intellect, the externalized, analyzing, dissecting faculty of the soul, applies itself also to politics. The results are a spate of theories, decline in the internal authority of all States, and the calling into question of the internal authority in all States.

The Law of Constancy
of Inter-Organismic Power

IT HAS BEEN SEEN that theories are a technic for weakening the State by trying to work up a friend-enemy disjunction on the basis of the theory. This technic is available not only to internal groups which aspire to attain to true political significance, but also to other States. The other State need not even have to carry out an intervention in order to reap the benefit of the activity of theorizing groups in another State.

We have seen that a State which fights a power not a real enemy is thereby fighting for a third power. This was but an instance of a law which is broader, and which is called the Law of Constancy of Inter-Organismic Power.

It may be thus formulated: *In any age, the amount of power in a State-system is constant, and if one organic unit is diminished in power, another unit, or other units are increased in power by the same amount.*

If a statesman, entrusted with the destiny of a State, moves with the sure consciousness of mastery which a feeling for organic laws confers upon him, he can never choose for the enemy of his State a power which his State cannot defeat, for such a power would not be a real enemy. He would know, even if only unconsciously, that the power which his own State would lose, in a war it could not win, would merely be transferred to some other power, either the one wrongly chosen as enemy, or a third power. One of the many phenomena which instance the Law of Constancy of Inter-Organismic Power is that of a given State being racked internally by groups using theories to work up internal contrasts. A point will be reached—short of the point of civil war, which of course dissolves the organism at least temporarily—in this process at which the external power of the organism will be diminished. The power lost passes thereby to another State or States.

The circumstances of the total situation determine which other power will be the beneficiary of this accretion of power. Even the particular theory which the agitating group is using plays often a certain role, for certain theories are owned by certain powers. France owned the theories of "democracy" and "equality" from 1789 to 1815. England owned the theory of "liberalism" in its many forms from the middle of the 19th century down to the First World War. Russia took over the theory of "dictatorship of the proletariat" in 1917.

II

In reality there is no such thing as a "political association" or a "political society"—there can only be a political unit, a political organism. If a group has real political significance, as shown by its ability to determine a real enmity, with the actuality or possibility of war, the political unity becomes decisive, and, even though it started out as a free intellectual association, it has become a political unit, and has lost entirely any "social" or "associative" character it may have had. This is no mere distinction of words, for the political is its own thought category. To be in politics is not the same as to be in a society, since a society involves no risk of life. Nor can a society become political by calling itself so. True political thinking, occasioned by the presence of a political organism will not take place in it, unless it acquires *real* political unity, and the only way it can do this is to be the focus of an enmity-opposition, with its possibility of war. The fact that a group in an "election" votes as a unit does not confer upon it political significance; usually the "election" itself has no political significance.

The Law of Constancy
of Intra-Organismic Power

IN THE MATTER OF "elections" which had a vogue of almost two centuries during the life of the Western Civilization, both in Europe and in its spiritually dominated areas elsewhere, an important law of political organisms is shown.

In "democratic" conditions—the origin and historical significance of "democracy" are shown elsewhere—occur the inner-political phenomena known as "elections." It was the theory of "democracy" arising about 1750 that the "absolute" power of the monarch, or the aristocracy, depending on local conditions, must be broken, and this power transferred to "the people." This use of the word "people" shows again the necessarily polemical nature of all words used politically. "People" was merely a negative; it merely wished to deny that the dynasty, or else the aristocracy, belonged to "the people." It was thus an attempt to deny the monarch or aristocracy political existence; in other words, this word implicitly defined them as the *enemy,* in the true political sense. It was the first time in Western history that an intellectualized theory became the

focus of political happening. Wherever the monarch or aristocracy were stupid or incapable, wherever they looked backward instead of adapting themselves to the new century, they
went down. Wherever they took over the theories themselves
and interpreted them officially, they retained their power and
their command.

The technique of transferring this "absolute" power to "the
people" was to be through plebiscites, or "elections." The
theoretical proposal was to give the power to millions of human
beings, to each his nth/millionth fraction of total existing political power. This was of course impossible in a way that even
the intellectuals could see, so the compromise was "elections"
through which each individual in the organism could "choose"
a "representative" for himself. If the representative did something, by a satisfying fiction it was agreed that each little individual "represented" had done that himself. In a short time it
became obvious to men interested in power, either for themselves personally, or to carry through their ideas, that if one
worked previously to one of these "elections" to influence the
minds of the voting populace, he would be "elected." The
greater one's means of persuasion of the masses of voters, the
more certain was his subsequent "election." The means of persuasion were whatever one had at hand: rhetoric, money, news-
print. Since elections were large things, disposing of large
amounts of power, only those who commanded corresponding
means of persuasion could control them. Oratory came into its
own, the Press stepped out as a lord of the land, the power of
Money towered above all. A monarch could not be bought;
what bribe could appeal to him? He could not be put under the
usurers' pressure—he could not be sued. But party politicians,
living in times when values became increasingly money-values,
could be bought. Thus democracy presented the picture of the

populace under the compulsion of elections, the delegates under the compulsion of Money, and Money sitting in the seat of the monarch.

So the absolute power remained—as it must in any organism, for it is an existential law of every organism that: *The power within an organism is constant, and if individuals, groups, or ideas within the organism are diminished in power, some other individuals, groups, or ideas are increased in power by that amount.* This Law of Constancy of Intra-Organismic Power is existential, for if a diminution of power in one place within does not pass elsewhere within the organism, the organism is sickened, weaker, and may have lost its political existence as an independent unit. The history of South America from 1900 to 1950 is rich in examples of triumphant revolutions against regimes that stripped them of power—which then moved to the United States of North America, and as long as that condition continued, the country in which such a revolution had occurred was a colony of *Yanqui imperialismo.*

The Political Pluriverse

WE HAVE SEEN what the "pluralistic State" is. There is, how-ever, another type of pluralism, one of fact and not of theory. There is a pluriverse *in fact,* which is not merely an attempt to prove one philosophy or to deride another. The world of pol-itics is a pluriverse. Although politics has been defined as activity in relation to power, and the inner nature, prerequisites, and invariable characteristic of politics have been set forth, nevertheless the nature of power itself remains to be shown. *Power is a relation of control between two similar organisms.* The degree of control is determined by the nature of the two organisms acting reciprocally on one another. Power appears, in its dim beginnings, in the animal world, where the beasts of prey exert something similar to power over their prospective victims. As something more than transitory, something *consti-tuted,* however, it begins with man.

Animals can be classified spiritually—and there is no point in any other classification, such as the materialistic Linnean one —into two great groups, herbivores and beasts of prey. If the materialistic thinkers had ever looked at it so, they would surely have put man down as a beast of prey. And they would have been correct for the animal part of him. This animal part is in constant tension with the spiritual part, the specifically human soul which sees symbolism in things and gives the symbol primacy over the mere phenomenon. For this is in very truth the deepest depth of all philosophizing whatever. Where does the question of a conflict between "appearance" and "reality" ever come from in the first place? All great philosophy in High Cultures, and there is none without High Cultures, has been saturated with the idea of establishing the true relationship between appearance and reality, and this was in obedience to an instinct which embodies the *essence* of man: his human *soul* tells him that *Alles Vergängliche ist nur ein Gleichnis.*

The will-to-power of the beasts of prey is limited and practical; it is fierce but unspiritual. Man carries within him this same will-to-power, but his soul infuses into it a purely spiritual intensity that raises its demands and its performances incomparably above the level of the beast. To the beast his will-to-power comes into play only in killing. Man, however, seeks not to kill, but to control. To control he will kill, but as Clausewitz correctly said, conquerors prefer submission and peace, it is the victim who makes the war. A man with a strong will-to-power wants control, not war as an end in itself.

But a display of will-power by one man calls forth opposition elsewhere. Similarly with superpersonal organisms—they do not and cannot exist alone, since, in their political aspect they are units of *opposition*. Each one exists as a *unit-with-the-power-to-choose-and-fight-enemies.* The ability to create a friend-enemy disjunction is the *essence* of the political.

But this ability necessitates opponents of similar rank. Hence it is quite total political stupidity to speak of a world with only one State, one Parliament, one government or however they put it. One could forgive Tennyson, but one can only say that if a politician talks about a world with "one State," "one Parliament," or "one government," he is the perfect type of the intellectual ass, and should be anywhere except in a position to distort the destiny of a State and bring misery to the individuals in it. He is an ass, even though he knows better, for—and this will sound self-evident to readers of 1980 and after—there is absolutely no necessity for a politician to deal in lies exclusively, as the Liberal school, the class-warriors, and the distorters believe. Men who are fighting against the Future perhaps have good reason to practice deception constantly, to throw clouds of theories over their actions, to say peace when they mean war, and war when they mean peace, and to keep elaborate classifications of "secret," "confidential" and the like.

The only secrecy that needs to exist in politics is that created by limitations of understanding on the part of individuals— and absolutely nothing can be done about this type of secrecy. For instance, the facts about the nature of politics and power which have been set down here will remain secret from the intellectuals and rationalists forever, even though they read this.

And similarly with lies: quite obviously the statesman who is the embodiment of the Spirit of the Age has no need of fundamental lies. He cannot fear the truth, since his actions are those of organic necessity, against which no force within the organism can prevail. Equally obviously he who sets out to strangle the Future, like Metternich and the *Fürstenbund,* or the Liberals, democrats, party-leaders of whatever nature, culture-distorters, and intellectuals of the period 1900–1975 have daily, pressing need of lies, ever bigger and better lies. They like to call this Macchiavellism, and to accuse others of it. But

Macchiavelli was certainly not a "Macchiavellian," or he would not have written his factual, truthful book. Instead he would have written a book about how good human nature is in general, and how extraordinarily good in particular is the nature of princes. Where Macchiavelli writes of deception he is thinking of deceiving the *enemy*—Liberals and distorters regard deception as the norm of conduct toward the populations whose destiny is in their hands, and over whose lives they hold the power of disposition.

The classic example in this realm is and will always remain the "election" in America in the Fall of 1940. There were two candidates, representing the same interests, and the populace was offered its "choice" between them. The issue which the populace would thereby "decide" was whether or not America would intervene in the Second World War. Both candidates said publicly in *totally unequivocal language* that they would not involve America in the War. Yet both of them were committed to the interests which made them candidates to involve America in the war as soon as possible. Both candidates were of course successful, for in late democratic conditions, the parties become trusts and no longer compete, since competition would injure them both. After the "election," the two successful candidates carried out their real commitment, took America to war, and sent to their deaths the very men whose lives they had vowed to spare from death in the Second World War, which did not affect American interests. One of the candidates explained after the "election" that his non-intervention promise to the populace was mere "campaign oratory."

In such a case, there is no doubt whatever that Macchiavelli would have counseled the rulers of America to have both candidates declare *for* intervention. But party-politicians deal in lies from inner compulsion, for their activity itself is an organic lie.

League of Nations

THE FACT that a world with "one State" or "one government" was an organic impossibility was well shown by two attempts on the part of what might be called the Holy Alliance of the 20th century to institute such a condition. After each of the first two World Wars the extra-European Holy Alliance against Europe established a "League of Nations."

The political organisms however remained organic, and thus subject to the Law of Sovereignty. If a political unit exists it is sovereign; the member units of these two "leagues of nations" continued to exist politically and thus were sovereign. Incidentally the organic Law of Sovereignty is not the "principle of sovereignty of nations" of Grotius and Pufendorff; that was a legal concept and thus subject to juristic quibbling, whereas the organic Law of Sovereignty describes all political units whatever since it belongs to their very existence.

Thus the dilemma was that the "leagues of nations" had no sovereignty—again I am speaking of factual, organic sovereignty, not legal sovereignty—and hence were not political units. There is no political unit without organic sovereignty; there is no organic sovereignty without a political unit.

What, then, were these two "leagues of nations"? They had two aspects, the ethical and the practical-political.

In terms of practical politics, they were polemical realities. Whatever power controlled them could thus speak for *all nations,* and thus any power opposing it was *hors-la-loi,* outside the comity of nations, not even human, for the league was *humanity.* They rapidly of course, needless to say, passed into the control of certain member-States, according to the Law of Sovereignty—where there is no sovereignty there is no independent political unit, and sovereignty must therefore reside elsewhere. And, in fact, the first league of nations, formed after the First World War, passed into the control of England. The second league of nations, formed in a time—after the Second World War—when politics had entered upon a more absolute stage, was seized by America.

This was foreseeable from the fact that Russia had allowed the geographical site of it to be established in America. This was not merely to keep out the undesirable swarms of ideologues, parasites, and holiday-makers, such as necessarily accompany every "league of nations," and to keep out the spies who pullulate in such a condition, but it actually showed a limited and secondary interest in the thing.

In the past, certain powers have owned certain theories. Conversely, there has never been an important theory that did not have practical, political ownership. A theory without a political unit to use it to practical purpose is not important; if the protagonists of a theory have sufficient passion and non-theoretical political skill to work up intense feeling with their theory, they will possibly attain power with such a weapon. If they reach a point just short of power, an already existing political unit will appropriate the theory for practical purposes. Example: Marxism, taken over in 1918 by Bolshevik Russia for political use against Europe, when its protagonists in Germany showed themselves politically stillborn.

The "league of nations" theory was, in *fact,* owned by America. Whoever spread the idea—even England, which seized the first "league"—was increasing the power of America, whether he knew it or not.

It was inevitable that politicians free of ideology, like the Kremlin Mongols, would see this. Since they understood how to use theories, it was obvious they would allow no political unit to hamstring them with its theory. Thus perished the second and last "league of nations."

There was also an ethical aspect to these leagues. They were another example of the deception that was still thought in the first half of the 20th century to be a necessity of political conduct. They were actually nothing but polemical attempts to deny Europe. The formation of Europe as a political unit was in the Spirit of the Age. Whoever agitated anything else was merely negating this idea. This explains the fact that though the two "leagues of nations" accomplished nothing else as a political fact, nevertheless they prevented—Europe. This is quite independent of whether all people participating were conscious of this. However, it is the organic task of the politician to be conscious of political reality and to understand and assess rightly the possibilities of the time. It is of course now known that many persons who participated in these world-frauds were quite conscious of the realities.

From what has been said about the nature of political organisms the relation of the statesman to his political organism is obvious: just as he calls on his populace to die, he cannot refuse if necessary to give his own life. To his political unit he owes all his physical energies and all his talent and genius. For him to be careless in researching a situation—and above all—for him to do that which he knows is contrary to the furtherance of the life of the organism is to forfeit his right to live. He can consider himself lucky indeed if he is able to die of a heart attack, brain concussion, blood clot or simply old age.

When the extra-European forces gradually increased their power to such an extent that the independent existence of the West became problematical—this was evident from 1920 onward, and was transparent from 1933—it was the collective duty to their States and to the Western Civilization for all statesmen in Europe to endeavor to save their respective States and Western States collectively from political annihilation by extra-European forces. Thus any statesman in a European State who sabotaged the general West-European understanding and final settlement that was sought by the custodians of the spirit of the Western Civilization was a strangler and distorter of the destiny of his own country and of that of the Western Civilization.

The ethics thus formulated is an ethics of *fact*. It is organic, political, factual and nothing else.

Its sole imperative is an organic-political one. It is distinguished from religious ethics in that it has no theological sanction. It is distinguished from all ethical systems whatever in that it only sees one relationship—that of the individual to the political unit. Nor does it have a sanction in the punitive sense. The organic relationship between the political unit and the statesman itself sets the ethical imperative. If the statesman violates it by injuring instead of furthering the life of the organism, the sanction is a matter for Destiny, the inner force of organisms. By doing so he forfeits his right to live, but often he is fortunate enough to escape with his life. The existential embrace of the lives of the individuals in it which has been shown to be an *essential* characteristic of a political unit makes no exception in favor of politicians. At its highest tension, this organic imperative causes a statesman in its service to tie his own life to the success of his own idea for the organism. Bismarck and Friedrich der Grosse also were determined to take their lives in the event of failure.

The Inner Aspect
of the Law of Sovereignty

THE LAW OF SOVEREIGNTY describes characteristics of all political units whatever. It places the decision in every matter having political significance with the organism. Depending on circumstances any one, or even more, internal issues may become important politically, i.e., may begin to assume the form of a political unit and determine a friend-enemy disjunction. The government of the organism will always intervene at this point if its understanding and will are unimpaired. Charles I of England allowed this critical juncture to pass, by allowing his first Parliament to send Montague to the tower for preaching the divine right of kings. From then on the situation deteriorated steadily, and a correspondingly increasing amount of force was necessary to attempt to change the direction events were moving. The actual significance of the struggle was seen from the very beginning by the contemporary political thinker Thomas Hobbes, who wrote against the State-destroying nature of the Parliamentary position. He was also sensitive enough to the situation to know when things had reached the stage of per-

sonal insecurity, and left England in 1640. During these years
of internal enmity, England did not exist as a political unit, it
was ignored in European power-combinations, and it can thank
the total European situation that it was not partitioned.

The Parliament considered itself the government, the mon-
archists considered themselves the government. A political outlook naturally does not concern itself with the question of
which was "right." Such a question has no political meaning.
It has only a legal meaning, and law is a reflex of politics.
Politics is concerned with assessing facts and acting upon them;
law comes afterward and has the function of consolidating a
given political fact-complex. Law formulates the disjunction
legal-illegal according to political dictate. If there is no political
unit to prescribe the law, there can be no law. Thus in time of
Civil War there is no law—there are two laws. If the result of
the War is a reconstitution of the former people and territory
again as a political unit, it will always turn out that the victor
was the one who was legally right all the time, and the defeated
was legally wrong. This *invariable* fact shows the nature of
law.

Nevertheless, Parliament and King stood opposed, each
claiming to be England. Politically, they were both wrong, for
there was no England. In political language, two Englands
equal no England. Each of the two groups was a political unit,
and had become such by determining an *enemy*. Each of them
was conducting itself as a government and each availed itself of
the organic political right—also, but *afterward* a legal right—
to determine the *inner* enemy. An organic characteristic of all
political units whatever—that they determine the inner enemy
when they feel it necessary—is the internal corollary of the
Law of Sovereignty. Thus Cavaliers in Parliamentary territory
were the enemy of the government, and their existence was that

of outlaws. Correspondingly with adherents of Parliament in Royal territory. It must not be supposed because of the example used of a Civil War, that such determination of the inner enemy only occurs then. On the contrary, if Charles I had declared his opponents to be inner enemies from the very beginning, and had treated them as such, there had been no Civil War. To do this however, he lacked the vigor and the understanding. He should have consulted Hobbes, who understood these things. But Charles was not a reading man, and did not know Hobbes's treatises on *Human Nature* and *De Corpore Politico.*

Every political unit in history has exercised in need, and sometimes not in need, its organic power to determine the inner enemy. If it does it soon and proceeds thoroughly, the danger is past. If it procrastinates and takes half-measures, it ceases to be a political unit.

If it exercises this power when there is no need, it is merely persecuting its own population, and is sowing seeds of hatred that will one day bear surprising fruit. The organic ethic of the relation of the statesman to his political unit applies also to conduct of this type. The statesman has no organic right to dispose wantonly of the lives of the populace. To send subjects to their death in a war against a power not a real enemy, a war which thus by its very nature *must* be unsuccessful, or to declare a group as an inner enemy when it does not contain the real possibility of constituting itself as a true political unit, is vicious, non-political conduct in both cases. Such a man exposes himself to the organic sanction that Destiny often imposes in such cases.

This organic right to determine the inner enemy is not always exercised in the same manner. It may be open: arrest, sudden attack, shooting down at home, butchery in the streets. It may be concealed: drawing up of punitive laws general in their

terms but applying in fact only to one group. It may be purely
formless, but nonetheless real: the ruler may attack verbally
the individual or group in question. Such a declaration may
be used only to intimidate, or it may be a method of bringing
about assassination. It may be economic pressure—such a tactic
is naturally the favorite of Liberals. A "blacklist" or boycott
may destroy the group or individual.

It goes without saying that the exercise of such a right has
no connection whatever with any written "constitution" which
purports verbally to distribute the public power in a political
unit. Such a "constitution" may forbid such a declaration of
inner enemy, but units with such constitutions have never hesi-
tated in need, and have often invoked such procedure independently of need. Thus the transatlantic part of the anti-Europe
coalition in the Second World War carried out, quite independently of necessity, since there was no real inner enemy as a
matter of fact, extensive inner persecutions directed against
groups and strata of its population. It does not affect the political nature of this activity that it was done by culture-distorting
elements, for the organic laws set out here describe all political
units whatever, even if they fall into the hands of political and
cultural outsiders.

II

This inward application of the Law of Sovereignty is of
course valid for political units in all the High Cultures. Our
information on it in the Classical Culture is sufficient to show
its development there. The best-known example is that of the
Resolution of Demophantos in the year 410 B.C. which declared
of every person who sought to destroy Athenian democracy that
he was "an enemy of the Athenians." In the same period the

Ephors of Sparta declared war on all Helots found living within the territory of Sparta. In our own Culture, the activities of the Grand Inquisitor Torquemada are instructive, and above all the famous document by which Phillip II condemned the entire population of the Netherlands to death as heretics represents about the ultimate development of which this organic right is capable. Calvin's theocracy in Geneva was outdone by Phillip only quantitatively.

In old Roman public law the undesirable was declared solemnly to be "hostis," which was the word describing the public enemy. The Imperial proscriptions, regardless of their economic motive, were an application of the same organic function. In the Holy Roman Empire, the *Acht und Bann* were directed against inner dangerous or unwanted elements. They were declared *Friedlos,* and placed outside all protection. Anyone aiding such a person fell thereby into the same category. The Jacobins and the *Comité de salut public* slew their thousands of victims, both with and without declaration of enmity.

In early democratic conditions, the weakening of the State *vis-a-vis* internal groups would have made it more difficult to invoke this right, but correspondingly, since all Western States were in more or less the same internal condition, the necessity for its invocation was not often present. In any case the triumph of theories of equality and freedom in the realm of political vocabulary made it inexpedient to invoke the right in the old open, declared, legalistic way.

The early democracy was, in the Western Civilization, from about 1800 to 1850. During this period internal sovereignty as exemplified by determination of the internal enemy was more refined, intellectualized, concealed. Examples: The American Alien and Sedition Laws, the Austrian measures against democrats 1815–1848. Bismarck's laws against class-warriors. Of course in war the right was as forcefully exercised as ever, but was usually legally formless: the Yankees in the American War of Secession, 1861–1865; French Communards, 1871.

With the sudden transition to non-democratic conditions marked by the First World War, began the Age of Wars of Annihilation. It could also be called the Age of Absolute Politics. The 19th century was the Age of Economics—not that economics was ever *prior* in a real sense in the world of action, but economics supplied much of the motivation of politics, as shown by phenomena like the Opium War, the American War of Secession, the Boer War. Economics wants a weak State, and in the Age of Economics, the States were on the defensive, but the new *Zeitgeist* changed the entire meaning of History and content of action. Because of the fact that the *Zeitgeist* of the 20th century did not attain to external triumph in all Europe, many supposed that the Age of Economics was not only continuing but was attaining to new victorious heights.

That this was not the case was shown by the war which greeted the opening of the century. The war in question was between the Boer State, a colony of the Western Civilization, and England. The War was not against savages, or aborigines of spoil lands and thus does not come into the same classification as the Australian war against the autochthonous tribes of Tasmania, when the victims were hunted down like rabbits to total extermination. We have seen that the armed contests between Western Culture-States were not true wars, but were agonal in nature. The turning point to Civilization was marked by Napoleon, the herald of absolute war and politics, but this tradition continued so strong that in the French War against Prussia, 1870–1871, victorious Prussia still did not think of annihilating the totally defeated foe, nor of subjecting it to an endless military occupation, but contented itself with re-incorporating two provinces and imposing an indemnity which was paid off in a few years.

England had also so conducted itself in intra-Cultural armed contests. And yet in 1900, it carried the war against the Boers to complete annihilation. This was in true 20th century style, and note that it was England, the organism which had brought forth the idea of the 19th century and was not destined to produce the idea of the 20th century, which thus acted completely within the spirit of the new age. So strong is the Spirit of the Age—it compels inner submission even though one use the formulae of the past and believe that he is leading a moribund idea to new life.

The Boer War was mentioned because it marked a turning point also in the matter of the internal aspect of the Law of Sovereignty. In this War, the English armies initiated the 20th century method of designating and handling the inner enemy. It is nonetheless an historical epoch in this matter that no real political need existed for what occurred, for we are interested in what did occur, and not in re-writing history. In this War, large numbers of civilian Boers, men, women and children, came into the custody of the English armies. They were taken into custody on the theory that they were a danger to the internal security of the territory controlled by the Empire, that thus they were inner enemies. The numbers involved were considerable, too great for the systems of prisons and jails there existing. The solution adopted was to place them into detention camps, hastily constructed *ad hoc*. These were called "concentration camps," and this word was to have a destiny of its own.

After the First World War, the Age of Absolute Politics showed its manifestations everywhere, and one way it did it was to introduce this "concentration camp" system into every country in the Western Civilization. The more dangerous its external situation, the greater was the necessity of firm inner control, unbroken and unbreakable inner peace, and thus those countries with the most political concern introduced large numbers of persons they declared inner enemies, or in any case treated as inner enemies, into prison camps. But since the word was connected with politics, it acquired polemical significance, and was used by some States as a method of attacking the "morality" of other States. And yet these concentration camps were similar in all countries, just as prisons are. It is not material that extra-European forces imprisoned Europeans in the camps they set up in England, or that Europe imprisoned Slavs, Jews and Bolsheviks in the camps it set up in Europe; the camps were essentially the same from the political standpoint.

They both illustrate the internal aspect of the Law of Sovereignty as it develops in the 20th century. The Age of Absolute Politics has a full century more in its course, and thus the number of prison camps and the number of inmates will increase and not decrease.

It remains to say a word on the future development of internal sovereignty. Since the spirit of these times and the next is no longer that of economics, but that of absolute politics, sly and veiled methods of acting against inner individuals and groups will fall into disuse. In their place will appear once more open and legally formulated inner enemy-declarations. Even economically motivated determinations will be quite openly pursued with political means.

Political Organisms and War

A POLITICAL UNIT has the *jus belli,* the organic right to make war on the enemy it has determined. Not moral right here—this organic right is a thing independent of morality, even though also the strictest Scholastic philosophers gave to political units the purely moral right to wage war. But it is in a purely political way that the word is used here: the right to make war is a part of the *habitus* of the organism. The existence as a political unit, the determination of an enemy, the making of war, the maintenance of the inner peace, the declaration of the inner enemy, the power of life and death over the life of all subjects—these are merely different facets of politico-organic existence. They cannot be separated; they are an indivisible whole; insofar as they can be defined at all, they can only be so in terms of each other.

In the exercise of its power to make war, a State disposes of the lives of its own subjects and of those of the enemy. This bloodshed is not a life-requirement of a State, but occurs merely as a part of the process of acquiring power. The State

directly seeking power is not the one that brings about bloodshed and war. No politician whatever would make war against
another unit if he thought it would submit to incorporation
without a fight. Thus war is always the result of *resistance,* and
not of political dynamism. War is *not* normative; it is existential only. In the entire panorama of the history of the High
Cultures, I doubt that there has been a case where the ruling
stratum of a political unit ever decided that, first of all, it
wanted war, and then cast about for someone upon whom to
make war. It would not be political.

Nor is the mere power over life and death generally, *jus
vitae ac necis,* the hall-mark of a political organism. Many
States in history recognized this power to be in family units. Old
Rome gave it to the *paterfamilias.* Some States have allowed the
master power over the life of the slave. Most states have permitted the victim of an imputation of dishonor to contest for
the life of his vilifier. Many States have recognized the right of
blood-revenge among clans—although this reaches the very
frontier in this matter, and is seldom found, and then only in
peace.

It is thus quite conclusive that politics, as such, seeks no
monopoly of taking life. Politics at its highest potential, war,
takes life only because resistance requires it. Politics is activity
in relation to power, and there is only one way organic instinct
behaves toward power: it seeks more. Metaphysically this is
the relation between the soul of man and the soul of the High
Culture on the one hand, and the *habitus* of the beast of prey
on the other hand. Although it permits subjects in certain cases,
which it determines, in accordance with the Law of Sovereignty,
to take life, the State never permits subjects to make war. If a
group of subjects assume this power, a new State has arisen. If
the right of blood-revenge turns into clan-warfare, the State

must intervene, for its existence is involved. That is why, in all States engaged in serious politics, the right of blood-revenge is abrogated.

The right to make war and in the process to dispose of life is purely political. No Church could possibly ask its members to die for the Church—this is quite different from insisting that martyrdom is preferable to apostacy—unless it is becoming a political unit. In critical times, many Churches, such as Abu Bekr's Islam, have become States, but then they are no longer Churches, and they are ruled by the political way of thinking and its basic inner, organic demand for more power, and no longer by the religious imperative of salvation and conversion.

It would be cruel and insane to ask men to die in order that the remainder would have an unimpaired, or higher standard of economic life. When war is motivated by an economic idea, the economics vanishes into the war-political situation; i.e., the test of success is the political one, the method of waging it is not reviewed as to its cost, the means used always are military-political, the leadership is always political, and would be so even if exclusively economists were used as the war leaders. Their thinking would indeed be curious, but it would not be economic. Politics and economics are two different directions of human thinking and are hostile to one another. For this reason no true politician and no true soldier would ever with full consciousness carry on or fight a war for an exclusively economic motive, no matter what grand opportunities it offered for personal distinction. Economically motivated wars like the American War of Secession, 1861–1865, the English Opium War, the Boer War were of necessity presented to the participants under an untruthful propaganda.

Economics lacks the strength in itself—i.e., "pure" economics —to rouse men to the level of action where they will risk their

lives. This is because economics *presupposes* life, and merely
seeks ways of securing, nourishing, perpetuating the life. It
simply does not make sense to buy life with death—when death
becomes a possibility, we are no longer in the sphere of economics. If economics wants a certain war, it can only bring it
about by political means, and then also—we are no longer in
the sphere of economics.

Morality has often been put forward as the motivation of
war, and many wars have been waged in the name of morality.
This however does not make sense—that is not according to
any Western system of morality—for States are not within the
purview of morality, which is valid only for individuals. Furthermore the materialistic morality of the 19th century denounced war as murder. Therefore when protagonists of this
type of morality—and they continue to exist and to do so—
demand a war to stop war, it is an obvious fraud. The most any
one man can do about stopping murder is to refrain from
murders himself, but these morality-warriors have not done
that.

A morality-war is impossible not only from the moral side,
but from the war-political side. War is not a norm—one cannot
fight *against* it. War is an existential disjunction, not a system
or an institution. There is no rational aim, program, for economic, moral, esthetic or other change, no ever-so-correct norm
that would justify one in killing. To adopt war and politics is in
fact to abandon the other things. One can retain non-political
ideas privately, but if they become public they vanish into the
political. The result is politics dressed in moral clothing.

Another fact emerges about politics mixed with morality.
There are, first, two possible mixtures: that of the Cromwell-
Torquemada type on the one hand, in which also the politician
believes that he is actualizing morality by his policies, and the

Lincoln-Roosevelt type, in which the morality is purely a deception. In the first case, in proportion as the politician thinks morally, his politics is faulty. Thus Cromwell refused in 1653 a Spanish Alliance which would have been highly advantageous to England because he abhorred the religion of Spain. His conduct was of course nonetheless politics, for he made with France the same alliance he refused with Spain and received considerably less from it than Spain had offered. In the second case, where it is not taken seriously, as in the case of Roosevelt, it is not morality at all and is repulsive to honor. Thus morality in politics makes bad politics if taken seriously, and if used cynically, it dishonors him who uses it.

The question may be asked why moral vocabulary is imported into politics in this Age of Absolute Politics. The answer is that it is done quite deliberately and politically. It is elementary that politics does not include within the idea *enemy* any subsidiary content of malice or hatred. Hatred is *private;* it occurs between antipathetical persons out of their own private hostility. Even though this terminology is different from that of Hegel, the idea is identical. He spoke of the hatred of the public enemy as being undifferentiated and totally free from personality. This is no longer hatred in the primary meaning of that word. War is between States, and when the enemy State is overcome—what overcome means is a reflex of the Age, and in an Age of Absolute Politics means total incorporation of the other State—there can be no more war. Enmity ceases, and if there ever was any animosity of any kind it must cease now, since it was directed, if it was political, against the enemy State. That State is gone.

But—if the population of a State has been given exclusively propaganda to the effect that the war was not political, but for moral, humanitarian, legal, scientific and other reasons, this population will regard the end of the war as the beginning of unlimited opportunities of oppressing the population of the former enemy State. Moral propaganda thus stands forth in its nakedness—in the 20th century it is a means of fighting a war after the war, a war not this time against a State with weapons in its hands, but against the survivors of the defeat. Herein is the true significance of a phenomenon that mystified many persons at that time—I refer to the "concentration camp" propaganda against Europe, which was developed to its full height *after* the Second World War. This propaganda was solely for the purpose of a war after the war, thus not a true war, since there was no opposing unit, but an attempt to rouse extra-European populations and extra-European armies of occupation to ever-renewed ferocity and personal hatred against a defenseless European population.

Thus a moral "war to end war" develops in actuality into an endless war. A war for humanitarian purposes develops into a war to exterminate by starvation the population of the former State. A war against concentration camps results in bigger and more numerous concentration camps. This must be so in an Age of Absolute Politics, for obviously *moral* reasons for a war are not necessary in such an age. Propaganda cannot bring more men on to the battlefield than can the Spirit of the Age. Therefore he who is using the vocabulary of morality wishes to import into the struggle a viciousness that the spirit of politics alone cannot develop. Proudhon observed: "Whoever says humanity wishes to deceive."

Only politics shows the *real meaning of war*. Economics, esthetics, law and the other forms of thought cannot supply its meaning, for war is politics at its highest intensity. The political meaning of a war is that it is waged against a *real enemy*. To be justified politically, the war must be an affirmation of the political organism or for the saving of the organism. To expend human life in any other war is distortion of the destiny of the State and treacherous dishonorable killing of the soldiers and civilians who die in it. The decision as to who is the enemy must be made by statesmen who embody the national idea, and if it is not, the result is political distortion. In the language of politics a just war is only that one waged against a real enemy.

It is immature thinking to suggest that military men should decide in such matters. It is possible for a politician to be also a soldier, but a soldier does not become ipso facto a politician. In Rome all statesmen generally speaking were ex-commanders, but they had gone into the field as part of their *political* careers. Caesar embarked late in life upon the military career, but how many professional soldiers could have gone into politics with corresponding attainment? In matters of politics, soldiers are circumstanced the same as the populace in general.

The Law of Political Plenum

THE ESSENTIALITY OF WAR to organic political existence is shown by the fact that a State cannot give up its *jus belli* without thereby giving up political existence. There have been in the history of the High Cultures very few examples of a political unit abandoning, either openly and consciously, or simply through submission, the organic right to make war. And in no case has a power that was important, or even considered itself to be important, renounced this right.

The famous Kellog Pact—what 21st century historians will designate as the high point of ideology-politics—did not even try to obligate its signatories to renounce war. The pact merely "condemns" war. The French version was "condamner," the German "verurteilen." Naturally in an age when many politicians were masquerading as clerics, most anyone was willing to "condemn" war. But the leading clerical powers made reservations to their condemnation. Thus England said that it could not condemn war in the case of its national honor, self-defense, implementation of the League of Nations or of neutrality treaties, or of the Locarno treaty, the welfare of spheres of interest like Egypt, Palestine and so on. France made similar exceptions, as did Poland. It was soon observed by political thinkers that the pact did not forbid, but sanctioned war, for the exceptions covered all possible cases. Thenceforward wars were to be legally formulated. Other political thinkers compared it to a New Year's resolution.

Organic realities were thus obeyed by this singular Kellog Pact, even though it purported to set them aside. Instead of law abolishing politics, politics used law, as usual, to prop up a certain political state of affairs.

The Pact also spoke only of war "as an instrument of national policy." As an instrument of some other idea however, nothing was said, not even of international policy. Thus the most vicious wars were not covered by the treaty. A war for an international policy, for "humanity," for "morality" and the like is the worst of all possible wars, for it dehumanizes the opponent, makes him into a personal enemy, sanctions any type of cruelty against him, and removes all restraints of honor from the person conducting such a war.

Nor is it possible to give up political existence entirely. Only a unit may disappear. The Organic Law of Political Plenum appears. If a given State should become tired through old age, and wished no longer to carry on war or politics, it could, if it desired, announce its idea to the world of States. It could say that it had renounced enmity and embraced all States as its friends, that it would make no more war and wanted only peace. Such conduct, no matter how logical it would be to effectuate such a wish, would not have that result. Logic does not obtain in politics. A State would by such conduct create a political vacuum, and other States not tired of war and politics would immediately abolish this vacuum and bring the area and population of the abdicating State into its own realm. Such a plenary action might be open and undisguised, or it might be veiled. In any case an abdicating power moves at once into a larger realm. *A political vacuum is an impossibility in a system of States.* This Law of Political Plenum describes actual political situations, and there need be no announcement of abdication by the disappearing State. If such a State merely by reason of the general development of the larger situation sinks into the place where it cannot wage war, i.e., engage in politics, the Law of Political Plenum is at once operative. It is not necessary for the incorporation of the disappearing State into the larger State to be accompanied by the marching in of troops. This is of course the 20th century method of doing it, for this is the Age of Absolute Politics, and any type of disguise for political action is both unnecessary and inappropriate. It occurs automatically with the lowering of political potential in the disappearing State.

Thus, for example, the American seizure of half Europe after the Second World War was a mixture of military and crypto-political means. The seizure of the other half of Europe by Russia was more open, but still loaded with 19th century talk of "justification," "non-interference," "security," "military necessity," and so forth. In both cases the fiction of independence of the former political units of Europe was maintained.

This dividing of the Western Civilization between the two extra-European forces occurred as an instance of the Law of Political Plenum. European, States were individually unable to wage war after 1945 because of the enormous requirements in industrial establishment and man-power. These existed only in Russia and America. Europe collectively thus became a political vacuum, because of the individual political incapacity of the States of the Western Civilization.

Inability to wage war is abdication in *fact* of political exist-ence, whether the abdicating State knows this or not. Thus, apart from all fiction, the frontiers which were maintained for a while in Europe after the Second World War were not power-frontiers, but administrative lines of demarcation. Thus America and Russia did not take these frontiers seriously each within its own half of Europe. The only frontier Russia and America took seriously was the one remaining power-frontier in Europe, that between them. The world of *actual* politics at any one time is described by powers capable of waging war.

Only political independence can be given up, not political existence. Politics still is present, with its existential embrace of the lives of the whole population. We stand before the Organic Law of Protection and Obedience.

The Law of Protection and Obedience

THE PURPOSE for which the great political thinker Hobbes wrote his *Leviathan* was to show the world once more the "Mutual Relation between Protection and Obedience," demanded alike by human nature and divine law. The Roman formula was *protego ergo obligo*. To him who supplies protection also goes obedience. It will go either voluntarily, as the result of persuasion, or as the result of force. Once more, there is here no *moral* content in this formula. It may have also a moral aspect, but nothing said about it here relates to any such aspect, or to any other aspect than the purely political. A 20th century outlook on politics is necessarily purely factual, and neither approves nor disapproves of political realities. Approval and disapproval on a moral basis is outside politics. Approval and disapproval on the basis of Culture-feelings, taste and instinct is, however, the driving-force of politics. But in examining realities as a prerequisite to acting upon the realiites, we put aside all pre-conceptions whatever.

Thus—Protection and Obedience. This organic law is again

a description of an *existential* reality. Without the relationship of protection in one place and obedience in another, there is no politics. Every political organism exhibits it, and the extent of protection and obedience describes the territorial frontiers of the organism. Wherever a power is under the protection of another power, the two are one for external political purposes. Whatever apparent anomalies have existed disappear as soon as political tension in the area in question heightens. Looking at the organism inwardly, the amount of protection and the amount of obedience, and the quality of these things, describes the inner strength of the unit. A high degree of protection and a high degree of obedience constitute an integrated organism that can stand the test of politics. Such an organism can often prevail against great odds. A low degree of the protection-obedience relationship describes a unit that is inwardly weak. It cannot stand a real hard struggle, and will often succumb in a test even to an organism with fewer material means and numbers.

Thus when in the 20th century an organism dare not conscript a population within its area, such an area is one of inner weakness, and cannot be counted part of the political body. Such a situation can only continue as long as such an area is not the focus of political tension. The law also describes the geographical extent of a political unit. Where protection and obedience stop, there are the actual frontiers.

Once more the words protection and obedience have also been used with an entire absence of any moral content. Thus "protection" can mean unlimited terror by military means, and "obedience" may be a reflection of the alternative of the concentration camp. The condition of occupied Europe under extra-European armies is protection within the meaning of this organic law. Even though these extra-European armies are

starving and torturing the populace, nevertheless they are protecting that part of Europe from incorporation by another
political unit. America protects its half from Russia and Russia
protects its half from America. Thus the word is neutral *vis-a-
vis* the disjunction of altruism-egoism. Protection is not kindli-
ness, it is acquisition of power. Obedience is not gratitude, it is
political submission from whatever motive.

Where the protecting force is within a Culture and the area
and populace protected also belong to the Culture, the obedience will be full, natural and voluntary, on the part of the
Culture-bearing stratum at least when the issue is the existence
of the Culture.

This Law describes Western feudalism, for instance. Feudalism is the strongest political system that can arise. It is integrated inwardly and outwardly. It is the system where political
activity is within a self-evident cadre of forms. It is an Internationale in the only true sense of the word; it is a phenomenon
of equal validity in the whole Culture. In our case, it was the
form and vessel of all Western happenings for 300 years. The
basic formulation of the feudal Idea is nothing but Protection
and Obedience.

Protectorates such as Western international law recognizes
are examples of the law. It also describes any federal units
that arise. The central government is the only political one, for
it protects and thus receives political obedience.

The existential nature of the Law is also shown by the fact
that if a State is unable to protect an area and population within
its system, that area and population will pass into the system of
another State that can protect and has the will to protect. The
passing may be by revolt, it may be by war. It may be by negotiation, particularly if the protecting State allows a quasi-govern-
ment to exist in the protected area, which can make a private

understanding with other powers to deliver to them the population and territory. This shows incidentally the danger of carrying fictions too far in politics. To boast too loudly that vassals are not vassals may be to transfer them to another allegiance. Similarly to describe one's fortresses as impregnable is dangerous; this will never convince a resolute State of equal rank, but may convince their owner.

A more inclusive way of saying this is that in an Age of Absolute Politics political appearances should correspond to political reality. In the century of economico-moral cant, mastery consisted in maintaining an elaborate pretense of freedom, and simultaneously therewith a rigid condition of servitude. This sort of thing becomes both impracticable and disgusting in this Age which will embrace the two next centuries. Impracticable because the danger constantly exists of deceiving only one's self, and not the political enemy. Disgusting because the more robust forces of this Age scorn sly deceits and veiled formulae for the fact of political subordination.

In a country where the cant of morality exercises a monopoly over political vocabulary, politicians cannot speak openly even to one another. The propaganda terror necessary to maintain such an absurd type of political terminology in contradiction to facts ends by weakening from within governments in such countries. Anyone making a purely factual remark becomes suspect, and some of the best brains have found their way thus into the concentration camps.

Internationale

IT HAS BEEN SEEN that the world of politics is a pluriverse.
This organic fact has within it fatal consequences for the league
of nations type of ideologist, and upon it his schemes founder.
Neither of the two "leagues of nations" which were established
by extra-European forces after the first two World Wars were
international organizations, but merely *interstate* organizations.
The English language does not permit of the clarity of the
distinction with the same self-evidence as the German language.
German "zwischenstaatlich" means occurring between States,
as self-contained impenetrable units; "international" in German means occurring inside of both States, and passing through
the State frontiers in every sense. Thus Macedonian terrorism
in the 19th and 20th centuries was truly international, but it
was not interstate. If the populations of the various States of
the world were represented in a "league of nations" quite independently of their various States, and if the States had no standing in it whatever, it could then possibly be called an international organization. When the sole membership is of States,

then the organization is merely "zwischenstaatlich," or in English, "interstate."

The importance of the distinction is that an interstate organization presupposes States. If they are true States and not States merely in name, they are described by the laws of Sovereignty and Totality. And in truth in both leagues at least some of the members were true States in this sense. In the first league, there were at various times five, six or seven such States. In the second league there were only two. But as long as there are two, such a league is merely an arena for the conduct of interstate politics.

An Internationale, provided it comes from the soul of the Culture, has the possibility of absorbing all States into it, provided it is an idea embracing life totally, i.e., a Cultural idea, and not merely a political scheme—and above all not a mere abstraction of some kind, an *ideal*—and feudalism was such an Internationale. Needless to say the various class-war revolutionary "internationales" were not this, for they had their origin purely in politics, and were purely negative. A Cultural Idea cannot be negative; such an Idea is not made by men, but comes from the development of the Culture, and represents an organic necessity of the higher organism. The phrase Spirit of the Age is transferable with the phrase Culture-idea. Both are superpersonal, and the most that a man can do is to formulate the Idea, try to actualize it, or try to strangle and distort it. Change it, or destroy it, he cannot.

An Internationale representing a Culture-idea is of course supra-national as well as international in the true sense, for nations are creations of the High Culture. Only such an Internationale could absorb States into it—and then only the States within the Culture. The idea would naturally have no inner effect on populations and areas outside its organic body. Thus no Western Internationale could inwardly touch China, India,

Japan, Islam or Russia. Their reaction to such an Internationale, provided they were affected by its external effects would of necessity be purely negative. If such an Internationale were to constitute the West as a unit also for *political* purposes—and the outer world has quite correctly always regarded the West as a unit for all other purposes—it would tend to create an anti-Western unity among the areas and populations outside. This would be only because the Western Civilization—the first one to do so—has made the whole world into its sphere of activity. For the first time in the history of the High Cultures, a Culture-political system embraced the entire world. For the politics of the extra-European forces is also in its depths motivated by the historically omnipotent force of our Western Civilization, in this way, that extra-European forces only derive their unity from the fact that they are a *negation* of Europe. If there were no Europe, Russia would merely be the scene of nomadic groups wandering with their herds, and engaging in small-scale inter-tribal warfare. Similarly, the famous "Chinese Revolution" of 1911 was a mere echo-phenomenon of Western currents, and its whole significance is that it had an anti-Western effect in the area the West calls China.

A true Internationale acts directly upon the entire Culture-area and all the populations in it. Capitalism was such a true Internationale—it was an expression of the Spirit of the Age. England was the vessel chosen by the Culture to actualize this idea, and England remained the spiritual home of Capitalism. The other nations were forced to orient their lives to this idea—which was also a world-outlook more than a system of economics. They could either affirm it, or negate it. This choice existed only because the Spirit of the Age also contained political nationalism, and thus Capitalism, belonging as it did to one nation, did not and never could have amalgamated all the

Western nations into one nation. Political nationalism was moribund even before the First World War, and thereafter the practice of political nationalism was simply Culture-distortion —every nation of the West was injured by it individually, and all of them collectively.

The Internationale of our times appears in a time when the Spirit of the Age has outgrown political nationalism. The Age of Absolute Politics will not tolerate petty-Stateism. The whole world is the spoils in this gigantic political age, and obviously tiny units, like the various former States of Europe, with a few tens of thousands of quadrate kilometers, with a few tens of millions of population cannot engage in a political struggle in a world filled with a population of 2,000,000,000 of human beings. The smallest possible unit that could even begin to participate in this world-struggle would have to have an area the size of Europe and hither Russia. Any struggle preliminary to this is local.

The two "leagues of nations" were merely interstate phenomena, thus pre-supposed States, thus were not themselves political units, thus could not engage in politics, thus did not exist as political realities. The Laws of Sovereignty and Totality, formulated herein, described the member-States of the leagues, but not the leagues themselves. Liberals and rationalists, moralists and logicians adrift in the world of facts, were not dismayed by the situation presented. They said that all that was necessary was to transfer sovereignty—mere legal sovereignty, for they knew nothing, and can know nothing, of the Organic Law of Sovereignty—from the member-States to the league itself. They thought that "sovereignty" was a word written down on a piece of paper, and was thus, according to the calculus of symbolic logic, manipulable at will. Sovereignty however, happens to be an existential characteristic of a political

organism, and these organisms are not subject to human control, but, on the contrary, control the human beings in their
areas politically. This is a *fact* and thus exists on a different
plane from logic, a plane which can never possibly intersect
that of logic. Logic deals with one phase of Culture-man, his
intellect, and that only. It can only dissect, analyze, conduct
spiritual post-mortems. Thus it cannot act, for action is creation. Politics in this light resembles art more than it does logic.
Logic is light, politics is chiaroscuro; logic is cameo, politics
is intaglio; logic is rigid, politics fluid. Creation is of the whole
soul, and logic is only one product of a small part of the soul.
Nonsense in logic may be sound politics; nonsense in politics
may be sound logic. Culture-political ideas precede reality; intellectual ideals bark at the heels of reality.

The basic idea of the leagues of nations was to abolish war
and politics. To provide a meeting place for war-political units
could hardly do it, and consequently these meeting places had
no political significance, which continued to reside in the
capitals.

We have seen that a world with one State is organic nonsense, since a State is a unit of opposition. But some of the
intellectuals wanted a world with no States whatever, singular
or plural. They spoke of "humanity," and wished to unite it for
the purpose of abolishing politics by politics, war by war. They
were thus affirming war and politics, but this remained hidden
from them. The name "humanity" became thus a polemical
word—it described everyone except the enemy. This was of
course nothing new, for this overworked word had appeared as
a political word in the 18th century, when it was used by the
intellectuals and equality-*ideologues* to describe everyone, except the nobility and clergy. It thus dehumanized the nobility
and clergy and when power came into the hands of the intellec-

tuals, in the French Terror of 1793, they showed that they considered their enemies subject to inhuman treatment because they did not belong to "humanity." Again, politics and logic separate out: humanity in logic means inhumanity in politics.

But yet the word humanity excludes no one, semantically speaking. The enemy is also human. Therefore humanity can have no enemy, and the "one State" liberals and the "humanity" intellectuals were involved in the very sort of thing they wished to abolish—politics and war. "Humanity" was not a peace word, but a war slogan. The "one State" remained in the world of dreams. Politics remained in the world and turned all of these anti-political things to its own use.

What would be a world without politics? Nowhere would there be protection or obedience, there would be no aristocracy, no democracy, no empire, no fatherland, no patriotism, no frontiers, no customs, no rulers, no political assemblies, no superiors, no subordinates.

For this world to come about or to continue to exist, there would have to be a total absence of men with lust for adventure and domination. No will-to-power, no barbarian instincts, no criminals, no superiority feelings, no Messianic ideas, no unpeaceable men, no programs of action, no proselyting, no ambition, no economics above the personal level, no foreigners, no race, no ideas.

We come to the fundamental disjunction between political thinking and mere thinking about politics. All intellectualistic thinking about politics posits a certain great non-existent characteristic of human nature.

The Two Political Anthropologies

THE TOUCHSTONE of any political theory whatever is its attitude to the fundamental ethical quality of human nature. From this standpoint there are only two kinds: those which posit a "naturally good" human nature, and those which see human nature as it is on the other hand. Good has meant reasonable, perfectible, peaceful, educable, desiring to improve, and various other things.

Every Rationalistic political or State theory regards man as "good" by nature. The Encyclopedists, the *Illuminati* and the devotees of Baron Holbach's philosophy were all symptomatic of the advent of Rationalism in the 18th century. All talked of "the essential goodness of human nature." Rousseau was the most forceful and radical of 18th century writers in this respect. Voltaire set himself apart by denying totally this essential goodness of human nature.

It is curious that a theory of *politics* could ever possibly ground itself on such an assumption, since politics actualizes itself only in the form of the friend-enemy disjunction. Thus a theory of hostility assumes that human nature is essentially peaceable and non-hostile.

The middle of the 18th century is the beginning of the word liberalism, and of the idea-complex liberalism. Since human nature is basically good, there is no need to be *strict* with it, one can be *"liberal."* This idea was derived from the English Sensualist philosophers. The Social Contract theory of Rousseau originated with the Englishman Locke in the previous century. All Liberalism predicates a sensualistic, materialistic philosophy. Such philosophies are rationalistic in tendency, and Liberalism is simply one variety of politically applied rationalism.

The leading 17th century political thinkers, like Hobbes and Pufendorff, looked upon the condition of "nature," in which States existed, as one of continual danger and risk, in which those engaged in action were driven by all the instincts and impulses of the beasts—hunger, fear, jealousy, rivalries of all kinds, desire. Hobbes observed that true enmity is possible only between men, that the friend-enemy disjunction is as much deeper between men than between animals as the world of men is spiritually above the world of the beasts.

The two political anthropologies are illustrated in the story, found in Carlyle, of the conversation between Frederick the Great and Sulzer, in which Sulzer was explaining the new discovery of Rationalism that human nature was essentially good. *Ach, mein lieber Sulzer, Ihr kennt nicht diese verdammte Rasse,* said Friedrich—"You don't know this damned race."

The assumption of the goodness of human nature developed two main branches of theory. Anarchism is the result of radical acceptance of this assumption. Liberalism uses the assumption merely to weaken the State and make it subservient to "society." Thomas Paine, an early Liberal, expressed the idea in a formula that remains valid for Liberalism to-day: Society is the result of our reasonably regulated needs; the State is the result of our vices. Anarchism is the more radical in proportion to the completeness of its acceptance of the human goodness assumption.

The idea of "balance of power," a technic of weakening the State, is Liberal throughout. By this means the State is to be rendered subject to economics. It cannot be called a State theory, for it is a mere negative. It does not deny the State completely, but wants it decentralized and weakened. It does not want the State to be the center of gravity of the political organism. It prefers to think of the organism as "society," a loose grouping of free and independent groups and individuals, whose freedom finds its sole limitation with the customary criminal law. Thus Liberalism has no objection to individuals being more powerful than the State, being above the law. What Liberalism dislikes is *authority*. The State, as the grandest symbol of authority, is hated. The two noble orders, as the symbols of authority, are likewise hated.

Anarchism, the radical denial of the State, and of all organization whatever, is an idea of genuine political force. It is anti-political in its theory, but by its intensity it is political in the only way that politics can manifest itself, i.e., it can bring men into its service and range them against others as enemies. During the 19th century, anarchism was a force to be reckoned with, although it was nearly always allied with some other movement. Particularly in 19th and early 20th century Russia was anarchism a powerful political reality. It was known there as Nihilism. The local strength of anarchism in Russia was owing to its coincidental attractiveness for the tremendous anti-Western feeling under the thin Petrine crust. To be anti-Western was to be against everything, therefore anti-Western Asiatic negativism adopted the Western theory of Anarchism as its vehicle of expression.

Liberalism, however, with its compromising, vague attitude, incapable of precise formulation, incapable also of rousing precise feelings, either affirmative or negative, is not an idea of political force. Its numerous devotees, in the 18th, 19th and 20th centuries have taken part in practical politics only as the ally of other groups. It could not create an issue; it could not line up men as friends or enemies; therefore it was not a political idea, but only an idea about politics. Its followers had to be for or against other ideas as a means of expressing their Liberalism.

Anarchism was able to rouse men to sacrifice of life, not so Liberalism. It is one thing to die to wipe out all order, all State; it is quite another to die in order to bring about a decentralization of State power. Liberalism is in essence nonpolitical; it is outside of politics. It would like to have politics serve as the handmaid of economics and society.

Liberalism

LIBERALISM is a most important by-product of Rationalism, and its origins and ideology must be clearly shown.

The "Enlightenment" period of Western history which set in after the Counter-Reformation laid more and more stress on intellect, reason and logic as it developed. By the middle of the 18th century this tendency produced Rationalism. Rationalism regarded all spiritual values as its objects and proceeded to re-value them from the standpoint of "reason." Inorganic logic is the faculty men have always used for solving problems of mathematics, engineering, transportation, physics and in other non-valuing situations. Its insistence on identity and rejection of contradiction are practicable in material activity. They afford intellectual satisfaction also in matters of purely abstract thought, like mathematics and logic, but if pursued far enough they turn into mere techniques, simple assumptions whose only justification is empirical. The end of Rationalism is Pragmatism, the suicide of Reason.

This adaptation of reason to material problems causes all problems whatever to become mechanical when surveyed in "the light of reason," without any mystical admixture of thought or tendency whatever. Descartes reasoned the animals into automata, and a generation or so later, man himself was rationalized into an automaton—or equally, an animal. Organisms became problems in chemistry and physics, and superpersonal organism simply no longer existed, for they are not amenable to reason, not being visible or measurable. Newton provided the universe of stars with a non-spiritual self-regulating force; the next century removed the spirit from man, his history and his affairs.

Reason detests the inexplicable, the mysterious, the half-light. In a practical problem in machinery or ship-building one must feel that *all* the factors are under his knowledge and control. There must be nothing unpredictable or out of control. Rationalism, which is the feeling that everything is subject to and completely explicable by Reason, consequently rejects everything not visible and calculable. If a thing actually cannot be calculated, Reason merely says that the factors are so numerous and complicated that in a purely practical way they render the calculation unfeasible, but do not make it theoretically impossible. Thus Reason also has its Will-to-Power: whatever does not submit is pronounced recalcitrant, or is simply denied existence.

When it turned its gaze to History, Rationalism saw the whole tendency as one toward Reason. Man was "emerging" during all those millennia, he was "progressing" from barbarism and fanaticism to enlightenment, from "superstition" to "science," from violence to "reason," from dogma to criticism, from darkness to light. No more invisible things, no more spirit, no more soul, no more God, no more Church and State. The two poles of thought are "the individual" and "humanity." Anything separating them is "irrational."

This branding of things as irrational is in fact correct. Rationalism must mechanize everything, and whatever cannot be mechanized is of necessity irrational. Thus the entirety of History becomes irrational: its chronicles, its processes, its secret force, Destiny. Rationalism itself, as a by-product of a certain stage in the development of a High Culture, is also irrational. Why Rationalism follows one spiritual phase, why it exercises its brief sway, why it vanishes once more into religion—these questions are historical, thus irrational.

Liberalism is Rationalism in politics. It rejects the State as an organism, and can only see it as the result of a contract between individuals. The purpose of Life has nothing to do with States, for they have no independent existence. Thus the "happiness" of "the individual" becomes the purpose of Life. Bentham made this as coarse as it could be made in collectivizing it into "the greatest happiness of the greatest number." If herding-animals could talk, they would use this slogan against the wolves. To most humans, who are the mere material of History, and not actors in it, "happiness" means economic well-being. Reason is quantitative, not qualitative, and thus makes the *average* man into "Man." "Man" is a thing of food, clothing, shelter, social and family life, and leisure. Politics sometimes demands sacrifice of life for invisible things. This is against "happiness," and must not be. Economics, however, is not against "happiness," but is almost co-extensive with it. Religion and Church wish to interpret the whole of Life on the basis of invisible things, and so militate against "happiness." Social ethics, on the other hand, secure economic order, thus promote "happiness."

Here Liberalism found its two poles of thought: economics and ethics. They correspond to individual and humanity. The ethics of course is purely social, materialistic; if older ethics is retained, its former metaphysical foundation is forgotten, and it is promulgated as a social, and not a religious, imperative. Ethics is necessary to maintain the order necessary as a framework for economic activity. Within that framework, however, "the individual" must be "free." This is the great cry of Liberalism, "freedom." Man is only himself, and is not tied to anything except by choice. Thus "society" is the "free" association of men and groups. The State, however, is un-freedom, compulsion, violence. The Church is spiritual un-freedom.

All things in the political domain were transvalued by Liberalism. War was transformed into either competition, seen from the economic pole, or ideological difference, seen from the ethical pole. Instead of the mystical rhythmical alternation of war and peace, it sees only the perpetual concurrence of competition or ideological contrast, which in no case becomes hostile or bloody. The State becomes society or humanity on the ethical side, a production and trade system on the economic side. The *will* to accomplish a political aim is transformed into the making of a program of "social ideals" on the ethical side, of calculation on the economic side. Power becomes propaganda, ethically speaking, and regulation, economically speaking.

The purest expression of the doctrine of Liberalism was probably that of Benjamin Constant. In 1814 he set forth his views on the "progress" of "man." He looked upon the 18th century Enlightenment with its intellectualistic-humanitarian cast as merely preliminary to the true liberation, that of the 19th century. Economics, industrialism, and technics represented the means of "freedom." Rationalism was the natural ally of this trend. Feudalism, Reaction, War, Violence, State, Politics, Authority—all were overcome by the new idea, supplanted by Reason, Economics, Freedom, Progress and Parliamentarism.

War, being violent and brutal, was unreasonable, and is replaced by Trade, which is intelligent and civilized. War is condemned from every standpoint: economically it is a loss even to the victor. The new war technics—artillery—made personal heroism senseless, and thus the charm and glory of war departed with its economic usefulness. In earlier times, war-peoples had subjugated trading-peoples, but no longer. Now trading-peoples step out as the masters of the earth.

A moment's reflection shows that Liberalism is entirely negative. It is not a formative force, but always and only a disintegrating force. It wishes to depose the twin authorities of Church and State, substituting for them economic freedom and social ethics. It happens that organic realities do not permit of more than the two alternatives: the organism can be true to itself, or it becomes sick and distorted, a prey for other organisms. Thus the *natural* polarity of leaders and led cannot be abolished without annihilating the organism. Liberalism was never entirely successful in its fight against the State, despite the fact that it engaged in political activity throughout the 19th century in alliance with every other type of State-disintegrating force. Thus there were National-Liberals, Social-Liberals, Free-Conservatives, Liberal-Catholics. They allied themselves with democracy, which is not Liberal, but irresistibly authoritarian in success. They sympathized with Anarchists when the forces of Authority sought to defend themselves against them. In the 20th century, Liberalism joined Bolshevism in Spain, and European and American Liberals sympathized with Russian Bolsheviks.

Liberalism can only be defined negatively. It is a mere critique, not a living idea. Its great word "freedom" is a negative—it means in fact, freedom from authority, i.e., disintegration of the organism. In its last stages it produces social atomism, in which not only the authority of the State is combated, but even the authority of society and the family. Divorce takes equal rank with marriage, children with parents. This constant thinking in negatives caused political activists like Marx, Lorenz v. Stein and Ferdinand Lasalle to despair of it as a political vehicle. Its attitudes were always contradictory, it sought always a compromise. It sought always to "balance" democracy against monarchy, managers against hand-workers, State against Society, legislative against judicial. In a crisis, Liberalism as such was not to be found. Liberals found their way on to one or the other side of a revolutionary struggle, depending on the consistency of their Liberalism, and its degree of hostility to authority.

Thus Liberalism in action was just as political as any State ever was. It obeyed organic necessity by its political alliances with non-Liberal groups and ideas. Despite its theory of individualism, which of course would preclude the possibility that one man or group could call upon another man or group for the sacrifice or risk of life, it supported "unfree" ideas like Democracy, Socialism, Bolshevism, Anarchism, all of which demand life-sacrifice.

II

From its anthropology of the basic goodness of human nature in general, Rationalism produced 18th century Encyclopedism, Freemasonry, Democracy, and Anarchism, as well as Liberalism, each with its offshoots and variations. Each played its part in the history of the 19th century, and, owing to the critical distortion of the whole Western Civilization entailed by the first two World Wars, even in the 20th century, where Rationalism is grotesquely out of place, and slowly transformed itself into

Irrationalism. The corpse of Liberalism was not even interred
by the middle of the 20th century. Consequently it is necessary
to diagnose even now the serious illness of the Western Civilization as Liberalism complicated with alien-poisoning.

Because Liberalism views most men as harmonious, or good,
it follows that they should be allowed to do as they like. Since
there is no higher unit to which all are tied, and whose superpersonal life dominates the lives of the individuals, each field
of human activity serves only itself—as long as it does not wish
to become authoritative, and stays within the framework of
"society." Thus Art becomes "Art for Art's sake," *l'art pour
l'art.* All areas of thought and action become equally autonomous. Religion becomes mere social discipline, since to be
more is to assume authority. Science, philosophy, education, all
are equally worlds unto themselves. None are subject to anything higher. Literature and technics are entitled to the same
autonomy. The function of the State is merely to protect them
by patents and copyrights. But above all—economics and law
are independent of organic authority, i.e., of politics.

Twenty-first century readers will find it difficult to believe
that once the idea prevailed that each person should be free to
do as he pleased in economic matters, even if his personal
activity involved the starvation of hundreds of thousands, the
devastation of entire forest and mineral areas, and the stunting
of the power of the organism; that it was quite permissible for
such an individual to raise himself above the weakened public
authority, and to dominate, by private means, the inmost
thoughts of whole populations by his control of press, radio
and mechanized drama.

They will find it more difficult yet to understand how such
a person could go to the *law* to enforce his destructive will.
Thus a usurer could, even in the middle of the 20th century,

invoke successfully the assistance of the law in dispossessing any numbers of peasants and farmers. It is hard to imagine how an individual could injure the political organism more than by thus mobilizing the soil into dust, in the phrase of the great Freiherr von Stein.

But—this followed inevitably from the idea of the independence of economics and law from political authority. There is nothing higher, no State; it is only individuals against one another. It is but natural that the economically more astute individuals accumulate most of the mobile wealth into their hands. They do not however, if they are true Liberals, want authority with this wealth, for authority has two aspects: power, and *responsibility*. Individualism, psychologically speaking, is egoism. "Happiness" = selfishness. Rousseau, the grandfather of Liberalism, was a true individualist, and sent his five children to the foundling hospital.

Law, as a field of human thought and endeavor, has as much independence, and as much dependence as every other field. Within the organic framework, it is free to think and organize its material. But like other forms of thought, it can be enrolled in the service of outside ideas. Thus law, originally the means of codifying and maintaining the inner peace of the organism by keeping order and preventing private disputes from growing, was transmuted by Liberal thought into a means of keeping inner disorder, and allowing economically strong individuals to liquidate the weaker ones. This was called the "rule of law," the "law-State," "independence of the judiciary." The idea of bringing in the *law* to make a given state of affairs sacrosanct was not original with Liberalism. Back in Hobbes's day, other groups were trying it, but the incorruptible mind of Hobbes said with the most precise clarity that the rule of law means the rule of those who determine and administer the law, that the rule of a "higher order" is an empty phrase, and is only given content by the concrete rule of given men and groups over a lower order.

This was political thinking, which is directed to the distribution and movement of power. It is also politics to expose the hypocrisy, immorality and cynicism of the usurer who loudly demands the rule of law, which means riches to him and poverty to millions of others, and all in the name of something higher, something with supra-human validity. When Authority resurges once more against the forces of Rationalism and Economics, it proceeds at once to show that the complex of transcendental ideals with which Liberalism equipped itself is as valid as the Legitimism of the era of Absolute Monarchy, and no more. The Monarchs were the strongest protagonists of Legitimism, the financiers of Liberalism. But the monarch was tied to the organism with his whole existence, he was responsible organically even where he was not responsible in fact. Thus Louis XVI and Charles I. Countless other monarchs and absolute rulers have had to flee because of their symbolic responsibility. But the financier has only power, no responsibility, not even symbolic, for, as often as not, his name is not generally known. History, Destiny, organic continuity, Fame, all exert their powerful influence on an absolute political ruler, and in addition his position places him entirely outside the sphere of base corruptibility. The financier, however, is private, anonymous, purely economic, irresponsible. In nothing can he be altruistic; his very existence is the apotheosis of egoism. He does not think of History, of Fame, of the furtherance of the life of the organism, of Destiny, and furthermore he is eminently corruptible by base means, as his ruling desire is for money and ever more money.

In his contest against Authority the finance-Liberal evolved a theory that power corrupts men. It is, however, vast anonymous wealth which corrupts, since there are no superpersonal restraints on it, such as bring the true statesman completely into the service of the political organism, and place him above corruption.

It was precisely in the fields of economics and law that the Liberal doctrine had the most destructive effects on the health of the Western Civilization. It did not matter much that esthetics became independent, for the only art-form in the West which still had a future, Western Music, paid no attention to theories and continued on its grand creative course to its end in Wagner and his epigones. Baudelaire is the great symbol of *l'art pour l'art:* sickness as beauty. Baudelaire is thus Liberalism in literature, disease as a principle of Life, crisis as health, morbidity as soul-life, disintegration as purpose. Man as individualist, an atom without connections, the Liberal ideal of personality. It was in fields of action rather than of thought that the injury was greatest.

Allowing the initiative in economic and technical matters to rest with individuals, subject to little political control, resulted in the creation of a group of individuals whose personal wills were more important than the collective destiny of the organism and the millions of the population. The law which served this state of affairs was completely divorced from morality and honor. To disintegrate the organism from the spiritual side, what morality was recognized was divorced from metaphysics and religion, and related only to "society." The criminal law reflected finance-Liberalism by punishing crimes of violence and passion, but not classifying such things as destroying national resources, throwing millions into want, or usury on a national scale.

The independence of the economic sphere was a tenet of

faith with Liberalism. This was not subject to discussion. There was even evolved an abstraction named "economic man," whose actions could be predicted as though economics were a vacuum. Economic gain was his sole motive, greed alone spurred him on. The technic of success was to concentrate on one's own gain and ignore everything else. This "economic man" was however man in general to the Liberals. He was the unit of their world-picture. "Humanity" was the sum total of these economic grains of sand.

III

The type of mind which believes in the essential "goodness" of human nature attained to Liberalism. But there is another political anthropology, one which recognizes that man is dis-harmonious, problematical, dual, dangerous. This is the gen-eral wisdom of mankind, and is reflected by the number of guards, fences, safes, locks, jails and policemen. Every catas-trophe, fire, earthquake, volcanic eruption, flood, evokes loot-ing. Even a police strike in an American city was the signal for looting of the shops by the respectable and good human beings.

Thus this type of thought starts from *facts*. This is *political thinking* in general, as opposed to mere thinking about politics, rationalizing. Even the wave of Rationalism did not submerge this kind of thinking. Political thinkers differ greatly in creative-ness and depth, but they agree that *facts* are normative. The very word theory has been brought into disrepute by intellec-tuals and Liberals who use it to describe their pet view of how they would like things to be. Originally theory was explanation of facts. To an intellectual who is adrift in politics, a theory is an aim; to a true politician his theory is a boundary.

A political theory seeks to find from history the limits of the politically possible. These limits cannot be found in the domain of Reason. The Age of Reason was born in bloodshed, and will pass out of vogue in more bloodshed. With its doctrine against war, politics, and violence, it presided over the greatest wars and revolutions in 5,000 years, and it ushered in the Age of Absolute Politics. With its gospel of the Brotherhood of Man, it carried on the largest-scale starvation, humiliation, torture and extermination in history against populations within the Western Civilization after the first two World Wars. By outlawing political thinking, and turning war into a moral-struggle instead of a power-struggle it flung the chivalry and honor of a millennium into the dust. The conclusion is compelling that Reason also became political when it entered politics, even though it used its own vocabulary. When Reason stripped territory from a conquered foe after a war, it called it "disannexation." The document consolidating the new position was called a "Treaty," even though it was dictated in the middle of a starvation-blockade. The defeated political enemy had to admit in the "Treaty" that he was "guilty" of the war, that he is morally unfit to have colonies, that his soldiers alone committed "war crimes." But no matter how heavy the moral disguise, how consistent the ideological vocabulary, it is only politics, and the Age of Absolute Politics reverts once again to the type of political thinking which starts from facts, recognizes power and the will-to-power of men and higher organisms as facts, and finds any attempt to describe politics in terms of morals as grotesque as it would be to describe chemistry in terms of theology.

There is a whole tradition of political thinking in the Western Culture, of which some of the leading representatives are Montaigne, Macchiavelli, Hobbes, Leibnitz, Bossuet, Fichte, de Maistre, Donoso Cortes, Hippolyte Taine, Hegel, Carlyle.

While Herbert Spencer was describing history as the "progress" from military-feudal to commercial-industrial organization, Carlyle was showing to England the Prussian spirit of Ethical Socialism, whose inner superiority would exert on the whole Western Civilization in the coming Political Age an equally fundamental transformation as had Capitalism in the Economic Age. This was creative political thinking, but was unfortunately not understood, and the resulting ignorance allowed distorting influences to fling England into two senseless World Wars from which it emerged with almost everything lost.

Hegel posited a three-stage development of mankind from the natural community through the bourgeois community to the State. His State-theory is thoroughly organic, and his definition of the bourgeois is quite appropriate for the 20th century. To him the bourgeois is the man who does not wish to leave the sphere of internal political security, who sets himself up, with his sanctified private property, as an individual against the whole, who finds a substitute for his political nullity in the fruits of peace and possessions and perfect security in his enjoyment of them, who therefore wishes to dispense with courage and remain secure from the possibility of violent death. He described the true Liberal with these words.

The political thinkers mentioned do not enjoy popularity with the great masses of human beings. As long as things are going well, most people do not wish to hear talk of power-struggles, violence, wars, or theories relating to them. Thus in the 18th and 19th centuries was developed the attitude that political thinkers—and Macchiavelli was the prime victim— were wicked men, atavistic, bloodthirsty. The simple statement that wars would always continue was sufficient to put the speaker down as a person who *wanted* wars to continue. To draw attention to the vast, impersonal rhythm of war and peace showed a sick mind with moral deficiency and emotional taint. To describe facts was held to be wishing them and creating them. As late as the 20th century, anyone pointing out the political nullity of the "leagues of nations" was a prophet of despair. Rationalism is anti-historical; political thinking is applied history. In peace it is unpopular to mention war, in war it is unpopular to mention peace. The theory which becomes most quickly popular is one which praises existing things and the tendency they supposedly illustrate as obviously the best order, and as preordained by all foregoing history. Thus Hegel was anathema to the intellectuals because of his State-orientation, which made him a "reactionary," and also because he refused to join the revolutionary crowd.

Since most people wish to hear only soporific talk about politics, and not demanding calls to action, and since in democratic conditions it matters to political technics what most people wish to hear, democratic politicians evolved in the 19th century a whole dialectic of party-politics. The idea was to examine the field of action from a "disinterested" standpoint, moral, scientific, or economic, and to find that the opponent was immoral, unscientific, uneconomic—in fact—he was *political*. This was devilishness that must be combated. One's own standpoint was entirely "non-political." Politics was a word of reproach in the Economic Age. Curiously however, in certain situations, usually those involving foreign relations, "unpolitical" could also be a term of abuse, meaning the man so described lacked skill in negotiating. The party-politician also had to feign unwillingness to accept office. Finally a demonstration of carefully arranged "popular will" broke down his reluctance, and he consented to "serve." This was described as Macchiavellism, but obviously Macchiavelli was a political thinker, and not a camouflageur. A book by a party-politician does not read like *The Prince,* but praises the entire human race, except certain perverse people, the author's opponents.

Actually Machiavelli's book is defensive in tone, justifying politically the conduct of certain statesmen by giving examples drawn from foreign invasions of Italy. During Macchiavelli's century, Italy was invaded at different times by Frenchmen, Germans, Spaniards and Turks. When the French Revolutionary Armies occupied Prussia, and coupled humanitarian sentiments of the Rights of Man with brutality and large-scale looting, Hegel and Fichte restored Macchiavelli once again to respect as a thinker. He represented a means of defense against a foe armed with a humanitarian ideology. Macchiavelli showed the actual role played by verbal sentiments in politics.

One can say that there are three possible attitudes toward human conduct, from the point of evaluating its motives: the sentimental, the realistic, and the cynical. The sentimental imputes a good motive to everybody, the cynical a bad motive, and the realistic simply seeks the facts. When a sentimentalist, e.g., a Liberal, enters politics, he becomes perforce a hypocrite. The ultimate exposure of this hypocrisy creates cynicism. Part of the spiritual sickness following the First World War was a wave of cynicism which arose from the transparent, revolting, and incredible hypocrisy of the little men who were presiding over affairs at that time. Macchiavelli had however an incorruptible intellect and did not write in a cynical spirit. He sought to portray the anatomy of politics with its peculiar problems and tensions, inner and outer. To the fantastic mental illness of Rationalism, hard facts are regrettable things, and to talk about them is to create them. A tiny politician of the Liberal type even sought to prevent talk about the Third World War, after the Second. Liberalism is, in one word, *weakness.* It wants every day to be a birthday, Life to be a long party.

The inexorable movement of Time, Destiny, History, the cruelty of accomplishment, sternness, heroism, sacrifice, super-personal ideas—these are the enemy. Liberalism is an escape from hardness into softness, from masculinity into femininity, from History to herd-grazing, from reality into herbivorous dreams, from Destiny into Happiness. Nietzsche, in his last and greatest work, designated the 18th century as the century of feminism, and immediately mentioned Rousseau, the leader of the mass-escape from Reality. Feminism itself—what is it but a means of feminizing man? If it makes women man-like, it does so only by transforming man first into a creature whose only concern is with his personal economics and his relation to "society," i.e., a woman. "Society" is the element of woman, it is static and formal, its contests are purely personal, and are free from the possibility of heroism and violence. Conversation, not action; formality, not deeds. How different is the idea of *rank* used in connection with a social affair, from when it is applied on a battlefield! In the field, it is fate-laden; in the salon it is vain and pompous. A war is fought for *control,* social contests are inspired by feminine vanity and jealousy to show that one is "better" than someone else.

And yet what does Liberalism do ultimately to woman: it puts a uniform on her and calls her a "soldier." This ridiculous performance but illustrates the eternal fact that History is masculine, that its stern demands cannot be evaded, that the fundamental realities cannot be renounced, even, by the most elaborate make-believe. Liberalistic tampering with sexual polarity only wreaks havoc on the souls of individuals, confusing and distorting them, but the man-woman and the woman-man it creates are both subject to the higher Destiny of History.

Democracy

ANOTHER IMPORTANT BY-PRODUCT of Rationalism is Democracy. The word has many meanings, and in the First World War it passed into the ownership of extra-European forces, and was declared synonymous with Liberalism. This was of course, a polemical meaning, and there are several variations on this side. But first the historical origin of Democracy.

It arose in the middle of the 18th century with the coming of Rationalism. Rationalism negated History as a basis for any thought or endeavor whatever, and therefore, Church and State, Nobility and Clergy had no rights based on tradition. Reason is quantitative, and thus the Estates were regarded as less important than the insignificant masses of the population. Previous centuries had referred to the monarch by the name of the country. Thus the King of France *was* "France." An assembly of the Estates was also called "France," or "England" or "Spain." But to Rationalism, not quality but quantity determines, so the mass became the nation. "The People" became a polemical word to shut out the Estates, and deny them the right to political existence. At first, the mass was called "The Third Estate," but later all Estates were denied.

The idea of Democracy was, however, saturated with will-to-power; it is not a mere abstraction, it is an organic idea, with superpersonal force. The whole development which produced Rationalism, the epoch at which Culture turned to Civilization, was of course a crisis in the Western organism. It was thus illness, and Democracy was illness, but it was a one through which every High Culture has gone, and was therefore impelled by organic necessity. Democracy seeks no compromise, no "balancing," no destruction of authority—it seeks power. It denies the Estates in order to supplant them.

One characteristic of Democracy was that it rejected the aristocratic principle which equated social significance with political significance. It wished to turn this around and make *social* dependent on *political*. This of course was merely the foundation of a new aristocracy, and in very fact democracy was self-destructive: when it attained power, it turned into aristocracy.

Napoleon has also in this respect the greatest possible symbolic significance. He, the great Democrat, the great Vulgarian, spread the Revolution against Dynasty and Aristocracy, but created his own Dynasty and made his Marshals into Dukes. This was not cynicism, nor faithlessness to conviction—Napoleon as Emperor was just as much a Democrat as when he cleared the mob from the streets of Paris. Democracy, by mobilizing the masses of the population, enormously raises the power-potential of the nations and of the Culture. Democracy is the idea that a Duke does not thereby become a Marshal, but a Marshal does thereby become a Duke. As a technic of ruling, it is solely and simply a new method of furnishing the political leaders. It makes social rank dependent on political-military rank, instead of vice-versa.

The new Dynasty of Democracy, and the new democratic aristocracy are filled with the same will-to-duration that animated the Hohenstaufen, the Capet, the Norman, the Hapsburg, the Welf, the feudal barons whose names and traditions still persist.

Historically speaking, Democracy is a *feeling,* and has nothing whatever to do with "equality," "representative government" or anything of the sort. The whole cycle of Democracy was compressed with intense symbolism into the comparatively short career of the great Napoleon. This man's formula *La carriére ouverte aux talens* expresses whatever "equality" sentiment Democracy contains, namely equality of opportunity. There is no thought whatever of abolishing rank or gradation of rights. Revolution, Consolidation, Imperialism—the history of Democracy.

But the expression of the whole cycle of Democracy in the short span of Napoleon's life, was symbolic only, for Democracy had most of its life span of two centuries ahead of it. Democracy is not a retreat from Reality, from War, History and Politics, like Liberalism. It remains within politics, but seeks to make politics a thing of *mass.* It seeks to make everyone subject to politics, and to make everyone into a politician. Napoleon's remark to Goethe "Politics is Destiny" expresses this widening of the base of political power that is Democracy. Up to the end of the 18th century, war and politics were for the Cabinets, the Kings, and small professional armies. Politics and war seldom touched the ordinary person. Democracy changed all this: it put the entire man-power of the nation onto the battlefields, it forced everyone to have an opinion on matters of government, it forced him then to express the opinion in plebiscites and elections. If he had no independent opinion—and more than 99% of men do not—it forced an opinion on him, and told him it was his.

It was Fate for the idea of Democracy that it was born at the same time as the Economic Age. It meant that its authoritarian tendency was, as it were, strangled, and it would have to wait for a political age to express itself again, after its brief flash of glory in Napoleon. But the end of the Economic Age was also the end of the Democracy Idea. Thus Democracy in fact was throughout most of its history a servant of Economics in its battle against Authority.

Democracy had two poles, ability and mass. It put everyone into politics, and allowed the successful ones an amount of power tenfold that of any absolute monarch. But Napoleon himself could not stand against the forces which Money mobilized against him in the Economic Age, and the lesser democratic dictators were more easily overwhelmed. In Spanish South America, where the money power was not absolute, a whole tradition of democratic dictators—Bolivar, Rosas, Francia, O'Higgins, some of the best known—show the powerful authoritarian tendency in popular government.

But in most countries only the vocabulary of democracy was retained, and this enabled the economic powers to conduct themselves in a more or less absolute fashion, for they had struck down the State with Democracy, and then bought Democracy. In later democratic conditions—in our case from 1850 —it was solely the financier whose interest was served by the constitutionalized anarchy called democracy. The word democracy thus passed into the possession of Money, and it was transformed from its historical meaning into its 20th century meaning. The Culture-distorters use it as meaning the denial of qualitative differences among nations and races; thus the for-

eigner must be admitted to the positions of wealth and authority. To the financier, it means the "rule of law"—his law,
which makes possible his unprecedented usury by means of his
monopoly of money.

But Democracy perishes with Rationalism. The idea of basing political power on the masses of the population was a technic at best. Either it proceeded to authoritarian rule like that of
Napoleon or Mussolini, or else it was a mere cover for un-
hampered looting by the financier. Authoritarian rule is the
end of democracy, but is not itself democracy. With the coming
of the Age of Absolute Politics, the necessity for pretexts falls
away. Plebiscites and elections become old-fashioned, and
finally cease altogether. The symbiosis of war and politics sup-
ports itself and does not claim it "represents" any class. In the
annihilation-war between Authority and Money, "Democracy"
may be a slogan for either side, but more than a slogan it cannot be.

II

History is cataclysmic; but it is also continuous. The superficial events are often extremely violent and surprising, but
beneath them the adjustment of one Age into the next is
gradual. Thus Democracy was not at all understood by its early
protagonists as the lowering of everything human to the level
of the least valuable human beings. Its first propagators came
from the higher strata of the Culture, in the main, and those
who did not, sought to give the impression they did: "de"
Robespierre, "de" Kalb, "de" Voltaire, "de" Beaumarchais.
The original idea was to make everyone, so to speak, into a
nobleman. Naturally in the blind hatred and passionate jealousy
of the Terror of '93 this was obscured, but Tradition does not

perish in one onslaught, and on the *social* side, the battle of Democracy versus Tradition was long and hard.

The authoritarian *political* tendency of Democracy was, as seen, strangled at birth by the power of Money in an Economic Age. But the word then became a slogan in the *social* battle, and in the *economic* battle. It always meant mass, quantity, numbers as opposed to quality and tradition. The first version of the idea was to make everything higher into common property, and as this was shown to be unfeasible, the next idea was to destroy all quality and superiority by merging it into the mass. The weaker Tradition was, the greater was the success of the mass-spirit. Thus in America, its victory was complete, and the principle of mass was applied even to the field of education. America with less than half the population of the home soil of Western Culture had in the 20th century ten times as many institutions of higher learning, so-called. For, in everything, Democracy must fail, even in success. The practice of giving everyone a diploma meant quite simply that the diploma became meaningless.

The ultimate in this direction was reached by an American writer who branded higher chemistry, physics, technics and mathematics as "undemocratic," because they were the possession of a few, and were thus tending to create some sort of aristocracy. It never occurred to this person that the theory of Democracy is also the possession of a few: these masses did not mobilize themselves, the Spirit of the Age, acting on certain individuals of the population, spread abroad the feeling that everything should be set in motion, everything should be externalized, de-spiritualized, rendered into "mass," numbered and counted.

And thus, with the coming of the 20th century, "democracy" has a different meaning from its original one. Its original two poles of Ability and Mass have become merged for the purposes of the powers of Economics, who own the word "democracy" in this century. They place upon it solely the meaning of mass, and use it to combat the new resurgent Authority-Idea. The economic lords of the earth mobilized the masses against the authority of the State, and miscalled it "democracy." The Age of Absolute Politics begins by mobilizing the masses against the power of Money and Economics, and will end Napoleon-wise in the restoration of Authority. But there will at last be no more plebiscites, no more elections, no more propaganda, no more mass audience attending the political drama. The two centuries of Democracy end in Empire. With the natural death of the idea of mass counting for something, Authority makes no intellectual appeal whatever to justify itself. It is simply there, and it is not a problem.

Communism

THE GRADUAL TRANSITION of the Spirit of the 18th century into that of the 19th century was manifested by the increasingly radical nature of the conflict between Tradition and Democracy. Rationalism became more extreme with each decade. Its most intransigent product is Communism.

In the century 1750–1850, Democracy had undermined the State and opened the way for the Economic Age. But the financier and the industrial baron replaced the absolute monarch. Communism is the symbol of the transference of the democratic struggle to the sphere of economics.

Communism fitted itself out with a Rationalistic philosophy: a materialistic metaphysic, an atomistic logic, a social ethic, an economic politics. It even offered a philosophy of history which said that *human history was the history of economic development and struggles!* And these people ridiculed the Scholastic philosophers for the nature of the problems they set themselves! Religion—that was economic, politics, of course, also. Technics and art were clearly economic. This theory was actually the crowning intellectual stupidity of the Age of Economics. The Age asserted thus its omnipotence and universality. "Everything within economics, nothing outside economics, nothing against economics" might well have been the slogan.

Just as the *political* aspect of Democracy had been directed against quality and, tradition, so the *economic* aspect was directed against even such quality and superiority as was engendered by economic differences. Political class war became economic class war. Just as the appeal in the first stage had been made to anyone not belonging to the two Estates, so later the appeal was directed to the non-possessors. Not all non-possessors, but only those in the great cities, and within this group, only the manual workers, for only these were physically concentrated so that they could be brought on to the streets for class war.

But Communism was *political*, unlike Liberalism, and named an enemy who must be annihilated—the bourgeoisie. The better to make the program of action go ahead, the picture was simplified: there are only two realities in the whole world, bourgeoisie and proletariat. Nations and States are bourgeois devices to keep the proletariat divided and thus conquered. This was the origin of the idea that Communism was an Internationale, but its strength as an Internationale was shown in 1914, when the class-war organizations in all countries threw themselves heartily into the fight among the nations. It was never an Internationale in the true sense.

Nevertheless it was an affirmation of politics, and was a force to be reckoned with during the Economic Age. It was able in various Western countries to bring about Civil War—e.g., France, 1871. Its high point was the Bolshevik Revolution in Russia, 1918, when the theory of Communism was actually adopted by a non-theoretical Asiatic regime as a weapon of foreign policy.

It was in the essence of Communism, as in every by-product of Rationalism, that its wish-picture could never become actualized. Using inorganic logic to construct a program for actuality does not change the fact that an organism has its own structure, development, and tempo. This can be injured, distorted, annihilated from without, but inwardly changed it cannot be. Thus Communism was purely destructive in effect, and this was why the Asiatic power on Europe's boundary adopted it as a program to disintegrate all European States. Communism, like all Utopias, is impossible of realization, because they are rational and Life is irrational. The sole novelty about the Utopia of Communism is that it proclaims itself as inevitable. This was a tribute to its will-to-power, but this vain boast had the same life span as Rationalism. With the advent of the Age of Absolute Politics, even class-war drops theory. History receives Rationalism and all its debris into its vaults of the dead. Death, and not refutation, is the fate of rationalistic theories of politics and economics. We who live in the middle of the 20th century will witness the final desuetude of Rationalism and its progeny.

Association and Dissociation
of Forms of
Thought and Action

IN DEVELOPING a 20th century outlook on politics, the first thing necessary was to dissociate politics from other directions of human energy, particularly from economics and morality. In view of the enormous vogue of theories which sought to explain political phenomena with ideational equipment derived from, and appropriate to, other fields of activity or thought, this was quite necessary. We have seen that politics is a type of activity *sui generis,* that its practice involves, often entirely unconsciously on the part of the actor, its own way of thinking in action. It remains to state definitively the separability and the inter-dependence of the various directions of human energy, and of Cultural energy.

A world without abstract thought—the world of the dog, for example—is a world wherein a complete continuity reigns. Each thing fits quite perfectly into its place or sphere. By comparison with the human world, it is non-problematical. Reality and appearance are one. The distinctively human soul sees the macrocosm however as *symbolic;* it differentiates between Appearance and Reality, the symbol and that which is symbolized. All constructive human thinking whatever contains this as its essence. But this separating of things into appearance and reality, this singling out of one thing from another and bestowing intense abstract thought on it, is itself a distortion of its quiet, non-problematical relation to other things. Thus to think is to exaggerate.

For Culture-man, the High Culture in which he is fated to be born, live and die, is the world of his spirit. The High Culture sets the spiritual boundaries of this world. The High Culture sets its impress on almost every form of thought and activity of the individuals and groups in its domain. Within this realm, the thought-forms and thoughts, action-forms and actions, all fit into their natural places and occupy their non-problematical relations to one another. These relations continue, even though thought is applied to a sphere to exaggerate its part in the destiny of the whole. To think is to exaggerate, but this exaggeration affects only thought and does not disturb the macrocosm. The same is true of any one man: the various directions of his energy stand in an organically unified, harmonious relationship to one another. There is no "economic man"—there is only this man directing his energy toward economics for the moment. Nor is there any "reasonable man," such as some Western legal systems predicate. There is only this man being reasonable for this occasion. The essential characteristic of the higher organisms, man, and High Culture, is the soul. Thus this particular man acts economically in quite a different fashion from another man, because his soul is different. This makes all of his thought and action peculiar to him. One man has strong interests and abilities in a certain direction, another man elsewhere. High Cultures are also differentiated from one another by unequal endowment in various directions. The *principium individuationis* applies also to the High Cultures.

Every organism, from the plants and animals to men and Cultures, has a multiplicity of functions, a diversity that increases in refinement and articulation as we proceed upward. This functional versatility does not however disturb the unity of the organism. It is the very unity of the organism that creates this necessity for expression in various directions. For one direction to be pursued at the expense of another is distortion and brings illness and death, if persisted in. I am concerned only with organisms in health here, and in these, the changing of direction of energy is governed by the inner rhythm of the organism. This rhythm is different in each organism, and is affected by individuality, age, sex, adaptation, and milieu. Each human being has his daily sequence of changes of direction of energy-flow. All organisms have their inner rhythm that governs which function is called into play at a given moment. A Culture has such a rhythm also, and at various stages of its development, this rhythm accents first one, then another, field of thought of activity. Similarly any man, and a Culture-man in particular, has his appropriate type of activity and of thought for each age of his development. It has been well said that a young man is an idealist, a mature man a realist, an old man a mystic. This rhythm in a Culture which gives primacy to a certain side of its life during a given period is the source of The Spirit of the Age.

It is only the accent, the beat, which is affected in this changing of direction. The various functions all continue, but one is primary. This describes both men and Cultures. Thus "economic man" continues to exist as a unit, even in his economic activity; his individuality continues, and his other spiritual sides still exist, even though not given primacy at the moment. Similarly with Cultures: all types of thought and activity exist in all ages, even though for a given Age a certain side of Life is uppermost. This is the meaning of "anachronism" in its historical use. Thus Fausto Sozzini is an anachronism in the 16th century, Carlyle in the 19th.

So much for the association of forms of thought and action. They are also dissociated.

The expression *change of direction* was used to denote the shifting of emphasis from one function to another. These changes of direction are forms of adaptation to different types of situations. It is the type of situation, of problem to be solved, that gives the uniqueness to a way of thinking or acting. Self-evidently one would not approach the problem of fixing a piece of machinery as a power-problem—that would end in the smashing of the enemy machinery. Nevertheless many Rationalists and Liberals tried to treat power-problems as mechanical in nature.

The various fields of thought and endeavor thus separate out. Considered by themselves, they are quite autonomous. Each has different conscious assumptions, and a different unconscious attitude. Some of the most important must be listed, with their fundamental structures.

First, there is *religion*. From the viewpoint of spiritual content, this is the highest of all human forms of thought. Religion has the great, ever-present characteristic that it sees the totality of things under a sacred aspect. It is *divine* metaphysics, and regards every other form of human thought and action as subsidiary. Religion is not a method of social improvement, it is not a codification of knowledge, it is not ethics—it is the presentation of a sacred ultimate reality, and all of its phases flow from this.

Philosophy, however, is essentially a different direction of

thought. Even a *theistic* philosophy has a different attitude
from the religions. In a theistic philosophy, the beginning of
religion sets the boundary to the philosophic endeavor. The
philosophy lies this side of religion and gives a purely natural
explanation to its subject-matter.

Science is yet another direction of thought: it is directed only
to finding interrelations between phenomena, and generalizing
the results, but it does not attempt to give ultimate explanations.

Technics has nothing to do with science, for it is not a form
of pure thinking at all, but thought directed to action. Technics
has one aim: *power over the macrocosm.* It uses the results of
science as its tools, scientific theoretical generalizations as
levers, but it discards them when their efficacy ceases. Technics
is not concerned with what is *true,* but with what *works:* if a
materialistic theory yields no results, and a theological one
does, technics adopts the latter. It was thus Destiny that Pragmatism should appear in America, the land of *worship of technics.* This "philosophy" teaches that what is true is what works.
This is simply another way of saying that one is not interested
in truth, and is thus the abdication of philosophy. This could
be called the elevation of technics or the degradation of philosophy, but the total difference of direction between technics and
philosophy is not thereby altered; it is merely that the age
placed strong emphasis on technics, and little on philosophy.
Nor can the alliance, in 20th century practice almost an identity, between practitioners of Science and Technics obliterate
the difference of direction between these two fields. The same
man can think at one time as a scientist, *seeking* information,
and in the next moment as a technician, *applying* it to get
power over Nature. Science and Technics are as different from
Philosophy as they are from each other: neither one seeks to
give explanations, these are for philosophy and religion. If

someone thinks he is founding a "scientific philosophy," he is mistaken, and on the very first page he is bound to abandon the scientific attitude and assume the philosophic. One cannot face two directions at once. If *precedence* is given to Science over Philosophy, this is something else; this merely reflects the Spirit of the Age as being an externalized one. But important is that all these forms of thought and action are imbedded in the flux and rhythm of the development of a High Culture; a given direction of thought has its vogue of supremacy just so long as the Culture-stage lasts which chose it for this role.

Economics is a form of *action*. Specifically, it is action designed to nourish and enrich private life. Any attempt to control other lives thus departs from Economics. When Cecil Rhodes thought primarily of making himself wealthy, he was thinking economically; when he proceeded to use his wealth for control over the populations of Africa, he was thinking politically. It is only rarely that a man of action is capable of mastery of both these different directions of endeavor, so different are their respective techniques. Economics again has two phases, production and trade, whose special techniques are again so different ordinarily one man does not master both.

The refinements of ways of thinking and acting are numerous. For instance, the data of metaphysics do not matter to ethics, even though one use a similar principle in both of them. Actually the data of ethics are its own. Mathematics also has its own attitude, related to but distinct from that of logic. Esthetics singles out one aspect of the totality of relationships, and this determines its basic assumptions.

II

Not only is there association and dissociation between forms of thought and action but there is also an order of rank between them, depending upon the problem of the moment. The duality of man, arising from the commingling in his nature of a human soul and of the instincts of the beast of prey, gives rise to the fact that his action almost never conforms to his abstract thought-systems. The abstract thought has its center of gravity on the soul side of him, the action on the beast of prey side. The man who, in a theological discussion, resorts to physical blows in order to prove his point, is confusing the two spheres of thought and action. So is the man who discusses politics in terms of morality. These two spheres of thought and action have their perfectly definite frontiers. Each man has abstract thought ability, and ability to act. When he is thinking abstractly, he does not act, and when he is acting, he does not think abstractly. His thought then is completely submerged in the action. Abstract formulation of action may come before action, or after action, but it does not come during action. As Goethe said: "The doer is always conscienceless; only the spectator has a conscience."

What is Life? It is the process of actualization of the possible. Actualization—and thus *action*. Life has its center of gravity on the side of action, and not on the side of abstract thought. For purposes of action, then, there is an order of rank which places practical skill above theorizing. It is this which makes Macchiavelli more valuable politically than Plato, Thomas More, Campanella, Fourier, Marx, Edward Bellamy or Samuel Butler. He wrote of politics as it *is*, the others as it *should* be, or as they *wanted* it to be.

It is fairly well known that nothing can be *proved* by violence—this is because the two spheres of abstract thought and action, *truths* and *facts*, do not intersect. It is not as well understood that the reverse is also true, that no violence can be done by proof; in other words, effects cannot be gained in the world of action by truths. Merely to start to try to actualize an abstract theory is to abandon it. The net result of the attempt to impose a way of thinking where it is not appropriate is *bungling*. There is no choice between a chemistry-artist and a physics-artist, but only between a good artist and a poor one. To approach a mechanical problem as though good and evil are involved in it is to prepare a failure. Each aspect of life yields its secrets only to the method adapted to it. Politics always has refused to give any power to the man who is out to "reform" it according to a morality. Nor can it be *understood* by trying to impose foreign methods of thought upon it. *Politics is the opposite of abstract;* derivatively abstract means "drawn away from"—away from what?—from action, reality, facts.

This whole outlook is one of the *fact* side of the human being. This work is concerned only with action, because the Age of Absolute Politics in which it appears is an age of action. No one has ever said politics *should* be immoral—but all political thinkers have said that politics is politics. Questions of *should* are on the other side of the soul, and are not treated here. The *fact* that politics and morality do not intersect is shown by the example of the Second World War. The American half of the extra-European coalition against Europe stated most decisively that it was fighting for Christian morality, yet after the war it carried out the attempt to exterminate physically the Culture-bearing stratum within its jurisdiction in occupied Europe. Beyond this, mass-starvation and looting were employed to destroy many millions of Europeans, physically, economically. The example is not unique: the victorious powers after the First World War had carried out a starvation blockade of the defeated enemy *after the War,* and that War also was conducted by those victorious powers in the name of Christian morality.

In the *practice* of politics, a moral approach can only result in inefficiency or disaster. It is destructive in exact proportion as it is taken seriously.

If the morality is used quite cynically, as propaganda to increase the brutalization of a war, it distorts war and politics in the direction of bestiality.

In the 20th century, politics reconquers once more its own realm. The motivation of politics is no longer derived from economics. Law, technics, economics, social organization—all reflect the great realities of politics. In this last formative age of a great Culture, which will last through the 21st century, the motivation of the perpetual power-struggle is supplied by the unity of the Western Civilization itself. The real front of the wars of this age is simply Europe versus anti-Europe. There are border areas, like those between Russia and Europe, like the northern countries of South America. Each side has its allies: the white populations strewn over the world belong to Europe; the Asiatic distorting elements of cohesion and power in the various Western countries belong to non-Europe. It is the struggle of a positive against a negative, of creation against destruction, of Cultural superiority against the envy of the outsider. It is the unrelenting battle against the master of yesterday by his liberated slaves, burning with vengeance for their centuries of slavery.

These wars of course will be true unlimited wars, like the Crusades, and not agonal like intra-European wars of the 17th and 18th centuries. They will be correspondingly absolute in their means and in their duration. For example, prisoner-of-war usages developed in the Western Civilization on considerations of humanitarianism and military honor. After the Second World War Russia abolished the first of these bases, by starving and enslaving prisoners, and America abolished the second by hanging prisoners-of-war en masse, and ignoring the Hague Conventions in its post-war occupation of Europe.

The coming wars will thus revive the older practices of enslaving and killing war prisoners, and remove the protections hitherto extended to the civilian population. Instead of the codified military honor of a High Culture, honor will eventually become a matter of inner personal imperative, and the individual will decide for himself, the importance of his decision depending upon his position. It is not dishonorable *per se* to kill prisoners, but only if they surrender and give up their arms on condition their lives are to be spared, as the European soldiers and leaders did who were later hanged by the Americans after the Second World War.

In the last act of our grand Western Culture-drama, the idea of the Culture itself demonstrates its unimpaired vigor—Destiny is always young, says the philosopher of this Age—by placing itself in the center of Life and defining all men as friends or enemies according as they adhere to it, or oppose it. *Culture-politics* is the end of the train of *religion-politics, family-politics,* and *faction-politics* from the Crusades to the Reformation, *dynasty-politics* to the Vienna-Congress, *national-politics* and *economic-politics* to the Second World War. The crisis of Rationalism subsides. Its attendant phenomena grow colorless, more forced, and one by one they fade away: Equality, Democracy, Happiness, Instability, Commercialism, High Finance and its power of Money, Class War, Trade as an end in itself, Social Atomism, Parliamentarism, Liberalism, Communism, Materialism, Mass-Propaganda. All these proud banners trail finally in the dust. They are nothing but the symbols of Reason's daring and bold, but hopeless, attempt to conquer the kingdom of the Soul.

CULTURAL VITALISM
(A) Culture Health

"I recognize only two nations, the Occident, and the Orient."

NAPOLEON

"It is want of race, and nothing else, that makes intellectuals—philosophers, doctrinaires, Utopists—incapable of understanding the depth of this metaphysical hatred, which is the beat-difference of two currents of being manifested as an unbearable dissonance, a hatred that may become tragic for both."

SPENGLER

"I wanted to prepare the fusion of the great interests of Europe, as I had accomplished that of the parties. I concerned myself little with the passing rancor of the peoples, for I was sure that the results would lead them irresistibly back to me. Europe would in this way have become in truth a united nation, and every one would have been, no matter where he traveled, in the same Fatherland. This fusion will accomplish itself sooner or later through the pressure of the facts; the impulse has been given which, since my downfall and the disappearance of my system, will make the restoration of balance possible in Europe only by merger and fusion of the great nations."

NAPOLEON

Introduction

FOR THE FIRST TIME is developed here the thesis of Cultural Vitalism, the physiognomy of the adaptation, health, or illness of a High Culture. Heretofore, a Culture has usually been looked upon as a result, a mere sum total of collective activity of human beings and groups of human beings. To the extent that its unity and continuity was perceived at all, this was regarded as purely materially-linked "influence" of individuals, groups or written ideas on contemporaries or posterity. But with the advance of age of the Western Culture, its unity began dimly to be perceived. This unity was formulated in very different ways, with different points of origin, different laws of development, but the essential idea was the *unity of the Culture*. Even in the home of Materialism, Benjamin Kidd recognized the inner unity of the West in his work "Western Civilization." Nietzsche, Lamprecht, Breysig. Meray, are only a few of those who sensed this idea. In an age which starts from facts, and not from programs, which submits to realities without trying to make them pass a rationalistic test, it has become self-evident, *spiritually compulsory* to think within this new framework. If two individuals, widely separated geographically, and in no contact with one another, develop similar inventions, similar philosophies, chose the same subject matter for drama or lyric—this is not "influence" nor "coincidence," but a reflection of the development of the Culture to which both belong. From the higher Cultural standpoint the arguments about who was the first to invent this or that device, who originated this or that idea, are quite barren. These questions are not on any higher plane than the legal, at best. If the development in question is one of superpersonal force, and not a mere personal amusement, it is the development of the *Culture,* and the fact that it was expressed simultaneously by more than one person only testifies to its Destiny-quality.

The nature of the unity of the Culture is *purely spiritual in its origin.* The material unity that follows is the unfolding of the precedent inner, spiritual unity. Life is the actualizing of the possible; the development of a High Culture is the unfolding, over the predetermined organic life-span, of the inner possibilities contained in the Culture-soul.

The one in which we live is the 8th High Culture to appear on this planet. The unity and inner relationship of the totality of forms and creations of any one of the others is apparent to us, because we stand completely *outside* it and cannot enter into the nuances of its soul, since we belong to another. This impenetrability of an alien Culture is part of a wider organic generalization: even the spirit of another age of our own Culture, of another nation, another individual, in the last analysis, presents difficulties to complete understanding. The technique of comprehension of other life-forms is *living into* them. To measure, time, and calculate the behavior of another organism is valueless to organic assimilation. Materialistic "psychology," with its heaps of results on paper, never aided one individual to understand another. If any identity was reached, it was in spite of the abstract equipment.

Difficulty in assimilating oneself into other organic forms, understanding them, *penetrating* them, is a matter of degree. A person with similar character is readily understood by us. If his character is dissimilar, but his background is similar, he can be understood with more difficulty. Different nationality, different race, different cultural origin, raise successively steeper barriers to mutuality. This sets out one of the problems of Cultural Vitalism.

The question is: to what extent can a Culture impress new populations entering its area with the Cultural idea? Subsidiary problems arise from the fact that such new populations may have one or all of various kinds of cohesiveness, that of a people, or of a race, or of a nation, or of a State, or of another Culture.

The further problem arises of the precise relation of the Culture to the populations in its service, and to those outside its area. It is formulated in this way because High Cultures are bound to a landscape, and the formative impulses appear always in the original landscape, even in the last phase, that of Civilization, in which the Culture externalizes itself completely and expands to its furthest limits. The expansive, externalizing tendency begins already in the middle of the life span, but it only becomes dominant with the sharp caesura marked by the crisis of Civilization. For us the symbol of this break is Napoleon. Since his time the populations of the entire Earth have been brought within the arc of the most unlimited Imperialism known to history. They stand however in varying relationships to the Mother-Idea of this Imperialism, and these relationships must also be examined.

The Articulation of a Culture

The nations, thought-forms, art-forms, and ideas which are the expression of the development of a Culture are always in the custody of a comparatively small group. How large this group is, how easily it can replenish itself, depends on the character of the Culture. In this respect, the Classical Culture is instructive. Its Ideas were one and all *exoteric:* Socrates conducts his philosophizing in the agora. In our case the picture of Leibnitz or Descartes carrying on such activity would be ludicrous in the extreme, for Western philosophy is the possession of a very few.

But any Culture, even the exoteric Classical, is restricted for its full expression, in whatever direction, to certain levels of the populations in its area. Culture is by its very nature selective, exclusive. The use of the word in the personal sense—a "cultured" man—describes a man out of the ordinary, a man whose ideas and attitudes are ordered and articulated. Cultured in the personal sense means devoted to something beyond oneself and one's own domestic well-being. In the 19th century world-picture, with its atomistic mania, only individuals existed, nothing higher, therefore the word was used to describe a practitioner or appreciator of art or literature. But patriotism, devotion to duty, ethical imperative, heroism, self-sacrifice, are also an expression of Culture—primitive man does not evince them. A war is just as much an expression of Culture as a poem, a factory as a cathedral, a rifle as a statue.

A high Culture in the course of its fulfillment acts in all directions of thought and action, and on every person within its area.

The intensity of its action in a given direction depends on the Culture-soul: some of the Cultures have been passionately historical, like the Chinese; some completely ahistoric, like the Indian; some have developed massive technics, like the Egyptian and our own, some have ignored technics, like the Classical and Mexican.

The intensity of the impression of the Culture on individuals is proportional to their receptivity to spiritual impressions. The individual of small soul and limited horizon lives for himself because he understands nothing else. To such a man Western music is merely an alternate up and down, loud and soft, philosophy is mere words, history is a collection of fairy-tales, even the *reality* of which is not inwardly felt, politics is the selfishness of the great, military conscription a burden which his lack of moral courage forces him to accept. Thus even his individualism is a mere denial of anything higher, and not an affirming of his own soul. The extraordinary man is the one who puts something else before his own life and security. Even as he faced the firing squad, William Walker could have saved his life by merely renouncing his claim to President of Nicaragua. To the common man, this is insane. The common man is unjust, but not on principle; he is selfish, but is incapable of the im-

perative of Ibsen's exalted selfishness; he is the slave of his
passions, but incapable of higher sexual love, for even this is
an expression of Culture—primitive man simply would not
understand Western erotic if it were explained to him, this
sublimation of passion into metaphysics. He lacks any sort of
honor, and will submit to any humiliation rather than revolt—
it is always leader-natures who revolt. He gambles in the hope
of winning, and if he loses, he whimpers. He would rather live
on his knees than die on his feet. He accepts the loudest voice
as the true one. He follows the leader of the moment—but only
so far, and when the leader is eclipsed by a new one, he points
out his record of opposition. In victory he is a bully, in defeat
he is a lackey. His talk is big, his deeds small. He likes to play,
but has no sportsmanship. Great thoughts and plans he casti-
gates as "megalomania." Anyone who tries to pull him up and
along the road of higher accomplishment he hates, and when
the chance offers, he crucifies him, like Christ, burns him, like
Savonarola, kicks his dead body in the square in Milan. He is
always laughing at the discomfiture of another, but he has no
sense of humor, and is equally incapable of true seriousness. He
denounces the crime of passion, but eagerly reads the literature
of such crimes. He herds in the street to see an accident, and
enjoys seeing another sustain the blows of fate. He does not
care if his countrymen are spilling their blood as long as he is
secure. He is everything mean and unheroic, but he lacks the
mentality to be Iago or Richard III. He has no access to Culture,
and, when he dares, he persecutes anyone who has. Nothing
delights him more than to see a great leader fall. He hated
Metternich and Wellington, the symbols of Tradition, he refused, as Reichstag, to send ex-Chancellor Bismarck a birthday
greeting. He makes up the constituency of all parliaments everywhere, and he invades all councils-of-war to advise prudence

and caution. If beliefs to which he was committed become dangerous, he recants—they were never his anyway. He is the inner weakness of every organism, the enemy of all greatness, the material of treason.

It is not such human stuff that an exacting High Culture can use to further its Destiny. The common man is the material with which the great political leaders in democratic conditions work. In earlier centuries, the common man did not attend the Cultural drama. It did not interest him, and the participants were not yet under the Rationalistic spell, the "counting-mania," as Nietzsche called it. When democratic conditions proceed to their extreme, the result is that even the leaders are common men, with the jealous and crooked soul of envy of that to which they are not equal, like Roosevelt and his coterie in America. In his cult of "The Common Man," he was deifying himself, like Caligula. The abolition of quality smothers the exceptional man in his youth and turns him into a cynic.

In earlier centuries there was no suggestion anywhere that the masses of the population had a part to play. When this idea does triumph, it turns out that the only role these masses can play is the passive one of unwieldy building material for the articulate part of the population.

What is the physical articulation of the body of the Culture? The more exacting the nature of the Cultural task, the higher the type of humanity required for its performance. There is in all Cultures a spiritual level of the entire population called the Culture-bearing stratum. It is this articulation of Culture-populations alone which makes the expression of a High Culture possible. It is the technic of living, the *habitus,* of the Culture. The Culture-bearing stratum is the custodian of the wealth of expression-forms of the Culture. To it belong all the creators in the domains of religion, philosophy, science, music, literature, the arts of form, mathematics, politics, technics, and war, as well as the non-creators who fully understand and themselves experience the developments in this higher world, the appreciators.

So, within itself the Culture-bearing stratum is articulated into *creators* and *appreciators*. It is in general the latter who transmit the great creations downward, insofar as this is possible. This process serves to recruit the higher material, wherever it appears, into the Culture-bearing stratum. The process of replenishment is continually going on, for the Culture-bearing stratum is not hereditary in any strict sense. The Culture-bearing stratum is a purely *spiritual* level of the populace of the Culture. It has no economic, political, social, or other hallmark. Some of its most luminous creators have lived and died in want, e.g., Beethoven and Schubert. Other souls, equally creative, but less rugged, have been strangled by poverty— Chatterton. Many of its creative members go through their lives entirely unnoticed—Mendel, Kierkegaard, Copernicus. Others are mistaken for mere talents—Shakespeare, Rembrandt.

The Culture-bearing stratum is not recognized by its contemporaries in any way as a unity, nor does it recognize itself as one. *As a stratum it is invisible,* like the Culture it carries. Because it is a purely psychic stratum, it can be given no material description to satisfy the intellectuals. Even the intellectuals would admit however that Europe or America could be thrown into a material chaos from which it would take years to emerge if the few thousands in the higher technical ranks were removed. These technicians are a *part* of the Culture-bearing stratum, although it is not merely occupational. Technicians of course, like economic leaders, or military leaders, play purely subordinate roles in the Culture-drama. The most important part of this stratum at any one time is the group which is the custodian of the highest Idea. Thus in Dante's time, Emperor and Pope were the two highest symbols of reality, and it was in the service of either one of these symbols that the leading members of the Culture-bearing stratum were then to be found. The highest symbolic force was then transferred to the dynasties, and dynastic politics claimed its lives during its centuries. With the coming of Enlightenment and Rationalism, the whole West goes into a crisis of long duration, and not less does the Culture-bearing stratum. It was split even more than usual, and only now, after two centuries, is it possible to restore its basic unity. I say more than usual, for it must not be supposed that the Culture-bearing stratum ever was a sort of international, a freemasonry. On the contrary, it supplied leaders on both sides of every war and every tendency.

II

Within this stratum there is constant struggle between Tradition and Innovation. The strong, vital part naturally represents the new, forward development, affirming the next age. It is the function of Tradition to assure continuity. Tradition is the memory of a superpersonal soul. It must see that the same creative spirit of the grand past is present at each innovation.

The crisis of Rationalism places the same frightful strain on the higher stratum that it does on the entire organism. The step forward—Democracy—is affirmative in the last analysis, because it is an historical necessity in the life of a Culture, as we know from history. But it is a difficult step for men to take who have given their lives to construction and creation, for to mobilize the masses is to destroy. The step from Culture to Civilization is a *fall,* it is the onset of senility. For this reason, leaders whose center of gravity was on the side of culture re-

sisted the Revolution of Democracy with all their power—
Burke, Goethe, Hegel, Schopenhauer, Metternich, Wellington,
Carlyle, Nietzsche. The Culture-bearing stratum, articulated
into creators and appreciators, is invisible as such. It corresponds to no economic class, no social class, no nobility, no
aristocracy, no occupation. Its members are not all public figures
by any means. But by its existence, this stratum actualizes a
High Culture on this earth. If a process had existed by which
members of the stratum could be all selected, the extra-European forces would probably have exterminated it in the attempt
to destroy the West. The attempt would not have succeeded,
for this stratum is produced by the Culture, and after a long
period of chaos—a generation or two, depending on circumstances—this Cultural organ would have been again present,
including in its numbers descendants of the invaders, who
would also succumb to the Idea. The possibilities in this direction will be more thoroughly examined later.

In a political age, it is natural that the best brains go into
politics and war. Those who are equal to renunciation and
sacrifice are the heroes of this realm. War-politics is pre-
eminently the field of heroism, and the sacrifices in this realm
are never in vain from the Cultural standpoint, for the war itself is an expression of Culture. Considered from the rationalistic standpoint, it is stupid to devote one's life to an idea, any
idea whatever. But once again, Life, with its organic reality
does not obey Rationalism with its urge to mediocrity. Thus
the best are culled from every generation and impelled into the
service of the Culture. The noblest of all are the heroes, who
die for an idea; but everyone cannot be a hero, and the others
live for an idea.

An invariable characteristic of this level is its *spiritual sensitivity,* which brings it more impressions than the others receive.

This is coupled with *more complex internal possibilities,* which order the volume of impressions. It can *feel* the new Spirit of the Age before it is articulate, before it triumphs. This also describes all great men, and one reason so many perish violently is that they promulgated things which were "ahead of their time." These men lived in a world more real than that of the "realistic" people, and these same "realists" are outraged and burn the Savonarola whom they would follow unquestioningly a generation or two later.

This vital plane is only a psychic-Cultural unity during the long centuries of the Culture, but with the coming of the late Civilization—mid-20th century—the dominant idea of the entire Culture is political. Napoleon's "Politics is destiny" is even more true now than when he said it. The two ideas of *Democracy* and *Authority* stand opposed, and only one of them belongs to the Future. Only Authority represents a step forward, and thus the strongest, most vital, creative elements in the Culture-bearing stratum are found in the service of the resurgence of Authority. It has become political-Cultural.

Since the Culture-bearing stratum has its highest importance in an age like the present one, when quality reasserts itself against quantity, it must be defined now as precisely as possible. The notion of mere *prominence* must be dissociated strongly from the idea of belonging to this stratum. Wagner, Ibsen, Cromwell, none of whom were prominent until middle life, were nonetheless in this plane of life and thought in their previous years. The notion of *prominence* is related to the idea of the Culture-bearing stratum in this way: every man who is prominent in any field, and who *also has inner gifts, of vision, appreciation, or creativeness,* naturally belongs to this stratum. Prominence however may be the result of accident of birth or fortune, and Europeans have seen two periods in recent history—after the first two World Wars—when nearly all the ruling politicians in Europe were simply common men thrown up by chance and the distorted life of the higher organism.

The Culture-bearing stratum has its highest importance now, rather than in previous centuries, because it is a relatively tinier minority. The vast increase of numbers in Europe—it *tripled* in population in the 19th century—did not increase the numbers of this stratum, nor of higher natures generally. This stratum was as numerous in the time of the Crusades as it is now. It is simply the way of Culture to choose *minorities* for its expression. Multiplication of population is *downwards*. *The tension between quantity and quality grows greater with the increase of numbers,* and the Culture-bearing stratum acquires a mathematically higher significance. The tension can be suggested in figures: there are not more than 250,000 souls in Europe who constitute by their potentialities, their imperative, their gifts, their *existence,* the Culture-bearing stratum of the West. Their geographical distribution has never been entirely uniform. In that nation which the Culture chose for the expression of The Spirit of the Age as it chose Spain for the expression of Ultramontanism in the 16th and 17th centuries, France for the Rococo in the 18th century, or England for Capitalism in the 19th, there was always a higher proportion of the culturally-significant than in countries which were not playing the leading Cultural role. This fact was known to the extra-European forces in their attempt to destroy the Western Civilization after the Second World War, and was utilized as far as it could be within the limits of expediency. The real purpose behind the mass-hangings, mass-looting, and mass-starvation, was to destroy the *few* by destroying the many.

The articulation of the Culture has three aspects: the Idea itself, the transmitting stratum, those to whom it is transmitted.

The latter comprise the vast numbers of human beings who possess any refinement whatever, who maintain a certain standard of honor or morality, who take care of their property, who have self-respect and respect the rights of others, who aspire to improve themselves and their situation instead of pulling down those who have enriched their inner life and raised themselves in the world. They are the body of the Culture *vis-a-vis* the Culture-bearing stratum as its brain, and the Idea as its soul. In each person who belongs to this numerically large group there is a quantum of ambition and appreciation toward the creations of culture. They furnish the instruments by which creators can carry out their work. By this means they give significance to their own lives, a significance which the underworld would not understand. The role of a Maecenas is not the highest, but it is of Cultural value. Who knows whether we would have Wagner's greatest works but for Ludwig II? When we read the results of a great battle, do we always realize that it was not simply a chess-game between two captains, but that hundreds of firm officers and thousands of obedient men *died* to write this line in history, to make this day and date forever remembered? And when a threatened sack of society is put down by the police and Army, the casualties on the side of order thus give by their deaths a higher significance to their lives also. Not everyone can play a great role, but the right to give meaning to his life cannot be taken from a man.

But beneath all this is the stratum totally incapable of cultural attainment, even the most modest: the mob, *canaille*. *Pöbel*, underworld, *profanum vulgus*, the "common man" of the American cult. These preside at every Terror, listen wishfully to every Bolshevik agitator, secrete venom at the sight of any manifestation of Culture or superiority. This stratum exists at all stages of every Culture as the Peasant's Wars, the Jac-

querie, Wat Tyler, Jack Cade, John Ball, Thomus Münzer, the
Jacobins, the Communards, the Spanish militiamen, the mob in
the square in Milan, are there to show. As soon as a creative
man makes his resolve and proceeds with his work, somewhere
else in a dark envious soul there rises a crooked determination to stop him, to smash the work. In his later years the
Nihilist Tolstoy gave perfect expression to this basic fact with
his formula that not even one stone should be on top of another. The slogan of the Bolshevik in 1918 was also illuminat-
ing: "Destroy Everything!" In our age this underworld is in
the possession of the class-warriors, the rear-guard of Rationalism. It is thus working, from the larger political viewpoint,
solely for the extra-European forces. Previous rebellions of this
stratum were all doomed because of the unity of the Culture,
the pristine vigor of the creative impulses, and the lack of
external danger of such crushing proportions as exists in this
age. Its history is not yet over with. Asia has use for this
stratum, and plans for it.

Tradition and Genius

THERE ARE TWO different ways in which the Culture-bearing stratum can perform its function. The first is through the presence of a high tradition of accomplishment along a given line, a "school"; the second is through the instrumentality of occasional genius. They can combine, in fact they are never completely separated, for individual genius is always present at the formation of a tradition in the first instance, and the presence of the tradition is not hostile to genius when it does appear.

Nevertheless they are different methods of Culture-expression, and both have importance to the 20th century world-outlook which is here formulated in its essentials.

Italian painting from 1250 to 1550 is an example of a tradition at work. The Flemish-Dutch school of the 17th century is another. It was not necessary for a painter in one of these schools to be a great master in order to express himself fully. The form was there, unquestioned, it was only required to master it and to contribute one's personal development of its possibilities. Spanish and German painting on the other hand

represent a collection of great originals, and not the sure forward progression of a tradition. The sublimest tradition of all
was the Gothic architecture to c. 1400. So powerful was the
tradition that the idea of a *work* of art, which pre-supposes a
personality creating it, did not even exist.

But traditions like this are not confined to arts. Scholastic
philosophy represented the same superpersonal unity working
itself out through many personalities all in the service and development of a tradition. From Roscellinus and Anselm
through Thomas Aquinas to Gabriel Biel, the problems and
their complete exploitation are continuous. Each thinker, regardless of his gifts, whether a man of genius, or merely a
hard worker, was trained by his predecessors and himself developed into his successors. It was not the solutions, and not
even always the questions which were continuous—it was the
method and thoroughness of investigation and formulation
which showed the presence of the tradition.

From Cromwell to Joseph Chamberlain—the beginning and
the end of that high political tradition which built the great
British Empire, which at its highest point exerted its control
over 17/20th of the surface of this earth—England was the
example of the possibility of *tradition in politics* as well as in
philosophy, music, and the arts of form. How many men of
political genius appeared in the Premiership during these centuries? Only the two Pitts. Nevertheless, England emerged
from all the general wars of those centuries with increased
power—Thirty Years War, 1618–1648, Spanish Succession
War, 1702–1713, Austrian Succession Wars 1741–1763, Napoleonic Wars, 1800–1815, Wars of German Unification, 1863–
1871. Only one serious blunder was made during these centuries, the loss of America, 1775–1783. The essence of this tradition was nothing other than applying only political thinking

to politics. Cromwell the theologian departed from this only occasionally, and more in words and expressions of sympathy than in actions. His successors in the tradition of Empire-building were not burdened with his heavy theological equipment, which they transformed into *cant,* a word translatable into no other European language. The technic of cant was what enabled English diplomacy to score continued successes in the world of facts, i.e., the world of violence, of cunning, of sin, while maintaining before itself the attitude of selfless morality. To enrich the country by new possession was thus "bringing civilization" to "backward" races. And so on, through the whole gamut of political tactics.

Traditions show in this example one of their prime characteristics: they are not efficacious unless *profoundly* mastered by the individuals. Thus other European statesmen during the 19th century, the century of the Anglicization of Europe, attempted to utilize cant and merely made themselves ridiculous. Wilson, the American world-saver who modestly offered himself as President of the World-as-Morality, went too far. A sure tact was the prerequisite of successful employment of cant, and this required for its mastery growing up in a cant-saturated atmosphere. In the same way the Austrian officer corps—whose ethical qualities Napoleon missed in his own officers—presupposed a life-long preparation and training in a certain atmosphere, and not three months military training on the basis of an "intelligence test."

The great thing about a tradition is that the leader of the moment is not alone—the qualities he lacks, and which the situation may need, are sure to be present somewhere in the entourage. The presence of a political tradition makes it extremely unlikely in the first place that an incompetent will be placed in a position of high political authority, and if it does

happen that a weak personality arrives on the heights by chance,
tradition again makes his early departure certain. It might be
supposed that this is contradicted by the case of Lord North,
but the initial blunders of his American policy were only seen
as such in retrospect. If he could have followed them up with
further strict measures, America would not have been lost, but
his domestic situation *vis-a-vis* the Whigs on the one hand and
the monarch on the other, was difficult in the extreme, and his
policy was hamstrung by the same type of Rationalist elements
who were preaching "Contract Social" and "Rights of Man" on
the continent. On the contrary, the successful avoidance of
Revolution and Terror from the Wilkes affair in mid-18th century through the horrors of '93, the general revolutionary waves
of 1830 and 1848, was attributable to the presence of an unimpaired tradition.

Tradition is not a rigid thing, a guarantee of certain results.
Not at all, for in History, it is the unexpected which happens.
The imponderables make their appearance. Incident plays
counterpoint to Destiny. A slight gap may appear also in a
tradition, but the health of the tradition-bearing stratum shows
itself by quickly closing the opening. A tradition of statesman-
ship is a sort of Platonic idea of excellence which molds men,
as far as possible, in each case, and serves as a form for their
personal expression. The results are shown by a *high average*
of training and ability. Fortunate is the political organism with
such leadership! What is missed in one place is picked up in
another; individual quirks are not allowed to become political
dogmas. The last result of the presence of a tradition in a
political unit is that *Destiny is kept on a sure path and Incident
is minimized.*

Genius

THE NAME *genius,* describing a certain small stratum of humanity, came into the effective vocabulary of the Western Culture only with the advent of Humanism. The 20th century means by this word what Emerson meant by "Representative Man," or Carlyle by "Hero." The comprehensive delineation of the subject of Genius by Lange-Eichbaum, the distinguished European scholar, has given the word its content for this age.

We no longer see genius under an aspect of causality or predestination. This was the only way Materialism could understand the word. Nietzsche pierced through this predestination idea of genius with his aphorism: the higher the type a man represents, the greater is the improbability that he will succeed, because of the increased diversity and difficulty of his life-conditions. The word genius thus has acquired through the centuries a large *objective* content, and has come self-evidently to contain within it the idea of *frame.*

If the word were to be used purely subjectively, it would describe simply a man with great creative force. There are

always some of these men at work, but their creative efforts may
be in any of the various directions of Culture. The test of creative force has come to be success, namely the personal success of
the man in translating his personal potentialities into creation,
whether of thought or deed. Not absolute success is meant, for
this would exclude nearly all men. Neither Wallenstein, Cromwell, Napoleon, or the Hero that we have seen, attained *absolute* success. The success of each was however *personal,* in the
sense that posterity can read his name in the skies at night.

It is the Spirit of the Age which influences greatly the direction of the creative ability of men of genius. Thus in the Gothic
religious time, many men of genius became religionists, philosophers, saints and martyrs. In the Enlightenment, men of genius
appeared as artists and universal men. In the time of Civilization men of genius appear mostly in the externalized pursuits of
technics, economics, politics and war. All tendencies exist in all
ages, but in each age one Idea is uppermost. High politics is
appropriate in every age and in the coming age it is the leading Idea. In our times, and the next times, the men of creative
force will be found largely concentrated in the service of the
Resurgence of Authority.

The crass stupidity of Rationalism and Materialism was nowhere more perfectly in evidence than in its attempt to make
the word genius into an *intelligence* term. Naive "tests" were
even devised to detect the presence of "genius," which could be
shown by a *number.* In the Age of Materialism, there was no
scruple about weighing and numbering the faculties of the
Soul. The *fact* is that intelligence is the functional opposite of
Genius. Intelligence is dissection, genius is creation; one is
analysis, the other is synthesis; the first is directed toward the
Part, the second toward the Whole. They are related as terrestrial and astral, counting and imagining.

It must be said that while Genius is *great* creative force, each man has some creative force, enough to make of his own life such a work that those who come after him need never be ashamed of him.

The interest of the 20th century is in politics, and hence the significance of Genius in this sphere will be examined here. It is best understood by comparison with Tradition in politics. Tradition secures the steady fulfillment of the Idea by training up the available talent to a high average level. It is superior to Genius as a vehicle for the actualization of an Idea, for the life span of the Tradition is also the life span of the Idea, while Genius is allotted only the usual three score and ten. The passing of Genius leaves a gap, but the Tradition only passes with the fulfillment of the Idea itself. In the larger sense, Cromwell is the beginning of the English national political tradition. Yet, in a narrower, *personal* sense, he did not found a tradition, for after his death, it was but a matter of months before the Dynasty was back, and Cromwell's body was exhumed and dragged through the streets of London by wild horses. But when once the English political tradition was founded in the Cromwellian spirit, it lasted right through to Joseph Chamberlain. What is Genius in politics? How does it manifest itself in this realm? In one thing simply: it represents the Idea of the Future. If one were to state the relation to the Present of the masses, a Tradition, and Genius, he would say that the masses are always behind the Present, the Tradition is alert at each moment adjusting to the Future, but the Genius represents the Promethean thrusting into the Future with unleased force.

Genius is dependent for its actualization on the appreciation of the Culture-bearing stratum, or nation-bearing stratum. Talent can understand anything that Genius can imagine or create, once it is actualized, but Genius always impresses at first as *fantastic*. Alexander the Great, Frederick the Great, Cromwell, Napoleon, the Hero of this age, all impressed most people at the beginning of their careers, as being unworldly, out of touch with Reality. There was some justification for this, for they were in touch with a *new* world, the *next* Reality.

In this connection, the use of the word Present is only a figure of speech. Actually, there is no Present in the world of politics: the Present is simply the point of tension between Past and Future. Genius in politics belongs *always* on the side of the Future. Genius is great creative force; in the realm of action, creation is of *deeds;* deeds are the form of the actualization of the Future.

At the very beginning of the Civilization period of the Western Culture, two extraordinary men stand opposed, Napoleon and Metternich. Only the Empire-builder had genius; his opponent, though equal in political skill, in assessment of the "realities" of the time, and in force of character, was a mere conserver, a servant of the Past. The "realities" he cognized were those of the immediately previous Reality, not those of the coming Reality. It is Genius of Napoleon's kind that occasionally appears and delivers the new Spirit of the Age, the new Reality. Talent of Metternich's kind lacks the vision of the Genius, and it is solely accidental whether or not he opposes him. If Metternich had been a Frenchman, he would have been a Minister of Napoleon.

What precisely are the qualities of Genius in politics, which constitute its maestria and its inner imperative? First, *vision*. It sees the possibilities of the Future, and its mind is thereby freed from the trammels which hinder the average man in his thinking. To the prosaic mind, everything which is, represents the end of all development, the Future is to be a mere extension of the Past. Second, *spiritual purity:* the ordinary man is an eclectic; he carries in his head hundreds of contradictory ideas and beliefs. Not so the creative man in politics: he thinks along *one* line, and *one* line only. This gives to his enemies the opportunity of convincing many that he is mentally ill, and they have never failed to do so, from Alexander to the Hero we have seen. But political Genius and its enemies pass into two different categories of History. His name is written in bronze letters as the symbol, meaning, apotheosis, and incarnation of the Spirit of his Age; his enemies turn out on this high plane to have been merely the material with which he hewed his deeds. Third, *intensity:* the voice of Genius commands, it is harsh, intolerant. It demands and impels upward. Genius is inseparable from the presence of a rushing inner chaos, the prerequisite of *formative* work. Under a Frederick, or a Charles XII, men will overcome tactical odds of 5 to 1, strategical odds of 30 to 1. But not under Laudon, or the Archduke Charles, or a Grant. These latter need crushing superiority to make up for their inner lack.

Fourth, the *sense of a Mission.* This vision, purity, and intensity are all brought into an ethical focus: the things which he sees are stamped with Necessity, and he *must* actualize them. This accounts for the powerfully *dramatic* influence of a political Genius upon the facts of History. His forceful mission compels everyone to orient himself to it. Everyone is either with him or against him. He becomes the center of the world.

Lastly, an Imponderable. Genius is Life at its highest human potential, and all Life is uncanny, irrational, mysterious. There is something about Genius that makes men *rise spiritually.* It is the Something that gave Napoleon victory on almost every field, that sat like an eagle on the shoulder of Moltke, as he worked quietly at his task of shaping the form of the 20th and 21st centuries. It may be merely the personality accompanying these extraordinary gifts. It may be a transcendental emanation from the higher organism—it is unknowable, but it is there.

Genius and the Age
of Absolute Politics

THERE CAN BE NO QUESTION that a Tradition, which makes use of the ever-present talent of the successive generations, is superior to Genius for the purpose of actualizing an Idea in its perfection. But the Idea will be actualized without either of them; their presence, together or separate, affects only the rhythmic sureness and external purity of the Life-process.

The soul of each Culture is an organism, and therefore possesses the mark of individuality. This is stamped on everything connected with the Culture, including its History-style. Just as persons differ in their way of expressing themselves—one man forceful and imperious, another quiet, but equally effective —so do High Cultures. The Classical offers a strong contrast to our own in this. Its historical style, in comparison with ours, is one of Incident. Accents are not sharp, transitions are not conscious, or marked by the intensely formed turning-points of the Western history. While their men of genius were not fewer, Genius played a smaller role in the working-out. Genius was the focus of less force.

Western nations have also seen great developments which

were unaccompanied by the phenomenon of direction of the whole Idea on to one man. For instance, the German Wars of Liberation, 1813–1815, England's transition to Democracy, 1750–1800.

But in the middle of the 20th century we see about us the wreckage of the two centuries of Rationalism: the high old traditions of the West have been mostly destroyed. The *horizontal* war of the banker and the class-warrior against the Western Civilization have laid the old quality low. But History has not stopped, and the greatest imperative of all in the political sphere is now operative. A new *quality*-tradition is arising. As the philosopher of this age has said, there are no longer in the world any sacred forms of political existence whose very age is an unassailable power.

Since an effective Tradition is absent in the political realm of the Western Civilization, we may expect that the Western demand for sharp accents in History will repose gigantic forces in the hands of individual men. The Hero whom we have seen was a symbol of the Future.

History does not stop; no one man is more important than History. The relationship of political Genius to the mass was misread by 19th century Materialism, and also by Nietzsche. Materialism regarded the great politician as bound to work for the—of course—*material* improvement of the mass. Nietzsche regarded the masses as existing only to produce the great men. But the idea of *purpose* cannot describe the process as it *is*. Apart from all ideology, the great man and the masses are a unity, both are in the service of the Idea, and each finds his historical significance only with regard to the counter-pole. Carlyle voiced the instinctive demand of this age when the idea of authority and monarchy has once again a good conscience: find the *Ablest Man,* and let him be king.

Democratic ideologists, with their heads buried deep in the sand, say that maybe a bad monarch will appear. But the imperative of History is not to produce a perfect system, but to fulfill the historical mission. It was this that produced Democracy and it is this that now pays no attention to the whining of the Past, but only to be the rumble of the Future. Good or bad, the monarchs are coming.

On the front of the tottering edifice is printed in gaudy letters: Democracy. But behind it is seen to be a cash-till, and the banker sits, running his hands through the money that was the blood of the Western nations. He looks up in terror, as the sound of marching feet is heard.

The Future of the West demands the committing of great forces into the hands of great men. The erection of a Tradition of politics is a hope; from the chaos of 1950 there is no hope. Only great men can bridge the gap.

Race, People, Nation, State

THE 19TH CENTURY concepts of race, people, nation, and State are exclusively of Rationalistic-Romantic provenance. They are the result of imposing a thought method adapted to material problems on to living things, and thus they are materialistic. Materialistic means shallow as applied to living things, for with all Life, the *spirit is primary,* and the material is the mere vehicle of spiritual expression. Since these 19th century concepts were rationalistic, they were basically *unfactual,* for Life is irrational, unamenable to inorganic logic and systematization. The Age upon which we are entering, and of which this is a formulation, is an Age of Politics, and hence an age of *facts.*

The broader subject is the adaptation, health and pathology of High Cultures. Their relationship to every type of human grouping is a prerequisite to examining the last problems of Cultural Vitalism. The nature of these groupings will therefore be looked at without preconceptions, with a view to reaching their deepest meanings, origin, life, and inter-connections.

Material inanimate objects retain their identity through the

years, and thus the type of thinking suited to dealing with
material things assumed that the political and other human
groupings in existence in 1800 represented something *a priori*,
something of the very essence of permanent reality. Everything
was regarded as a creation of one of these "peoples." This
applied to the arts of form, literature, State, technics, culture
generally. This view is not in accordance with historical facts.

The first concept in order is Race. The materialistic race-
thinking of the 19th century had particularly heavy consequences for Europe when it was coupled with one of the early
20th century movements of Resurgence of Authority.

Any excrescence of theoretical equipment on a political movement is a luxury, and the Europe of 1933–2000 can afford none
such. Europe has paid dearly for this Romantic concern with
old-fashioned racial theories, and they must be destroyed.

II

Race has two meanings, which will be taken in order, and
then their relative importance in an Age of Absolute Politics
will be shown. The first meaning is an objective one, the second
subjective.

The succession of human generations, related by blood, have
the clear tendency to remain fixed in a landscape. Nomadic
tribes wander within larger, but equally definite, bounds. Within this landscape the forms of plant and animal life have local
characteristics, different from transplantations of the same
strains and stocks in other landscapes.

The anthropological studies of the 19th centuries uncovered
a mathematically presentable fact which affords a good starting-
point to show the *influence of the soil*. It was discovered that
for any given inhabited area of the world there was an average

cephalic index of the population. More important, it was learned, through measurements on immigrants to America from every part of Europe, and then on their children born in America, that this cephalic index adheres to the soil, and immediately makes itself manifest in the new generation. Thus long-headed Jews from Sicily, and short-headed ones from Germany, produced offspring with the same average head measurement, the specifically American one. Bodily size and span of growth were two other characteristics in which all types whatever in America, Indians, Negroes, white men, were found to have the same average, regardless of average size and growth-span of the countries or stocks from which they came. In the case of immigrant Irish children, coming from a country of a very long growth-span, the response to the local influence was immediate.

From these and other facts, both comparatively new and of ancient observation, it is apparent that the landscape exerts an influence on the human stocks within its bounds as well as on the plant and animal life. The technic of this influence is beyond our ken. The source of it we do know. It is the cosmic unity of the totality of things, a unity which shows itself in the rhythmic and cyclic movement of Nature. Man does not stand out of this unity, but is submerged in it. His duality of human soul and Beast-of-prey is also a unity. We separate him thus to understand him, but this cannot disturb his unity. Nor by separating in our thoughts the aspects of Nature can we destroy its unity. The moon cycle stands in a relationship to many human phenomena, of which we can know only *what,* but never *how.* All movement whatever in Nature is rhythmic—the movement of streams and waves, of winds and currents, of appearance and disappearance of living individuals, of species, of Life itself.

Man partakes of these rhythms. His particular structure gives
these rhythms their peculiarly *human* form. The side of his
nature that expresses this connection is *Race*. *Race in a man is
the plane of his being which stands in relationship to plant and
animal life, and beyond them, to the great macrocosmic
rhythms.* It is, so to speak, the part of Man that is generalized
into, absorbed into the All, rather than his soul, which defines
his species, and sets him off from all other forms of existence.

Life manifests itself in the four forms: Plant, Animal, Man,
High Culture. Distinct though each is, yet it is related to all the
others. The animals, subject as they are to the soil, retain thus in
their being a plane of plantlike existence. Race is the expression
of the plant-like and also of the animal-like in Man. The High
Culture, by being fixed for its duration to a landscape, retains
also a connection with the plant world, no matter how defiant
and free-moving are its proud creations. Its high politics and
great wars are an expression of the animal and human in its
nature.

Some of the totality of human characteristics are soil-determined, others are stock-determined. Pigmentation is one of the
latter, and survives transplantation to other areas. It is not possible to list all of even the physical characteristics according to
such a scheme, for the data has not been gathered. But even so,
it would not matter to our purpose, for the most important element also in the *objective* meaning of race is the spiritual.

Some stocks are undoubtedly more highly endowed than
others in certain spiritual directions. Spiritual qualities are as
diverse as physical qualities. Not only average height of body
varies, but also average height of soul. Not only skull-shape
and stature are soil-determined, but so must be some spiritual
properties. It is impossible to believe that a cosmic influence
which puts its mark on human bodies passes over the essence,

the soul. But so thoroughly mixed have all the stocks been, or so repeatedly skimmed by History, that we can never know original soul-qualities of landscapes. Of the racial qualities of a given population on the spiritual side, we can never know which are soil-bound, and which have been produced by the amalgamation of stocks through the generations. To a practical century like this, and the next, origins and explanations are less important than facts and possibilities. Therefore our next concern must be with race as a practical reality rather than with its metaphysics.

To what race does a man belong? We know at first glance, but exactly what sign tells us this cannot be materially explained. It is accessible only to the feelings, the instincts, and does not yield itself to the scale and balance of physical science.

We have seen that race is connected with landscape and with stock. Its outer manifestation is a certain, typical expression, a play of features, a cast of countenance. There are no rigid physical indicia of this expression, but this does not affect its *existence*, but solely the method of understanding it. Within wide limits, a primitive population in a landscape has a similar look. But closer scrutiny will be able to find local refinements, and these again will branch down into tribes, clans, families, and finally individuals. *Race, in the objective sense, is the spirituo-biological community of a group.*

Thus races cannot be classified, other than arbitrarily. The materialistic 19th century produced several classifications of this arbitrary kind. The only characteristics used were, of course, purely material ones. Thus, skull-form, was the basis of one, hair and speech type of another, nose-shape and pigmentation of another. This was at best mere group anatomy, but did not approach race.

Human beings living in contact with one another influence

one another, and thus approach one another. This applies to individuals, where it has been noted through the ages in the fact that an old married couple come to resemble one another physically, and it applies to groups as well. What is called the "assimilation" of one group by another is not at all *merely* the result of commingling of germ-plasm, as materialism thought.

It is mostly the result of spiritual influence of the assimilating group on the newcomers, which is natural and complete when there are no strong barriers between the groups. The lack of barriers leads to the disappearance of the racial boundary and thereafter a new race is present, the amalgamation of the two previous ones. The stronger one is influenced usually but slightly, but there are various possibilities here, and an examination of them belongs properly to a subsequent place.

III

We have seen that race, objectively used, describes a relationship between a population and a landscape, and is essentially an expression of cosmic beat. Its prime visible manifestation is the *look,* but this invisible reality expresses itself in other ways. To the Chinese, for instance, smell is a hall-mark of race. Certainly audible things, speech, song, laughter, also have racial significance. Susceptibility to disease is another racially-differentiated phenomenon. The Japanese, Americans, and Negroes have three different degrees of resistance to tuberculosis. American medical statistics show that Jews have more nervous disease, more diabetes, and less tuberculosis than the Americans, and that in fact the incidence of any one disease shows a different figure for the Jews. Gesture, gait, dress, are not without racial significance.

But the *face* is the great *visible* sign of race. We do not know what it is that conveys race in the physiognomy, and attempts to reach it by statistics and measurements must fail. This fact has caused Liberals and other materialists to *deny that race exists*. This incredible doctrine came from America, which is veritably a large-scale racial laboratory. This doctrine really only amounts to a confession of total inability of Rationalism and scientific method to understand Race or subject it to order of the type of the physical sciences, and this inability was known before by those who have clung to facts and resisted anti-factual theories. Suppose that a man were to familiarize himself *thoroughly* with the measurements—length of nose, brows, chin, width of brow, jaws, mouth, etc.—of every face he knew until he could fairly well say from a new face what its measurements would be. If he were then given a set of measurements merely written down as such, does anyone think that even such a specially trained person could form any idea in his mind of the *racial expression* of the face from which the measurements were taken? Of course not, and the same is true of any other expression of race.

Another important objective aspect of race finds an analogy in the fashions of female physiognomy which come and go in a Late urban civilization. When a given female type is held up as an ideal, it is a fact that the kind of woman who is sensitive to this sort of thing very soon develops the facial expression of this type. In the domain of Race a similar phenomenon exists. Given a race with a certain, distinct cosmic beat, its members develop automatically an *instinct for racial beauty* which affects the choice of mates and also works on each individual soul from within, so that this double impetus forms the *racial type* pointing toward a certain ideal. This instinct for racial beauty, needless to say, has no connection with the decadent erotic-cults of the Hollywood type. Such ideals are purely individual-intellectual, and have no connection with Race. Race, being an expression of the cosmic, is informed throughout with the urge to continuity, and a racially ideal woman is always thought of, quite unconsciously, as the potential mother of strong sons. The racially ideal man is the master who will en- rich the life of the woman who secures him as the father of her children. The degenerate eroticism of the Hollywood type is anti-racial: its root-idea is not Life-continuity, but pleasure, with the woman as the object of pleasure, and the man as the slave of this object.

This striving of a race towards its own physical type is one of the great facts with which one cannot tamper by trying to substitute ideals of amalgamation with types totally alien, as Liberalism and Communism tried to do during the reign of Rationalism.

Race cannot be understood if it is inwardly associated with phenomena from other planes of life, such as nationality, politics, people, State, Culture. While History in its advance may bring about for a few centuries a strong relationship be- tween race and nation, that is not to say that a preceding racial type always forms a subsequent political unit. If that were so, none of the former nations of Europe would have been formed on the lines they were. For example, think of the racial differ- ences between Calabrian and Lombard. What did they matter to the history of Garibaldi's time?

This brings us to the most important phase of the objective meaning of Race in this age: *History narrows or widens the limits of race-determinacy.* The way this is done is through the *spiritual* element in Race. Thus a group with spiritual and his- torical community tends to acquire also a *racial* aspect. The community of which its higher nature partakes is transmitted downward to the lower, cosmic part of the human nature. Thus in Western history the early nobility tended to constitute itself as a race to complement its unity on the spiritual side. The extent to which this proceeded is still apparent wherever historical continuity of the early nobility has been maintained to the present day. An important example of this is the creation of the Jewish race that we now know in the millennium of ghetto-existence in Europe. Leaving to one side for the moment the different world-outlook and culture of the Jew, this sharing by a group, whatever the basis of its original formation as such, of a common fate for centuries will hammer it into a race as well as a spiritual-historical unit.

Race influences History by supplying its material, its treasures of blood, honor, and strong instincts. History in turn influences Race by giving to units of high history a racial stamp as well as their spiritual one. Race is a lower plane of existence, in the sense that it is closer to the cosmic, more in touch with the primitive yearnings and urges of *Life in general.* History is the higher plane of existence where the specifically human, and above that, the High Cultural, represent the differentiation of *forms of Life.*

The method of *racialization* of an historical unit, as the Western nobilities were racialized, is through the inevitable cosmic rising in such a group of an ideal physical type, and the instinct for racial beauty, which work together through the germ-plasm and inwardly in each soul to give this group its own *look,* that individualizes it in the stream of history. Once this community of fate departs, through the vicissitudes of History, this race vanishes also, never to appear again.

IV

From this point the fundamental misunderstanding of the 19th century materialistic interpretation of race appears clear and distinct:

Race is *not* group anatomy;

Race is *not* independent of the soil;

Race is *not* independent of Spirit and History;

Races are *not* classifiable, except on an arbitrary basis;

Race is *not* a rigid, permanent, collective characterization of human beings, which remains always the same throughout history.

The 20th century outlook, based on facts, and not on the preconceptions of physics and mechanics, sees Race as *fluid,* gliding with History over the fixed skeletal form determined by the soil. Just as History comes and goes, so does Race with it, bound in a symbiosis of happening. The peasants now tilling the soil near Persepolis are of the same race as those who planted or roamed there a thousand years before Darius, regardless of what they were called then, or what they are called now, and in the time between, a High Culture fulfilled itself in this area, creating races now gone for ever.

This last error—the confusing of names with unities of history or race—was one of the most destructive made by 19th century materialism. Names belong to the *surface* of history, not to its rhythmic, cosmic side. If the present-day inhabitants of Greece have the same collective *name* that the population of the same area had in Aristotle's time, is anyone deceived into thinking that there is historical continuity? Or racial continuity? Names, like languages, have their own destinies and these destinies are independent of others. Thus from the common language, it should not be inferred that the inhabitants of Haiti and those of Quebec have a common origin, but this result would occur of necessity if 19th century methods were applied to the present, which we know, as well as to interpretation of the past from left-over names and languages. The inhabitants of Yucatan to-day are racially the same as in 100 A.D., even though they now speak Spanish, and then spoke a now-vanished tongue, even though they have a different name now from then. In between occurred the rise, fulfillment and wiping out of a High Culture, but after its passing, Race became once more the primeval, simple relationship between stock and landscape. There was no high History to influence it, or for it to influence.

In the time of the Egyptian Culture, a people called the Libyans gave their name to an area. Does that mean that whoever inhabits this are from then on related to them? The Prussians in the year 1000 A.D. were an extra-European people. In 1700 the name Prussia described a nation in the Western style. Western conquerors merely acquired the name of the tribes they displaced. That which went under the various names of Ostrogoths, Visigoths, Jutes, Varangians, Saxons, Vandals, Norsemen, Danes, came from the same racial material, but the names do not show it. Sometimes a group gives its name to an area, so that after it is displaced, the old name passes to the conquering group; this was the case of Prussia and Britain. Sometimes a group takes its name from an area, like the Americans.

As far as the Race-History symbiosis is concerned, *names are accidental.* They do not indicate any sort of inward continuity by themselves. The same is true of language.

Once the idea is grasped that what we call history really means High History, that this is the history of High Cultures, and that these High Cultures are organic unities expressing their inner possibilities in the profuse forms of thought and happening which lie before us, a deep understanding follows of the way in which History uses whatever human material lies to hand for its fulfillment. It puts its impress on this material by creating *historical units* out of groups hitherto often very

diverse biologically. The historical unity, in harmony with
cosmic rhythms governing all Life from plant to Culture,
acquires its own racial unity, a *new* racial unity, removed, by its
spirituo-historical content from the former, primitive, simple
relationship between stock and soil. But with the departure of
High History the fulfillment of the Culture, the spiritual-historical content recedes forever, and the primitive harmony resumes its dominant position.

The previous, biological, history of the groups taken by a
High Culture play no role in this process. Previous names of
indigenous tribes, previous wanderings, linguistic equipment—
none have any meaning for high History, once it sets upon its
course. It starts, so to speak, from a clean slate. But it remains
this way also, in its ability to take in whatever elements enter
into its spirit. New elements, however, can bring nothing to the
Culture—it is a higher *individuality,* and thus has its own unity,
which cannot even be influenced, other than superficially, by an
organism of equivalent rank, and *a fortiori* cannot be changed
in the slightest in its inner nature by any human group. Thus
any group coming within the area of a Culture is either within
the spirit of the Culture, or without it—there is no third
alternative.

Organic alternatives are always only two: Life or Death,
sickness or health, forward development or distortion. When
the organism is put off its true path by external influences, crisis
is bound to follow, crisis which will affect the entire life of the
Culture, and will often involve the destiny of millions in confusion and catastrophe. But this is an anticipation.

The objective meaning of race has other aspects important
to a 20th century outlook. It has been seen that races—meaning here primitive groupings, simple relationships between soil
and human stock—have different gifts for historical purposes.

We have seen that Race influences History as well as the converse. We come to *the hierarchy of races.*

V

'The materialists could, of course, not succeed with all their attempts to make an anatomical classification of races. But races can be classified according to *functional* abilities, starting from any given function whatever. Thus a hierarchy of races can be based on physical strength, and there is little doubt that the Negro would stand at the top of such a hierarchy. There would however be no point in such a hierarchy, because physical strength is not the essence of human nature in general, and even less of Culture-man in particular.

The fundamental impulse of *human* nature—above the instincts toward self-preservation and sex, which man shares with other Life-forms—is the will-to-power. Very seldom is there any struggle for *existence* among men. Such struggles as do occur are nearly always for control, for power. These take place within couples and families, clans, *tribes,* and among peoples, nations, States. Therefore *the basing of* a hierarchy of races on strength of will-to-power has a relation to historical realities.

Such a hierarchy can have, of course, no eternal validity. Thus the school of Gobineau, Chamberlain, Osborn and Grant was on the same tangent as the materialists who announced that there is no such thing as Race, because they could not discover it with their methods. The mistake of the former was to assume the permanence—backwards and forwards—of races existing in their time. They were treating races as building-blocks, original material, and ignoring the connections of Race and History, Race and Spirit, Race and Destiny. But at least they recognized the existing racial realities of their time, their sole mistake consisting in regarding these realities as *rigid, existing* rather than *becoming*. There was also in their approach a remnant of genealogical thinking, but this sort of thinking is intellectual and not historical, for History uses the human material at hand without questioning its antecedents, and in the process of using it, this human material is placed in relation to the vast, mystical force of Destiny. This remainder of genealogical thinking tended to create divisions in thought between Culture-peoples corresponding to no divisions in actuality. The further materialistic tendency developed to extend the principles of heredity which Mendel had worked out for certain plants to the subject of human Race. Such a tendency was doomed to be fruitless, and after almost a century of barren results, it must be abandoned in favor of the 20th century outlook which approaches History and its materials in the historical spirit and not in the scientific spirit of mechanics or geology.

Nevertheless the school of Gobineau at least started from a *fact,* and this brings it much closer to *Reality* than the learned fools who looked up from their rulers and charts to announce the demise of Race.

This fact was the hierarchy of races for Cultural purposes. In their day the word "culture" was used to designate literature and the fine arts as distinct from the ugly, brutal things like economics, technics, war and politics. Hence the center of gravity of these theories was on the side of intellect rather than on the side of the soul. With the coming of the 20th century outlook, and the clearing from the air of all Materialistic-Romantic theories, the unity of Culture was perceived through all its various manifestations of arts, philosophy, religion, science, technics, politics, State-forms, race-forms, War. Therefore the hiearchy of races in this century is one based on degree of will-to-power.

This classification of races is also arbitrary, from the intellectual standpoint, just as much as one based on physical strength. It is, however, the only one suitable for us in this age.

Nor is it rigid, for the vicissitudes of History are more important in this realm than heredity-transmitted qualities. There is to-day no Hindu *race,* although there once was. This *name* is a product of accomplished history, and corresponds to no racial group. Nor is there a Basque race, a Breton race, a Hessian race, an Andalusian race, Bavarian race, Austrian race. Similarly, races existing to-day in our Western Civilization will also disappear with the advance of history over them.

The source of a hierarchy of races is History, the forces of happening. Thus when we see a European population, with its own racial stamp, the English, hold down a population of hundreds of millions of Asiatics for two centuries with only a handful of its own troops, as the English did India, we call that race one with a high degree of will-to-power. During the 19th century, amid 300,000,000 Asiatics, England had a tiny garrison of 65,000 white troops.

The mere numbers would mislead if we did not know that England was a nation in the service of a High Culture and India a mere landscape with primitive millions teeming in it, a landscape that had been also at one time the area of a High Culture such as our own, but had long since returned to its pre-Cultural primitivity within the ruins and monuments of the past. Knowing this, we know thereby that the source of this stern will-to-power is at least partially in the force of the Destiny of the Culture of which England was an expression.

When we see a race like the Spanish send forth two bands like those of Cortez and Pizarro, and read of their accomplishments, we know we are in the presence of a race with high will-power. With a hundred-odd men, Pizzaro set out to overcome an empire of millions. The project of Cortez was of a like boldness—and *both achieved military success.* It is not a slave race that can do such things. Aztec and Inca were no raceless populations, but were themselves the vehicle of another High Culture, a fact which makes these exploits almost incredible.

The French race in the time of the Revolutionary and Napoleonic Wars was in the service of a Cultural idea, the mission of changing the whole direction from Culture to Civilization, of opening the Age of Rationalism. The enormous force which this living idea lent to the armies of France is shown by the 20-year succession of military victories over all the armies that repeated coalitions of all Europe could throw against them. Under Napoleon's personal command, they achieved victory in more than 145 out of 150 engagements. A race equal to such a test was one of high will-power.

In each of these cases, the race was one created by History. In such a unit, the word *race* contains the two elements: the stock-landscape relationship, and the spiritual community of history and Cultural idea. They are, so to speak, *stratified:* beneath is the strong, primitive beat of the cosmic rhythm in a particular stock; above is the molding, creating, driving Destiny of a High Culture.

When Charles of Anjou beheaded Conradin, the last Hohenstaufen Emperor, in 1267, Germany disappeared from Western history, as a unit with political significance, for 500 years, reappearing in the 18th century in the double form of Austria and Prussia. During these centuries, the high history of Europe was made by other powers mostly with their own blood. This meant that—in comparison with the vast expenditure of blood over the generations of the others—Germany was *spared.*

To understand the significance of this fact, we must go back to the purely biological origin of races of Europe.

VI

The primeval population-streams which came out of the North of the Eurasiatic land-mass from 2000 B.C. right down to 1000 A.D.—and after—were probably of related stock. Barbarians called Cassites conquered the remains of the Babylonian Culture, about 1700 B.C. The next century Northern barbarians called Hyksos by the Egyptians threw themselves at the ruins of the Egyptian Civilization and subjected it to their rule. In India, the Aryans, also a Northern barbarian horde conquered the Indian Culture. The populations which appeared in Europe over the millennium and a half ending 1000 A.D. under the various names, Franks, Angles, Goths, Saxons, Celts, Visgoths, Ostrogoths, Lombards, Belgae, Norsemen, Northmen, Vikings, Danes, Varangians, Germani, Alemani, Teutones—and other names—are all of similar stock. It is very probable that the conquerors of the older Civilizations eastward were of similar stock with the Western barbarians who threatened Rome for centuries and finally sacked it. The great sign of this stock was blondness. Wherever to-day blonde traits are found, elements of this Northern stock have at some past time found their way. These Northern barbarians conquered the indigenous populations of all Europe, constituting themselves an upper stratum, supplying the leadership, fighting-men, and laws, wherever they went. Thus they represented the ruling-stratum in the territories now known as Spain, Italy, France, Germany, England. Their numerical proportion was greater in some places than in others, and with the arising of the Western Culture, c. 1000 A.D., it was on this strong-willed primitive stratum that the idea took hold. From having been the conqueror of fulfilled Civilizations, this stock now was itself selected to fulfill the Destiny of a High Culture.

That which distinguished this primitive biological population-stream is its *strong will*. It is also this strong will—and not only the inner Idea of the Culture itself—that contributes to Western history the unique forcefulness of its manifestations in all directions of thought and action. Think of the Vikings, in the gray dawn of our history reaching America from Europe in their tiny ships! This is the sort of human material which contributed its blood to the Western races, peoples and nations. It is to this treasure of being that the West owes its prowess on the battlefield—and this *fact* is known all over the world, whether it is theoretically denied, or not. Ask any general in any army whether he would rather have under his command a division of soldiers recruited from Pomerania, or a division of Negroes.

Unhappily for the West, the Russian populations contain also a strong strain of this Northern barbarian stock. It is not in the service of a High Culture, but stands to us as did the Gauls to Republican and Imperial Rome. *Race is material for events,* and it is available to the will-to-annihilate as freely as it is to the will-to-create. The Northern barbarian stock in Russia is still barbarian, and its negative mission has given it its own racial stamp. History has created a Russian race, which is steadily widening its racial boundaries by taking up into it and impressing with its historical mission of destruction the population-streams of its vast territory.

In the hierarchy of races based on will-to-power, the new Russian race stands high. This race needs no moralistic propaganda to fan its militancy. Its barbarian instincts are *there,* and can be relied on by its leaders.

Because of the fluid nature of Race, even the hierarchy of races based on will-to-power cannot succeed in ordering all races now existing. For instance, would the Sikhs stand above the Senghalese, or below, the American Negroes above or below the Aymara Indians? But the whole purpose of understanding the varying degrees of will-to-power in different races is a *practical* one, and applies in the first instance to our own Western Civilization. Can this knowledge be *used*? The answer is that not only it *can*, but it *must* be, if the West is to live out its life span and not to pass into slavery to Asiatic annihilation-hordes under the leadership of Russia, Japan, or some other militant race.

Before this information can be applied with full insight and with no danger of old-fashioned misunderstanding, the subjective meaning of Race must be examined, and beyond it the ideas connoted by the terms *People, Nation* and *State*.

Subjective Meaning of Race

RACE, as has been shown, is not a *unit* of existence, but is an *aspect* of existence. Specifically it is the aspect of existence in which the relation of the human being to the great cosmic rhythms is revealed. It is thus the non-individual aspect of Life, whether it be the life of a plant, animal, or human being.

The plant exhibits—at least, not to us—no consciousness, i.e., no *tension* with its environment. The plant has thus only race, so to speak, for it is totally submerged in the cosmic flow. The animal exhibits tension, consciousness, individuality. Man has in addition self-consciousness and the ability and necessity of living a higher life in the realm of symbols. All men have this, but the difference in degree between primitive man and Culture-man in this respect is so vast that it seems almost a difference in kind.

It is the racial beat which informs primitive impulses, which informs *action* generally. Opposed to it is the illuminated part of the mind, the rootless reason, the intellect. The stronger these things are in relation to the racial plane, the more the existence bears an intellectual instead of a racial stamp.

Each individual, as well as each higher organic unit, has these two aspects. Race impels toward self-preservation, continuance of the cycle of generations, increase of power. Intellect decides the meaning of the Life, and the aim, and this may, for various reasons, deny one or all of these fundamental urges. The celibacy of the priest and the sterility of the libertine both come from intellect, but one of them is an expression of High Culture, and the other is the denial of Culture, an expression of total degeneracy. Intellect may thus be in the service of Culture, or opposed to it.

Race is, in the first instance—in its subjective sense—what a man *feels*. This influences, whether immediately or eventually, what he *does*. A man of race is not born to slavery. If his intellect counsel him to a temporary submission, rather than an heroic death, in the hope of future changes, it is a mere postponement of his breaking out. The man without race will submit permanently to any humiliation, any insult, any dishonor, so long as he is permitted to *live*. The continuance of breathing and digestion are Life to the man without race. To the man of race, Life itself represents no value, but only Life under the right conditions, affirmative Life, rich, expressive and growing.

Heroism can be motivated from either side of the soul: the martyr dies for the Truth which he *knows,* the fighting man who dies with weapons in his hands rather than submit to his enemies dies for the honor that he *feels.* But the man who dies for something higher shows that he has race, regardless of his intellectualized motives. For Race is the faculty of being true to one's self. It is the placing of a beyond-value on one's own individual soul.

In this subjective sense, Race is not the way one talks, looks, gestures, walks, it is not a matter of stock, color, anatomy, skeletal structure, or anything else objective. Men of Race are scattered through all populations everywhere, through all races, peoples, nations. In each unit they make up the warriors, the leaders of action, the creators in the sphere of politics and war.

Thus in the subjective sense, there is also a hierarchy of race. *Above* the men of race, *below*—those without race. The first are swept up into action and events by the great cosmic rhythm of motion, the second are passed over by History. The first are the materials of high History, the second have outlasted every Culture, and when the stillness resumes its sway over the landscape after the whirlwind of events, these are the great mass. The Chinese mothers counsel their children with the ancient admonition: "Make thy heart small." This is the wisdom of the man without race, and of the race without will. The men of race are skimmed off every population that is caught up into the course of motion of a High Culture, and this process continues through the generations of History on the heights. What is left is the fellaheen.

Race in the subjective sense is thus seen to be a matter of *instinct*. The man with strong instincts has race, the man with weak or bad instincts has it not. Strength of intellect has nothing to do with the *existence* of race—it may merely, in some cases, such as that of the man who takes a vow of celibacy— influence the *expression* of a part of race. Strong intellect and strong instincts can co-exist—think of the Gothic bishops who led their flocks to war—they are merely opposed directions of thought and action, but it is the instincts that furnish the driving force for great intellectual accomplishments also. *The center of gravity of ascendant Life is on the side of instinct, will, race, blood.* Life which places rationalistic ideals of "individualism," "happiness," "freedom" before the perpetuation and increase of power is *decadent*. Decadent means—moving toward extinction, extinction of higher Life in particular, and finally even of the life of the race. The intellectual of the great city is the type of the man without race. In every Civilization, he has been the inner ally of the outer barbarian.

This quality of having race has, obviously, no connection with which race one feels community. Race in the objective sense is a creation of history. One's destiny must express itself within a certain framework—the framework of Fate. Thus a man of race born in Kirghizia belongs by Fate to the barbarian world of Asia with its historical mission of destruction of the Western Civilization. Rare exceptions are of course possible— Life submits to no generalization entirely. Some Poles, Ukrainians, or even Russians, might be impelled by their souls to share the spirit of the West. If so, they belong to the Western race, and every healthy, ascendant race accepts recruits who come in on its terms and who have the proper feeling. In the same way, there are numerous intellectuals in the West who feel community with the outer idea of Asiatic Nihilism. How numerous they are is indicated by the journalism, novels and plays that live from them. But the converse would not be true of men without race—they are not even acceptable to the enemy. They have nothing to contribute to an organic group—they are the human grains of sand, atoms of intellect, without cohesion upwards or downwards.

Every race, no matter how transitory it may be contemplated from the viewpoint of History, expresses a certain idea, a certain plane of existence by its life, and its idea is bound to be attractive to some individuals outside it. Thus in Western life, we are not unfamiliar with the man who, after associating with Jews, reading their literature, and adopting their viewpoint, actually becomes a Jew in the fullest sense of the word. It is not necessary that he have "Jewish blood." The converse is also known: many Jews have adopted Western feelings and rhythms, and have thereby acquired Western race. This process —contemptuously called "assimilation" by the Jewish leaders —threatened during the 19th century the very existence of the Jewish race by ultimate absorption of its total racial body into the Western races. To halt it, the leaders of the Jews evolved the program of Zionism, *which was solely an expedient for maintaining the unity of the Jewish race,* and maintaining its continued existence *as such.* For this reason they also recognized the value of anti-semitism of the social type. It was serving the same purpose of preserving the racial unity of the Jews.

II

The dying out of racial instincts means the same thing to an individual as it does to a race, people, nation, State, Culture: unfruitfulness, lack of will-to-power, lack of ability to believe in or follow great aims, lack of inner discipline, desire for a life of ease and pleasure.

The symptoms of this racial decadence in various parts of the Western Civilization are manifold. There is first the ghastly distortion of the sexual life arising from the complete dissociation of sexual love from reproduction. The great symbol of this in the Western Civilization is everything suggested by the name Hollywood. The message of Hollywood is the *total* significance of sexual love as an end in itself—the erotic without consequences. The sexual love of two grains of sand, two rootless individuals, not the primeval sexual love looking to the continuity of Life, the family of many children. One child is permitted, as being a more complicated toy than a dog, perhaps even two, one boy and one girl—but the family of many children is a subject for humor to this decadent outlook.

The instinct of decadence takes many forms in this realm: dissolution of Marriage by divorce laws, attempts to discard, through repeal or non-enforcement, the laws against abortion, preaching in the form of novel, drama, journalism, the identification of "happiness" with sexual love, holding it up as *the* great value, before which all honor, duty, patriotism, consecration of Life to a higher aim, must give way. An erotomania is abroad through our civilization, not indeed like the sexual obsession of the 13th century which was at least racially affirmative, in that it increased the Western Peoples, but always a purely rootless erotic-without-consequences. This spiritual disease is the suicide of the race.

The weakening of the will—Nietzsche called it "paralysis of will"—another symptom of dying out of racial instincts, leads to a total deterioration of public life in the afflicted races. Government leaders dare not offer a stern program to their masses of human grains of sand: they abdicate, but remain in office as private men. Government ceases; the only functions that continue are the ones that have always gone on, no new aim, no sacrifices. Keep the old going; no creation! No effort! That would be too hard. Keep the pleasures going, *the panem et circenses*. Never mind the necessities of life, we are willing to renounce them as long as we have the pleasures.

This weakening of the will leads to voluntary abandonment of empires conquered with the blood of millions over ten generations. It leads to abysmal hatred of whoever and whatever represents sternness, creation, the Future. One of its products is Pacifism, and the only way a racially-dissolving population can be driven to war is through conscription coupled with pacifist propaganda—"This is the last war—actually it is a war against war." Only an intellectual could be taken in by such stark Unreality. The weak will of society manifests itself in the Bolshevism of the upper classes, the sympathy with the enemies of society. Anyone with unimpaired will however is really felt to be the enemy—even cogent reasoning is hated: ideals are so much less demanding.

Mediocrity rises over the horizon of a dying race as its last great ideal, total mediocrity, renunciation of all greatness and distinction of any kind whatever; also mediocrity of the racial blood-stream—anyone can come in now, not only on our terms, for there are no more terms, and there are no racial differences, everything is one, dull, eventless, *mediocre.*

The weakening of the will is not hard put to find an ideology which rationalizes it as "progress," everything desirable, the aim of all previous history. The democracy-liberalism complex lies to hand, and it acquires in such times the meaning of *Death*—of race, nation and Culture. There are no human differences, everyone is equal, men are women, women are men, "the individual" is everything, Life is a long holiday whose main problem is devising new and more stupid pleasures, there is no God, no State, off with the head of anyone who says there is a mission, who wishes to resurrect Authority.

These symptoms, or similar ones, will be found present at the demise of every upper stratum whose will is weakened. Thus Tocqueville has described for us how the French upper stratum of 1789 had no suspicion whatever of the impending Revolution, how nobility waxed enthusiastic over the "natural goodness of Humanity," the "virtuous people," the "innocence of Man" while the Terror of 1793 lay before their very feet— *spectacle terrible et ridicule.* Did not the Petrine nobility of Russia up until 1917 go through the same performance? The Tsar resisted pleas to leave while there was time with "My people will not hurt me." Their picture of the Russian peasant was that of a happy, simple muzhik, basically good. Similarly the weakening of the Western will in certain countries was shown by the deluge of pro-Russian propaganda spread, sometimes with official encouragement, in those countries from 1920 to 1960.

Horizontal Race v. Vertical Race

WE ATTAIN NOW to the grand formula of the 20th century outlook on Race: *Race is a horizontal differentiation of men.* The materialism of the 19th century, confusing race with anatomy, regarded Race as a vertical differentiation of men. It was "abstract"—away from Reality—and started from the will-to-systematize, rather than from quiet contemplation of the living facts. Such contemplation was made difficult for them by the existence of political nationalism, which tried to build walls of all kinds between the Western races and peoples.

But had they been able to pierce through to a view of the facts, these materialists would have seen that the races of Europe were the creations of History and not a mere continuation of the aboriginal material that was present in 900 A.D., before the beginning of high History in this area. Viewing the process of creation of races, they would have seen the far greater significance of Race in the subjective sense than in the objective sense. For it is always men of race that create the deeds of History, and the units they are leading are of secondary importance.

The attempt to create a vertical system of races was *Apollonian*—it was an effort of the intellect. Actually Race has the primary meaning of presence of strong cosmic rhythm—a *Dionysian* meaning.

The 20th century viewpoint in this matter starts from facts, and the observed fact is that all strong minorities—both within and without a High Culture—have welcomed into their company the outsider who was attracted to it and wished to join it, regardless of his racial provenance, objectively speaking. The racial snobbery of the 19th century was *intellectual,* and its adoption in a too-narrow sphere by the Resurgence of Authority in Europe between the first two World Wars was a grotesquerie.

What matters to a unit engaged upon a mission is the *strength of will* which other groups can bring to it. To interpret the historical mission as one of "safe-guarding the purity of the race," in a purely biological sense is sheer materialism. Race, in both its meanings, is the material of History, not the reverse. Race supplies the fruitfulness, sureness, and will-to-power to the Mission. The Mission can never be to make the race "pure" in a biological sense, however satisfying such a result would be *esthetically.* And with this last word is touched upon the other factor in the tragic connection of this old-fashioned outlook on Race with the strong, vital movement of Resurgence of Authority: We have seen that all the 19th century concepts in this sphere—Race, People, Nation, State, Culture—were of Rationalistic-*Romantic* derivation. Romantic—half of this misalliance of the Future and the Past is traceable to romantic-esthetic notions. Esthetics is however a domain of its own, and does not have sufficient vitality to supply the motivation of a political struggle. Its presence there can only be superfluous.

The stark *historical* value in this matter is simply this: It only matters that the Cultural Mission be accomplished, even though in the process everything else is wiped out. And after that? Did Darius ever think that lions would one day be roaming his terrace of Persepolis? And if he had, what could he have done about it? History, with its great rythms—the widest and deepest we know—is also submerged in the Cosmos, and for Culture-man to think that he can impose his will on the millennially remote future is only a tribute to his pride of intellect, but no compliment to his wisdom. We are thinking here in centuries, not in months or years. One must oppose the attitude of *après moi la deluge* which prevails at this moment. It is not a shirking or evading of duty to say that only the historical Mission matters, but the highest possible affirmation of Duty.

To Race there is no duty. Race in the vertical sense is an abstraction, corresponding to nothing existing. If taken seriously, it leads the victim off the path of History and into an esthetic *cul-de-sac*.

To the 20th century outlook, a man does not *belong* to a race —he either *has* race, or does not. If the former, he has value to History, if the latter, he is valueless, a lackey.

The attempt to interpret History in terms of Race must be abandoned. The 20th century sees it quite otherwise. That attempt was a fad, historically speaking. It had a vogue of a century. It is now quite dead. Its last formulation, and its most radical, attempted even to intervene in the sphere of action. That was the last such attempt. An Empire of a thousand years duration—yes, that has been actualized—in India, China, Egypt. But the last nations that laid the foundations of these Empires could not know whether the barbarians would come soon or never. Montezuma's Empire would also have lasted a thousand years—but the Spaniards appeared. There is no guarantee of duration, racial or other. Actually it is Race that must be interpreted in terms of History, for that is the factual developmental-sequence. This viewpoint is not a fad, an arbitrary abstract picture, but one reflecting the facts of history.

Race and Policy

Both MEANINGS of Race, the objective and the subjective, have a meaning for policy in the 20th century.

The objective meaning of Race describes a group which shares a certain basic, instinctive rhythm. This racial stamp has been given to it by History, which narrows or widens the limits of this Race, depending on the character and magnitude of the historical Mission.

Such a race is the creation of *History,* and not of a text-book scheme first planned on paper and then put into actuality. It is not a creation of a man, as such—although a man may by his personality be the vehicle of History, and may be the focus of historical energy on to the creation of a race. But important is: as far as policy is concerned, one can only work with the races *existing.* They cannot be created or disposed of by human fiat.

Existing races are a *mixture,* as far as *stock* is concerned. There is nothing to be done about this. Such a mixture of stock is not "impurity," in any true, factual, meaning of that word. "Purity" in racial matters means inclusiveness of the entire population within the same historical feeling and cosmic beat. "Purity" is directed to *feeling,* and not to anatomical derivation. This is true even in the most objective meaning of the word Race, and *a fortiori* is it true of Race in the subjective sense.

The hierarchy of races is a *fact* of which policy must take cognizance. The strength of will of the Russian race is an ominous fact which cannot be explained away by intellectualizing. This strength is reflected in physical stamina which enables the Russian soldier to recover from wounds which would be fatal to a Western soldier. The will-to-power diffused through the Japanese race places it high in the hierarchy of races. The force this gives to the body of a nation is shown by the physical performance of Japanese infantry, matched by only one of the Western races still existing. The two general physical types which make up the body of the Japanese race show perfectly the fact that purity means prevalence everywhere of the same *feeling,* cosmic rhythm, and not of the same physical structure, pigmentation, or shape of head, for spiritually these two physical types are both *Japanese.*

The lower degree of will-to-power of the populations in the areas called China, India, and Africa generally is also a fact for policy to apply. This is, of course, no attempt to contradict that some tribes in these areas have strong will-to-power, but only a general observation of these large areas. Anything that is a *fact* is material for policy, no matter how general, or how specific, so long as it relates to action.

Important as these general facts as to the hierarchial ordering of extra-European races are, Race has a vastly more important aspect for policy, and that is *the strength of our own race.*

Race is the material of History, it is the treasure which a

population brings to an Idea. The stronger the racial instincts of the population, the greater its promise of victory. Consequently anything which strikes at the strength of these instincts is the enemy of the highest significance, and even of the very existence, of the race. These instincts are self-preservation, fruitfulness, increase of power. Without these there is no Idea, no History—there is only the collection of human grains of sand—and later a pyramid of skulls erected by outer barbarians.

Thus the whole liberal-democratic ideology, with its "individualism" that is a mere negation of everything superpersonal, its "happiness" ideal that encourages every weakness and self-indulgence, its erotomania which distorts the whole sexual life into a barren disease of the will, its "tolerance" which seeks to break down the cohesion of the race by denying its existence, its materialism which denies all spiritual values, all higher significance of human life, its pacifism which values weakness above virility, its ideal of Mediocrity by which it opposes every creative man and the Idea he represents in History, its cult of the proletarian as the highest element, its total renunciation of the Soul of Man—this is the great enemy of Race.

Part of this degeneration is organic—more of it is deliberately spread abroad within our Civilization by alien distorting elements which either belong to, or sympathize with, Asia in the annihilation battle for Western survival that will take up this century and the next. It is quite obvious that anything that undermines the will-to-power and the virility of the West ripens it for Asiatic slaughter. It should be equally obvious that the world-outlook that is thus eating away at the Western soul must be ruthlessly eradicated wherever it lurks by whatever means necessary. Thus even if one may have clung to his little ideal of "freedom" or "happiness" during the 19th century—the century of security, of comfort, of money-making and money-spending—he must renounce it now in the century when the very foundations of the life of our Culture are under attack from below and without—an attack in each case that means to *destroy everything.* To retain such ideals is to become the *inner enemy* of the West.

Thus Western policy must declare this outlook and its adherents to be the inner enemy. It must supplant its superannuated ideology by the strong, manly one appropriate to this Age of Absolute Politics. It must root out its ideas, its leaders, its techniques. Any groups that are committed to this outlook by their inner constitution and spiritual existence must be proscribed.

Western policy has the duty of encouraging in its education of the youth its manifestations of strong character, self-discipline, honor, ambition, renunciation of weakness, striving after perfection, superiority, leadership—in a word—Race.

The man of race disciplines himself—because he *needs* discipline. Strong instincts need a strong will. Race is also a residue of inner chaos, for only out of chaos can come creation, whether of thought or deed. Strong instincts are the prerequisite of every outstanding performance even the creation of a work for the intellect. The raceless, rootless-intellectual attitude has no inner imperative—it shrugs its shoulders and says "So what?" Such an attitude is that of *finished* men—they are used up before they start. They can insist on nothing, compel nothing, perform nothing. A hundred men of race without particular intellectual qualifications can accomplish more under the same leader than a thousand intellectuals from the pavements of the great cities. A man of race is *not yet* finished—he offers material for performance.

An intellectual cannot be *inspired*—enthusiasm he regards, quite seriously, as pathological, as mania. He prefers to sit in his cocktail lounge or his sidewalk cafe, sipping his alcohol and preserving the degagé manner. The talk is of pathetic ideals of social and sexual atomism, of "new artistic tendencies," of "the subconscious," of "democracy"—but over it all is the perfume of decay. It is a world of boredom, a blasé degeneration, the casual bumpings and connections of grains of sand—in one word, *the sarcophagus of the race*. Baudelaire, with his preoccupation with corpses, is its perfect expression: the world of the intellectual is the putrescence of the superpersonal soul. Where this sort of material has influence, the barbarian has easy conquests.

Western policy must recognize these facts. Education policy, propaganda, public life, must form the race away from this charnel outlook. To keep away from all these forms of decadence is to safeguard the strength of the race. To allow them is to promote the death of the race.

II

We have seen the power of a race imbued with an historical idea to take up alien human material into it, and imbue it with its own rhythm. This phenomenon must be more closely examined.

We have seen this sort of thing throughout all history. Thus the Romans accepted into their racial body whoever was capable of Romanness, and wished to be able to say with the same inner pride as the dwellers on the Seven Hills—*Civis Romanus sum*. Up until 1933, America had thus taken up into its race many millions of immigrants from Europe and from the Balkans. The Russians have been thus increasing their numbers steadily through the past three centuries.

In each of these cases, the essence of the ingress of the alien into the proper racial body is his *total* absorption into the new idea, his *complete* adoption of the new plane of existence, his *total* loss of the old existence. With human beings, the word "total" refers to the *soul*. If his soul can assimilate, his body can. Thus Frenchmen settled in Brandenburg en masse during the 18th century. Thousands upon thousands of Germans have settled in France. Frenchmen settled in America in great numbers. So did Englishmen. Italians have moved to France in enormous numbers. The examples are almost endless. In each case, the newcomers disappeared as a group. As individuals, their blood-stream continued in the new landscape, but it now had a new cosmic beat. French Huguenots in Brandenburg became Prussians, in Ireland they became Irish. Spaniards in Ireland became Irish. English in America became Americans. Germans in France became Frenchmen, in Argentina, Argentines; in America, Americans. The newcomer in this process, as individual or as group can contribute nothing on the superpersonal level. His contribution is limited to his personal qualities of instinct or talent as individual, of healthy instincts as group. Cultural things he cannot contribute, because they cannot be received.

A unit itself under the impress of a High Culture cannot assimilate anything on the cultural level from a group under the impress of another High Culture.

This explains why the various European races were so easily assimilable one in the other, how they disappeared in a generation into the new pulse and feeling—*they shared the same Culture*. Although they belonged to separate races, nevertheless there was a higher stratum of Life that included all these races as manifestations of its superpersonal Life. Thus *these vertical divisions of mere race did not separate Western men*.

Nor did they separate non-Westerners from Westerners

when the incoming non-Westerners sought to preserve no barrier of their own: during the youth of our Culture, on the Eastern Marches of Europe, many thousands of Slavs were assimilated into the European races, disappeared into them and became completely European. Western policy of the future must remember facts of this kind.

Actually, this is no blending, no amalgamation; it is simply the increasing of the receiving race. They bring only their blood and numbers; they can bring no Idea, for it already is an Idea. Only a superficial view could attach importance to words, phrases, even vocabularies, or to quaint social customs that the receiving race may adopt from the newcomers in the process of assimilating them. These things are merely the traces by which one can trace the influx after the passage of generations. Thus some Irish family names are "de la" this or that, Spaniards "di," Frenchmen and Americans "von," Germans "de." It is no sign of any continuity other than that of the germ-plasm, this of foreign family names, after assimilation has occurred. In fact it is noticeable, and is part of old European wisdom that— in the beginning, at least—this new element has a higher racial potential than the absorbing race generally. Hence the old expressions: *Hibernis ipsis Hiberniores, päpstlicher als der Papst*. The man who comes from the periphery to the center of an Idea has an enthusiasm that the older members do not feel. What they take for granted is to him inspiring in its excellence. It is the zeal of the convert.

But there are cases where this assimilation does not occur. They are the cases where there is a cultural bar between the two populations. Either they are each under the impress of a Culture, or else one group is and the other is not, and is negative.

Thus, during the reign of Catherine the Great, and at her

invitation, thousands of German farmers and craftsmen came to Russia. Land on the Volga river was given to them, and there they remained until very recent history. By the 20th century, their numbers were about 350,000. But—during the generations of their residence in Russia, they had retained their orientation to Europe. Their Russian environment, culture-less and primitive, had been unable to deprive them in any way of their character as a fragment of a High Culture. The Bolshevik regime did what time never could have done: it exterminated them by starvation and dispersal through Asia. Other German colonies preserved their European Culture along the Baltic shores of Russia, and in the primitive Balkan area. The new Asiatic will to annihilate the West has now exterminated them all whether in Rumania, Serbia, Bohemia, Poland, Bulgaria.

The best-known example of this organic regularity, and the most Fate-laden for all concerned, was the contact between the group called Jews and the Western Culture. Until the discovery of the organic unity of a High Culture, and its inner articulation, no final understanding of what has come to be called "the Jewish problem" was possible. At this point, only the racial aspect of this problem is touched on, and it is only necessary to explain the origin of the Jewish race now existing.

The Jew is a product of another Culture. When the Western Culture arose, the Jews were distributed through a part of its area, mostly in Spain and Italy. The Arabian Culture, then in its very last stage, had created the Jews as a unity, and they were in the form of this expiring Culture. Hence the stirrings of the Western Idea could not touch them inwardly at all. They held themselves entirely aloof from anything Western. They had an entire world-outlook and world-feeling of their own, which needed no impulse from without, that could only resist any other Culture. This basic fact kept the Jew entirely separate from the West spiritually and racially—the West rejected his world-feeling, he rejected its. Mutual hatred and mutual persecution only strengthened the Jewish race, sharpened its cunning, and increased its resentment.

Thus we see that while mere race cannot prevent assimilation of new stock from outside, Cultural barriers will. Certain numbers must of course be present for an alien group to maintain its identity within the body of a culturally-alien host. A tiny group could not so preserve itself.

That there is nothing about the Jewish race physically that is unassimilable is shown by what happened in Spain. There late in the 15th century the monarch compelled them either to adopt Christianity or leave the country. Most Jews left, but the descendants of those who adopted Christianity and raised their children among Westerners disappeared into the Spanish race.

Another example of a Cultural barrier is the relation of Russia and the West. There it is the purely negative will to destroy Culture that has prevented assimilation of Russia by the West, despite the fact that Peter the Great and his dynasty after him tried by every means to Westernize Russia for three centuries. The outburst of 1918 was primarily an expression of the great fact of the failure of the Petrine effort—it had been only superficially successful and had not penetrated to the depths of this powerful negative soul. The *Western* Culture is the great barrier that also prevents racial assimilation either way in large numbers.

For this same reason, Chinese and Japanese, who have behind them and in their souls the Chinese Culture that was fulfilled by 1000 B.C., cannot be assimilated by Westerners racially in numbers. The converse is also true: if a colony of Westerners were planted in the middle of China, 1000 years hence it would be still Western surrounded by the totally alien Chinese. This is the explanation of the anti-Chinese and anti-Japanese laws and activity of the Americans from the middle of the 19th century to the present.

It is the numbers that create these racial questions. If a tiny group is involved, it will disappear; if a group of significant numbers is present, separated by a Cultural barrier from the surrounding population, it will not.

III

To think is to exaggerate; to separate a thing into elements is to give a picture that is bound to disturb the natural order of the relationships. And yet it is a necessity of thought and presentation to examine and set forth things serially. Thus constant precedence has been given to Culture as a barrier to assimilation of populations, because it is an immensely more important one, since it is race-creating. Cases exist, however, where race-difference in the physical sense is so vast that assimilation seems to be impossible. There are no such problems in Europe, but they occur in various Western colonies, such as America and South Africa.

Race in the subjective sense influences the choice of a mate. If racial instincts are strong, they prevent the taking of a mate belonging to a race of totally alien characteristics, even physically. Thus the Negro in general rejects the white race, and the white generally rejects the Negro. The Culture barrier is also present, for the Negro is below our Culture, even though he has lived within its area for centuries. It is those whose racial instincts are attenuated in both cases who accept the totally alien physically.

The case of America shows the limits of racial assimilability between populations totally alien physically. There the liberal-democratic-communist-ideology has openly sought by all possible means to promote a blending of these two races. The only result it has had is to arouse racial bitterness that finds expression in bloody riots which proceed to mass-killings on both sides.

The only reason the subject of the Negro is touched here— its political significance is treated with America—is that it seems to be the extreme case of race-difference preventing assimilation. How much of this is due to the primitivity of the Negro, and how much to his total physical difference, we do not know.

The touching of this racial-frontier case of the Negro however, shows to Europe a very important fact—*that race-difference between white men, which means Western men, is vanishingly small in view of their common mission of actualizing a High Culture.* In Europe, where hitherto the race difference between, say, Frenchman and Italian has been magnified to great dimensions, there has been no sufficient reminder of the race-differences outside the Western Civilization. Adequate instruction along this line would apparently have to take the form of occupation of all Europe, instead of only part of it, by Negroes from America and Africa, by Mongols and Turkestani from the Russian Empire.

We have reached now the last and deepest relationships between Race and Policy:

Policy is charged with actualizing an historical Mission, the saving of the Western Civilization from decadence within, and from the barbarian without.

Whether this is to succeed will depend on the strength of racial instinct left, by which is meant the instincts of self-preservation, fruitfulness, and will-to-power.

Any man who shares the feeling of this Mission, and any

group which shares it, belong to us in this greatest of all battles in 5,000 years of history, regardless of the derivation of the man or group.

Any group or idea which does not share this feeling, and wishes to further its own aims within the West is an inner enemy. Any group or idea which weakens in any way the racial strength of the West is an inner enemy.

Policy has the great double task of eradicating the inner enemy in order to salvage the racial instincts of the West, and of training this race into a sure and firm unit for a century of warfare.

The two great mistakes of materialism in the field of Race must be a cast into the dead past of Materialism: on the one hand the denial of Race, on the other hand the primacy of Race before Culture.

The aim of Policy is to actualize our Western Imperium— whoever introduces racial theories of materialistic provenance, whether in the name of "tolerance," which means we should abandon our instincts, or in the name of "racial purity," which means we should abandon our Cultural unity, is prolonging the crisis and division of the West.

One *result* of the coming warfare for the liberation of the West and the creation of the Empire of the West will be the creation—in the long and desperate fight—of a new race, the Western race, which will embrace the populations which made up the 19th century nations or England, Germany, France, Italy, Spain, Scandinavia.

Those populations of the West which have the least impaired racial bodies and racial instincts will respond most intensely to the demands of the coming century of warfare, and will play the largest formative role in this greatest of all struggles, but the new race will be a *unity*, not a collection of dead races, but a new and grander creation from the human streams now existing.

The races of 19th century Europe are, *as such,* dead. Policy starts from this. Provincial patriotism of the 19th century type can evoke no response. The unity of the West which the barbarian has always recognized is recognized at the last hour by the West itself.

The barbarian is astride the prostrate West. This is not the end, but the beginning of Western unity.

People

THE CREATION of a race by History is clear. It is an example of the biological following the spiritual. For this process to reach its highest potential a certain time is necessary—two or three generations are needed for the type of the racial ideal to fasten on to a population-stream and give it its own distinct outer look, corresponding to its inner unique superpersonal soul.

People is a word on a different plane of thinking from this. We are familiar with its polemical use by the democratic mob to deny existence to qualitative elements and assert pure and simple quantity as "the People." We seek, however, facts. What is a people? What is its articulation?

Two French thinkers contributed to the 19th century valuable insight into the nature of all human groups whatever. Gustave le Bon and René Worms both saw and set forth with Cartesian clarity the *organic* nature of human groups, the *superpersonal* unity which was the custodian of the Destiny of the group. Worms applied it upward—to the State. Le Bon applied it downwards—to the crowd. Their presentation was not entirely free of materialistic tendencies—"Truth belongs to the individual, Error belongs to the Age," said Goethe—but they gave to the West a glimpse along the path of History. Their contribution was ignored by the Age of Rationalism. The *pure* materialism of William Paley was preferred: a people is "only a collection of the citizens who compose it." Again: "The happiness of a people is made up of the happiness of single persons." This stupid anti-factual picture could not be refuted, for it was a *faith*. The picture reflected the Spirit of the Age, and could only pass away with the expiration of that spirit. It was a picture that sprang from a certain *soul*, and even though it denied the soul, yet it was tied to the existence of that one certain soul.

The new age is one of Resurgence of Authority, both spiritual and political. This Age bases its political formula on facts, on the actualizing of the possible. It does not dream up an ideal picture, and then try to change the vocabulary of the world-of-action. It does not wish to delude itself into thinking that changing words will transform fact. It wishes to orient itself to facts, and above all to the repository of facts, History, and the driving force of facts, Destiny.

To understand what a people is, one must begin with the smallest human group, the crowd. It strikes one immediately that there are two types of crowds. There is the crowd assembled on an intellectual basis—the attendance at a lecture, at a drama, at a social function. Then there is the crowd assembled on a spiritual basis—a political meeting, a religious agitation, a protest, a riot.

The first type is a mere collection. The individuals repel one another, figuratively and literally. These crowds have as many viewpoints as there are individuals in them. They are not unities, but only potential unities. The outbreak of fire in a theater immediately turns such a collection of independent individuals into *one* soul, with *one* thought, a thought directed downwards, it is true, but it is a *unity*. The *unity of panic* is a fact which political and military leaders must know how to exploit. It is one way of inspiriting when other methods may fail.

The second type is not a collection, but a *unity*. The first is unarticulated—all the human atoms are on the same level. The second is articulated—it has a *leader*. If there is no leader, there is no unity, and a few mounted police may disperse it. No individual will risk anything for a mere gathering, because his individuality is uppermost. The unity of the crowd submerges the personalities of the components; the unity is a *super-personal soul*. The unity must be on the basis of an *idea*, a wordless feeling strong enough to cause individuality to subside. When this idea is present, the human beings present become mere cells, as it were, of the higher organic unity. Men of strong intelligence who have been in crowds united for action have described how their own faculties were transformed and how the detachment that intelligence gives was suddenly in abeyance, overcome by a force as mystic in its power as in its origin.

This crowd is a *people*. It is a higher organism, it is informed by a superpersonal soul. The individuals will sacrifice themselves in the process of this higher soul actualizing itself, what they would never do alone.

The technique of this process is quite invisible, mystical, but its results are just as visible. Not only do crowds arise by themselves in conditions of great super-personal excitement when a leader appears, as Camille Desmoulins did to the gathering in the Palais Royal in 1789, *to activate the* mere *sum* into a *unity* —but they can be created. Thus, anyone so situated as to be able to bring a mass into one place can transform the mass into a unity by leadership.

As far as the individuals are concerned, the crowd is an attitude of mind. The man in a crowd would not dream of thinking for himself—the results of thinking are presented to him by the leader, and thenceforth these thoughts are his.

With this emerges a very important fact about crowd unity. It only reached expression with the results of the new propaganda technics of the First World War. It is this: Through constant, unremitting propaganda of all possible types, and with unbroken continuity, the unity of the crowd can be maintained even though the members are physically separated. Mass propaganda converts the population of a continent into a crowd. Individual thought occurs very rarely under such conditions. Constant bombardment with cinema, press and radio-wireless removes all individuality from the units of vast populations.

The crowd thus presents the articulation of leader-led. This is existential: without it there is no unity, with it any gathering becomes a unity. But the decisive part of the articulation is the leader, and not the led. All understanding is transferred to him. All decision is with him. This is totally independent of any theory or ideal in the name of which the crowd may be mobilized, even the theory of individualism. The crowd is a higher unity; the leader represents it.

Where a High Culture is present, any crowd whatever is affected by it, even though only negatively. By that is meant that even a protest against Culture, such as the Peasant's Wars, Jack Cade's rebellion, Marxian class-war, and the like, only gain their unity from their desire to annihilate Culture. Whether the crowd is in the service of Culture or not depends on the leadership. Crowds as masses are *neutral*. Leadership is decisive: creative leaders like Napoleon lead a crowd upward and forward; leaders of the negative and devious type, like Roosevelt, lead a crowd downward and backward.

The crowd is a soul-unit. Its significance and potentialities belong to its articulation, its leader. This is true both of street-crowds within the range of one eye and one voice, and also to crowds on a continental scale, like America.

The leader has a dual significance: he is part of the crowd, he must also be against the crowd. It has no individuality save his; if he also becomes lost in the crowd mind, there is no individuality present, no will, no brain. He is part of the super-personal unity as the brain is part of the body. The brain serves the soul, the body serves the brain.

This smallest superpersonal unit, the crowd, shows the *polarity of instinct and intellect* that extends up through all *ascendant* organisms to the highest, High Culture. Instinct is the content of the Life, Intellect is the technic of actualizing it. Instinct tells *what,* Intellect tells *how.* Instinct says: Preserve! Multiply! Increase power! Intellect seeks methods of preserving Life and increasing power. Intellect is charged with the mission of actualizing Life, of expressing the instinctive imperatives of Life.

They can only be understood in relation to one another. Their separation is distortion and illness. They increase together in healthy man. That is why the intellectuals in Late Civilizations exhibit such egregious stupidity—they have attenuated instincts, and *hence* no intellects. Instinct is the ship bound for a destination, intellect is the rudder that steers it; another figure: instinct is the passengers who are to be transported, intellect is the master of the vessel, who must deliver them.

Their relationship can be formulated from the negative side: Instinct furnishes the will-to-power, but must not decide the moment for attack. Instinct cannot decide on the policy by which Life is to actualize its inner imperative. It is blind—it always counsels attack. Thus General Hood threw away the

Army of Tennessee in the American War of Secession. Intellect
must decide between the posture of defense and the movement
of attack. Instinct may succumb to defeat, Intellect can still dis-
cern the elements of hope. Instinct sees everything else and
everyone else as enemy, Intellect coldly decides from the situation who is the enemy, and seeks to make all the others friends.
Instinct is subject to intoxication, the function of Intelligence is
to remain sober. Instinct loves and hates, Intellect, neither.

In Gothic times, the Empire and Papacy were formulated as
the two perfect bodies. Each was supposed to exhibit absolute
balance and harmony in its inner unity, as distinct from Man,
who is imperfect and contains the inner struggle of Instinct and
Intellect. In those times, the problem for the man of action
seeking to actualize a great idea was to keep instinct within its
bounds. Thus Henry the Lion acted instinctively in his defection
from Barbarossa and destroyed the Hohenstaufen Empire, from
which destruction the West has suffered ever since. In this time
of transition, the problem is the reverse: now it is intellect
which must be firmly held in place. In the pride of Rationalism,
Intellect announced that it was Life—all else was retrograde,
aberrant. The result of Western Intellect denying Western Instinct was the division of the World between Washington and
Moscow.

II

The crowd has been seen to be a *submerging* of individual
souls into a superpersonal soul. It is the creation of a *unity* out
of a *sum*. In the process intellect moves out of the components
and becomes vested in the articulation, the leader.

The street-crowd is the smallest *people*. A people is a unity
for action. Whenever, in its great rhythmic swirls, History pulls

a group into its vortex, the group immediately articulates itself as a people, or disappears. The group may be religious in origin, economic in origin, cultural in origin. But when it becomes an object of happening, it must respond by constituting itself as a people, or simply vanish from the pages of history. Peoples may be tiny, or they may be vast. The population living in the area between the Adige and the Kurisches Haff felt itself a people at the dawn of our Culture. This vastness of landscape at its origin was unique to the Western Culture. The same feeling was abroad then *that in its maturity, in the custody of* Spain, made the *whole world* into the object of Western politics. Or a people may be tiny—the Mormons in America, a mere group of converts to a religionist, asserted themselves strongly and were opposed from without. They responded by becoming a people. Their unity persisted until their leadership decided in favor of Intellect and compromised the doctrines of the religion, whereupon the Mormon people disappeared.

What is it that creates a people? It is first a difference between a group and its human environment, and secondly a *tension* worked up by this difference. A *tension* is a *frontier*. The frontier sharpens the feelings on both sides, and results in a new action-unit, a *People*.

Just as this tension may arise out of religion, economics, culture, race, so may the new unit contain all kinds of people, if the population affected is heterogeneous. Language is no bar to the formation of a people; in fact all existing Western languages came *after* the formation of their respective peoples.

A People is a spiritual unit. It is created by History, and if it is able to survive its first tests, it becomes a unit which carries History further. Just as the excited street-crowd only becomes a unit by virtue of the leader-led articulation, so a people is only such by virtue of *leadership*.

The distinction between crowd and people is only one of duration and magnitude, and not one of kind. Thus one man can exercise, for the few hours necessary, the entire leadership functions of a crowd. A people is more elaborately articulated than a crowd, has a more complex existence, a larger Life-task, and hence, a *stratum* of leaders. Any absolute monarchy or dictatorship also has a leader-*stratum*.

A people may be weak, or it may be strong. During the recent centuries of Western history, since the Peace of Westphalia, a handful of weak peoples have managed to maintain a *nominal* independence, politically speaking, by virtue of the tense situation between larger powers. But weak peoples, like weak individuals, cannot create great deeds or great thoughts. A strong people, by the intensity of its imperative, maintains the frontier between it and other populations, refuses to compromise its unique idea. By frontier is meant here of course, spiritual frontier. Whether this develops into a territorial frontier is for events to show, and is also a matter of what Culture we are talking about.

Thus, in neither the Arabian Culture, nor the Classical Culture, was the idea of a people bound up with a land area. In neither of these Cultures was it repugnant to the spiritual feeling of unity of a people to have a strange people living in the same area, having its own government and laws. Imperial Rome administered foreign laws in cases involving foreigners. In the Arabian Culture, the independence was even more marked. Thus Nestorians, Muslims, and Jews lived side by side, but belonged to different nations, and did not intermarry. Foreign meant: of a different belief. These peoples and nations would have regarded the Western doctrine of the Reformation-times *cuius regio, eius religio* as the most Satanic possible inversion of the natural order. To make belief dependent upon the

land of residence would have seemed monstrous to them. The
Jew brought this feeling with him from this alien Culture. He
regarded his next-door Western neighbor as *foreign*. The public
life of his Western host-nation was a matter of indifference to
him, and he had his own public-life, unnoticed by the West.
Their laws were not his, nor their religion, nor their ethics,
customs, thoughts, or habits, and above all, their political life
did not touch him with its ideas of Fatherland, patriotism, military service, self-sacrifice.

In Turkey and China it was not felt as a humiliation that by
the "Capitulations" Westerners were under the jurisdiction of
their own consular representatives, and not under local courts.

Thus the relation of a people to other peoples is a matter
determined by the symbolic inner-life of the High Culture in
which it may arise. This is not to say that a People can only
arise in a High Culture. For phenomena like Tamerlane and
Gengis Khan are also people-creating.

As *concepts,* Race and People are quite separate; in life they
are not so separate. We have seen the formation of a Race. It
begins with the formation of a People. Every people with a
strong idea and good leadership will develop also into a racial
unity if it lasts long enough. The converse is also true: a race—
using the word now with its maximum of anatomical content,
e.g., the Negro—may be the focus of happenings that will force
it to assume the form of a people.

A People is a unit of the soul. Wherever there is a soul-unity
gestating, a people is forming. The entire 20th century West
can now see what Nietzsche discerned in the 80's of the 19th
century—the arising of a *Western People.* His expression "We
good Europeans" was understood by few of his time. They were
too busy with their petty games: in the Cabinets they were playing national-atomism; in the salons they were talking social-

atomism and "happiness"; in the cellars they were plotting in class-atomism.

The strength and health of a People depends upon the definiteness of its articulation. We have seen how in a street-crowd, all will and intellect mystically devolve upon the leader. If this breaks up, through mistakes by the leader, or crushing by external force, the crowd is dead, and reverts to a sum of individuals.

The decentralization of will and intellect in the West generally is thus seen to be a grave Cultural sickness. The Authority and Unity of the West was gradually undermined for centuries by the slow increase of the intellectual content of the Culture. Nevertheless this Culture preserved its unity before the world, generally speaking, until the cataclysm of 1789, which Napoleon, and after him the Vienna Congress, were unable permanently to undo. The Concert of Europe was replaced by a progressing Discord of Europe.

The more will and intellect that passed downwards and outwards in the Culture, the greater was the decline in the Cultural health. Nationalism was the disease of the Culture; Class War was the disease of the Nation; Parliamentarism was the disease of the State; the Rule of Money was the disease of Society; sterile Pleasure was the disease of the Race; the new selfishness was the disease of the Family; Divorce was the disease of Marriage.

Every Culture has gone through this terrible crisis, and each has stood where the West now stands in 1948. This means, of course, inwardly, for never before at the height of its crisis has an entire Culture been occupied by barbarians and distorters. The previous seven Cultures surmounted this critical time: the creative forces of Instinct and Intellect, working in harmony brought about the Resurgence of Authority, and formed, in each case, the Empire of the Culture.

The beginning of this resurgence of synthesis and creation after the long orgy of Intellect-run-wild manifests itself in diverse phenomena. Nietzsche and Carlyle were symbols of the resurgence. Characteristically both were Europeans, and despised the petty-statism of their times. Their lives and ideas were an expression of organic necessity. Both were heralds of the next Age. The appearance of a spate of *cultural* histories was another sign. The appearance of *State*-Socialism was another. The biological theories of de Vries and Driesch, the abandonment of the materialistic cliches by a whole group of physicists was another. For political purposes, the most important was the beginning of the formation of a *People of the West.*

Nation

THE WORD *People* describes a group which has become a soul-unit, through an idea and the presence of the polarity of leader and led. The word is neutral as to the duration of such a group, its inner strength, its intensity, or the magnitude of its mission in life.

A nation is a people—and something more. It is more highly articulated. A people can arise outside of a Culture; a nation cannot. A people may be a unit of short duration, or inwardly weak. A nation has a life span and belongs to the strongest organic unities within a Culture. With the word Culture, we touch upon the hall-mark of the Nation: *a nation is a people containing a Cultural Idea.*

When a High Culture is born into a landscape, after a gestation period of several generations, it works with mysterious effect upon the populations in its area. Previous names and groupings vanish into new spiritual unities. In the West, around 1000 A.D., the names Swabian, Frank, Lombard, Visigoth, Saxon, become dead terms for practical purposes, and men begin to feel themselves as Germans, Italians, Frenchmen, and Spaniards. Each of these groups is an *Idea*—it is the vehicle of a certain part of the soul of the Culture, it is a plane of existence, an aspect of the Culture-spirit. This is the basis of their differences. Their similarity is that they are the creations of the same Culture.

Their differences beget different racial rhythms and styles of thinking and doing. A different inner accent shapes the same general linguistic material into various tongues, each one the expression of a different soul. The separate souls react in distinct fashions to similar outer experiences, and thus events also contribute their part to shaping the character of the nations that arise.

To understand what a nation is, one must first entirely dissociate in his mind the connection—so self-evident to the 19th century—between nation, political unity, and language. To the era of Rationalism and Capitalism, these units were the very primordial material of history. But these nations were only expressions of a certain stage of the Nation-Idea in Western history.

In the dawn of our Culture, language had no relation to nation, nor had politics. A Nation in those days was a spiritual unity which expressed itself as such in the Spirit of the Age. That Spirit was one of religious feeling, Scholastic philosophy, Gothic architecture, Imperial-Papal politics, Crusades. There was a sharp and distinct feeling of *the foreigner,* but the word did not relate exclusively to politics, or language. In the 11th and 12th centuries, English, German, French methods of thinking appear in the various Scholastics. Varying honor-imperatives, varying moral-feelings, different ways of manifesting religious feelings, variations in the Gothic cathedrals, degrees of attachment to Empire or Pope—all show the different national ideas.

Vis-a-vis the foreigner—the Moor, the Slav, the Turk, the Saracen—these nations *unconsciously, self-evidently,* were *one People.* However strong their feelings of separation toward one another, instinct welded them into a unity for assertion against the *Cultural alien.* Thus when the Crusaders established a Western State in the Levant, it was not English, French, German—but simply Western. The instinct of the Culture is strong, its rhythms compel virtually, its superpersonal unity is felt in the blood, and hence recognized by the intellect.

All Cultures express themselves in the form of nations, as well as art-forms, religions, languages, technics, knowledge-systems and the other Culture-forms. Just as all the other forms are distinct within each Culture, so is the style of the Nation. In the Arabian Culture, just as its conception of History was the actualization of a World-Plan by God beginning with a Creation and ending with a Cataclysm, so the Nation-style was one of *belief.* Members of a belief were constituted as *nations.* The notion of territory, Fatherland, was not present. The nation had a spiritual, and not a physical, extent. This Nation-idea created in this alien Culture the Jewish nation, which in that Culture was one among others of a similar structure. In our Culture, it was so completely alien that no one realized what its essence was until we reached our period of Late Civilization with its historical sensitivity.

In the Classical Culture, the Nation-idea was expressed in the form of a City-state. The Nation was not an area, but only the City and its population. Any further territorial control was negative in origin; e.g., to control was to deny possession of the area to a potential enemy in war. To these nations, our idea of a Fatherland with distant frontiers that one never sees during his whole life would have been a fantastic and repellent hallucination.

II

The Nation is an Idea. Its material manifestations are the actualizations of this Idea as it fulfills itself. We can, for purposes of understanding, divide the Nation into three strata. On top is the Idea itself. It is incapable of expression in words, for it is not an abstraction, not a concept, but is a soul. It can only be expressed in lives, deeds, thoughts, events.

Under it is the minority which embodies the Idea at high potential, the nation-bearing stratum. It represents the Idea in History. For *practical* purposes it is the nation. It is, as actuality, what the mass of the population, the body of the nation, is as possibility.

The lowest stratum is the mass. It widens out toward the base, becoming ever less differentiated as one goes down. Finally one reaches the level where an eternal stratum is reached, that takes no part whatever in the national Idea, which does not experience the History which is playing its drama higher up on top.

Just as, in a crowd, the leader is the decisive part of the unity, so is the nation-bearing minority in the national unity. Both minority and mass are in the service of the Idea, just as both leader and led are of the crowd-idea. If the leader is killed or removed, another will arise, if the idea is strong. Similarly in a nation, the mass contains, in most of its individuals, a spark of the national feeling. Those who are more moved by this inner quality than others are a part of the minority, the nation-bearing stratum.

Dissociate nation-bearing stratum and mere political leadership. In organic health the political leadership contains only members of the nation-bearing stratum—but not all of them, by any means, for nation-bearing stratum is much wider than political administration. But the political leadership may contain, owing to weakness of the national idea and aggressiveness of an inner alien group, few or even no members of the nation-bearing stratum. The members of the nation-bearing stratum are those who by the strength of their national feelings and their willingness to sacrifice for this Idea are the custodians of the Idea before the world and against inner alien and anti-national elements.

If this stratum were to be removed from a healthy nation with a future, after a period of spiritual chaos in the body of the nation, a new one would arise from the mass. If the mass were *totally* devoid of national feelings, the minority could not accomplish the Idea.

That there is nothing whatever abstract about this is shown by the case of Russia. There the Romanov dynasty and its upper stratum tried to make Russia into a Western people, a Western nation. But the mass was quite devoid of possibilities in this direction. They did succeed in making Russia into a Western nation, for appearances, and for political purposes, and this shows that the minority is decisive. But when the Bolsheviks exterminated or drove out this entire minority, there was nothing to replace it, for the mass did not even contain a spark of this idea.

Thus *from the standpoint of History,* the nation serves the Culture, the minority serves the nation, the mass serves the minority. The quaint transposition of thought known as Rationalism saw it otherwise: there is no Idea, there is only mass, anything else must serve the mass. But Rationalism only affected terminology in this matter, for even those nations most heavily undermined by Rationalism still appeared in History in the custody of a minority, and the mass was only called upon to obey, to think a certain way, to vote a certain way. It is important in the 20th century to know that denying facts does not remove them, nor does changing their names change their nature. In the 19th century the Nation was still an Idea, even though it was supposed to be merely a huge collection of individuals. It was an Idea that infected even the most rationalistic of the Rationalists, the Communists. Thus French Communism was entirely different from German Communism—the difference between Paris in 1871 and Berlin in 1918. They may have read from the same book, but the pulse in the blood was different.

Nation and History

A NATION is an organic part of a Culture, it expresses by its life and development a certain inner possibility of the Culture-soul. It is never independent of the Culture, and this condition of dependence is shown by the expression *Spirit of the Age*. It has long been recognized by thinkers and men of action that there are certain things which simply must be done, others which simply cannot be done, during a certain age. One may, or may not, agree with these things with his intellect, but he must observe them. *The Spirit of the Age is the phase of development of the Culture*. It subjects all nations to it. Since each nation has its own character, and since each Age has its own stamp, it follows that one nation may be more adapted to one given Age than another. This is the explanation of why we have the Age of "The Holy Roman Empire, German by nation," 1050–1250, the Spanish Age, 1500–1650, the French Rococo, 1650–1750, the English Age, 1750–1900.

Within this framework of its own subjection to the Culture, the Nation-Idea compels everything in its realm to submit to its force. Thus each Western nation had its own type of social behavior, its own articulation of society, sharp and clear in England, Prussia, Spain, vague and nebulous in France and Italy. The religiousness of England differed from that of Spain, both from Germany. The orientation to economics is different in each place, strongest in England. Even in the field of erotic, the nations are differentiated, and France is the nation that developed the most elaborate culture of sexual love. Literature is distinctly national, so is drama, so is architecture, so is even music. Philosophy did not escape nationalization: the two greatest Western schools are the English Sensualist school, 1600–1900, and the German Idealist school, 1650–1950. Orientation to religious doctrines is different: Spain has been the stronghold of Catholicity, England of Protestantism. The great men that have arisen in the various nations have expressed national qualities at high potential: Think of Richelieu, Cromwell, Alva, Wallenstein. An oil painting discloses the nationality of its painter during the great era of Western painting, 1550–1850.

It is thus easy to understand how Materialism could convince itself that nations were the creators of Culture, instead of seeing the fact that it is the reverse.

A Culture begins in Faith and Mysticism, with its thought-world and its action-world both subject to self-evident order and authority. It develops along the path of increasing intellectuality until it reaches the caesura of Rationalism, when intellect frees itself entirely from faith and instinct, analyzes, distintegrates, and mobilizes everything. In its very last stage, that of Late Civilization, it gathers itself once more together, asserts its unity by impressing all forms of its life with a final form which returns once more to the symbolic Authority and Mysticism of its origins.

This biography of the Culture is traceable in every life-form, including its nations.

The Culture created its nations through *dynasties*. The idea
of a dynasty is repulsive to the Classical Culture, unknown to
the Arabian.

But Western nations, imbued with the unique force and intensity of expression of the Western Culture are dynastic, even
when they abolish a dynasty. They either want another dynasty,
or else they wish the dynastic feeling to be freed from the personality of the sovereign. *Dynasty is the affirmation of political
continuity from Past to Future.* The political history of the
West from its origins is the history of dynasties.

The diverse tribes of Swabians, Franks, Saxons, Bavarians,
and Thüringians became united into the German nation
through the dynastic Empire-Idea, the creation of Karl der
Grosse. Similarly the French people and nation were formed by
dynasties. Out of diverse Frankish and Visigothic elements, the
Capetian dynasty created a nation and a language. If Dynasty
had followed speech, there would have been two Frances:
Frankish-Romance France in the North, Provencal France in
the South.

The Dynasties created the nations, by focusing these mystic
feelings onto a passionate symbol. The nations created Race
and Language. The Italian written language is attributable
chiefly to Frederick II of the Hohenstaufen dynasty, a German
Emperor who preferred the South, and caused this language to
be used officially and socially in the Empire. The Portugese
people and language are the result of the fact that Alfonso VI
of Castile gave that territory as the marriage portion of his
daughter to Henry of Besancon in 1095. To this creation of a
dynasty is due the fact that Brazil speaks Portugese to-day. The
House and kingdom of Lorraine came to an end with the child-
lessness of Lothar II in the 9th century. Had his dynasty continued, there probably had been a nation, people, language,

kingdom and State of Lotharingen in Western history. The English people, nation and language are all the result of the Norman Conquest with its founding of the House of Normandy which continues to this time. The Prussian nation is the creation of the Hohenzollern dynasty, and the Austrian was that of the Hapsburg.

The form of Western politics was always dynastic, and increasingly so as the Culture attained to greater heights. The rhythmic cycles of great wars took a dynastic form: a vacant throne somewhere called forth a Succession-War. Even in 1870 the pretext which Napoleon III adopted for his war against Prussia was a dynastic one. And the great Napoleon too, was brought down by a millennium of dynastic tradition that he roused against him by driving out old dynasties and putting his brothers and Marshals on thrones as new dynasts.

In this stage of Western history the idea of the dynasty is only apparently gone. A thousand-year Empire is itself a dynastic idea. The genealogical continuity of the ruling house is merely a powerful symbol of continuity. This symbol satisfies instinct. Western intellect demands this same continuity during its reign, 1750–1950, but merely changes the symbol: instead of a blood-stream of a royal House, it puts up a piece of paper, a Constitution.

Readers in 2050 can see about them the final form of the expression of Western dynastic feeling. In Rationalist times the symbol of the Royal House became unsatisfactory, and was merely tolerated, if not abolished altogether. The piece of paper was much more real to a Rationalist. Now the piece of paper has become unsatisfactory, as History quietly submerges Rationalism. We stand at the next epoch, that of Resurgence of Authority.

Nation and Rationalism

THE NATIONAL STYLE of a High Culture is so strong that it pulls even neighboring populations into its form. Examples of outer populations that adopted the Western national style because of their geographical proximity are the Balkans, Poland, Bohemia and Russia. This adoption is quite enough to deceive certain elements in the Culture that these border-streams are within the Culture-organism. This is strongly reinforced in the minds of superficial people if, for instance, one or two highly gifted men from beyond the border come under the spirit of the Culture and produce works of thought, or deeds, in the Culture-style. The year 2050 will hardly believe that *Russia* was referred to as a Western nation as late as the middle of the 20th century. This mistake was merely one of the results of the impact of Rationalism on the Nation-style of the Culture.

Reason is the form of thought adopted to solving mechanical problems, and cannot be applied to organic things, in its free, rootless form. Thus to every organism there is a birth, and a death. For what *reason*? The question is senseless from the organic standpoint. Why must an organism die? No one can give a *reason*. This refers, of course, to emancipated, inorganic, reason. Religion employs reason, but within the framework of Faith. Emancipated reason—Rationalism—recognizes no superior discipline, neither that of organic regularities, nor beyond them, of Faith or Religion. But yet, the organism dies, even though Rationalism loudly insists that it is not necessary. The human life span of 70 years represents no *logical* necessity. It would not offend *logic* if organisms were perpetual. This same unadaptability of logic and reason to organic rhythms affects fundamentally the Nation-Idea during the period of Rationalism.

The laboratory-logic which denied God and the human soul was certainly not going to allow the Nation-Idea. The most it was willing to concede was the existence of a great number of individuals. Actually this pose was impossible for even the most intransigent rationalists to maintain, and in their writings, they continually slip into figures of speech which betray that they are thinking in terms of a higher Idea which is imminent in each of these individuals.

Thus to Rationalism, Nation means—Mass. There must be no articulation—no nobility, no clergy, no monarch, no group raised above the others by virtue of its higher Idea-content. There is also no Idea which forms all the individuals, even though there is the mechanico-logical concept of the totality.

The concept of Nation-as-Mass is coeval with Democracy and Class War. The three notions are merely different aspects of Rationalism. If the nation is the mass, there should be no social stratification, and if the old-traditional structure does not give way, one must make class-war against it.

Rationalism is born at the same time also as the decisive turn of Culture toward Civilization, the fulfillment of the inner

form-world, and the unequivocal turning to *activity* as the
prime content of Life. This means the vast increase in the public
power available to political leaders, larger wars, more intense
economics, more physical energy, enormous development of
technics. No Western thinker ever had a better technical brain
than Roger Bacon, or Leonardo da Vinci, but the technical
works of these men came in an age of *inner* activity, which regarded technics as a branch of knowledge, not as a form of
unleashing power for industrial and war purposes. The Civilization expanded in power and in extent. Anything opposing this
organic rhythm was doomed to frustration and defeat. The
old traditions could only survive if they would take up the new
tendencies and lead them onward. This was done in England,
but the feat was not so remarkable as has been generally supposed, for the English national-Idea was actually the vehicle of
this change of direction from Culture to Civilization. The Rationalist Idea was born in England. English Sensualist philosophers enunciated its basic doctrines, English parliamentarians
applied them to theory of government, English technicians invented the new power-unleashing machines, English merchants
created the forms of 19th century Capitalism, English thinkers
first announced the idea that the nation was the mass. The
French Encyclopedists were all under English influence, and
many of them lived for years in England. Thus there were
plenty of persons in high places who were in contact with the
new ideas and felt the necessity of adopting them verbally.

The doom of Napoleon symbolizes the deep fact that he was
both representing and opposing this idea at the same time.

Rationalism could only say: the nation is the mass; it only
denied the articulation of the Nation. These nations were not
yet dead, and could not be denied. The emphasis passed to the
external differences between the nations, which means, political

differences. Nation becomes for the first time in Western history, *primarily* a political idea. The word "nationalism" acquires an exclusively *political* meaning.

Nation had not been, even in Frederick the Great's Wars, a purely political thing. Under Frederick had fought Russians against Russia, Frenchmen against France, Swedes against Sweden, Saxons fought both for and against him. An early acquaintance of Frederick tendered to him his military services. Frederick offered him a majority. Reluctantly the man took service with an enemy army, because a colonelcy was available there. Such conduct was not considered monstrous at that time. 19th century interpretation of history—ignoring the soul and following the surface continuity of names—merely took current politics and applied it backwards. The foreigner was not *liked* during previous Western history, but politics was not oriented to this one fact alone. Politics was a thing of dynasty— or as in the case of the microscopic nations, revolt against dynasty. German condottieri like Froberger, and English like Sir John Hawkwood led foreign mercenaries in the wars in Italy. The German Emperor Frederick II was more Italian than German, and found no difficulty in being both politically. Allegiance was not a thing of geography of birthplace, but of attachment, common destiny, oath, honor. Thus, treason in those days did not refer to birthplace, but to obligation of honor. Not until allegiance was given was honor involved. The great Emperor Charles V had a German father, a Spanish mother, grew up in the Netherlands, was educated by a Flemish churchman, whom he later appointed Pope Adrian VI, spoke French as a native tongue, was King of Spain, and Holy Roman Emperor. Spaniards had dukedoms in England, an English queen was married to the King of Spain, the English King was Elector of Hanover. Armies consisted of men of mixed nation-

ality, and commands changed often among generals of different
nationality. It suffices to mention Maurice de Saxe, Prinz Eugen,
Marshal Conde, Montecuculi. Dynastic-politics cut straight
across nations, just as nationalistic politics cut clean across
dynasties.

But the old spiritual significance of Western nations was
replaced by a purely political one after the triumph of Rationalism. The linkage in those days between the new idea of the
nation-as-mass and nation-as-political instead of dynastic,
caused nationalism to be looked on in 1815 as Communism was
in 1915—the height of radical destruction.

Napoleon represented both ideas to Europe. He was anti-
dynastic, and thus unlocked everywhere the new feeling of
political nationalism. But to countries occupied by French
armies, political nationalism meant revolt, and it was the Prussian rising of 1813 that destroyed Napoleon.

Rationalism saw a nation thus as a political mass. But why
just this mass and not another? There had to be some visible,
mechanical, determinant of nationality. This was found in—
Language. If a man spoke French, he was French; Italian,
Italian. What determines this? Where he was born. It does, or
it should. Allegiance became something owed to a language
and a piece of ground, not to an Idea or the dynastic symbol
of the Idea.

This concept triumphed, publicly and privately. It determined a man's national feelings, and changed the nature of
wars. Instead of the Succession-Wars, which arose from dynastic-politics, came now wars for a territory and population which
one could assimilate by language policy in the schools.

The populations of the Balkan countries were a reflection
of the school-policies of the preceding generation. It reached a
grotesque height when it was employed in theory at the Ver-

sailles conference, 1919. Language was supposed to be the indication of the presence of a nation. The principle was of course only used where it suited the political purpose, but nevertheless everyone paid lip-service to this materialistic stupidity.

This concept of the Nation-Idea had many important consequences. The Italian Wars of linguistic Unification created what never had existed before, a political unit Italy. The Austrian nation was annihilated by this concept, and the attempt by extra-European forces to resurrect it as a nation after the Second World War as a part of the general plan to Balkanize Europe was doubly ludicrous, *for a new Nation-Idea was coming.* The linguistic idea of Nation also enabled England to bring about the entry of America into the First World War on its side, because the written language was more or less common to both. Suppose that—as narrowly missed by vote—the American Constitutional Convention in 1787 had adopted the resolution to make German the official language of America. Western history, 1914–1918 had been quite different. Instead of Europe controlling in 1950 *no part* of the globe, not even its own area, it would have controlled—the *entire* globe.

But the Nation is always an Idea, it can be nothing other. Only one's *concept* of the Nation can change, but the Idea is something in the blood and soul, and not merely in the mind. It permeates a man's way of understanding what a Nation is, and what everything else is. Even though, say, French and English Rationalists had agreed *precisely* on what the Nation is, each would have behaved in his distinct national way.

Rationalism looked at the nation from within and said: it is mass. It looked at it from without and said: it is language. Both were materialistic stupidities. Nation is, first, the Idea; second, the nation-bearing stratum; lastly, the mass who are the *object,* the mere *body* of the Nation. From without, the Nation is a *different* soul from other souls. It is contact with the foreign that develops the sense of the proper.

Rationalism liberated the Nation-Idea from the Dynasty-Idea. Dynasties changed their names to try and cover up their connections with other nations. In most countries the dynasty was dethroned as being anti-national, since nation was mass, and Dynasty was symbol. Above all, Rationalism accomplished the identification of *nation* and *politics*. Nationalism became primarily a *political* term.

II

The Dynasties reacted as a group to the new concept of the nation, both in its politicization of the Idea, and its identification of Nation and Mass. The making of Nation into *the* unit of politics was an attack on every dynasty. Dynasties hitherto had exercised a monopoly of politics—were they now to be supplanted by mob-leaders who wished to tear up everything and set it in motion? At the Vienna Congress, 1815, and in the Holy Alliance, the Dynastic Idea of Politics gained its last great victory *on the surface*. But only on the surface, for repression of the Spirit of the Age only dams it up, as it were, and a dam cannot be built against Destiny. This is the tragedy of every aging woman, and of every effete, backward-looking, ruling class. Talleyrand—alone at the Congress in his political superiority—was however working with the 19th century Nation-Idea, and not that of the 18th century, like the Kings. He stimulated their conservatism, and brought out of a total French military defeat a stronger France. Boundaries were secondary to the Dynasts, primary to Talleyrand.

Readers in the 20th century find it difficult, those in the 21st century more difficult, to believe that even in the 50's of the

19th century nationalism was considered a radically destructive force by the traditionary elements in European Nations. In Germany, it took a man of political genius, Bismarck, to transform the idea of nationalism from a destructive, class-war idea into a conserving, creating idea, serviceable to Tradition and forward development.

This changing of the meaning of the word nationalism from destructive and levelling to creative-conservative and hierarchical showed that despite their surface-victory, the Dynasts at Vienna had lost their contest against Destiny. Whether or not they continued, the dynasties were politically dead. They became, more in some places than elsewhere, mere pageantry. The force of the dynastic idea—the passionate affirmation of eternal duration—was transferred on to the Nation. The dynasty became merely a part of the general public property of the Nation—like the public buildings, and the national museums. At one time the monarch owned the nation—in the 19th century the nation owned the monarch. If the monarch did take part in politics, he was subject to the same inner limitations as any Premier.

The question will be asked: how did nationalism change its significance from Tradition-destroying to Tradition-conserving? It was another development of the Rationalist stock of ideas that brought this about, namely the transference of class-war from the political-social sphere to the economic sphere. Nationalism had done its work on the destructive side: it had destroyed Dynasty and Estates. Now its place in the center of History was challenged by Economics. Economics—Money—is hostile to politics generally, whether dynastic or nationalistic. *Authority* is the prime enemy of Money. Authority means responsibility, and Money means irresponsibility. Authority means Public; Money means Private.

The Master of Money is the second of the class-warriors. First was the ideologue on the barricade with a copy of Contrat Social in his hand. He cleared the stage for the Master of Money. The third in this succession of Culture-termites is the Master of Labor.

Vis-a-vis all three of them, any form of political nationalism is conservative, and contains possibilities of creativeness if the responsible stratum has sufficient vision and energy. But it takes Genius to see the obvious, and a Bismarck was necessary to show the conserving value of nationalism, and its creative possibilities. Metternich stood with his feet in the old Europe of Dynasty, and had thus seen the struggle of Nationalism against Dynasty as one of Chaos against Order. The year of his passing, 1848, was the epoch of Nationalism from its old meaning to its new one. Had he lived to see the economic class war of the forces of Money and Proletariat against Politics, he also would have chosen nationalism as the alternative.

In the field of politics, Rationalism accentuated the differences between the nations. In the field of economics its effect was even more disintegrating. It wished to break up the nation into classes, and the classes into individuals. Liberals, financiers, Communists, Anarchists were the coalition against the remnants of Authority embodied in the nationalistic State. In its first century, Rationalism affirmed the nations as the ultimate units of history and warred against the subjection of the nations to the dynasts. In its second, more radical, century, Rationalism denies the nations altogether. The professors and "political economists" conceived of the nation as a mere economic convenience in a world-wide "division of labor." Thus one nation could grow crops, another could make machines. It was to be solely *economic* differentiation. This idea was the darling of the financier, for in the flow of trade in such a world—there must be no autarchy—he would be the great gainer, for it would all flow *through* him.

On the other side, the Communists said that nations were only a capitalist trick to separate the "workers of the world." Only *classes* were real—all else is illusion—and there are only two of them, bourgeois and proletaire.

These two world-pictures point to total chaos, the dissolution of the Civilization, and submission to the barbarian. Hence Nationalism, from having been destructive became conservative, and even, in the right hands, creative.

Nation in the 20th Century

EACH AGE passes into the succeeding Age gradually in the depths. On the surface the transition may be gradual, or it may be sudden. This is only another way of saying that there is struggle between Young and Old. The old try to preserve that which is familiar to them, the young wish to actualize the new which is beating in the pulse. A tradition bridges the gap and maintains surface gradualness corresponding to the gradualness beneath. If the tradition has decayed—France, 1789—the break opens, and becomes a front for fighting. England was ready sooner than France—the Wilkes agitation contained the possibility of a Terror in London in the 60's—but the ruling class was not decadent and knew what to take over and when to be firm.

The 20th century Nation-Idea can be understood by applying the Hegelian-Fichtean Triadic Law of Thought. The thesis of Nation as Dynastic-Unit, and the antithesis of Nation-as-Linguistic-Unit are both submerged into the creator of them both, and become Nation-as-Culture-Unit, the gigantic synthesis whose irresistible actualization is the inner motive force of History in this century. We who live in the middle of the 20th century cannot understand the excitement of 1848, for we only know the hither side of it. Those in 2050, living in the Western Nation-Idea of the 20th century style, will not be able to understand how anyone could have opposed the obvious Destiny of the Western Nation-Idea. Yet the opposition was as effective as that of Metternich and the Fürstenbund was to the entry of the 19th century Nation-Idea.

One great difference exists however. The Russia that the Western Nations called in to help against Napoleon and the new Nation-Idea he represented considered itself a Western Nation, and so conducted itself. The Russia that the party-politicians called in against the 20th century Nation-Idea was the primitive barbarian in all his vigor and will-to-annihilate. The America that intervened in Western politics was entirely in the grip of Culture-distorters, and thus removed by such a regime temporarily from the areas of Western influence. The only difference between them to the Europe they divided after the Second World War, 1939–1945, was that no Western possibilities existed in Russia, and America did present a possibility —in the future—of a revolution which would restore America to the West. Both were completely alien, both could only destroy.

The 20th century sees the end of Rationalism. Even now— 1948—it is pale and emaciated. Scientists and philosophers are falling away. Mysticism is reappearing, both in its authoritative-religious form, and in the form of theosophistic fads. Mechanism in biology has yielded to Vitalism. Materialism fights desperately, hopelessly against the resurgence of the Soul of Culture-Man. Relativity has placed the determination of phenomena with man, precisely where German Idealistic philos-

ophy had put it in the 18th century. Even matter has been liberated from Causality—we now allow the "electrons" and their
relatives to dance freely about, no longer in subjection to the
strict Culture-physics of Western tradition. That which would
have been regarded with horror a generation before quietly
asserts itself in defiance of Rationalism—clairvoyancy, disguised as "extra-sensory perception." The Psyche intrudes even
into physiology.

But in this year 1948 the world of action remains, chained
by its stupidity, in the dead past. Synthesis replaces analysis in
Western thought, but Western action remains disintegratory:
classes, tiny "nations," *division* of powers, economic obses-
sions, parties, trade-unions, "rights," parliaments, elections,
frontiers every few miles in Europe, opposition, hatred of
authority, lack of respect and dignity, mutual economic strangulation by customs boundaries. This while the extra-European
world agglomerates itself into great, world-embracing masses
of territory and population. The Cultural impetus of Imperialism is carried forward by the non-Culture peoples, the barbarians, while the sick, backward-looking West thinks in ever-
smaller space-terms. While the barbarians build empires, Europe abandons old conquests. While the barbarians proclaim
their superiority, voices in Europe are raised saying that Western Imperialism—that mighty inner imperative of the most
passionate, intense High Culture the world has yet seen—only
existed in order to prepare the under-races of the world for
"self-government." They continue to say it as the extra-Europeans divide the Mother-soil of European Culture between
them, and loot and starve European populations on a mass-
scale.

It might be thought that the 20th century Idea of the Nation
is disintegration, when one hears fools in Bavaria announce

that the solution for them is to constitute themselves a "little
Switzerland." One wonders that is it *possible* for extra-Europeans to find such people down below the Western Culture.

But this atomizing of the Soul of the West is *not* the 20th
century Idea. These voices of submission to the barbarian, and
abandonment of Culture, of disintegration into ever-smaller
particles of territory and population are the illness of the West,
not its Future, its crisis, not its health. They are the pseudo-
victory of 18th and 19th century Rationalism over the Resurgence of Authority of the 20th and 21st centuries. They are
the extrapolation of the Rationalistic twins, finance-Capitalism
and snarling Communism, the desire to extend into the Future
old diseases of the European will, to perpetuate feelings that
are dead and can no longer inspirit the soul of the West.

It is known however that the life of a Culture has its own
rhythm, its own inner law of development, its own imperative.
This cannot be changed by the will or rationalistic ideal of
human beings. These ideals are themselves the expression of a
great Culture-crisis, and with the disappearance of the crisis,
the ideals are suddenly entirely empty. No one is willing to die
for them. The crisis is now coming to an end, as is manifest by
the developments in other Culture-directions. The history of
previous Cultures shows the duration of this great crisis,
through which they all had to go, and from their history, we
know at what point we stand.

That point is the transition to the new idea of the Nation, the
Nation as Empire, Nation as Culture-unit. The tests of race,
people, and language have no validity, for the 20th century will
shape its own race and people exactly as the 19th century races,
peoples, and nations were the products of History. It sounds
much more fantastic to 1950 ears than to the ears of 2150 to say
that the creation of a new language by the 20th century Nation

in process of arising is not impossible. It may be one of the old languages, modified by the new spirit; it may be a new language, containing elements of pre-existing languages.

The Second World War represented the surface victory of the Past over the Future. Metternich, Burke, Wellington, would have read this situation correctly, but would have cast in their lot with the Future, for the Future is Order, and the Rationalistic Past is Chaos and Disintegration. They fought Rationalism in its inception, and their heirs who fight it to-day fight a Rationalism stricken with *rigor mortis,* for which no one will mount the barricade, and which only sits leering upon its throne by virtue of its serviceability to the Barbarian. It divides Europe, and Europe divided is Europe conquered.

The fight against the Past is thus seen to be the fight against the extra-European forces, for it is they who are perpetuating the atomizing of Europe, the Balkanization of a Culture, the Switzerland of the West.

It is characteristic of any phase of development of a Culture that it is historically necessary. It is precisely the same force that causes one Culture phase to succeed to another that makes the youth inevitably into a man. To attempt to interfere with the one process is the same as interfering with the other. So far no way has been discovered to stop the development of an organism, except killing it. The caterpillar *must* become a butterfly, the bud *must* become a flower, the youth *must* become a man, the man *must* express his mature possibilities. This force which impels this forward development is called Destiny. It is operative at every moment from conception to death in every organism. It is the hall-mark of the organic which distinguishes it from the inorganic, the permanent, the historyless. Every organism has its own life-task, and the fulfillment of this task is inwardly necessary. The extent to which an outer force can affect the process is different for various organisms. The phenomena of outer forces attempting to warp a High Culture from its Life-path come under the heading of Culture-distortion.

The subject of the State must precede a treatment of Culture-distortion. Race, People, Nation, State are manifestations of Cultural *health*. Distortion is the *illness* of the Culture.

State

WITH THE STATE we come to the first purely political Idea in the life of the High Culture. Race, People, Nation have all of them political potentialities, deep connections with politics, but State is a political term. It is a word whose content changes quite completely during the development of a Culture. The States which philosophers, scholars, and theoreticians project are not States for the purposes of this work. These things belong to literature, whereas this is concerned with the actualized and the possible. Plato and Campanella, More and Fourier, Rousseau and Marx, all designed Utopias which *should* exist, and it is this moral imperative, this *should,* which shows that the center of gravity of these States lies in thought and not in action. The State as an actuality is a manifestation of the development of a High Culture. Outside of a High Culture there is no State, but only leadership of more or less permanence. The content of the State-Idea is a reflection of the stage of development of the High Culture, and thus the State can only be comprehended organically. It cannot be made the object of logical operations, for being living, it is irrational, unamenable to logic. If such attempts reach the level of politics, of actuality, they throw the State into crisis, since the State, like every phase of the Culture, can only be itself, or be sick and distorted.

The State is the form of a nation for action. The content of this form changes, and each change is a crisis in the Culture-development. In the earliest time of the Culture, the time of the Crusades, of the conflict of Empire and Papacy, from 1000 to 1300, the Culture-unity is so strong that the Culture itself is constituted more or less as a nation, with all the lesser sovereigns holding of the Emperor. *Vis-a-vis* the barbarian, all Westerners are of one nation, and are welded into one State.

The first social articulation of the Culture is into Estates. The two Estates, Nobility and Priesthood, represent the two aspects of the Culture-soul with the highest possible symbolic purity. Nobility represents war, politics, law, race. Priesthood represents religion, knowledge, science, philosophy, the world of thought. The rest of the population is just that—the rest. Seen from above, it has only an economic function. Out of it develop the beginnings of trade-organization, free cities, and merchant-princes.

The meaningful idea of life is, however, represented by the Estates and the symbols of Empire and Papacy. This political form is known as *the feudal-State,* the first State-idea of the West.

The first great political form-crisis of the West occurs when this idea loses its self-evident power, and there appears in the feelings of men the idea that there is something *higher,* to which even the noble blood and the feudal organization is subordinate. It is the dim beginning of the State-idea. The dissolution of the feudal State occurs in the 13th and 14th centuries. It takes the form of breaking down the overlordship of the highest lords, the Pope, Emperor, Kings. The Papacy, on the temporal side, was organized as a feudal hierarchy, with the great spiritual dignitaries holding their investitures of the Pope as overlord. After the death of Innocent III, under whom for a short time, the whole Western Culture had acknowledged the feudal supremacy of the Pope, the great archbishops and bishops forced through representative institutions for themselves, and reduced the temporal power of the Papacy gradually to a mere shadow power by 1400.

The greater German Princes made the Imperial throne dependent upon them as Electors, and this idea was formally constituted in the Golden Bull of 1356, although actually long before that. Magna Charta, 1215, the General Privilege of Saragossa, 1283, the Estates-General, 1302, have corresponding significance in England, Spain and France. In each case it is the breakup of the feudal concept of the State, and the arising of the pure State-Idea. It is the beginning of the Dynasty-Idea. The highest feeling heretofore was that of Life as deriving its significance from noble blood, but henceforth the idea is one of a *task*, a labor for the Future. The Dynasty is the symbol of this new idea.

From this crisis, we in the 20th century learn first of all that State-crises in a High Culture are not things of a few years duration, but of a century or more. We learn further that the surface of History does not reflect at once the underlying idea-forces at work which provide the impetus of History.

The end of the crisis finds the State-idea established everywhere in Europe. Even though everywhere the State remained entirely aristocratic, nevertheless Sovereignty did not reside with the Estates, but with the higher idea, the State. The word treason changes its meaning and becomes more absolute, more heinous. Henry the Lion had received but mild punishment for his defiance of the feudal Emperor. The Emperor was after all but *primus inter pares,* and the relationship between him and his vassals was *personal.* With the triumph of the State-idea, the obligation of loyalty to the State becomes superpersonal, once it is undertaken. It is loyalty to an Idea, not to the person of the monarch.

The State progresses in its development from the aristocratic State to the Absolute State. Absolute means: *independent of any other form.* As applied to the State, this means independent of the Estates who had everywhere asserted their independence of the dying feudal power of Emperor and Kings. This development brings forth the second great State-crisis of the West, the transition to the Absolute State. It lasts a century in its severest form and dominates all political events from 1550 to 1660.

Feudal politics had been the struggle for power among families, lords and vassals, factions. The dynasties had to rely on their political talent, for none of them rested so strongly that it could not be challenged by a powerful duke with a claim to kingship. It was the time of Lancaster and York, of the German Princes, of Renaissance city-politics and condottieri.

But the Absolute State-Idea was at work in the depths, and by about 1500 it becomes articulate, and engages everywhere in a struggle with the idea of the aristocratic State. Two ideas of the State are at war: the aristocratic State and the Absolute State. Since the Absolute State is the one which attained in history to identify with the State generally, we may call this second State-crisis of the West the battle of State against Estate, for, indeed, the form of this crisis was a defensive fight by the Nobility against the encroachments of Absolutism. The *new* idea is the State, it represents the Future in 1500, and therefore it prevails. The generic name of the wars entailed by this crisis is the Wars of the Fronde. The Fronde is the collective name of the noble Estates. This crisis lasts a century, and ends in France and Spain in the victory of the State over the Estates. The great names associated with this historical development are Richelieu and Olivarez. In England the State was represented by Charles, the Fronde by Cromwell. The defeat of the State-Idea was final in 1688, and thereafter England had no State in the sense of the State of Louis XIV, of the Spanish Phillips, of the Saxon, Würtembergian, Bavarian, or Prussian Kings. The aristocratic Parliament was the Nation, not the State.

In the Empire, the greater Princes overcame the State-idea in the Thirty-Years War. The name Wallenstein and its tragedy symbolize the defeat of the Imperial State-idea by the German Princes. After the Thirty Years War, Germany developed a whole collection of petty States, each modeled on the Versailles State. The defeat of the State-idea in Germany meant that Germany was out of condition for the great political contest.

II

The experience of England and of Germany in the Wars of the Fronde is of high importance for the surface of subsequent European history and must be examined.

The Absolute State idea represented the Future. It was a centralizing of politics, and therewith of power. It enlarged the arena of politics, and increased the amount of public power, and meant consequently that powers not adopting the new idea would drop out of the great combinations and become mere battlefields, objects of the great politics of the States. This is precisely what happened to Germany. Since there were 300 Germanies, there was no Germany, and the other powers fought their wars in German territory. Only Austria was a power, and it was constituted as a State. The other German States were too small to be able to play an independent role in Western politics, and thus were not true political units.

England is the only power in which the Fronde triumphed but which nevertheless was able to stay in condition for the greater political battles introduced by the State-idea. This was owing *solely* to England's island situation. The geopolitical security conferred on England by its insular existence enabled it to dispense with the strict centralization of inner power demanded by the State-idea, without at the same time ceasing to exist as a political unit, as did Germany. When Wallenstein and the Imperial State-idea lost, all was lost for Germany for two centuries. But Cromwell's victory, which destroyed the State-Idea in England, substituting for it the Idea of "Society," did not spell ruin for England, simply because other better-organized States were not able to invade it as long as it maintained an adequate naval establishment. To keep up a sufficiently large fleet did not require political centralization, and thus England survived the era of Absolutism without an Absolute State.

England, because of this island situation, did not become acquainted with the Slavic border-barbarian. It experienced, for instance, no Hussite Wars as did Germany. For 16 years, 1420–1436, the Hussite armies, first under the blind Ziska, and later divided, flooded over half Germany, burning, ravaging, killing. This destruction was vandalism, unconnected with any constructive political idea. It was 15th century Bolshevism—annihilation of everything Western.

The situation of Germany, on the border against Asia, was one of constant danger of invasion by barbarian Slavic, Turkish, Mongolian and Tartaric armies. Fighting against these armies was not colonial warfare, in the meaning of one-sided warfare that the expression acquired in the later centuries. These border barbarians were in contact with the West and adopted its purposefulness, its higher organization, and its centralized will.

While Germany in the East, and Spain in the South, were protecting the body of the Western Culture from the Barbarian, England was forming a national feeling based purely on contrast with other Western nations, and without feeling for the deep, total contrast between the Culture-peoples and the Barbarian. This exaggerated national feeling was to have fateful consequences for the entire West, including England, in the era of World Wars.

III

The great formula for the transition from the feudal union to the aristocratic State is that in the former the State existed only with reference to the Estates, and in the latter the Estates exist only with reference to the State. The slow externalizing of the Western soul—shown by things like gunpowder and printing, voyages of exploration, increasing elaboration of the economic life, demise of Scholastic philosophy through the triumph of Nominalism, growth of cities, growing strength of the idea of the Nation—progressively weakens the States, and the Wars of the Fronde were their last great assertion against the growing power of the Absolute State.

But the Absolute State represented the Future, and the Estates went down. In the main body of the West, after 1650, the State rules in politics. Its expression is dynastic, but the monarch derives his significance from the fact that he is the prime symbol of the State. When his entourage arrived at the formula that Louis XIV was *the State,* they were clothing him with the highest formula to which their thought could attain. In England, where there was no Absolute State, the substitute idea of the Nation was the leading idea, and the noble order ceased gradually to be an aristocracy, and finally even a nobility, and became finally *the Peerage,* a stratum whose significance was purely social. Its political possibilities were greater by reason of its social ascendancy, but it was still politically subordinate, and not sovereign as in the days of Magna Charta.

The political form-world of the Culture moves onward, and the next great political form-crisis is that of the transition from the Absolute State to Democracy. The crisis begins around 1750 and lasts a century in intense form. It broke out violently in France in 1789, and rapidly progressed to the Terror of 1793. The Rationalistic provenance of the ideas of the democrats showed that the Democracy-Idea is only politically-applied Rationalism.

The Absolute State-versus-Democracy crisis is different from the others in several ways. The decisive externalization of the soul of the West, brought about by the epochal change of Culture into Civilization, generated an amount of power for political purposes that dwarfed anything previous. Armies are numbered no longer in thousands or tens of thousands, but within decades pass to hundreds of thousands, and their numbers on both sides total millions. Instead of decisions being made by a few ambassadors or ministers, new leaders appear with the might of mobs at their backs. The form of the Absolute State had been unquestioned for more than a century, and now suddenly the new idea is in the air that *Reason* will examine all things anew and re-form the world. Since it is an organic fact that living things must obey their own inner laws or become sick, the attempt to subject the world of action to Reason could never succeed in its aim. Success merely meant the putting of

the State out of condition. But actually Reason simply turned
into a political weapon, and political leaders obeyed the dictates
of the situation without regard to Reason. The pretense of logic
had to be maintained, and the extreme divergence between conduct and principle equates Democracy with Hypocrisy. The
type of the party-politician is of necessity a charlatan-type. Lincoln, the American party-leader masquerading as a saint, is the
new idea of a politician. His pretense was humanitarianism, his
result was unlimited finance-capitalism over a continent, his
technic was the spoils-system.

Reason is a product of Life, and the attempt to turn the
tables and make Life into a creature of Reason was doomed in
practice. In theory, however, it lasts two centuries in all High
Cultures. The sole effect is to *destroy*. It destroys culture, in the
narrower sense of art forms and literature, it destroys traditions
of service, dignity, loyalty, honor. It destroys the State-idea as
embodied in its last refined form, the Absolute State. It lays the
Civilization waste from within, politically speaking. Having
leveled all the political and social powers, Rationalism can now
look upon the monster of its own creation, the absolute power
of Money. This new power is unformulated, anonymous, irresponsible. The most powerful money-magnates are not well-
known to the masses, nor do they wish to be. Fame, responsibility, and sanctions go together. The Master of Money desires
no limelight, no risk of life, but only money and ever more
money. Party politicians exist only to protect him and his operations. The courts are there to enforce his usury. The remnants
of the State are there to do him service. Armies march when his
trade system is challenged. He is subject to nothing, he is the
new Sovereign. He is above nations, and his banking operations
transcend national laws. It is during his tenure of power over
the Western Civilization that the phrase "power behind the

throne" acquires its sinister and private meaning. His is action without risk. To him a hero is a fool, a patriot an idiot. They may bleed, but he will profit. If his system is threatened, he mobilizes the masses of continents, supplementing nationalistic slogans with universal conscription which is more effective than the slogans.

This new creation shows what the great catchword "Freedom" means. Freedom was attractive to two great groups, the intellectuals and the trading-class. To both of them, the State was a burden. For its *one* pulse, *one* imperative, which impressed the life of everyone with its majesty, the pavement-intellectuals wish to substitute universal criticism, and the traders introduce universal trade without any restriction whatever. *These two new orders are the old nobility and priesthood in caricature.* The intellectual with his atheist pamphlet and the trader in his counting-house are respectively the masters in the democratic world of thought and action.

IV

For the purpose of recapitulating with the utmost clarity the biography of the State-Idea in the Western Culture, I append here a paradigm. The dates given must of course be taken as approximate. The exact year given is arbitrary. Historical transitions are gradual in their depths. An idea is born, slowly grows, finally enters the field of action, where its ultimate success may be delayed for many decades. Crises are perceptible, but the beginnings of the slow developments toward, and away from, a crisis, can have no exact date assigned them. Even in the life of a man, there is no date at which he becomes mature, nevertheless 21 has been selected as the *ideal* age of this transition.

	Duration of	Duration of Crisis in Transition to
Form of the State-Idea	Form	Next Form
Feudal State	1000–1300	1200–1300
Aristocratic State	1250–1660	1550–1660
Absolute State	1600–1815	1750–1850
Democracy	1750–1950	1900–19—

The table shows the State-forms overlapping one another, and the crises overlapping the forms, because the facts *do* exhibit this phenomenon in actuality. In one place the idea has already triumphed, in another this does not occur for fifty years. Or the new idea may appear and lose on the surface of history, and decades may be necessary before it again contends for power. We living in the middle of the 20th century know well what a transition period means. The old idea is quite dead, but party-leaders continue to repeat the old catch-words, like senseless parrots doing something for its own sake.

The last entry in the paradigm has been left blank. Succeeding the Democracy-idea of the State comes the last State-form of the Culture.

The old traditions of the Culture and their highest political expression, the Absolute State, have been swept away by two centuries of destruction under pressure from below. The class-war of mob-leading doctrinaires attacked and defeated the old social powers in the first century of Rationalism, 1750–1850, and finance-capitalists and labor-leaders defeated the productive economic leaders in its second century, 1850–1950, dissolving the whole collective life into a miserable, soulless, endless battle for money.

The entire population of the Western Culture is weary to death of this vile scramble, of this chaotic lack of leadership, of authority, or a strong, commanding voice. A deep yearning is going through the Western world to be free from the dirt and uncleanness of party-politics, class-war, financial usury, and complete absence of the heroic spirit. This yearning is the current form—1948—of the State-idea of the Future. It has already expressed itself in the body of Europe. Its form for the immediate Future is the Resurgence of Authority. It attains finally to Caesarism, in which authority is free from all defensiveness and is once more self-evident, as in the pre-Rationalist millennium. In its first stages the new State-idea is anti-democratic, anti-Rationalistic, but the further these ideas sink into the past, the less is it concerned with them.

The new State-form, corresponding to the slowly rising European race, European nation, European people, and European language, is also universal. It is a State whose home-soil is co-terminous with the boundaries of the West: Scandinavia, England, France, Germany, Italy, Spain. The details of whether this State in its first phase drags along some of the outdated Rationalistic forms with it—such as written pieces of constitution paper purporting to have something to do with government, parliaments, elections—are unimportant to its great inner meaning.

This State ends the inner anarchy of the West, which has become self-evident from long usage. Public power can no longer be held by individuals; public enterprises pass under public control and ownership; the money-monopoly of the few individuals is transferred to the State. Capitalism vanishes, in both of its aspects, the finance-capitalism of the supra-national usurer, and the capitalism of the labor-dictator. The emphasis on inner-politics passes away with the undertaking of the greatest wars the world has ever seen against the Barbarian for the survival of the Western Civilization. The heroic spirit replaces the spirit of profiteering. Honor replaces cant, and the trader gives way to the soldier. Unlimited Imperialism is the task of this State, not the Crusading Imperialism which vanished with feudalism, nor the Ultramontane Imperialism of Spain in its glory, nor the economic Imperialism of England, 1600–1900, but a new, total, political, organizatory, authoritarian Imperialism, which will plant the Western banner on the highest peaks and the most remote peninsulas. The new State will not have the party-leader's horizon of the next election but will think in centuries, and will build for a millennium. It will dissolve the selfishness of individualism in a new Socialism, not the old-fashioned class-war Socialism of "rights," but a stern Socialism oriented to the outer danger. The old attempts to tamper with Reality by means of theories are forgotten in the new unity of Culture, Nation, People, Race, State. Since the new State negates Rationalism, the enemy of the soul of Culture-man, it has an affirmative attitude toward the spiritual development, the Rebirth of Religion, which accompanies the arising of the new State.

The last entry on the paradigm illustrating the biography of the State-idea in the Western Culture thus is:—

    Authoritarian State   1900–2——   None, final
                                                Western
                                                State-form

CULTURAL VITALISM
(B) Culture Pathology

Culture Pathology

ALL OF THE four forms of life—plant, animal, man, High Culture—exhibit the organic regularities of birth, growth, maturity, fulfillment, death. Each form contains within it the essence of the less elaborate, less articulate forms and the new soul is a superstructure, as it were, on the general foundation. Thus the plant exhibits a close connection with the cosmic rhythms, the animal has geographic distribution over a certain landscape, large or small, and shows also immediacy of instinct coming from its close connections with cosmic rhythms. Man has attachment to the soil, both spiritually and materially, possesses beast-of-prey instincts, and shows in his rhythm of sleep and waking the alternating supremacy of the tensionless plant-element in him. A High-Culture is *plantlike* in its attachment to its original soil, which lasts from its beginning to its latest period; *animal-like* in its ruthless devouring of other life-forms; *man-like* in its spirituality, and *original* in its power to transform human life, its great life span, and the forcefulness of its destiny.

To everything living belongs sickness as well as health. In his classification of the sciences, Bacon provided a place for the science of deviations, and after him D'Alembert, in his classification for the *Encyclopédie* listed "Prodigies, or deviations from the usual course of Nature." Life is regular in its phenomena, and when it deviates, it is regular in its deviations. Illness of whatever sort, exopathic or autopathic, comes under Pathology. Plants have their pathology, as have animals and man. High Cultures also have their pathology, which is only being realized for the first time by the new Age, with its incorruptible eye for facts, and its freedom from the prejudice of Materialism. Pathology follows the organism, and thus plants cannot suffer from liver trouble, nor dogs from psychosis. But the process works upward, just as the planes of life are stratified, one above the other, as life increases in complexity. Thus parasitism, a form of plant pathology, exists as well for all the higher life-forms. The growth of a plant can be thwarted by unfavorable conditions, just as the development of an animal can be stunted by outside interference. Weaker human organisms can be spiritually retarded and stultified by complete domination of their souls by stronger-willed humans.

Human pathology is a science of the becoming, not a science of the become, like physics. It can never succeed in its program of organizing the field of life-deviations, for Life defies all classification whatever. The invisible components dominate the visible. The soul, the will, the intellect, the emotions, are all *uncanny* in their effects, and cannot be treated in the systematic fashion appropriate to the data of physics or geology.

The pathology of High Cultures was naturally a blank to a scientific method which asserted as a basic dogma that Life was mechanics, man was soulless, that there must be a chemical formula for consciousness. To this outlook which denied God and Soul, High Culture was an abstract name for the collective efforts of single men. A nation was a collection of individuals with only mechanical connections, economics and "happiness" were the entire content of Life, everything which put spiritual content or meaning into Life was the prime enemy. This view simply could not understand Life. It produced a psychology hardly complex enough even for animals, and called it human psychology. It placed the barren intelligence in the center of the inner world, and denied the mystical nature of human creativeness.

This viewpoint was itself a product of a certain Age, the Age of Rationalism, and with the passing of this prejudice, we stand before a whole new world of soul-relationships, entry into which was forbidden during the last two centuries. We are liberated from the oppressive drabness of Materialism, free to step forth once more into the multi-colored and infinitely varied realm of the Soul. In its final phase, the Age of Rationalism turned its knife on itself: with its refusal to recognize psychic phenomena proved by its own methods, it showed its own nature as a Faith, an irrationality, and moved into History's collection of temples, legends, and memories.

Materialism approached Life from its under side. In actuality, the Soul uses the material as the vehicle of its expression. Materialism, seeing only the results, and not the invisible Destiny which was bringing them about, said that the *results* were primary, the Soul a null. Failing to grasp the invisible *Necessity* which rules the organic and its relationship to the Cosmos, it reached the conclusion from a hundred different directions that Life is an *accident.* Not to catalogue these interesting reasons, take for example, the presence of dust in the air. The laboratory-thinkers discovered that *if* dust were not present in the air, all Life would be impossible. It never occurred to

them that Life and all the other phenomena were connected by
mystical necessity. By treating everything separately, by ever-
finer analysis of ever-smaller things, they lost all connection
with Reality, and were surprised when connections among
things did appear. It could only be an accident, said these profound thinkers.

I X 95

II

The *conditions* of Life form a starting point for us. Not the
conditions of all Life, but only that particular form of Life
called High Culture.

Each variety of life-form has its own ideal conditions. Some
plants require much water, others little. Some grow in salt
water, others need fresh water. Animals have a habitat, each
species has its own area or areas which furnish the conditions
of its health and survival. Human beings as a whole have certain areas, and various types of human beings have their respective landscapes which further their life-needs.

Corresponding to the ideal life-conditions of the various life-
forms, each form of life, and each organism, possesses power
of *adaptation*. A plant can continue to live—at a lower potential—if given less than the ideal amount of water. But a point
is reached at which the amount of water is minimal, and if less
is given, life ceases entirely. This is the *limit of adaptation*.
Both animals and man have adaptivity and a limit thereto. Men
can live in the dense air of valleys and in the rare air of high
mountains. The human body adapts itself to mountain conditions by increasing the size of the chest and the lung-surface.
But this ability to adapt is not indefinite, and a rarity of air is
reached to which men cannot become adapted because of inherent bounds of the human life-form.

The treatment of this subject in this work is not meant to be anything more than the minimum presentation of fundamentals necessary to understanding the nature of Culture-phenomena generally, as the basis for *action*. This is politics, not philosophy of history, nor yet natural philosophy of organisms. The whole subject of Culture-pathology is comparatively new. What in 2100 will be a completed discipline is now only an outline, and this is even less than an outline. But politics cannot be separated from Culture, and any effort which lights its *necessary* path forward for Western politics at this critical juncture is justified culturally and historically.

A High Culture is different from other organisms in that it actualizes its material manifestations through lower organisms, namely through Culture-man. Its body is a huge aggregate of many millions of human bodies in a certain landscape. The question of whether the prime symbol of the Culture is spiritually adapted to the particular *landscape* is outside our scope.

It is apparent that the question of *physical* adaptation does not exist for a Culture. Its only adaptation is *spiritual*. Nor can it have a *physical* disease like men can. Disease to a Culture can only be a *spiritual* phenomenon.

Life itself is a mystery, that is, something which is not fully understandable. Perhaps this is because the faculty of understanding is only one manifestation of one type of Life, in other words a part of a part, and is thus unadapted to assimilating the Whole. Every manifestation of Life is a mystery, including disease. Some men, when brought in contact with certain micro-organisms, develop a definite disease. Other men do not react at all to these micro-organisms. The serum that may be beneficial to one man may kill another. It is possible to discuss disease-phenomena like these in terms of adaptation and inability to adapt. The last reason why a species, or an individual,

finds its limits of adaptability precisely *here* and not at a further
point, will always be unknown.

And so with Cultures. Just why the soul of a Culture retains
its purity and individuality is hidden. Nevertheless inwardly
it follows its own life-course, and cannot follow the life course
that an alien life-feeling, deriving its motivation from extra-
Cultural sources, might wish to have it.

Just why Destiny impels an organism to actualize its possibilities, compels continuous transition from one phase into
the next, is also a mystery. Nevertheless it does. The materialistic 19th century, having completely lost touch with the real
world of the spirit in its obsession with the sub-real world of
the material, felt in consequence a nameless terror of death, and
rationalistic medicine announced its intention of doing away
with Death. This sort of thing reflects credit on the intellectual
courage of the rationalists, but shows their rootless intelligence
to be synonymous with stupidity. We cannot do away with
Destiny, since even our protest against it is a phase of development.

The entire subject of Culture-pathology is too wide to be
treated here, and it will be the subject of many volumes in the
coming centuries. All that is necessary for the 20th century
action-outlook is to understand three phenomena within this
larger field of Culture-pathology, namely, Culture-parasitism,
Culture-Retardation, and Culture-distortion. All of these Cul-
ture-illnesses exist in the West in the middle of the 20th century, and have existed for some time. It is only this sick condition of the Western Civilization that makes the current grotesque world-situation possible. Current refers to the first two
World Wars and their hideous aftermath. The home soil of
the Western Civilization is the site of the strongest brains and
characters, the most intense moral force, the highest technical

creativeness, the only positive high Destiny, in the world, but yet despite the fact that all these spell the world's greatest power-concentration, the Western Civilization today is simply an object of world-politics. It is spoils, booty, for marauding powers from without. This situation did not come about by military means, but by critical Culture-disease.

Culture Parasitism

IN THE chapter on the outlook on politics, the condition in which persons thinking privately affect public affairs was called parasite-politics. The example was given of La Pompadour throwing France into a war against the great Frederick because he had dubbed her with an uncomplimentary name before all Europe. In this war, France lost its overseas empire to England, because it was fighting in Europe, and devoting less effort to the great imperial war than to the local European war. This is the usual result of parasite-politics.

A nation is an Idea, but it is a mere part of the greater Idea of the Culture which creates it in the process of its own actualization. But precisely as a nation can be the host to groups and powerful individuals who think in complete independence of the fulfillment of the national Idea, so can a Culture.

Everyone is familiar with parasite politics in a nation, and everyone understands it when he becomes aware of it. When the Greek Capodistria was Secretary for Foreign Affairs in Russia, he was not expected to execute an anti-Greek policy. During the Boxer Rebellion in China, no Western power thought of giving a command to a Chinese general. In the American war against Japan, 1941–1945, the Americans did not use their Japanese conscripts, just as Europe discovered in the first two World Wars that it could not use Slavic Bohemians against Russia. American generals would not dare to use their Mexicans against Mexico, or their Negroes against Abyssinia. Nor in a period of war preparation against Russia would a known Russian sympathizer be given public power in America. Much less would the Americans turn over the entire government to known Russian immigrants.

Phenomena of this type reflect the general fact that a man or group remains what it is even though taken into another group unless assimilated. Assimilation is the demise of a group *qua* group. The blood-stream of the individuals comprising it continues, but the group is gone. As long as it was a group, it was foreign.

In our examination of race we saw that physical differences are no barrier to assimilation, but that a Cultural barrier is. Examples are the Baltic Germans and the Volga Germans, cut off in primitive Russia, Chinese and Japanese in America, Negroes in America and in South Africa, the British in India, the Parsees in India, the Jews in the Western Civilization and in Russia, the Hindus in Natal.

Culture-parasitism arises in the same way that parasitism arises in politics. A parasite is simply a life-form which lives in or on the body of another life-form at its expense. It involves thus the direction of part of the energy of the host into a direction alien to its interest. This is quite inevitable: if the energy of an organism is being spent for something other than its own development, it is being wasted. Parasitism is inevitably harmful to the host. The harm increases in proportion to the growth and spreading of the parasite.

Any group which takes no part in the Culture-feeling, but which lives within the Culture-body, necessarily involves a loss to the Culture. Such groups form areas of anesthetic tissue, as it were, in the Culture body. Such a group, by standing outside the historical necessity, the Destiny of the Culture, inevitably militates *against* that Destiny. This phenomenon is in no way dependent on human will. The parasite is spiritually without, but physically within. The effects on the host-organism are deleterious both physically and spiritually.

The first physical effect of non-participating groups within the body of a Culture is that the numbers of the Culture-population are thereby reduced. The members of the alien group *take the place of* individuals belonging to the Culture, who thus *never come to be born.* It reduces artificially the numbers of the Culture-populations by the numbers of the parasitic group. In animal and human parasitism, one of the numerous effects on the host is the loss of nourishment, and Cultural parasitism is analogous. By reducing the numbers of Culture individuals, a Culture-parasite is depriving the Cultural Idea of the only form of physical nourishment it needs—a constant supply of human material adequate to its life-task.

It is only in the light of recent studies of population trends that this anti-reproductive effect of immigrating groups is established. Thus from comparative study of American population trends, it emerged that the 40,000,000 immigrants to America from other continents from 1790 up to now—*did not serve to increase the population of America at all,* but only to change the quality of it. A superpersonal Idea, clothed as it is with the force of Destiny, must fulfill its life-task, and if this involves populations of a certain size, increasing at a certain rate, these externals will come into existence.

Materialism found itself with the data of population trends

on its hands but no explanation for them. These data showed for the Western nations gradual increases, rising rapidly to a peak, and then a stabilizing and slow falling off. The curve that describes this population movement of nations—it is the same curve, roughly speaking, in each case—will be found also to describe the population movement of a High Culture. At the stage where a High Culture passes over into Civilization—the stage marked for us by Napoleon—the increase of numbers is rapid and rises to figures which dwarf anything previous. The same Spirit of the Age which externalized the whole energy of the Culture into massive industrialism and technics, great revolutions, gigantic wars, and unlimited Imperialism, also called these numbers into being. The life-task of the Western Civilization is the mightiest the world has ever seen, and it needs these numbers in order to accomplish it.

Culturally parasitical groups are not available to the Idea. They use the energy of the Culture inwards and downwards. Such groups constitute weak spots in the body of the Culture. The danger of this internal weakness increases in direct proportion as the Culture is threatened from without. In the 16th century when the existence of the West was threatened by the Turks, it would have been perfectly evident to every Westerner that large inner groups of Turks—had there been such—were a serious menace.

A second way that Culture-parasitism wastes the substance of the Culture is through the inner friction that their presence *necessarily* creates. In the body of the Arabian Culture around the time of Christ, a large number of Romans was present. Their cultural-stage was that of Late Civilization, complete externalization, and the cultural stage of the Aramaean population which was there at home was that of the earliest Culture. The tension which was naturally engendered—racial, national and cultural, finally culminated in the massacre, in 88 B.C., of 80,000 Romans. This brought on the Mithradatic Wars, in which more hundreds of thousands perished in 22 years of fighting.

Another phenomenon closer to our times is that of the Chinese in California. The racial tension between the white and Chinese populations there during the 19th and 20th centuries resulted in mutual persecution, hatred, riots, and bloody excesses.

The Negro population both in America and South Africa has been the occasion of similar outbreaks of hatred and violence on both sides.

All these incidents are manifestations of Culture-parasitism, the presence of a group which is outside the Culture totally. These phenomena have no connection whatever, as the analytic approach of Rationalism thought, with hatred or malice on either side. Rationalism always looks downward: it saw merely a group of individuals on both sides. If these individuals were massacring one another, it was the desire of these particular individuals at this particular time to kill one another. Rationalism did not understand even the simple organic phenomenon of a crowd, much less the higher forms of people, race, nation, Culture. It never occurred to the Liberals that since these tensions throughout 5,000 years of history had always manifested themselves thus, that there was any *necessity* at work. Liberals could not understand instinct, cosmic rhythm, racial beat. To them a race riot was a manifestation of lack of "education," of "tolerance." A bird flying over a street-disturbance would understand it better than the materialists, for they voluntarily adopted the viewpoint of the earthworm and held to it with determination.

So far from these excesses being the result of malice or hatred, the contrary is true—demonstrations of good-will and "tolerance" actually increase the tension between totally alien groups, and render it more deadly. Focusing attention onto the differences between utterly alien groups works these differences up into contrasts, and hastens outbreaks. The closer the two groups are brought into contact, the more insidious and dangerous grows the mutual hatred.

Theoretically it sounds perfect to say that if each individual is "educated" to "tolerance" there can be no racial or cultural tension. But—*individuals are not the units of this type of happening;* individuals do not bring these things about, higher organic unities do this, and impel the mere individuals. The process has nothing to do with consciousness, intellect, will, or even emotions, in its inception. All these come into play only as a manifestation of defense on the part of the Culture against the alien life-form. Hatred does not begin the process, nor does "tolerance" stop it. This sort of talk is applying the logic of the billiard table to superpersonal organisms. But logic is out of place here. *Life is irrational,* and so is every one of its manifestations: birth, growth, illness, resistance, self-expression, Destiny, History, Death. If we wish to keep the word *logic* we must distinguish inorganic logic from organic logic. Inorganic logic is causality thinking; organic logic is destiny-thinking. The first is aware, illuminated, conscious; the second is rhythmic and unconscious. The first is the laboratory-logic of physical experimentation; the second is the living-logic of the human beings who carry on this activity, and who are in no way amenable, in their lives, to the logic which they apply in their workshops.

I I

The most tragic example of Culture-parasitism for the West has been the presence of a part of a nation from the Arabian

Culture scattered through the entire body of the West. We have already seen the entirely different content of the nation-idea in that other Culture—nations there were State, Church, and People all in one. The idea of a *territorial* home was unknown. Home was wherever the believers were. Belonger and believer were interchangeable ideas. This Culture had attained to its Late Civilization phase while our Gothic West was barely emerging from the primitive.

Into the tiny hamlets—there were no cities—of the awakening West, these finished cosmopolitans built their ghettos. Money-thinking, which seemed evil to the deeply religious West, was the *forte* of this highly civilized alien people. Interest-taking was forbidden by the Church to Christians, and this conferred a monopoly of money on the strangers. The *Judengasse* was a millennium ahead in Cultural development of its surroundings.

The legend of the Wandering Jew arose at this time, expressing the feeling of *uncanniness* that the Westerner felt in the presence of this landless stranger who was everywhere at home, although it seemed to the West that he was nowhere at home. The West understood as little of his Torah, Mishnah, Talmud, Kabbalism, and Yesirah, as he of its Christianity and Scholastic philosophy. This mutual inability to understand generated feelings of alienness, fear and hatred.

The hatred of the Westerner for the Jew was of religious motivation, not racial. The Jew was the *heathen,* and with his civilized and intellectualized life, he seemed Mephistophelean, Satanic to the Westerner. The chronicles of the time record the horrors which the contact of these two utterly alien groups begot. Jews were massacred in London on the day of coronation of Richard I in 1189. The next year 500 Jews were besieged in York castle by a mob, and to avoid its fury, resorted to cutting each other's throats. King John had Jews imprisoned, their eyes or teeth plucked out, and hundreds butchered in 1204. When a Jew in London forced a Christian to pay him more than 2s. a week on a loan of 20s., mob action killed 700 Jews. Crusaders, for centuries, massacred whole Jewish populations of towns, when they stopped on their way to the wars in Asia Minor. In 1278, 267 Jews were hanged in London, accused of clipping coins. The outbreak, in 1348, of the Black Death, was attributed to the Jews, and massacres were the result all over Europe. For 370 years, the Jews were banished from England, until readmitted by Cromwell.

Although the motivation of these excesses was not racial, it was race-creating. What did not destroy the Jews made them stronger, and separated them further than ever from the host-peoples, physically and spiritually.

During the centuries of our Western history, the problems and developments which roused *fundamental* excitement in the West did not touch the problemless Jew, whose inner life had passed into fixity with the completion of the Culture which created this Jewish Church-State-People-Nation. Empty for him were the conflict of Empire and Papacy, the Reformation, the Age of Discovery. He looked upon them purely as a spectator. His only question was what they might mean to *him*. The idea of his taking part in them, or making sacrifices for one side or another, never came up. The British in India looked upon disturbances among the indigenous populations with the same eye.

In his ghettoes distributed over Europe, all was uniform: the food-prohibitions, the Talmudic dualistic ethics, one for the *goyim* and another for the Jew, the legal system, the runes, the phylacteries, the ritual, the feeling. His Sufism, his Hasidim sect, his Kabbalism, his religious leaders like Baal Shem, his

Zaddikism, are equally unintelligible to Westerners. Not only unintelligible, but uninteresting. The Westerner was absorbed in the intense conflicts of his own Culture, and did not observe, except in relation to himself, the life of the Jew in his midst.

Not until the externalized, fact-sensitive 20th century, did the Western Culture notice the Jew as a Cultural phenomenon. In Gothic times, until the Reformation, it saw him as a heathen and usurer, in the Counter-Reformation as a shrewd business-man, in the Enlightenment as a civilized man of the world, in the Age of Rationalism as a fighter in the van of intellectual liberation from the bonds of the Culture and its traditions.

The 20th century saw for the first time that he had his own public life, his own world down to the details. It realized that the comprehensiveness of his outlook was the equivalent of its own in breadth and depth, and therefore alien in a *total* sense which was never before suspected. In its previous centuries, the viewpoint of the West toward the Jew was limited by its stage of development at the time, but with the 20th century and its universal outlook, the *entirety* of what has been called "the Jewish problem" is seen for the first time. Not race, not reli-gion, not ethics, not nationality, not political allegiance—but something which includes them all, separates the Jew from the West—Culture.

Culture embraces the totality of world-outlook: science, art, philosophy, religion, technics, economics, erotic, law, society, politics.

In every branch of the Western Culture, the Jew has devel-oped his own taste and preference, and when he intervenes in the public life of the Western peoples, he conducts himself in a distinct fashion, namely in the style of the public life of the Jewish Church-State-Nation-People-Race. This public life was invisible to the inward West until the 20th century.

Like all nations at the end of their Civilization, *e.g.,* Hindus, Chinese, Arabs, the Jewish nation passed into a caste system. The Brahmins in India, the Mandarins in China, the Rabbinate in Jewry, are three corresponding phenomena. The Rabbinate were the custodians of the Destiny of the Jewish unity. When freethinkers appeared among the Jews, it was the duty of the local Rabbinate to prevent a schism. In the case of Uriel da Costa, a freethinking Jew of Amsterdam, the local Synagogue had him imprisoned, and subjected him to such persecution that he finally took his own life. Spinoza was excommunicated by the same Synagogue, and an unsuccessful attempt was made on his life. Large bribes were offered him to return to Judaism, and when he refused he was cursed and pronounced anathema. In 1799, the Hasidim leader in Eastern Jewry, Senior Salman, was handed over by the Rabbinate to the Romanov Government after a trial by his own people, much as the Western Inquisition turned over convicted heretics to the State for disposal.

The contemporary West did not even see these phenomena, and would not have understood them if it had. It looked at everything Jewish with its own preconceptions, just as the Jews looked at the West in terms of its advanced outlook.

The Parsee in India is another fragment of the Arabian Culture strewn abroad among aliens. The Parsee possessed *vis-a-vis* his human surroundings the same superior business acumen as the Jew in the early West. His inner life was entirely apart from the aliens around him. His interests were different in every way. In the disturbances and revolts during the centuries of the British Raj, the Parsee took no part.

In the same way, the Thirty Years' War, the Succession Wars, the conflict of Bourbon and Hapsburg, did not in any way touch the Jew. Difference of Culture-phase creates complete spiritual insulation. The attitude of the Jew toward Western

tensions was that of Pilate at the trial of Jesus. To Pilate the
religious issue there involved was utterly hidden—he belonged
to a Civilization in its last phase, a thousand years away from
the religious excitement of his own Culture.

With the stirrings of Rationalism in the West, however, a
caesura is marked in the collective life of that part of Jewry
cut off in the Western Culture.

III

Around 1750, new spiritual currents begin to move in the
West. English Sensualist philosophy assumes the ascendancy
over the European soul. Reason, empiricism, analysis, induction
—this is the new spirit. But *everything* becomes folly when
examined in the light of reason unleavened by faith and instinct
—Erasmus had demonstrated in his malicious work *In Praise of
Folly* that *everything* is folly, not only greed, ambition, pride,
and war, but Church, State, marriage, child-bearing and philosophy. The supremacy of Reason is hostile to Life, and brings
about a crisis in any organism which succumbs to it.

The Culture-crisis of Rationalism was a part of the Destiny
of the West. All previous Cultures have gone through it. It
marks the turning-point from the inwardness of Culture to the
externalized soul-life of Civilization. The focal idea of Ràtion-
alism is *liberty*—which means liberty from the bonds of Culture. Napoleon liberated war from the style of Fontenoy, 1745,
where each side courteously invited the other to fire the first
shot. Beethoven liberated music from the form-perfection of
Bach and Mozart. The Terror of '93 liberated the West from
the idea of the sacredness of Dynasty. Materialistic philosophy
liberated it from the spirit of religion, and ultra-Rationalism
then proceeded to liberate science from philosophy. Waves of

revolution liberated the Civilization from the dignity of the State and its high traditions into the dirt of party-politics. Class war was liberation from social order and hierarchy. The new idea of "humanity" and "The Rights of Man" liberated the Culture from its old pride of exclusivensss and feeling of unconscious superiority. Feminism liberated women from the natural dignity of their sex and turned them into inferior men.

Anacharsis Cloots organized a deputation of "representatives of the human race" which presented its respects to the Revolutionary Terror in France. There were pig-tailed Chinamen, black Ethiopians, Turks, Jews, Greeks, Tartars, Mongols, Indians, bearded Chaldeans. Actually however, they were Parisians in disguise. This parade had thus at the very beginning of Rationalism a double symbolic significance. First, it symbolized the idea of the West that it now wished to embrace all "humanity," and secondly, the fact these were disguised Westerners showed the exact amount of success that this intellectualizing enthusiasm would have.

The Jew had of course seen these things coming. Persecution does not diminish intelligence and awareness of one's surroundings. As early as 1723 the Jews had acquired the right to possess land in England, and in 1753 they acquired English citizenship, only to have it revoked the next year on the petition of all the cities. In 1791 they were emancipated in France, and in 1806 the Great Sanhedrin was summoned by the Emperor Napoleon, thus giving official recognition to the existence within the West of the Jewish Nation-State-People.

Only one thing prevented the new situation from being as idyllic as the new liberal sentiment would have it. Eight hundred years, of robbery, hatred, massacre, and persecution on both sides had roused within the Jew traditions of hatred of the West even stronger than the old Western hatred of the

Jew. In its new outburst of generosity and forgiveness, the
West renounced its old feelings, but the Jew was unable to
reciprocate. Eight hundred years of resentment were not to be
removed by a New Year's Resolution on the part of the alien
West. Superpersonal organic unities were here opposed, and
these higher unities do not share with human beings things like
reason and sentiment. Their life-task is hard and colossal, and
excludes feelings of "tolerance" except as a symptom of crisis.
In a great battle of this kind, human beings are in the last
analysis mere spectators, even though they play an active role.
Human malice and desire for revenge play only the smallest,
most superficial part in such conflicts, and when they appear,
they are the mere expression in the individual of the higher
incompatibility, deep and total, between the superpersonal
Ideas.

The new movements—capitalism, industrial revolution, democracy, materialism—all were tremendously exciting to the
Jew. In the middle of the 18th century already, he had sensed
their potentialities and had fostered their growth in every way.
His position as the outsider forced him to act secretly, and the
secret societies of the Illuminati and its offspring were his creations, as their Kabbalistic terminology and ritualistic equipment show. More than two thirds of the Estates-General which
paved the way to the French Revolution in 1789 consisted of
members of these secret societies, committed to undermine the
authority of the State and introduce the idea of Democracy. The
Jew responded to the invitation of the West to participate in
his public life, but it was impossible for him to lose his identity
overnight, and so he had from now on two public lives, one
before the West and one before his own Nation-State-People-
Church-Race.

With the crumbling of the old Western traditions before the

onslaught of the new ideas, the Jew forged ahead. The Roths-
childs became—what would have been simply fantastic to both
sides a century before—barons of the Austrian empire in 1822.
Jews penetrated the English bar in 1833, and a Jew was
knighted by the Queen—the first one—in 1837. The West
acceded to the duality of the Jew and a statute of 9 Victoria re-
lieved Jews elected to municipal office from taking oaths. Jewish Members of Parliament appeared from the forties onward,
and a Jew became Lord Mayor of London in 1855. All of these
things were resisted by traditional elements of the West, and
on each occasion the Jew gained a triumph. The experiment of
"tolerance" was visibly failing on both sides.

The amount of power and importance the Jew was gaining
was shown by the incident of the boy Mortara. This child was
forcibly taken from his Jewish parents, ordinary private persons, by the archbishop of Bologna in 1858, on the plea that
he had been baptized by a serving maid. In the same year *the
French government* officially urged restoration of the boy to its
parents. The next year, the Archbishop of Canterbury, bishops,
noblemen and gentlemen of England signed a petition presented by Lord John Russell asking return of custody of the
child.

The persecution continued—there were outbreaks in Bucha-
rest, 1866, Rome, 1864, Berlin, 1880, Russia through the whole
century and into the 20th century. This persecution in Russia
was an index of the strength of the Jew in the Western nations.
Protests, petitions, committees, sought to alleviate the lot of
the Jews in Russia and to obstruct the government of Russia.
The pogrom in the Ukraine after the Russo-Japanese War,
1905, *caused the American government to break off diplomatic
relations with Russia.*

Hatred or intolerance in no wise explains the numerous unfortunate results attendant upon the Jewish dispersion through the Western nations. The hatred on both sides was a mere result. The more tolerance was talked about, the more atten-tion was focused onto the differences, sharpening them into *contrasts*. The contrasts led to opposition and action, either covert or open, on both sides.

Nor is it an explanation to *blame* the Jew for failing to assimilate. This is blaming a man for being himself, and the notion of ethics does not extend to what one *is*, but only to what one *does*. The "Jewish problem" is not to be explained ethically, racially, nationally, religiously, socially—but only *totally*, cul-turally. From having seen at each phase only that aspect of the Jew which his own development permitted him to, Western man now sees the whole relationship, for his own Cultural unity is uppermost in Western man. In Gothic times, he saw the Jew as different only in religion, because the West was then in a reli-gious phase. In the Enlightenment with its ideas of "humanity," the Jew was seen merely to be socially different. In the materi-alistic 19th century with its vertical racism, the Jew was re-garded as merely racially different. In this century, with the West passing into a unit of Culture, nation, race, society, eco-nomics, State, the Jew appears clearly in his own *total* unity, a complete inner stranger to the soul of the West.

IV

The materialistic 19th century saw this phenomenon of Cul-ture-parasitism only as nation-parasitism, and thus it was mis-understood in each nation as merely a local condition. For this reason, the phenomenon in each country called *anti-semitism* was only a partial reaction to what was a Cultural, and not merely a national, condition.

Anti-semitism is precisely analogous in Culture pathology to the formation of anti-bodies in the bloodstream in human pathology. In both cases, the organism is resisting the alien life. Both are *inevitable, organically necessary,* expressions of Destiny. In fulfilling the proper, Destiny combats the alien. It cannot be said too often that hatred and malice, tolerance and goodwill, have nothing whatever to do with this fundamental process. A Culture is an *organism,* an organism of a different class from man, just as man is an organism of a different class from animals. But the fundamental regularities of organic life are present in all organisms, of whatever class, plant, animal, man, Culture. This hierarchy of organisms is obviously part of the divine plan, and it cannot be changed by a process of propaganda, no matter how continuous, "tolerance," no matter how self-renouncing, or self-deception, no matter how complete.

A treatment of anti-semitism raises questions which belong with Culture-distortion, rather than Culture-parasitism, and so it may suffice to say here that anti-semitism—again, precisely like the human pathological phenomenon of formation of antibodies in the blood—is the other side of the existence of Culture-parasitism, and is only to be understood as one of its effects. Anti-semitism is completely organic and irrational, just as is reaction to human disease. Culture-parasitism is the phenomenon of the totally alien in co-existence with a host, and is also entirely irrational. There is no *reason* for Culture-parasitism.

On the contrary, Reason would seem to dictate that the alien group dissolve and flow into the surrounding life. This would end all the bitter persecution, the sterile hatred, the wasted fighting. But Life is irrational, also during the Age of Rationalism. In fact the only way Rationalism can come onto the stage is in the form of a religion, a Faith, an Irrationality.

The phenomenon of Culture-parasitism is not confined in a High Culture, to the mother-soil of the Culture. This is well shown by the history of America.

America originated as a colony of the Western Culture. This one sentence contains the whole Fate of America. It sets in advance the limit to the potentialities of America. The idea of the *Colony* must be examined. What is a Colony? It is a *creation* of a Culture, it is a work, by its mere successful plantation it is something spiritually completed. This is another way of saying it has no inner necessity, no mission. It is thus dependent for its spiritual nourishment on the Mother-Culture. This is as true of America in the Western Culture as it was of Syracuse and Alexandria in the Classical, of Granada and Seville in the Arabian. While fruitful impulses can, albeit rarely, come from the periphery of the Cultural Body, they find their significance in their development in the Culture-center. This spiritual dependence of colonies is *weakness*. This weakness is expressed by lack of resistance to the Culturally alien, and one would expect to find less organic resistance to the Culturally alien in a colony, for the sense of Cultural mission is not generally present at all, but exists only in isolated individuals or tiny groups at best. The history of Colonies shows us—Syracuse is one example—that Culture-crises, even autopathic ones like the appearance of Rationalism, produce greater effects in them. A colony can be more easily disintegrated, because it lacks the articulation that the Culture has. There is not, cannot be, a Culture-bearing stratum in a Colony. This stratum is an organ of the land-bound High Culture. The Culture cannot be transplanted, even though its populations migrate and remain in contact with the body of the Culture. Colonies are *products* of a Culture, and represent Life at a less complex and articulate level than the creating Culture.

The comprehension of this elementary fact has always been unconsciously quite complete in America, and in the 20th century has been just as vehemently *consciously* denied. American men of letters in the 19th century, assimilated Western Culture inwardly, and were assimilated by it. The phenomenon of Edgar Poe has always generated wonder by reason of his complete mastery of Culture-thinking and total independence of his colonial environment. In its higher branches, American belles-lettres has figured as a part of English literature, and quite correctly, as regards most of it. The poverty and meagerness of American letters is attributable to the colonial fate, while its few great names are expressions of Western Culture.

Americans of all callings through the past two centuries, insofar as they were, or wished to be, men of significance, have had their center of gravity in Europe—Irving, Hawthorne, Emerson, Whistler, Frank Harris, Henry James, the finance-plutocracy, Wilson, Ezra Pound. A tradition in America makes a European tour a part of education. Europe continued to possess spiritually those American elements with Culture feelings or Culture ambitions.

In every generalization of organic subject matter, it is sought only to state the *great regularity*. The deviations always exist in living matter, but find their place only with respect to the larger rhythms. Rationalist thought attempted to disintegrate organic thinking by concentrating on the *deviating incidents,* in the attempt to destroy the great, sweeping, organic rhythm. It had not even the depth sufficient to grasp the wisdom contained in the saw "the exception proves the rule."

Even though it became the fashion in America, after its appearance as a world-power, following the Spanish war, 1898–1899, to *deny* its spiritual dependence upon Europe, the fact continued to exist. By this time we are not surprised when a

Culture-fact shows its disregard of human wishes, intentions, demands, statements. America is a subject that needs to be treated separately, as the Culture-disease of the West has given it a new significance in world-politics. In this place, the presence of Culture-parasitism in America is the only aspect under consideration.

V

From the early 17th century onward, continuing to the early 19th century, slave-trading brought millions of African aboriginies to America. These formed, during the 18th and first half of the 19th century, a large, prolific, and totally alien parasitic body. It is a good example of the *Cultural* meaning of the term parasite that it has no reference to work, in the economic sense. Thus the Africans in America were *economically* important, and, after an economy was built on them, necessary, in a practical sense. Class-war made it the mode to refer to all persons other than manual workers as "parasites." This was a polemical term, and has no community of any kind with the phenomenon of Culture-parasitism. The Negro in America was the expression of Culture-parasitism despite *economic* utility.

The first result of the presence of such a Culture-parasitic body is known. He displaced unborn white men in America. By performing part of the life task, he made unborn millions unnecessary, and therefore this great mass of Africans has reduced the population of America by ten per cent, for at the present moment—1948—the African makes up 14,000,000 out of a total of 140,000,000. The fashionable, materialistic way of explaining this displacement in America is to say that white people will not bring children into the world to compete economically with the blacks and their lower living-standard. Naturally economic obsession explains everything economically, but the facts of population trends show that the population of an organic unity follows a life-path that may even be described mathematically. It is entirely independent of immigration, of the wishes of individuals, and of non-organic explanations given for it. The displacement is Cultural, *i.e.*, total, and is not to be fully explained by economics.

The Colonial mentality, more thoroughly disintegrated by the Rationalist crisis, has been able to oppose no effective defense to the increasing displacement of the white population, the vehicle of America's attachment to the West, by the African. With equal inability either to comprehend, or to oppose, America has not resisted while the rear-guard of the Arabian Culture, which was strewn throughout the West even at its Cultural origins, has assumed larger numerical proportions and a vastly larger role than it ever had in Europe.

Beginning around 1880, the Jews embarked upon what Hilaire Belloc aptly termed an invasion of the United States. The numbers alone would justify the figure. While they cannot be exactly given, because of the fact that American immigration statistics reflect only *legal* origins, *i.e.*, nation of legal allegiance, nevertheless they can be approximated from a study of current American population figures, and study of the Jewish birth-rate. How typical this is, of the total *incongruence* between two different Cultures, that a mass movement of the members of one can occur within the other Culture, and leave no statistical trace. The immigrant was asked where he was born. This was determining of everything for 19th century materialism. It was supposed to fix his language, which then was supposed to govern his nationality. And nationality was supposed to pre-ordain everything else. Such things as petrifacts

of dead Cultures—India, China, Islam, Jewry—were regarded
as "nations" in the Western sense of the word. In form,
Rationalism was definitely a religion, but a bloodless, materialistic caricature of true religion. Religion is properly directed
toward the great, higher, things of man's spirituality, but
Rationalism tried to turn things like economics, State, society,
nation, into the object of its own religious concern.

America began its independent political existence as a creature of Rationalism. Its politicians agreed to the proposition—
externally—that "all men are created equal," and even said this
was "self-evident." To call it self-evident, and thus dispense
with proof, was easier, and perhaps wiser, than to prove it.
Proof would have spoiled what is actually a tenet of a Faith,
and thus above Reason. The religion of Rationalism dominated
America in a way that it was never able to dominate Europe.
Europe always had resistance against Rationalism—based on
tradition until the middle of the 19th century, and after that
based on anticipation of the coming anti-rationalist spirit of the
20th century—as exemplified in Carlyle and Nietzsche. But
America did not possess the first because it had no tradition,
and had not the second, because Cultural impulses and Culture-
forwarding phenomena come from the Mother-soil and are
thence radiated outward, as the Rationalistic religion of America came from England, through France.

America acquired even its section of Jewry from Europe,
whence it had acquired its materialistic philosophy, to both of
which it succumbed. This was no coincidence. The word spread
rapidly through the Jewish population of Europe that anti-
semitism was less of a threat in America, and that other opportunities, such as the economic, were equal to those Europe
offered to the Jew. This was perfectly sound, and was a tribute
to the collective Jewish instinct. America did undoubtedly

represent in the late 19th century a country with the greatest possibilities for the Jew. From 1880 to 1950, approximately—remember, no *exact* figures exist—five to seven million Jews arrived in America. They came mostly from the Eastern, or Askkenazic, section of Jewry.

At the present time, the Jews in America number approximately eight to twelve millions. An exact figure cannot be given, because the number is not reflected in any statistics, but must be approximated from religious statistics and study of the birth-rate. At any rate, it is a considerable number, and displaces its own number of Americans from existence. The American writer, Madison Grant, in 1916, described how the American of the old stock was being driven off the streets of New York City by the swarms of Jews. He calls them "Polish" Jews, as the older custom was to give the Jews a Western nationality. Westerners thus used to differentiate between English Jews, German Jews, and so forth. It was a compulsion of the Western Civilization at that stage to see all other people outside the Civilization in its own image.

America, as the country most completely disintegrated by Rationalism, exhibited the least understanding of the nature of the Jew, while there were always some people in Europe—for instance, Carlyle—even during the 19th century who realized the total, and not merely political, alienness of the Jew. But in America, with its complete lack of tradition, there were no Carlyles, no de Lagardes. Thus America decided, in the middle of the 19th century, that a Chinaman born in the United States thereby acquired exactly the same American citizenship as the white native population of European derivation. Characteristically, the decision was not made in a responsible fashion, but as the result of a lawsuit. This was in pursuance of an American custom of deciding political questions in a pseudo-

legal form. Obviously a regime which did not differentiate between Chinese and native American would oppose no political
barrier to the Jew. And so, by 1928, the French writer on historical and world-political topics, Andre Siegfried, could say
that New York City had a semitic countenance. By the middle
of the 20th century, this development had gone further, and
New York City, the largest city in America, perhaps in the
world, was almost half Jewish in population.

VI

America, with its total lack of spiritual resistance, springing
from the inherent *soul-weakness* of a Colony, became the host
to other large Culturally-parasitic groups. The period of dense
immigration which had begun before the turn of the 20th century, and in which the Jews came, brought in also many *millions*
of Balkan Slavs. Between 1900 and 1915 alone, 15,000,000 immigrants came to America from Asia, Africa and Europe. They
came mostly from Russia, the Levant, and the Balkan countries.
From the Western Civilization came a fair number of Italians,
but the rest of the human material was from outside the West.
These millions, by their very numbers, created phenomena of
Culture-parasitism. On the edge of each group, individuals
passed into the American feeling, but the groups continued to
exist *as such*. This was shown by the existence of a newspaper-
press for each group in its own language, unity of the groups
for political purposes, geographical centralization of the various groups, and social exclusiveness of the groups.

In examining the nature of race, we saw that Slavs could be,
and have been, assimilated by European Culture-populations.
Two features distinguish the American relationship to the Slav,
and explain why the Slavs have retained their group existence,

even though surrounded by an American population under the influence of Western Civilization. First, the fact of its *colonial* style of existence meant that America could not transmit to entering populations the forceful impress of the Cultural idea that the Western nations on the Mother-soil could. Secondly, the enormous masses, numbering many millions, created, by their mere *bulk* a pathological condition in the American organism. Even if these millions had been of Western antecedents, such as French, or Spanish, they would have created a *politically* parasitic group. Naturally such a group would have dissolved eventually, but in the process it would have had a distorting effect on policy in America. Slavic groups, on the other hand, in masses of millions, whose leaders are allowed facilities of welding the group into a firm unity, will only slowly, if ever, dissolve into the American host population, under such conditions.

America has other smaller parasitic groups, each of which displaces unborn Americans, and calls forth the unfortunate displays of hatred and bitterness which waste and twist the superpersonal life. There is a Japanese group, various Levantine groups, and the Russian group.

Superficially it might seem that the case of America militates against the 20th century view of Race, set forth above, but actually it does not. The American example is no criterion for Europe, for being a colony, it is an area of low Cultural sensitivity, with correspondingly less Cultural force and assimilative power. In other words, its power of *adaptation* is slighter than that of the Mother-soil.

The case of America is not a case of assimilating too much —it is a case of not assimilating enough. Alien groups— whether merely politically alien, such as a Western group in another Western nation, or totally alien, like the Jew in a West-

ern host—are parasitic only so long as they are groups. When
they dissolve, the totality of the assimilating population has
increased. The fact that this has come from immigration rather
than from increase by birth-surpluses of the native population
is not important. The mere fact that they could assimilate shows
that they were not alien in a parasitic sense.

Nor must this be ignored in examining Culture-parasitism
in America: this American population during the 19th century
assimilated many millions of Germans, Irish, English and Scan-
dinavians into its own bloodstream. The 20th century immigration did not come mainly from these European countries, but
to the extent that it did, complete assimilation occurred. In the
case of the *immigrant* Germans and Irish, the Yankee armies
in the War of Secession employed them in great numbers, and
with good success—what never could have been done with
Culturally alien groups, *e.g.*, Jews, or Slavs.

America has been called a melting-pot. This it is not, for
the massive groups of Culturally-alien provenance have not
"melted," but have remained distinct. Groups not Culturally
alien *have* assimilated at once—which means, in one generation—and thus the 20th century view of Race applies also to the
facts of the American scene.

These unassimilated groups in America comprise between
one-third and one-half of the population of America. The
Slavic groups are apparently slowly being assimilated, but even
if they disappeared entirely, the remaining Culturally-parasitic
groups would comprise a pathological condition of the utmost
seriousness for America.

The old-fashioned view of vertical racism can derive no
instruction from the case of America, for what we see there
is not the *mixture* of races, but their *non-mixture.* All of the
parasitic groups have been torn loose from old landscapes, but

have no new spiritual connections. Only the landless Jew, who carries Nation, Church, State, People, Race and Culture within him, has preserved his ancient roots.

The phenomenon of Culture-parasitism, even though divorced from ethics, is not outside the realm of policy. It does no good whatever to talk about Culturally alien groups in terms of praise and blame, hatred or "tolerance."

Wars, riots, massacres, destruction, the entire waste of senseless domestic conflict—all the phenomena which inevitably rise when a host entertains a Culture-parasite, remain as long as the pathological condition lasts.

Culture-parasitism, by calling forth resistant phenomena, has a doubly injurious effect on the body of the Culture and its nations. A fever is a sign of resistance to a disease in a human, but this does not confer a positive health-value on the fever. Its sole value is negative, and the fever itself is a part of the disease, even though the saving part. Resistant phenomena like the anti-Japaneseism and anti-semitism and anti-Negroism of America are as undesirable as the conditions they are combating. Similarly, European anti-semitism has no positive value and moreover it can, if exaggerated, easily develop into another type of Culture-pathology, that aggravated condition which may proceed also from Culture-parasitism under certain conditions, namely, Culture-distortion.

Culture-Distortion

THE MIGHTY DESTINY of a High Culture has the same power over the Culture organism as the plant-destiny over the plant, the human-destiny over a human being. This power, vast and inwardly undeniable though it be, nevertheless is not absolute. It is organic, and an organism is a relationship of an *inner* to an *outer*, a microcosm to a macrocosm. While no inner force can prevail against the destiny of the organism, outer forces sometimes can—on all planes of Life—bring about disease and death of the organism. The micro-organisms that penetrate into the body of a man bring about illness by reason of the fact that their life-conditions are entirely different from those of the man. Their welfare means his doom. They are an *outer* force, even though they are working from the *inside* of the human organism. *Outer* is thus seen to be a spiritual, and not a spatial term. That is outside which has separate existence, no matter how it may happen to be physically. Everything with one Destiny is one; anything with another Destiny is other. It is not geography which determines, but spirituality. In war a traitor within the fortress may be as valuable to the besieging army as half of its numbers. He is outer, even though he is within.

Life is the process of actualizing the possible. But Life is multiform, and organisms, by actualizing their own possibilities, destroy other organisms. Animals devour plants, plants destroy one another, human beings lay waste entire species and slaughter millions of animals. High Cultures by their existence evoke negative impulses from outside populations. Those who do not share this Culture-feeling, which confers such unquestioned superiority on its possessors, instinctively determine to annihilate it. The more powerful the pressure of the High Culture on the outer populations, the more nihilistic is the negative feeling which forms in the under-populations. The more extensive the Culture-expansion geographically, the wider is spread through the world the external will-to-annihilate among the extra-Cultural peoples. Life forms are hostile to one another; the fulfillment of one is the demise of a thousand others. This is another way of saying that Life is war.

A High Culture is no exception to this great Life-regularity. Its existence destroys other forms, and on the other hand, throughout its entire existence, it is engaged in an existential battle against the outsider. On this high plane of contemplation, the attempt to distinguish between offensive and defensive, aggressive and resisting, is seen clearly to be nonsense. It is a pseudo-legal trick of Rationalist conjurers, lost in hyper-intellectualism, and hostile to Life. Defense is aggression, aggression is defense. The question of who strikes first in a war is on the same level as who strikes first in a boxing contest. The 20th century leaves all this cant, stupidity, hypocrisy, and legalistic legerdemain behind it as it strides forward to a century of warfare, the most powerful and unrelenting of all wars hitherto.

But as it faces its most trying period, the period that will demand every fiber of its spiritual reserves, and every atom of its physical resources—it is gravely ill. It is suffering from Culture-distortion.

Culture-distortion is the condition in which outer life-forms are warping the Culture from its true Life-path. Just as a human illness may render a man *hors de combat* so may a Culture illness, and this is precisely what happened to the West, after the turn of the 20th century. Culture-distortion must be clearly understood by the Western Civilization.

It has already been seen that the word *outer* does not have a geographic meaning when used in the domain of the organic. The phenomenon of Culture-distortion is the result of outer forces at work *within* the body of the Culture, participating in its public life and policy, directing its energies to problems that have no relation to its inner task, turning its forces, physical and spiritual, to alien problems.

A moment's thought shows the impossibility of such a Culture-illness arising during the time of the strict Culture, before the turn of Civilization. During those days, the forms of the Culture—in all directions of Life—were so highly developed that they not only required highly gifted souls to master them, but they mastered these souls in the same process. No European thinker, artist, or man of action, could, in the 17th century, have tried to focus European energy onto Asiatic thought, art, or action-forms. Such a thing might have existed as an imaginative possibility, but it is doubtful whether it was possible in actuality. At any rate, it did not occur for 800 years in the West, except in its rudimentary beginnings. We cannot see Cromwell, Oxenstierna, or Oldenbarneveldt concerning himself with the restoration of the Abassid dynasty in Asia Minor, or the driving out of the usurping Manchus from the ruins of the

Chinese petrifact. But if a European statesman had successfully directed Western energy into such a totally alien, sterile enterprise, it would have been Culture-distortion. If an artist had managed to turn Western oil-painting into the style of Egyptian linear painting, or of Classical sculpture, that would also have been Culture-distortion. Future volumes of Western history-philosophy in the 20th and 21st centuries will trace out fully the superficially distorting effects in architecture, literature, and economic theorizing, of the Classicist mania introduced by Wincklemann in the 18th century.

They will also list the innumerable distortions arising from Culture-parasitism, during the Rationalist period 1750–1950, of the various life-aspects of the West, artistic, religious, philosophical, scientific, and in the realm of action. This work is concerned with actions, and directs itself mainly to the phenomena of distortion of the Present and the immediate Future, that is the next hundred years.

In the presentation of the articulation of a High Culture, it was seen that not all of the population in the Culture area is available to the Idea. This is quite exclusive of parasitic phenomena. The higher, psychically more sensitive stratum which bears the Culture-Idea, and translates it into progressive actuality, is completely available to the Idea, but the availability is progressively less as one moves downward in the body of the Culture. Downward means, of course, not economically or socially, but spiritually. Thus a man from the lowest possible spiritual stratum may be found in a high position, like the monster Marat. Such individuals belong to no other Culture, even a dead one of the past, and apparently are members of the Culture, but in their souls they wish to destroy all formative Life. Their motives do not matter, for their orientation is obvious.

Such individuals—who make up a whole, large stratum during these centuries—are simply below the Culture. They are only physically within the body of the Culture. They expressed themselves in England in the phenomena of the order of Wat Tyler's Rebellion and Jack Cade's Rebellion; in the 16th century Peasant's Wars in Germany; in the French Terror of 1793 and the Commune of 1871. When Germany existed as a 19th century nation, this stratum below the Culture was known as *der deutsche Michel*. Phenomena of this type must not be confused with Culture-parasitism. Things like the Michel element —which exists all through Europe, and not alone in the former German nation—are simply below, but they are not *per se alien*. They are an organic part of every Culture, but parasitism occurs only fortuitously, and not with necessity. The Michel element of a Culture is not a pathology, and is not a Cultural menace in itself. Its sole danger is that it is serviceable to the will-to-annihilate, whether this springs up autopathically, as in Liberalism, democracy, Communism, or exopathically as in the case of the extra-European forces which brought about, during the Age of World Wars, the nadir of the Western Civilization.

In that very situation, the European Michel showed its potentialities for destruction. One section of it worshiped the primitivity of Russian vandalism, the other the spiritually-putrefying disease of Hollywoodism. It was solely by virtue of this European Michel-stratum that the extra-European forces were able to split Europe between them, physically and spiritually. This European Michel, with its attachment to the formless, brought Europe down before the Barbarian and the distorter. In its supreme hatred of grandeur and creativeness, it even allowed itself to be formed into military movements within Europe to sabotage Europe and work for the military victory of the barbarian during the Second World War.

After the War, it learned that its fate was after all bound up with the creative forces of the Culture, for this element was starved, frozen, and looted along with the collective body of Europe in the gruesome aftermath of the victory of the barbarians and distorters.

II

The Destiny of a living organism must not be confused with the entirely opposite idea of predestination. The latter is a *causal* idea, both in its religious form of Calvinism, or in its materialist form of mechanism and determinism. Destiny is not *causal,* but *organic,* necessity. Causality is a form of thought, but Destiny is the form of the living. Causality claims absolute necessity, but Destiny is only *inner* necessity, and every child who is accidentally killed at play shows that Destiny is subject to outer incident. Destiny merely says: if it is to be, it will be this way, and no other. Every man is destined to grow old, but many will not fulfill this destiny. Let no one claim to understand the Destiny-idea if he regards it as a sort of hidden causality, a form of predestination.

At the beginning of this treatment of the subject of Cultural Vitalism, it was said that if the extra-Cultural forces had succeeded after the Second World War in destroying the entire Culture-bearing stratum of Europe, this stratum would have once again been present in thirty to sixty years. The statement was of course, hypothetical, for this did not occur. The mere fact that someone is writing and someone is reading this is proof that they did not succeed.

The basis of that statement was the tremendous, ever-youthful, vigor of a High Culture. The West has a Future, and this Future must be *inwardly* fulfilled. Inwardly is distinguished from outwardly, for whether or not the West fulfills its outward potentialities is as much a matter of Incident as it is of Destiny.

The inner Future of the West contains many necessary developments, such as the Rebirth of Religion, the attainment of new heights in technics and chemistry, perfection of legal and administrative thinking, and others. These could all be fulfilled under a permanent occupation by barbarians from other continents. The grandest, mightiest side of Life, that of action, of war and politics, would express itself in such a regime in inexorable, continuing, bitter revolt against the Barbarian. Instead of planting the flag of the West at the antipodes, it would be reduced to trying to free the sacred soil of the West from the heel of the primitive. It was therefore no causal-predestination thought when it was said that the Culture-bearing stratum would reconstitute itself even though every one of its contemporary members were entirely wiped out by scaffold-trials.

Contained in that statement was this: either the West will fulfill its tremendous, world-embracing Destiny of unlimited, Absolute Imperialism, or else—all this energy will go into warfare on European soil against the alien, and whatever European elements he finds serviceable to him. As is true of all wars, hatred is dissociated from the necessity of this process. Wars do not come from hatred, but from organic rhythms. The choice is not between War and Peace, but between a Culture-forwarding war, or a Culture-distorting war.

If Europe remains under the outer forces, they will be sending their soldiers into a graveyard, for the might of the West is not to be annulled by a mountain of propaganda, mass-armies of occupying "soldiers," nor by millions of traitors in the Michel stratum. For two centuries the streams of blood will flow, irrespective of the wish of any human being. It is the nature of superpersonal organisms to express their possibilities. If it cannot be done in one way, it will be done in another. This idea conscripts men, and it discharges them only by their individual deaths. It has no legal hold on them, no formal allegiance, no threat of court-martial: its claim on them is *total*. It is a *selective* conscription: the higher a man's gifts, the stronger is the bond which the Idea lays on him. What have the barbarians and distorters to oppose *this*? Against their murderous Russian slaves, their savage Negroes, their hapless, go-home conscripts from North America, Europe pits its unconquerable superpersonal superiority. Europe stands at the *beginning* of a world-historical process; the end is not in sight. When —or even whether—complete success will come is not visible. Perhaps before it is over, the outer forces will have mobilized the swarming, pullulating masses of China and India against the body of the Western Civilization. This kind of thing does not affect the continuation of the conflict, but only its size.

It is *absolutely necessary* to the continuance of the subjugation of Europe that the outsiders have large numbers—whole societies, groups, strata, remnants of dead 19th century nations —of domestic European populations available for their purposes. Against a united Europe, they could never have made their way in, and only against a divided Europe can they maintain themselves. Split! divide! distinguish!—this is the technique of conquest. Resurrect old ideas, old slogans, now quite dead, in the battle to turn European against European. But work always with the weak, Culture-less stratum against the strong bearers and appreciators of Culture. These must be "tried" and hanged.

This availability of the under-strata of the Culture to outside forces is one type, and the most dangerous, of that form of Culture-pathology called Culture-distortion. It is closely related however to another type called Culture-retardation.

Culture Retardation as a
Form of Culture Distortion

IN THE STUDY of the articulation of a Culture, the ceaseless battle between Tradition and Innovation appeared. This is normal and accompanies the Culture from the feudal union to Caesarism, from Gothic cathedral to skyscraper, from Anselm to the philosopher of this age, from Schütz to Wagner. The unending struggle takes place within the form of the Culture and is thus not a disease-form, for even the conflict itself in each case is strictly cast in the Culture-mold. It occurred to no one during the period 1000–1800 when engaged in a battle against another Western idea that he must prevent it from realization even at the cost of destruction of the Culture. To be specific, no European power and no European statesman would have delivered all Europe to the Barbarian merely in order to defeat another power or statesman. On the contrary, when the Barbarian appeared at the gates, all Europe opposed him, as it finally united against the Turk at the moment of greatest danger. After the defeat of the European army at Nicopolis at the turn of the 15th century, the Osmanli Sultan Bayazid swore an oath that he would not rest until he had turned St. Peter's into a stable for his horse. At that period of Western history that was not to be. This total domination of the West by the outer forces of annihilation had to wait until almost the middle of the 20th century.

It only came about because certain elements in the West preferred to ruin all Europe rather than allow Europe to pass into the next Cultural stage, the Resurgence of Authority.

Any such historical phenomenon as this does not appear in a moment. The beginnings of this terrible division of the West are found in the origins of Rationalism. Even in the Wars of the Austrian Succession, there is a new ferocity which presaged the coming split. In that war, the Allies actually planned completely to partition the territory of the Culture-nation of Prussia. Participating were to be Sweden, Austria, France—and *Russia.* It is true that during the Romanov regime, from the 17th to the 20th centuries, Russia figured as a State and Nation of the Western style. Nevertheless, there were open misgivings on both sides, and there was a difference between partitioning of Asiatic border-land like Poland between Western powers and Russia, and the sharing of the Mother-soil of Europe with Russia.

In the battle of the Dynasts and Traditionalists against Napoleon, the tendency went further, and in 1815 at the Vienna Congress, the Tsar with his troops occupying half Europe—a fact of which he frequently reminded the European monarchs—was able to pose as the *savior of the West.* Thus the *Fürstenbund* and England were actually on the verge of the Culturally pathological when they pushed their battle against a Western sovereign, Napoleon, to the point where they admitted Russian troops to European capitals. It is however quite certain that the Western veneer of Russia was determining in the matter: the *Fürstenbund* and Pitt's England would not have admitted a nihilistic Russia or the Turk to Europe as a means of defeating Napoleon and therewith themselves.

But the tendency did not stop there—in the First World War, between the two European nations, both in 19th century style, England and Germany, England again embraced Russia as an ally, and painted the Romanov despotism as a "democracy" before Europe and America. Fortunately for the West there was a counter-tendency, and when the Bolshevik started his westward march after the war, he was thrown back by a Western coalition before Warsaw in 1920. In the armies against Bolshevism were Germans, French, English, but yesterday enemies, today united against the barbarian. Even the Americans sent two expeditions against the Bolshevik, one to Archangel, and one to Eastern Siberia.

During the period of preparation of the Second World War, 1919–1939, it appeared at several moments as though the coming war could take the form of a struggle by certain of the powers of the West—for the West was still divided at that time into a collection of tiny States—against Russia, while others of these petty States would remain neutral, giving economic assistance. Such a moment occurred in June, 1936, when the leading four among these petty States signed a protocol embodying a general understanding among themselves. This protocol was never ratified. No less than *twenty* separate efforts were made between 1933 and 1939 by the bearers of the 20th century Idea to effect a general understanding with those of the petty States still in the grip of the 19th century Idea, which was already by then manifesting *rigor mortis*. Naturally, the leading elements of the Culture-bearing stratum in these latter petty States were in contact with the new Idea, but certain elements were opposed by reason of their spiritual insensitivity, their

materialistic shallowness, their negativistic jealousy, their firm
roots in the Past, and—to put the most important reason last—
by reason of their material interests in the perpetuation of the
19th century type of international and domestic economy, from
which they alone were profiting, and from which the entire
Western Civilization was suffering.

These latter elements decided to allow the division of Europe
between Asia and America rather than to embrace the Future
of the West.

When the struggle between Tradition and Innovation, the
Old and the New, natural and normal in every Culture, reaches
this *degree,* it is Culture-pathology. This form of Culture-
pathology is definable by the intensity of the hatred of the
Future of the Culture it shows. It reaches the point of self-
destruction rather than giving up the rigid Past to the vigorous
Future. When the conservative elements come to hate the creative elements so intensely that they will do *anything* to encom-
pass their military defeat, including self-destruction, it becomes
Culture-treason, and is classified as an acute form of Culture-
pathology.

The hallmark of this Culture-disease is solely the question of
degree. Every new Idea in the Culture has been opposed—in
architecture, music, literature, economics, war, and statecraft.
But until this horrible outbreak of Culture-sickness in the 20th
century, the opposition to the creative had never attained to a
totality that can only be adequately described as maniacal.

Culture-pathological also was the base and servile truckling
throughout the Second World War of this sub-Western element to the parasitic forces and barbarian forces to which it
had voluntarily submitted in its hatred of Europe and its
Future. With unforgettable dishonor it threw millions of Western soldiers to the Russian savages, to disappear forever into

the unmarked graves of Siberia. This Michel element cooper-
ated with and aided the Barbarian enthusiastically, and naively
gave him all its secrets, but this same Barbarian accepted all the
aid without thanks and returned for it suspicion, sabotage, and
hatred.

The Michel element of the West went down with the defeat
of the West and its passing under the Barbarian and the distorter. The pathology of Culture-retardation had in this case
tragic consequences for the representatives of the Past as well as
for those of the Future. Actually they are more tragic, for in the
battle of the Past against the Future, the Past is doomed.
Eventually the Idea of the Future will triumph inwardly even
if its external Destiny is frustrated. Mechanism in politics will
give way to the Future just as mechanism in biology has long
since yielded. The idea of individuals having power over the
gigantic economies of superpersonal organisms is doomed, and
this is one of the things the sub-Western, Future-hating elements wished to save for themselves. Materialism, their world-
outlook, has given way almost everywhere in the West to historical skepticism, which will make way for mysticism and the
Rebirth of Religion. The most they have salvaged from the
general destruction is an accumulation of small personal advantages for themselves. To show their appreciation, the Barbarian and the distorter have appointed them their deputies in
Europe. How symbolic it was that the puppets who were placed
in the formerly important positions in Europe after the Second
World War were old men! They were even old, biologically
speaking, but spiritually they were two centuries old, rooted in
the dead parliamentaristic past. It did not matter to the new
rulers of Europe that these superannuated appointees lacked
vigor and creativeness—that is in fact precisely why they were
chosen. Anyone with vigor of any sort was carefully scrutinized

by the new rulers. Lethargy coupled with oratory was preferred to the will-to-accomplishment *sans* the stream of 19th century patriotic verbiage.

This is the result of Culture-Retardation. Without it, the outer forces could never have succeeded in grinding the flower of Western Culture under the heel of their primitivity and stupidity. It played, however, only a subordinate role. The study of pathology of other organic life-forms, plant, animal, and human, offer numerous examples of simultaneity of disease, in which the damage done by one promotes the spread of another. The simultaneity of pneumonia and tuberculosis in the human organism is but one case. The more serious disease which was running its course contemporaneously with the Culture-retardation illness, and which was promoted by the latter condition was an aggravation of Culture-parasitism, which becomes Culture-distorting when the parasite takes an *active* part in the life of the Culture.

Culture Distortion Arising
from Parasitic Activity

THE ELEMENTARY EFFECTS on the Culture-body of Culture-parasitism have already been seen: reduction of the Culture-population by displacement, loss of Culture-energy in friction. These effects arise from the mere *existence* of the parasite, however passive it may be. Far more deadly to the healthy realization of the Culture is the mingling in the Cultural life of parasitic elements, the *activity* of the Culture-parasite, his participation in creation and formation of Culture-tasks, ideas, and policy. The activity of the parasite generates at a higher level of intensity the repetition of the frictional phenomena which accompany the passive presence of the parasite. In California, every accretion of economic strength, every public display of collective energy on the part of the Chinese called forth new outbreaks of anti-Chinese activity among the Americans. The same applied to the Japanese group. The worst riots have been those attendant on the progressive advance of the Negro into American public life. As long as the Negro was passive, there was a minimum of bitterness between the races. The year 1865 marked the beginning of a transition from passivity of the Negro to his activity. It was naturally not spontaneous; white Rationalist elements, Liberals, "tolerance" enthusiasts; Communists, created the movement to ignore the distinction between the races, and under their direction it grew to dimensions where recurrent race riots caused temporary cessation of public life in the largest cities of America. Tulsa, Beaumont, Jersey City, Chicago, Detroit, New York—these are only a few of the scenes of mass riots during the past quarter of a century. Each riot is preceded by a deluge of "tolerance" propaganda and senti-mentalizing, and afterwards a public investigation is held which decides that the cause was lack of "tolerance" and "education."

During the American occupation of England, 1942–1946, several large race battles occurred, with both sides using automatic weapons, between American troops and Negro troops, both of whom were there on a mission against England and Europe. The limited utility of Culturally-parasitic groups for purposes of military conscription is shown by this example. Actually, these Negro troops were a part of an American command engaged in the destruction of Europe, but a slight social incident in a public-house was enough to cause a flaming-up of the racial hatred developed by the sharing of the same life by parasite and host. Troops from parasitic groups have little value if they are always two steps away from a race riot, and the Rationalists and Liberals discovered this by experimentation, rather than by looking at the chronicles of 5,000 years of the history of High Cultures. These Negro troops showed their willingness to destroy America as well as Europe. These examples of heightened tension between host and parasite are but the simpler form of the disease of Culture-distortion arising from parasitic activity. They differ only in degree from the

resistance to Culture-parasitism. Much more serious is that form
in which the parasite moves squarely into the public life of the
Culture, or the Culture-nations, and directs their policy into his
own channels. Neither in America nor in South Africa has the
Negro attained to this significance. Nor yet have the Japanese,
Chinese, Levantine, or Indian groups in America.

One group, however, has brought about a major Culture-
distortion throughout the entire Western Civilization and its
colonies on every continent, and that is the rear-guard in the
West of the fulfilled Arabian Culture, the Church-State-Nation-
People-Race of the Jew.

From the Arabian Culture, which was inwardly fulfilled by
about 1100 A.D., the Jew derived his world-outlook, his religion,
State-form, Nation-Idea, People-feeling, and unity. From the
West however he has derived his race and his Life-mission. We
saw the developing of this race in the ghetto-existence during
the first 800 years of our Western Culture. As Rationalism became more articulate—from 1750 on—and the Jew sensed the
wider possibilities for him of the new Life-phase of the West,
he began to agitate against the ghetto which he had created for
himself in the early days as symbol of his unity, spiritual and
physical. This race had a different *ideal type* from the Western,
and this influenced the material which passed into the collective blood-stream of the ghetto-race. In the middle of the 20th
century one sees Jews with Nordic pigmentation, but the racial
purity has adapted the new material to the old racial look. To
19th century vertical racism, these phenomena were uncanny,
but the 20th century has seen the primacy of the spiritual in
race-formation. When it is said, therefore, that the Jew derived
his race from the West, it is not meant that he drew entirely
on the stock of the Western peoples to recruit his own—although this did, and does, go on to some extent—but that by

serving, through its own Cultural imperative, as a totally alien mass around the Jew, the West prevented the dilution and disappearance of the Jewish unity.

For, it must be said, that while contact with the foreign is harmful to an organism when the foreign is *within* the organism, it is the opposite when the foreign is *without*—such contact strengthens the organism. That generates war, and war is strengthening to an organism. The Crusades, the birth-cry of the West, made the new organism firm, proved its viability. The wars of Castile and Aragon war against the Barbarian gave Spain the inner strength to bear its grand Ultramontane mission. England's victories on colonial battlefields all over the world gave it the compelling sense of a mission. Rome's wars in its national infancy gave it the inner firmness which enabled it to undertake the Punic Wars which gave it mastery of the Classical Civilization at last.

Thus it is obvious that the mutual contact of the West and the Jew had an opposite signification for the two organisms. To the Jew, it was a source of strength, and informing; to the West it was a drain of strength, and deforming. The Jew was within the West, but the West was not within him. Persecution *strengthens*, if it stops short of extermination. The quotation which stands at the beginning of this work is as true for the West now as it was for the Jew in the early days.

When the subject of persecution is touched upon, the source of the Life-mission of the Jew has been named. A millennium of massacres, robbery, cheating, burning, insults, mistreatments, expulsions, exploitation—these were the gift of the West to the Jew. They not only strengthened him, made him race-hard, but gave him a mission, the mission of revenge and destruction. The Western peoples and monarchs were storing up explosives in the soul of the alien in their midst.

The great organic regularity of war governs Life: even primitive tribes in Africa engage in war, when they have, as far as a Culture-people can see, nothing whatever to fight about. The appearance of a High Culture on the earth, and the concentration of power which its high organization and articulation give to it, bring about in the human surroundings a *counter-will* to destroy, balancing the will-to-create of the High Culture. In Life, not-to-belong is the same as to oppose. The opposition may be in abeyance long or forever because of other, stronger oppositions, but it remains, latent and potential. The contact of two superpersonal organisms can only engender opposition and war. The West and the Jewish organism were engaged during the millennium of their contact in constant, unremitting war. It was not the warfare of the battlefield, of the clash of ships-of-the-line, but a different form of war.

The total alien-ness of the Jew made him *politically invisible* to the West. It did not regard him as a nation, for he had no dynasty, no territory. He spoke the prevailing language of whatever landscape he was in. He had no visible State in the Western style. It seemed that Jewry was simply a religion, and as such not a political unit, for even in the Thirty Years' War, 1618–1648, religion played a subordinate role to dynastic politics, and Fronde politics. Therefore, even though the West itself had given the Jew his political mission of revenge and destruction, it could not see him as a political unit.

And so the war between the Western Culture and the Jew was a subterranean one. The Jew could not emerge in his unity and fight the West openly, for the reason of the odds involved. The West would at once have united against an open Jewish attack, and destroyed him utterly. The Jew had perforce to carry on his politics by the method of penetrating the conflicts among Western forces, ideas, States, and trying to influence the outcome in his favor. He favored always the side pointing toward materialism, triumph of economics, opposition to absolutism, opposition to the religious unity of the West, freedom of trade and usury.

The tactics of this Jewish warfare was employment of money. His dispersion, his materialism, his finished cosmopolitanism, all precluded him from taking part in the heroic form of combat on the field, and he was thus confined to the war of lending, or refusing to lend, of bribing, of gaining legally enforcible power over important individuals. Since the early days when the Western Popes had forbade Christians to take interest, the Jew had enjoyed a favored economic position. Cromwell brought them back to England when he decided there was "not enough money in the land." Theirs were the largest banking houses in the West in the 17th century. The Bank of England itself was founded on concessions granted to Ali-ben-Israel by Cromwell. This bank proceeded to give 4½ per cent on deposits and re-lent to the Government at 8 per cent.

This tactic had not been freely available to him before the middle of the millennium. Scholastic philosophy, the laws of the Church, the Spirit of the Age, the power of the feudal barons to rob him—all were against the Jew. St. Thomas Aquinas, for instance, in the 13th century, taught that trade was to be despised, as being the creature of desire for gain, which tends to become measureless, that the taking of interest was injustice, that the Jews should be deprived of the money they had taken through usury, and forced to work and give up their lust for gain. Various Popes directed bulls against the economic practices, the materialism, the rising influence, of the Jew.

But the Soul of the West itself was slowly externalizing. The decisive turning-point of 1789 was prepared for by centuries of slow changes. The old inwardness of the West, which gave to the feudal centuries their self-evident spiritual cohesion, gradually was undermined by new conflicts especially those of town versus country, of trade-nobility versus land-nobility, of materialism against the spirit of religion. The Reformation was a schism in the whole soul of the West. In it appeared as a symbol of the coming triumph of materialism the system of Calvinism. Calvin taught the sanctity of economic activity; he sanctioned usury; he interpreted wealth as a sign of Election to salvation. This spirit was abroad; Henry VIII legalized usury in England in 1545. The old Western doctrine of the sinfulness of usury was rejected.

This represented liberation for the Jew, accessibility to power, even if disguised, invisible power. In the Reformation time, the Jew was found everywhere fighting against the Church, and, as between Luther and Calvin, supporting Calvin, for Luther also rejected usury. The victory of Puritanism in England, an adaptation of Calvinism, gave the Jew favorable conditions. The Puritan writer Baxter even recognized a religious *duty* to choose the more gainful of two economic choices. To choose the less gainful was to disregard the will of God. This atmosphere protected and increased the Jew in his possessions, so that none of the old robbery by monarchs and barons could occur again.

II

From the beginning of the 17th century, an undercurrent appears in Western history, a twist, a distortion. It had its greatest effect in England, and there in the economic life. Many of the most rapacious aspects of the ascendancy of usury and finance-capitalism were not English at all, but ascribable to the rising influence of the Jew. Again, these effects do not redound to the *blame* of the Jew. The religious side of the Jewish unity

permitted the taking of interest, and prescribed a different
ethic as between Jews and *goyim* from that between Jews. It
was meritorious according to the religion of the Jew to inflict
injury on the *goy*. This religious tenet might have remained a
dead letter, but for the life-mission of the Jew, whose formation in the centuries of persecution has been seen. The Jew was
merely being himself, but his influence was not Western, and
was a *distortion* of Western Culture. Even in the 19th century,
after this sanctification of greed had been firmly established,
Carlyle, a high representative of the Western soul, cried out in
horror at the spectacle of universal thievery and throat-cutting
with cunning economico-legal weapons, at the utter lack of
social conscience which sacrificed whole strata of nations to
want and misery.

The distorting effects of the presence of the Jew on Western
economic life from the very beginning have been comprehen-
sively set forth by the oustanding European economic thinker
Werner Sombart in his *Jews and Modern Capitalism*. After the
awakening within the Western soul of a stronger interest in the
material world, the Jew became more secure, more indispensable, and more powerful. Even if he had wished to go into
callings other than usury, they were closed to him, for the Western guilds admitted only Christians. His original economic superiority was thus maintained, and highly-placed Westerners in
many cases became dependent on him. They in turn could not
attack him, for the new commercial laws, reflecting the growing
spirit of trade, protected him in his possessions, his bonds, and
his contracts. The story of Shylock shows the dual picture of the
Jew—socially cringing on the Rialto, but emerging as a lion in
the courtroom. It was the West that cast him into these two
roles. It expected him to play a purely subordinate part, and
at the same time it gave him a path to a leading part.

The more materialistic the Culture became, the more it approached the Jew, and the greater was his advantage. The West gradually abandoned its exclusivensss, but he retained his, invisible to the West.

The epoch is the appearance of Rationalism, the radical affirmation of Materialism. Around 1750, the new ideas are ascendant in the West: "freedom," "humanity," Deism, opposition to religion and to absolutism, "democracy," enthusiasm for "the people," belief in the goodness of human nature, "Return to Nature." Reason challenges tradition, and slowly the old, highly-refined Western structures of thought and statecraft go down. Lessing, in this period, put the Jew into a leading role in his play *Nathan der Weise*, what a century before would have been ridiculous. The intellectuals became enthusiastic for the ghetto man with his highly refined caste system, his private religion existing side by side with his external materialism. He was the cosmopolitan and, as such, seemed to the Western intellectuals to be pointing toward the Western future. For the first and last time, Westerners and Jews worked together on Cultural tasks—the spreading of the new ideas. The Cultural distortion now spread to the political life. The form of the French Revolution was due to Culture-distortion. The particular epoch that this great episode marks is, of course, an organic Western development. The distortion is manifest in these *particular facts*, occurring in this particular way, in this particular time and place. Otherwise put—the distortion occurred on the *surface* of history, not in its depths, for there distortion cannot occur. A human analogy is offered in incarceration: it distorts the surface of a man's life, by changing all the facts of it, but it does not touch his inner development, physical or spiritual. Distortion is twisting, warping, frustration; it is not killing, nor can it kill. It is a chronic illness, a running sore, a waste, an impurity in the Cultural life-stream.

The philosopher has treated in full outline the best known example of Culture-distortion in the Arabian Culture. There it was the old, civilized, Romans who permeated the new up-springing life of the Aramaean world. This new Culture had to force its way through the entire corpus of life-forms of the Roman world in order to express itself. Its early centuries are a progressive emancipation from Culture-distortion, a fight against Culture-distortion. The Mithradatic Wars are an early outbreak of this fight. The Romans were the "Jews" of that world, *i.e.*, the finished economic thinkers, with complete Cultural unity, in the midst of an area of awakening religion. The distortion extended into every direction of Life—law, philosophy, economics, politics, literature, war. Its occurrence was at the very inception of the Culture, which slowly freed itself from the completely alien world of the Roman. But the inmost soul of this new Culture was not touched by the distortion—it was its actualization, its surface, its expression, its facts, that were distorted.

Similarly, it is only the *facts* of the period 1775–1815, the period of the French Revolution, that were distorted. The great transition which was symbolized by this horrible event—the change of direction of the soul of the West from Culture to Civilization—could have happened in innumerable other ways.

It was the policy of the distorters to make the French public finance dependent on debts and interests, as they had long since made the English government. An absolute monarchy, however, with its centralization of power, militates against the subservience of the State to the power of Money. Therefore the idea was to introduce constitutional monarchy into France, and for this purpose, the distorters and their instrument, Necker, forced the summoning of the Estates-General. Its membership was also determined by the distorters to a large extent, and a constitutional monarchy was instituted.

Necker immediately tried to raise two large loans, without success. A solution of the financial crisis was suggested by Talleyrand in the form of confiscation of the real property of the Church. Mirabeau supported this and further suggested the issue of currency against the confiscated property. Necker refused, since such money, non-interest bearing and unconnected with debt, would not serve the distorters.

In the financial crisis, Necker was exiled, and Mirabeau became dictator. He immediately issued land-money to save the country from the panic the distorters were trying to bring about. But outside France, Necker, representing the power of Money and the distorters, then launched a continental war against France, exciting it from both within and without. The idea was that a war would necessitate large foreign purchases by France in England, Spain, and elsewhere; that the land-money, the assignats, would be refused by the Money powers outside of France, and that France would be forced to succumb to the gold-monopolists. From this war a straight line led to the Terror.

At the very beginning of the Civilization we see the same gigantic conflict between Authority and Money that lasts for generations into the Future. It is the battle of Napoleon against six coalitions. Napoleon has been painted by a distorted history-writing as a mere conqueror; his State-philosophy is ignored. But his autarchic economic ideas were clearly outlined by him to Las Casas and to Caulaincourt. He saw economy as production, not trade, and based *primarily* on agriculture, *secondarily* on industry, and *lastly* on foreign trade. He was opposed to interest-bearing money.

The battle of the distorters against these ideas contributes

much to the form of the facts of Western history from Napoleon's assumption of the Consulate to 1815. Regardless of what
these facts would have been otherwise, it was a distortion of
Western history that a Culture-parasite engaged actively and
decisively in the expression of the Western soul. In the battle
between Western forces, the outcome of which is organically
shaped by the progressive development of our Culture-soul, the
casting of totally foreign power into the balance is a warping
and frustration.

We do not know what Western history had otherwise been,
but it is quite obvious that the power of Money never would
have enjoyed its absolute sway during the 19th century if it had
not been for the disease of Culture-distortion. There would
have been two poles in the Western soul—reaching down into
every individual—the pole of money-thinking, and the pole of
authority and tradition. The absolute triumph of Money exacted
a horrible toll of Western lives and health. It sacrificed the
agricultural class of whole countries to the selfish interest of
Trade. It let loose wars for private interests with the blood of
patriots. The Opium War is enough to name—a war in which
English soldiers and sailors had to die in order to force upon
the Chinese Emperor recognition and protection of the opium
monopoly enjoyed by distorters based in the Western Civilization.

The debt system was forced onto every European State.
Prussia borrowed from Nathan Rothschild in 1818. Russia,
Austria, Spain, Portugal, followed in order. But the shallow
materialistic Spirit of the Age, hostile as it was to deep thinking and probing beneath the surface remained blind, Philosophy, which had produced Berkeley and Leibnitz, was contented
now with Mill and Spencer. Economic thinking was satisfied
with Adam Smith, who taught—in the face of the ruin and

destitution of millions—that the pursuit of his own selfish economic interests by each man would advance the collective life.
When amazing propositions like these were accepted generally,
it is not surprising that but few Westerners were conscious of
the distortion of the Cultural life of the West. Byron was one
of these few, as The Age of Bronze, and lines in Don Juan and
other poems, show us. Charles Lamb and Carlyle were also
aware, but for the most part Westerners were bent upon execution of the command of Louis-Phillipe: *Enrichissez-vous!*

III

The economic life, although influenced in its forms by Culture, is really only the raw material of Culture, a preliminary
condition of the higher life. The role of economy in a High
Culture is precisely analogous to its part in the life of a creative
man, like Cervantes, Dante, or Goethe. For such a man to be
tied to a bench is a distortion of his life. Every High Culture is
creative—its whole life is a continuous superpersonal creating.
Thus to place the economic life in the center, and to say that
it is Life, and all else is secondary, is a distortion of Culture.

But that was the effect of the distorters from two sides. The
masters of money worked solely for the spread of the Sovereignty of Money over the old traditions of the West. From
the under side, the distortion of Marxism denied everything
else in the world except economics, and said that the proletariat
must exploit the Western Civilization for its own benefit.

From the examination of the articulation of a High Culture,
the Cultural importance of the "proletariat" is known. In one
word, it is—*nihil*. This is a plain *fact*, not an expression of an
ideology, and because it is a fact, the distorter Marx, with his
abysmal, snarling hatred of the Western Civilization, chose it as

an instrument of destruction. From above and below, the distorters sought to employ the only techniques they understood, economic ones, in an instinctive attempt to destroy the body of the hated West. This, it cannot be said too often, is outside praise and blame: the distorters were acting from *compulsion,* their conduct was irrational, unconscious, springing from organic necessity.

The idea of Money, and the idea of class-war on an economic basis, both appear in other Cultures at a corresponding time. The distortion of our life was not manifest in the mere existence of these phenomena, but in their universality, their absolute form, and the bitterness with which they confused and divided the entire West. The presence of the distorter, a sort of organic catalyst, is interwoven into all these disintegrating, shattering ideas and developments.

The West only succumbed to this Culture-distortion because of its own externalization. Once the West began to dabble with Materialism, the distorters aggravated it. The breaking down of some barriers led the distorter to work for the removal of all distinctions. He turned Deism into atheism—but kept his own runes and phylacteries. In the battle of Rationalism against Tradition, he enhanced the division of the West by ever more absolute demands.

The very status of the distorter was the occasion of bitter discord in the Western nations. In England, public life was distorted over the question, which continually came up, of Jewish status. This question had nothing whatever to do with the English organism, but in battle after battle, Englishmen wasted themselves fighting for or against things like Jewish citizenship, membership in Parliament, in the Bar, the professions, government offices. Similar struggles divided Western society everywhere. The result of the steady financialization of the economic

life, substituting the idea of *Money* for the idea of *goods,* was
the steady ruination of the material and spiritual life of the
working people and farmers in all the Western lands. The
death of millions through the 19th and 20th centuries from conditions of dirt, malnutrition and sub-human living conditions,
through typhus, hunger, and tuberculosis, is traceable to the
transformation of the economy of production into a battlefield
of the Master of Money against the entrepreneur and the industrialist. The Master of Money was the one who brought
about the triumph of the corporate form of business ownership.
This forced every business owner into interest servitude to the
Master of Money, for it was the latter who bought the shares
and then proceeded to grind the employees of the enterprises
by turning the proceeds of the industry entirely into dividends.
To a banker, wages paid to living human beings as the economic basis of their lives are merely a "cost of production." To
lower this "cost" was to increase his own profits. It did not
matter whether rachitic children, starvation of families, debased
national life, was the result—the aim was *Profit.*

The ideology was that each working-man could, if he wished,
become a Master of Money. If he did not, it was his own fault.
The Money Masters owed no duty to anyone, for they had made
themselves. Not the converse, however, for if their foreign
holdings were attacked, it was the patriotic duty of the starvel-
ings to rescue the Money Masters.

The terrible results of the ascendancy of Money in throwing
whole sections of the population into existence on the margin
of starvation, had, as was to be expected, a counter-effect. The
resultant seething discontent of these masses was also rendered
into an instrument of the policy of the distorters.

In between was the enemy—the body of the Western Civilization. Above was the financial technique of mastery over this

body. Below was the trade-union technique. The millions of the others were the spoils of this war on two fronts. The role of the distorter was to increase the division, render it sharper, make it work for his advantage. No historian has ever presented the policy and effect of the Culture-distorters better than Baruch Levy presented it in his famous letter to Marx:

"The Jewish people, taken collectively, will be its own Messiah. It will attain to mastery of the world through the union of all other human races, through abolition of boundaries and monarchies, which are the bulwarks of Particularism, and through the erection of a universal Republic, in which the Jews will everywhere enjoy universal rights.

"In this new organization of mankind the sons of Israel will spread themselves over the whole inhabited world, and they, since they belong all to the same race and culture-tradition, without at the same time having a definite nationality, will form the leading element without finding opposition.

"The government of the nations, which will make up this universal Republic, will pass without effort into the hands of the Israelites, by the very fact of the victory of the proletariat. The Jewish race can then do away with private property, and after that everywhere administer the public funds.

"Then shall the promises of the Talmud be fulfilled. When the time of the Messiah has come, the Jews will hold in their hands the key to the wealth of the world."

This was the expression of the foreign body in the Western organism. There is nothing sinister about it to the distorter—to him the West is a brutish monster of pride, selfishness, and cruelty. The life-conditions of the two organisms, or any two organisms of this rank, are simply different. For the distorter to promote the economic obsession within the West, which undermines its soul and opens a path for him, is only obedience to the obvious. It is the eternal relationship of host and parasite, which is found in the plant world, the world of animals, and the world of human beings. For the West to be itself is to stifle the expression of the distorter and restrict his soul: for him to be himself is to frustrate the expression of the Western soul.

It must be clearly understood that Culture-distortion cannot kill the host, for it cannot reach to the Soul, but can only affect the expressions of that Soul, as they reach the phase of actualization. If distortion could reach into the Soul, it would no longer be felt as such, for the Soul would be changed. But the Soul continues in its purity and intensity, and its externalizing only is distorted. Here is the source of the tension: the disjunction between that which was possible and that which has become actual is *visible*. Reaction begins: with each victory of Culture-distortion, the feeling of frustration grows, and the more determined is the hostility of the Culture-bearing elements. Propaganda cannot touch this process, for it is organic, and *must* occur, while Life is present.

IV

Culture-distortion affects the Culture life on every plane. When the Culture is in a politically nationalistic stage, as the West was during the 19th century and the first part of the 20th century, not only the life of each nation may be distorted, but also the relations between the nations themselves.

The simplest illustration would be hypothetical. The Chinese parasitic group in America was never able to attain to the level of Culture-distortion, but let us suppose it had. If it had possessed public power in America at a time when, let us say, England was marking out spheres of influence for itself in China, the Chinese element in America would have inevitably worked for a war by America against England. If its degree of public power had been sufficient, it would have succeeded. This would have been distortion of the international life of the Western Civilization. It would have been an intra-Western war on a Chinese issue. This hypothetical case did occur, repeatedly, with other participants, throughout the 19th century. Whatever country was engaged in persecution of the Culture-distorter in Europe, or whatever country was slow in granting him the civil rights, legal protection, and financial possibilities that he needed, found itself the object of the policy of the Culture-distorter. The distortion was never *absolute,* for the public power of the distorter was never that. It was always a mere twisting, not a transformation; an influence, not a command; hidden, not visible; a deviation, not a straight line. The distorter never appeared as himself, for so to do would have been to destroy himself, a tiny parasite in a gigantic host. Distortion was always masked by Western ideals—freedom, democracy, liberty, and the like. This, again, was not sinister, for it was a life-necessity of the distorter thus to conduct his policy. His small numbers precluded a challenge of the entire West on the battlefield.

During the entire 19th and early 20th centuries there was, in addition to the surface history of Western politics and Western economics, another history—that of the advance of the Culture-parasite through his own politics, with consequent distortion of Western politics and economics. The contemporary Europe could only catch glimpses of this second history. Because of its political nationalism, it could not conceive of a political unit without a definite territory, a definite language, a "Constitution," an army, a navy, a Cabinet, and the rest of the Western political equipment. It was not acquainted with the history of the Arabian Culture and its Nation-idea, nor with the unity of its remnant that was strewn through the West.

Within each nation it worked for the adoption of constitu-

tions, the attenuation of the old aristocratic forms, the spread
of "democracy," the rule of parties, the extension of the franchise, the breaking down of the old exclusiveness of the West.
All of these transformations are quantitative, the negation of
quality. The democratization of a land was a prerequisite to the
conquest of power therein. If the resistance was too great
within, other nations where power had already been gained
were mobilized against the recalcitrant nation, and war was
the result.

Throughout the 19th century Russia—which still figured
then as a member of the Western State-system—Austria, and
Prussia resisted Culture-distortion. The Church of Rome also
stood out, and was marked down as an enemy.

By 1858 the point had been reached where the Culture-distorter could mobilize the government of France and the public
sentiment of England in the case of the Mortara child. When
an international incident among Western nations could be
created by the case of one private Jewish child, it is not surprising that much larger Jewish affairs could bring about much
greater international results in the Western political system.

The greatest enemy of all was Russia, the land of the pogrom.
It has been seen that when there was a large pogrom in Kiev in
1906, the Roosevelt government in America broke off diplomatic relations with the Russian government. No Americans
were concerned in any way in the pogrom, and so the case is
indicative of the strength of the distorter. If the victims of the
pogrom had been Laplanders, Cossacks, Balts, or Ukrainians,
it would have passed unnoticed by Washington.

The First World War, both in its original form, and in its
development, was not at all indicative of the Western problems
of the time. The treatment of this great turning-point belongs
to another place, but here the result for Russia, the great enemy

of the distorter, can be shown. The connection of the Culture-distorter with Bolshevism was the subject of loud boasting in his press in the early days of Bolshevism. Romanov Russia was paid back a thousandfold for the pogroms of three centuries. The Tsar and his family were shot against a wall in Ekaterin-burg, and a Kabbalistic symbol was scrawled above their bodies. The entire stratum which had been the vehicle of the Western Civilization in Russia was massacred or driven out. Russia was lost to Europe, and became the greatest threat to the Western body. In the Bolshevist wars, plagues, and famines, immediately following the Revolution, a number between ten and twenty millions perished. The slogan was: Destroy everything!—which meant—*everything Western.* Among other changes in Russia, anti-semitism was made a crime.

This example shows the magnitude to which Culture-distortion can attain. The tremendous formative power of the Western Culture had pulled Russia into its spiritual orbit. The instrument of this development was Peter the Great. The Romanov dynasty he founded in the 17th century had been the great symbol of the ascendancy of the Western spirit in the vast subcontinent called Russia, with its teeming millions of primitive populations. The transformation was, of course, not complete. It could not have been, since a High Culture has a situs, and does not move about. Nevertheless the Romanov dynasty and the Western stratum it represented in Russia gave Europe for three centuries comparative security in the East. Bolshevism removed this security.

When the armies of Alexander occupied Paris in 1814, they were compelled by the Western veneer of their leaders to behave as Western troops. It was somewhat as though Western troops were occupying a foreign Western capital. But the Bolshevist troops which planted the red flag in the heart of Europe in 1945 had nothing in common with the West whatever. In their primitive blood and instincts was the wordless imperative: destroy everything!

V

The phenomenon of Culture-distortion is not confined to the sphere of action. The ascendancy of the Classical Civilization over the early Arabian Culture, up to about 300 A.D., showed a complete distortion of the expressions of the new, rising, Culture. The philosopher has described the situation—which lasted for centuries—as a "Pseudomorphosis," a "false-forming" of all the manifestations of the new Culture-soul.

The high refinement of our Western arts, and their esoteric nature, which made them accessible only to a few, made their distortion by Cultural outsiders impossible. Westerners themselves occasionally—for instance Chippendale, the Classicists in *belles lettres,* philosophy, and the arts of form—sought to introduce extra-Cultural motives in Western things, but they transformed them in their very using of them, adapting them to our feeling. But there are no Culture-distorters in a great Western art during its period of highest development. Calderon, Rembrandt, Meister Erwin von Steinbach, Gottfried von Strasburg, Shakespeare, Bach, Leonardo, Mozart, have no counterparts with extra-Cultural backgrounds. Oil painting and music remained entirely Western as long as they were in process of fulfillment. When, with the end of the 19th century, both of these great arts had become history, the distorters emerged with atrociousness in the pictorial realm, and clangor in the world of music.

Because of the extent of their public power, they were able to hold up these horrors as worthy successors to Rembrandt and Wagner. Any minor artist continuing to work in the old traditions was smothered, while a Culture-distorter was praised as a great artist. The tendency in the middle of the 20th century finally became simply to take old works of art and distort them, without any pretense as to the process. A form of "music" taken from the primitive culture of African aborigines was adopted, and the works of Western masters were forced into this form. The pretense of originality was given up. When a Culture-distorter produced a drama, it was often simply a Shakespearean play, distorted, twisted, and made to convey the social propaganda of the distorter. Any other drama was stifled by the total ascendancy of the Cultural outsider, and his control of the channels of publicity.

In this realm, as in the realm of action, it was exclusiveness that kept the Western soul pure in its expressions, and it was the victory of quantitative ideas, methods, and feelings that laid the life of the West open to the entrance of the Culture-distorter.

In the domain of action, Money, Democracy and Economics —all quantitative, none of them exclusive—had admitted the outsider to public power. Without Western materialism, money-thinking, and liberalism, the entry of the outsider into Western public life had been as impossible as the mastery of Talmudic casuistry would have been to a Westerner.

And with this, we come to the Future.

The coming developments of the Western Soul are known. Authority is re-appearing, the old Western pride and *exclusiveness* are back. The spirit of Money is giving way to Authority; parliamentarism is yielding to order. Social disarticulation will be replaced by cohesion and hierarchy. Politics is destined to move into a new realm: the Western nations are gone, and the Western nation is coming. The consciousness of the unity of the West supplants the petty-stateism of the 19th century.

Sternness and discipline are the characteristics of the Western soul in the 20th century. Gone are the pathological individualism and feebleness of will of 19th century Europe. Respect for the mystery of Life, and for the symbolic significance of living Ideas take the place of 19th century Materialism. Vitalism has triumphed over mechanism, the soul over Rationalism.

Ever since the appearance of Calvin the West has been steadily moving toward more absolute Materialism. The apogee of the curve was reached by the First World War, and this powerful epoch into a new world marked also the reappearance of the Western soul in its unimpaired purity. It had come through the long Cultural crisis of Rationalism, and its ever youthful Destiny produced the Resurgence of Authority and the unification of Europe in such a self-evident form that no force in Europe save retarders and distorters—both pathological— even opposed it.

This movement toward Materialism was a movement *toward* the Culture-distorter in the sense that it made his entry into Western affairs possible. When men were *counted,* naturally he too was included. But the counting-mania has ceased, and the old exclusiveness is coming back. The phenomenon of Disraeli, a Culture-distorter as prime minister of a Western State, would have been simply unthinkable a century previous, in Pitt's time, and it is just as unthinkable now and for the Western Future.

The movement away from Materialism is a progression *away from* the Culture-distorter. In the realm of thought, Materialism is fighting a desperate rear-guard action. It is vanquished in every realm: physics, cosmogony, biology, psychology, philosophy, *belles lettres.* This *irresistible* trend simply makes distortion impossible to him, for it makes the affairs of the West inaccessible to him. The Western was always esoteric: when Goethe's *Collected Works* were published in 1790, only 600 copies were subscribed. Yet this public was enough for his fame over all Europe. Buxtehude, Orlando Gibbons, Bach and Mozart wrote for a small public, including no Culture-distorters. Napoleon's policy was understood in its last ramifications by few persons in his contemporary Europe. The distorters could only see so much as touched *them*. The Culture-bearing stratum of the West is drawing together over the crumbled walls of vertical nationalism. The West is shedding the skin of Materialism, returning to the purity of its own soul for its last great inner task, the creation of the Culture-State-Nation-People-Race-Empire unity of the West, as the basis for the fulfillment of the Inner Imperative of Absolute Imperialism.

The problem of Culture-distortion is therewith fundamentally altered. The very possibility of a parasite being admitted to the public life of the West is fast passing away. With a sound instinct, the distorter has given up Europe, and bases himself henceforth outside Europe.

The old tools of finance-capitalism and class war have lost their efficacy in the presence of the Resurgence of Authority, and only armies matter now. From without, he carries on his same compulsory revenge-mission. In one Western colony, America, Culture-diseases are still present which from there have exerted and continue to exert a decisive influence on world-happening.

AMERICA

"America's battle is yet to fight; and we, sorrowful though nothing doubting, will wish her strength for it. New Spiritual Pythons, plenty of them, enormous Megatherions, as ugly as were ever born of mud, loom huge and hideous out of the twilight Future on America; and she will have her own agony, and her own victory, but on other terms than she is yet quite aware of."

—CARLYLE

"Will the intellectually primitive upper class, obsessed as it is with the thought of money, reveal all at once, in face of this danger, dormant moral forces that will lead to the real construction of a State and to spiritual preparedness to sacrifice posessions and blood to it, instead of regarding war as a means of gaining wealth, as hitherto?"

—SPENGLER

Introduction

THE POINT has now been reached when the historical-organic method which has been developed in the foregoing must be applied to the immediate Future. The thought-method has been perfected, it has shown us our historical position, our affinities, that from which we are forever inwardly dissociated, our organically-necessary inner imperative. It will now be brought to the material of happening of the immediate Future. Having answered the *what,* there remains yet the *how.* The first step in practical politics is the assessment of *facts.* Next is the intuition of possibilities. This is as true of the cheap practical politics of a self-seeking party-leader as it is of the practical politics of a great statesman like Pitt, Napoleon, or Bismarck. The facts and possibilities of Western politics in 1948 cannot be arrived at without a complete understanding of the significance and potentialities of America. Up to now, this has usually been absent in Europe. The time has come when all policies, ideas, and viewpoints, must be referred to *facts.* Prejudices, whims, abstractions, and ideals are out-of-date, and even if they were

not ludicrous, they would still be a luxury, for a straitened,
looted, occupied Europe must think *clearly* if it is to capture
once more the custody of its own Destiny. Up to the Second
World War, the mistake and confusion about America was
well-nigh general in Europe. It was greater in some European
countries than in others, but there is no point in separating
them, since Europe is a *unit* for world-historical purposes,
whether this fact is widely appreciated or not. Europe *suffers*
as a unit, it *loses* in World Wars as a unit, and when it realizes
its own unity, it can also *win* in World Wars and impose its
inner imperative on the form of the Future. There is only one
way this age can understand phenomena, and there is only one
method to which organic units yield up the secrets of their Past
and Future—that is the organic-historical method. The character and potentialities of America are found in its history. The
theses of Cultural Vitalism afford the means of understanding
the significance, both to itself, and to the Western Civilization,
of the history of America.

The Origins of America

THE AMERICAN continent was populated by *individual* migration. The greater number of the immigrants came from the Northern races of Europe during the period 1500–1890. During the early, the Colonial, period (1500–1789), the life-conditions under which the incoming settlers lived were rigorous in the extreme. The hinterland was populated by hostile savages. The secure territory was a narrow strip of seaboard some 1500 miles long. Beyond that was the vast, unexplored, unknown "frontier." This word, an important one in understanding the national souls of the former nations of Europe, had an entirely opposite significance in America. Instead of a *boundary* between two power-units, it referred to an *area*, vast, dangerous, and almost empty. It needed only to be conquered in order to be incorporated, and in this process, the greatest enemy was Nature, rather than the savages, for in no case were the latter highly organized. Thus America did not develop in the early centuries the consciousness of *political tension* which arises from a true frontier.

Whether or not a man penetrated into the hinterland to take land there for his own was a matter of his personal will. These millions of quadrate kilometers were not developed by State action, but by *individual imperialism*. This fact also is of the highest importance for subsequent American history. In the first place, these immigrants had in general the characteristic Gothic urge into the distance which had given to Western history its unique intensity. Whether they were adventurers or religious refugees, merchants or soldiers, they nevertheless left their European homes for an unknown and dangerous land of privation and primitive conditions. The new conditions under which they lived perpetuated and developed the instincts which had brought them there.

In small groups these early Americans cleared the forests, built forts and homes. The farmers ploughed the fields with rifles slung over their shoulders. The women worked in the homes with weapons at hand. The human characteristics encouraged were self-reliance, resourcefulness, bravery, independence.

Cities grew up along the coast—Boston, New York, Philadelphia—and in these cities arose in the 18th century something resembling society, and even a sort of American Encyclopedism.

The early colonies, thirteen in number, were organized as independent parts of the British Colonial Empire. The main connection with England was the defense it afforded against the French, whose colonial empire embraced Canada and part of the hinterland of the colonies. With the defeat and expulsion of the French armies from Canada, in the 1760's, the centrifugal forces in the colonies gained in strength, and French policy aided in every way to separate the colonies from England. Commercial and political motives were both present in the motivation of the American Revolutionary War, 1775–1783, but the thing of greatest interest at the present day was the ideology in which the colonial Encyclopedists formulated their war-aims. Most of the colonial propagandists—Samuel Adams, Patrick Henry, Thomas Paine, John Adams, John Hancock, Thomas Jefferson, and Benjamin Franklin—had been in England and France and had thus absorbed the new Rationalistic Idea which had triumphed in English society, and was conquering the French State and Culture. The colonials adopted the French form of the Rationalist doctrines, demanding "The Rights of Man," rather than the rights of Americans.

It was not the ideologists—as usual—who fought the war. It was the soldiers who did that, and this war was the most difficult America has ever fought. The entire population of the colonies was only three million, and these were stretched the entire length of the Atlantic seaboard. Their only common bond was opposition to England, and hope of mutual independence. The British were stronger on the sea than the French, who were aiding the colonials, and the British not only enlisted the savages on their side, but also hired mercenary troops from the European continent for this war. Owing to Prussian and French assistance, the colonials were finally successful in concluding the war on the basis of complete independence from England.

The war had been a civil war as well as a war for independence, and the leaders of the Revolution had to conduct a terror at home against the Loyalist elements of the colonial population. After the War, most of these emigrated to Canada, which remained British. If the Revolution had been unsuccessful, the colonial leaders would have all been hanged for treason, but their success meant that they are regarded as the Founding Fathers in America.

Owing to a small group of patriots and creators—History is always in the custody of a minority—the thirteen colonies were united into a federal union. The leaders who brought about the union were principally Washington, John Adams, Franklin, Pinckney, Rutledge—and, above all, Alexander Hamilton, the greatest statesman ever to appear in America. If this great soul had not there been at work, the subsequent history of the American continent would have been the history of a series of wars, which by now would have reached the stage of annihilation wars, and might not yet have united the continent.

The union was on the basis of a federal state, and the allocation of power between it and the component "States" was sought to be expressed by a written document, a "constitution." The leading French political theories of the time had developed an opposition, which exists only in literature, between "the State" and "the individual." The American Constitution, and also the various constitutions which were adopted by each component colony, tried to codify this "opposition" and listed a series of individual rights *vis-a-vis* the State.

It has not been noted sufficiently how totally different these developments were from contemporary phenomena on the home soil of the Culture. In the colonies, there had never been a State except as a word. Hence, the Constitution represented a *beginning,* and not a *denial* of tradition, with the attempt to replace the old form of the State by a piece of paper. In America there was no tradition. Hamilton wanted a monarchical State, on European traditionary lines, but Rationalist ideology and propaganda was too strong to be overcome and these demanded a republic.

The "individual rights" that were set down in the various documents had no analogy to European conditions. Since there had never been a State in America, and had never been a frontier in the European sense, there had been *only* "individuals." Land could be acquired by claiming it and settling on it. Any man who wished could at any time take his gun and go into the hinterland, and there live as farmer or trapper. Thus the talk of "individuals" was nothing new, and furthermore it represented no parallel to European conditions, since the State was the basis of *the life* of persons in Europe. It was only because there was a State in Europe that the "individual" was able to live and prosper. If there had been no Prussian State, half the population of Europe would have passed into Slavic conditions.

There had been no State in America—the closest thing to a State had been the far-away English government—and hence the American anti-State ideology was not denying any fact of life, but was merely affirming the *fact of individualism,* which had grown out of the empty and vast landscape. *State* is a unit of *opposition*—there were no other States on the North American continent, and thus no American State could arise.

1 X 95

The American Ideology

THIS *organic* individualism was formulated in written constitutions and in a literary-political literature. Typical of the spirit of this literature is the Declaration of Independence. As a piece of Realpolitik, this manifesto of 1776 is masterly: it points to the Future, and embodies the Spirit of the Age of Rationalism, which was then ascendant in the Western Culture. But, in the 20th century, the ideological part of this Declaration is simply *fantastic:* "We hold these truths to be self-evident: that all men are created equal; that they are endowed by their creator with inherent and inalienable rights; that among these are life, liberty, and the pursuit of happiness; that to secure these rights, governments are instituted among men, deriving their just powers from the consent of the governed; that whenever any form of government becomes destructive of these ends, it is the right of the people to alter or to abolish it, and to institute new government, laying its foundation on such principles, and organizing its powers in such form, as to them shall seem most likely to effect their safety and happiness." In 1863, the charlatan Lincoln delivered an address in which he speaks of America as "a nation, conceived in liberty, and dedicated to the proposition that all men are created equal." He then went on to say, referring to the War of Secession, then in progress, ". . . we are engaged in a great civil war, testing whether that nation, or any nation so conceived and so dedicated, can long endure."

This ideology continued right into the middle of the 20th century, and was even, after the First and Second World Wars, when a totally different and utterly incompatible outlook was in the ascendant, offered to the home of the Western Civilization as a model to imitate somehow. It was only the entirely fortuitous material success which attended American arms that enabled this ideology to survive late into a century which had outgrown it, and, not because it is important as a political outlook, but solely because it is an effective technique for splitting and disintegrating Europe, must this archaic ideology be examined here.

The Declaration of Independence is saturated with the thinking of Rousseau and Montesquieu. The basic idea, as in all Rationalism, is the equating of what *ought* to be with what *will* be. Rationalism begins with confusing the rational with the real, and ends by confusing the real with the rational. This arsenal of "truths" about equality, inalienable and inherent rights, reflects the emancipated critical spirit, devoid of respect for facts and tradition. The idea that governments are "instituted" for a utilitarian purpose, to satisfy a demand of "equal" men, and that these "equal" men give their "consent" to a certain "form" of "government," and then abolish it when it no longer serves the purpose—is pure Rationalistic poetry, and corresponds to no facts that have ever occurred anywhere. The source of government is the *inequality* of men—this is the fact.

The nature of the government is a reflection of the Culture, the Nation, and the stage of development of both. Thus any nation may have one of two forms of government, an efficient or an inefficient government. An efficient government carries out the Idea of the nation—not the "will of the masses," for this latter does not exist if the leadership is capable. Leadership goes down, not when "the people" rationally decide to abolish it, but when that leadership becomes so decadent as to undermine itself. No government anywhere is "founded" on "principles." Governments are the expression of political instincts, and the difference between the instincts of various populations is the source of differences in their practice of government. No written "principles" affect the practice of government in the slightest, and the sole effect they have is to furnish the vocabulary of political struggles.

This is as true of America as it is of every other political unit that has ever existed in five millennia of the history of High Cultures. Contrary to a certain messianic feeling in America, America is not *completely* unique. Its morphology and destiny are readable in the history of other colonies, in our own, and in previous Cultures.

The reference in the Independence Declaration to government as having the purpose of effecting the "safety" and "happiness" of the population is more Rationalistic nonsense. Government is the process of maintaining the population in form for the political task, the expression of the Idea of the Nation.

The quotation from Lincoln still reflects the Age of Rationalism, and his contemporary Europe could feel and understand such ideology, although, since State, Nation, and Tradition existed still in Europe, even if weakened, there was always resistance to Rationalist ideologies, whether of the Rousseau, Lincoln, or Marx variety. No nation was ever "conceived in liberty," and no nation was ever "dedicated to a proposition." Nations are the creations of a High Culture, and in their last essence are mystical Ideas. Their coming, their individualities, their form, their going, are all reflections of higher Cultural developments. To say that a nation is "dedicated to a proposition" is to reduce it to an abstraction that can be put on a blackboard for the instruction of a class in logic. It is a Rationalistic *caricature* of the Nation-Idea. So to speak of a Nation is to insult and debase it: no one would ever die for a logical proposition. If such a proposition—which is also claimed to be "self-evident" —is not convincing, armed force will not make it more so.

The numen "liberty" is one of the main foci of the American ideology. The word can only be defined negatively, as freedom from some restraint or other. Not even the most rabid American ideologist advocates total freedom from every form of order, and similarly the strictest tyranny has never wished to forbid *everything*. In a country "dedicated" to "liberty" men were taken from their homes, under threat of prison, pronounced soldiers, and despatched to the antipodes as a "defense" measure on the part of a government which did not ask the "consent" of its masses, knowing perfectly well such "consent" would be refused.

In the practical sense, American freedom means freedom from the State, but it is obvious that this is mere literature, since there never was a State in America, nor any necessity for one. The word freedom is thus merely a concept in a materialistic religion, and describes nothing in the world of American facts.

Important also to the American ideology is the written constitution adopted in 1789, as a result of the labors of Hamilton and Franklin. Their interest in it was *practical*, their idea being to unite the thirteen colonies into a unit. Since the union could never have been brought about at that time on any sort of central basis, the most they were able to bring about was a weak federation, with a central government that could hardly be described as government at all, but only as a formulated anarchy. The ideas of the constitution were mostly derived from the writings of Montesquieu. The idea of "separation of powers" in particular comes from this French theorist. According to this theory, the powers of government are three, legislative, executive, and judicial. Like all crystal-clear Rationalistic thinking, this is muddy and confused when applied to Life. These powers can only be separated on paper, in Life they cannot. They were never actually separated in America, although the theory was retained that they were. With the onset of an internal crisis in the 30's of the 20th century, the entire power of the central government was openly concentrated into the executive, and theories were found to support this fact, still calling it "separation."

The various colonies retained most of the power that mattered to them—the power to make their own laws, keep a militia, and conduct themselves in economic independence of the other colonies. The word "state" was chosen to describe the components of the union, and this led to further confused ideological thinking, since European State-forms, where the State was an Idea, were thought to be equivalent to American "states," which were primarily territorial-legal-economic units, without sovereignty, aim, destiny, or purpose.

In the union, there was no sovereignty, that is, not even the *legal* counterpart of the State-Idea. The central government was not sovereign, neither was any state government. Sovereignty was represented by the agreement of two-thirds of the states and the central legislative, or in other words, a complete abstraction. If there had been fifty or a hundred million Slavs, or even Indians, on America's borders, there would have been a different notion of these things. The whole American ideology presupposed the American geopolitical situation. There were no powers, no strong, numerous, or organized hostile popula- tions, no political *dangers*—only a vast empty landscape, sparsely populated with savages.

Also important to the American ideology was the feeling— expressed above in Lincoln's address—of *universality*. Al- though the War of Secession had nothing whatever to do with ideology of any kind—and in any case, the Southern legalistic rationale of the War was more consequent than the Yankee idea—Lincoln felt impelled to inject the issue of ideology into the War. The opponent could never be simply a political rival, bent upon the same power as the Yankee—he had to be a total enemy, intent upon wiping out the American ideology. This feeling informed all American Wars from that time onward— any political enemy was regarded *ipso facto* as an ideological opponent, even though the enemy had no interest whatever in American ideology.

In the Age of World Wars, this ideologizing of politics was extended to a world-scale. The power that America chose for enemy was perforce against "freedom," "democracy," "liberty," and all the other magic, but meaningless, words of that cate- gory. This led to strange results—any power fighting against the power America had gratuitously chosen for enemy became *ipso facto* a "liberty," or "freedom" power. Thus both Roma- nov Russia and Bolshevik Russia were "freedom" powers.

American ideology led America to claim countries as allies which did not return the compliment, but American ardor was not thereby dampened. This type of politics can only strike Europe as *adolescent,* and in truth, any pretense that 20th cen- tury forms and problems can be described in a 19th century

Rationalistic ideology is immature, or to be more blunt, *silly*.

In the 20th century, when the Rationalist type of ideology had been discarded by the advancing Western Civilization, the American universalizing of ideology turned into *messianism*— the idea that America must save the world. The vehicle of the salvation is to be a materialistic religion with "democracy" taking the place of God, "Constitution" the place of the Church, "principles of government" the place of religious dogmas, and the idea of economic freedom the place of God's Grace. The technic of salvation is to embrace the dollar, or failing that, to submit to American high-explosives and bayonets.

The American ideology is a religion, just as was the Rationalism of the French Terror, of Jacobinism, of Napoleonism. The American ideology is coeval with them, and they are completely dead. Just as inwardly dead is the American ideology. Its principal use at the present time—1948—is in splitting Europe. The European Michel element battens on to any ideology whatever which promises "happiness" and a life without effort or sternness. American ideology thus serves a negative purpose, and that only. The Spirit of a bygone Age can give no message to a subsequent age, but can only deny the new age, and attempt to retard, distort, and warp it from its life-path. American ideology is not an instinct, for it inspires no one. It is an inorganic system, and when one of its tenets gets in the way, it is promptly discarded. Thus the religious doctrine of "separation of powers" was dropped from the list of sacred dogmas in 1933. Before that the holy tenet of Isolation had been put aside in 1917, when America entered into a Western War which did not concern it in any way. Resurrected after the First World War, it was again discarded in the Second World War. A political religion that thus switches the changes on its supernatural doctrines is convincing neither politically nor religiously. The

"Doctrine" of Monroe, for instance, announced early in the 19th century that the entire Western Hemisphere was a sphere of American imperialistic influence. In the 20th century, this passed into the special status of an esoteric doctrine, being retained for domestic consumption, while the external dogma was called the "good-neighbor policy."

The ideology of a people is merely intellectual clothing. It may, or may not, correspond to the instinct of that people. An ideology may be changed from day to day, but not the character of the people. Once that is formed, it is definite and influences events far more than they can influence it. The character of the American People was formed in the Secession War.

The War of Secession, 1861–1865

POLITICS IN AMERICA in the European sense there was none. The American union was formed before the 19th century style of inner-politics was developed. Political parties in their later form were unknown to the authors of the Constitution. The word Party described a dangerous thing—factionalism, near-treason. George Washington in his farewell to public life, counselled his people against "the spirit of Party." But ambitious men will always seek to have power, even the limited and irresponsible power available within the bounds of a loose federation. When tenure of power is limited to a few years (four years in the American union) the main inner-political problem becomes remaining in power. When the power is obtained by majorities in elections, the science of "electioneering" develops. Voters must be *organized* in order that the leaders may perpetuate themselves in office, and the technique of organization is the *party*. Organization takes funds, and it takes ideals. The ideals are for the masses of voters, the funds make it possible to spread them. The funds are more important because they are

difficult to procure, whereas ideals are plentiful. This dependence of party-organization upon a supply of funds brought
about the situation in which rich men were able to make the
party-leaders and party-organizations run things to please them.
Even a party-leader in *office* was not independent, for the rich
man alone could keep him there. The name given in the books
to this type of government is plutocracy, the rule of money.
This was the American form during the whole 19th century,
and it continued to the year 1933.

The source of the wealth of the richest men in America during the period 1789–1861 was manufactures and trade. The
richest men were found in the Northern states, the manufactur-
ing and trading places. The Southern states had a totally non-
plutocratic organization. A society arose there on a patriarchal
and hierarchical basis. Half of the population belonged to the
African race and was held as slaves by white land-owners and
planters. Slavery was less efficient than industrialism, for capitalistic purposes, because the slaves enjoyed complete security—
protection against illness, unemployment, old age—whereas the
Northern factory-workers were as completely unprotected in
these respects. This gave the Northern industrialist one more
advantage over the humanitarian slave-owner. The industrialists' "cost of production" were cheaper. Factory-workers who
were wiped out by illness or other catastrophe were not the
responsibility of the industrialists—they had only the disad-
vantages of slavery, whereas the Africans in the South had its
advantages as well.

The South was thus less mobilized economically than the
North and consequently desired the cheapest possible manufactures, which meant, at that time, English imports. Northern
industry could not compete well with English imports, and
demanded a high protective tariff. The tariff issue was the

focus of a political struggle for three decades before the War finally broke out.

Once any issue, from whatever sphere of Life it derives, becomes of sufficient intensity to become *political*, other motives come in to support it. Thus Yankee ideologists fastened on the idea of slavery and made it a war-issue for the masses in the Northern states. The financial labor-exploitation of the Northern capitalists was held up as humanitarianism, and the patriarchal care of the Southern planter was branded as cruelty, inhumanity, and immorality. The ideological side of this war presaged coming American war-conduct.

The Secession-War arose on the issue whether the Southern states, comprising a unit based on an aristocratic-traditional life-feeling, with an economic basis of muscle-energy, could secede from the union, which had been captured by the Yankee element. The Yankee territory was organized on a financial-industrial basis, with an economic basis of machine-energy. For three decades, the main political issue in the union had been the balancing of the number of representatives in the central government from Northern states against those from the Southern states. The South was on the defensive, for the North was outstripping it in wealth, power, and control of the central government.

But because of its aristocratic tendency, the South had supplied a disproportionate number of the officers in the central army, and most of the war-material was in the South at the start of the War. The anti-financial heroic attitude of the South gave it an immense advantage in the field against the Yankee armies, who were innoculated with a war propaganda of jealousy of the superior life in the South. The War was a contest—not the last in Western history—between quality and quantity. The North had all the war-industries, most of the railroads, and four times the population available for military purposes.

The material weakness of the South was too great to be compensated for by its spiritual superiority on the field of battle, where its heroic spirit gained victory after victory over superior numbers. The South could not replace its human losses however, and this the Yankees could do, utilizing German and Irish immigrants in particular. This War was the largest-scale war in the Western Civilization up to the First World War. The armies numbered millions, the theater of war embraced more than a million quadrate kilometers. Railroads and ironclads entered tactics for the first time.

Napoleon had calculated, from his experience on 150 fields, that the ratio in warfare of the spiritual to the material is as three is to one. Assuming this to be true, the defeat of the South was the result of Yankee material superiority of more than three times. This war had many lessons for Europe, but was mostly ignored in the European capitals, which were still in the nationalistic petty-state period, and not capable of large-space thinking. It showed the enormous military potentiality in America, it showed the Yankee character, which was thenceforth to be the American spirit, it showed the enormous will-to-power of the New York plutocracy—it showed, in short, that a base for a world-power had been laid here. The only European power which noticed it was the only one capable at that time of large-space thinking—England, and England's attitude toward the War was throughout one of benevolent neutrality toward the South, to say the least. England was prevented only by the attitude of Russia from declaring war on the Yankee government. Southern commerce raiders were fitted out in English ports, and the *Alabama* was even manned with English mariners. Yankee strength on the seas meant that the military task would have been too great for England. This was showed that America had passed the period when it needed to fear the intervention of any European power in North American or Caribbean affairs. No European power could afford to ignore the European-Russian situation, and thus could only commit its surplus power, so to speak, to transatlantic affairs. American power had now become greater than the surplus power of any possible European combination, considering the situation of the European powers *vis-a-vis* one another.

This was the beginning of the *fact* of American isolation. Quite independent of any formulation of it, America was politically isolated from Europe as a fact, and furthermore it was the only power in a hemisphere. This fact, coupled with the vast inner landscape of America, developed the possibility of large-space thinking in America, as contrasted with the petty-stateism of Europe, which considered a hundred kilometers to be a great distance.

It was, of course, European petty-stateism which permitted the development of America, in the beginning, and at every subsequent stage. This is more fully treated in the history of American imperialism.

The American Practice of Government

THE ACTUAL FORM of the government of America was a plutocracy, but the technique through which this government was maintained was usually taken by superficial thinkers to be the real government. The great epoch in the history of practice of government in America is 1828. In that year Andrew Jackson was elected President of the central government, and he immediately announced the new conception of office-holding as private economics. With his slogan "To the victor belongs the spoils" he dethroned forever the Federalist idea of a tradition of State-service. Government henceforth was "spoils" for successful party-politicians. The election of 1828 was the last appearance of the Federalist party in an election. It retained for itself, however, control of the Federal judiciary until the middle of the 19th century. Jackson's election also put an end to the aristocratic "congressional caucus" method of choosing the presidential candidates. Thenceforth the parties had nominating conventions for this purpose. The forces of tradition,

which had been concentrated in the Federalist party, no longer
appeared in inner-politics as an organized group. Their only
remaining significance was social. Thus, all during the 19th
century in America, there was no conflict of the European
variety between Party and Tradition, between the Constitution-
mongers and the aristocratic forces of Monarchy, State, Army,
Church. The Constitution-idea meant three different things in
America, in England, and on the Continent. In America the
Constitution was the symbol of the beginning of the People. In
England, the "unwritten" Constitution represented the organic
link of the history of the English national soul binding together
Past and Future. On the Continent, Constitution represented
the gathering point of all anti-traditionary forces, the break
with the organic Past, and the attempt to destroy State and
Society. In America, there was no tradition, but only a Constitution; in England Constitution and Tradition were synonymous;
on the Continent, Constitution and Tradition were antitheses.

In America, the practice of government was determined by
the great fact that there was no State in America, and hence
only private- and party-politics. In England, the practice of government was slowly developed over the centuries and the English Constitution merely is the record of this development. On
the Continent, the practice of government, developed through
centuries of tradition, was challenged root and branch by the
Rationalistic Idea of substituting quantity for quality, wiping
out History and Tradition, and substituting the rule of a reasonable piece of paper which would guarantee forever the rule of
Reason, Humanity, Justice, and the rest of it. Consequently
there were no forces opposed to the Constitution as such in
America, and there are not today, while in Europe the traditionary forces were opposed to Constitutionalizing as such, since it
was simply the symbol of anarchy.

Historical thinking is more interested in what is done with a written constitution than what it says, and the practice of government in America was actually quite independent of the Constitution, even though that document was constantly invoked by all party-politicians. In the first place, the Constitution did not recognize Parties, but only individuals. It did not foresee that political businesses would develop which would coerce the masses through employment of ideals, promises, and money. Nor did the Constitution recognize universal suffrage, since it was thought quite unnecessary to forbid a thing which was regarded by everyone at that time as synonymous with anarchy. If the Founding Fathers were to return, they would demand the abolition of Parties and their coercion of individuals, and forbid group participation in politics, as well as severely restricting the franchise by property, educational, racial, and social qualifications, since these restrictions were the actualities whose continuance was assumed by the authors of the American Constitution.

The first administration in America was the Federalist government of Washington and Hamilton. Hamilton established already in 1791 the doctrine of "implied powers" in the central government, as a measure for strengthening the central government. This was, of course, entirely against the letter and spirit of the Constitution, which "delegated" certain powers to the central government, and reserved all other powers to the States. Thenceforth, two ideas separated out: the idea of a strong central government, and the "states' rights" idea. This issue was the focus of secessionist movements, first in the Northern States, and later in the Southern States, and theoretical formulation of the War between the States, 1861–1865, was based on the right of a State to secede from the Union.

The Federalist Chief Justice Marshall was the last representa-

tive of the Federalist tradition in the government. He established the unique idea in America that laws can be upset by the
judicial system, which can declare them "unconstitutional."
This device was to play a large role in American inner-politics
during the 19th and 20th centuries. More than anything else,
the decisions of this Justice strengthened the central government. But the technique he developed was of necessity limited;
its efficacy was purely negative. It could unmake laws, but could
not make them. This too was entirely against the Constitution,
like Parties, conventions, wide suffrage, "implied powers" and
the rule of private persons. This judicial usurpation was one
more refutation of Rationalistic theories that Life can be
planned on a piece of paper and then actualized, for the piece
of paper had specified that the judiciary was to be separate from
the legislative.

Again, it was not logic, but History, which enabled Marshall
to usurp this function of the judicial veto. Far back in colonial
history, the idea of "paramount law" had emerged. At that
time, it was simply an expression of the centrifugal political
tendency in all colonies, for "paramount" law meant domestic
law, as opposed to the law of the English King, which was supposed to be personal. The royal governors in the colonies came
from Europe, while the judges in the colonies were native-born.
Hence "paramount law," and the establishment of the unique
institution of "judicial review."

A corollary development of this old colonial idea was American *legalism. Law* in the colonies meant opposition to the
Crown, and hence the lawyer became a sort of defender of the
public. The Founding Fathers were mostly lawyers; the membership of the Constitutional Convention comprised almost exclusively lawyers. The Constitution was a lawyer's document,
with legal phraseology, and complete absence of political wis-

dom. Judicial veto of legislation thus seemed quite natural in America and conquered a place for itself. Consequently the strange usage developed of referring all manner of problems to the legal system, to be handled on common law principles. The theory was that political, social, economic, racial, and other problems would thus receive an impartial treatment, free from any human bias.

Law however is the result of politics. Every judiciary is created by a political regime. If the judiciary usurps power which makes it more or less independent, it has become political itself. But in either case, its decisions are the result of politics, cast into legal form. And thus the history of legalism in America, in the form of constitutional law, is simply a reflection of the economic-political history of America. Its first phase was a series of decisions strengthening the central government, an expression of Federalist policy. In the same tradition was the Dred Scott decision in 1857, which reflected the Southern viewpoint on slavery, since the Federalist idea was not abolitionist. After the complete victory of industrialism and Money, 1865, the decisions represent the viewpoint of industrial—and finance —capitalism. The rising capitalism of the labor-unions was continually frustrated by the Supreme Court. No less than 300 times, between 1870 and 1933, it struck down laws made by various States and the central government which were aimed at the plutocracy.

The institution of judicial review could not have developed if there had been a strong central government or a true State. Nor could it have arisen except in a country dominated by economic activity, and lacking any real political issues. Before 1861, there was only one critical political issue, that of the balance of power between North and South. Between 1865 and 1933 there was no true political issue, but only party-politics, which is merely private or group business in the *form* of inner-politics. The Dred Scott decision would not have been allowed to stand, had not the War of Secession broken out, since the North-South issue was really political, which means that it could not possibly be settled otherwise than by political negotiation or by war, but absolutely not by legalistic ritual. In 1933, a real political issue again took shape, and there was an unsuccessful attempt to solve it by legalistic means.

In that year occurred the fateful Revolution, the seizure of the central power by the Culture-distorting group in America. The new regime did not at once dominate the judiciary, since it has life tenure of office. The judiciary vetoed every one of the principal internal measures of the new regime, until, in 1937, it was intimidated by the threat of creating enough new judges to outvote the opponents of the regime. Grant had successfully done this in 1870 to coerce a hostile Supreme Court, showing that judicial review was merely tolerated by the ruling forces in America so long as it was in their interests.

After 1936 the Court soon passed into the control of the Revolution, and judicial veto of political measures was terminated. It may possibly be used as a slogan, or resurrected as a show, but the forces which the 20th century has let loose do not take legalism seriously. The weapon of judicial review in America possessed some conservative efficacy during the first onslaughts of the Revolution of 1933, but it was a negative defense. Only a creative movement can prevail against a determined Revolution, only politics can defeat politics.

The "separation of powers" theory has worked out in practice to mean either the domination of all branches of the government by the same interests, or else the splitting of the branches between two opposing groups. The authoritarian spirit of the 20th century spells the end of attempts to "separate" the powers of government. Empty theorizing may continue, but this method of politics is dead, in America as well as elsewhere.

II

During the whole 19th century—except for the political issue which created the Secession-War—America was a country without true politics. Inner-politics was simply business, and any group could engage in it to further its own economic or ideological interest. In addition to parties, the usage of "lobbies" developed. The lobby is the means of exerting pressure on legislators after election. Private groups send private representatives to the legislature and there they persuade office-holders, by bribes of votes and money, to support, introduce, or oppose, legislation. Agrarian groups, racial groups, economic groups, societies of every description, use this method. By this means the anti-alcohol societies introduced nation-wide prohibition of the manufacture, sale or transportation of alcoholic liquors. This political technique continues. After the defeat of the Federalist party, early in the 19th century, there was a constant trend toward widening the suffrage, supported by all parties, and only opposed by social-traditionary forces. Party always wants the widest possible suffrage, since this completely deprives the electorate of power. If ten men decide an election, they all have some power, at least, but if ten million comprise the electorate, the masses deprive the higher elements of any significance. The inner development of America has followed the invariable pattern of Democracy, observable in all Cultures and all States.

Party-politics is tied to commercialism, Rationalism, Materialism, economic activity. With the Spirit of the Age of Resurgence of Authority, party-politics gives way to author-

itarian forms, regardless of theories or techniques employed.
The power is simply there for an ambitious man or group to
take. As the American Revolution of 1933 shows, this group
can even be Culturally alien. The actual technique for institut-
ing authoritarian rule in America was instructive: the two established parties, Republican and Democratic had enjoyed, under
various names, a monopoly of inner-politics for a century. It
was simple for a group determined on the seizure and maintenance of absolute power to penetrate both of these older formations, and so bring under its control the entire means of expression of internal politics. Only two candidates—or, rarely, three
—could be nominated for the Presidency. If the same group
nominated them all, it was secure against all means of eviction
save revolution by force. This was done, and the result was
shown by the elections of 1936, 1940, 1944 and 1948.

During the 19th century of economic obsession in America,
the idea of instilling efficiency into any phase of the public
political life occurred to no one. The situation was allowed to
develop in which forty-eight administrative units, theoretically
"sovereign," are maintained, each making its own laws on all
subjects, levying its own taxes, operating its own educational
system, judiciary, police, and economic program. Within the
continental United States, there were, in 1947, 75,000 units
levying taxes. Each unit can create a public debt, and this must
be done through the great private banking houses. In 1947, the
total public indebtedness of America was a greater figure than
the total assessed tax-valuation of the country. This wide distribution of the apparatus of public power has meant that exactly
the opportunities of corruption and misrepresentation which
inhere in the central government are reproduced in miniature
thousands of times over.

The American Revolution of 1933 was not directed toward

reorganizing this state of affairs, but was interested primarily in external affairs. The background of the intervention of this regime in world affairs is the history of American external affairs, after which the aims of the regime will be shown in detail.

2 Oct 95

The History of American Imperialism

AMERICA ACQUIRED its far-flung empire with less bloodshed than any previous conquering nation in the history of the planet. Every other power that has ever held sway over subject peoples has purchased its position with long and heavy warring. An empire cannot remain at peace. Peace and Empire exclude one another. The hardest war America ever fought was its first one, from 1775 to 1783. From Lexington to the Treaty of Paris was a long, bloody road, and one that at any time could have taken the opposite turning. The American regime of those days was not one of full coffers and vast resources that could join late in a war on the winning side of a world-wide coalition against one power. It was not in the enviable position of a gambler who can keep his winnings, but need not pay if he loses. Those leaders actually risked their lives in that war, and if they had lost a hangman's noose would have been waiting for them.

The people who have supplanted the descendants of these proto-Americans would in that case call them "war criminals," which is the name they devised for the defeated leaders in a war. For were they not "conspirators against humanity," "wagers of aggressive war," and the rest of it? Could not this small band of generals, propagandists, statesmen, ideologues, financiers, have been easily fitted into a courtroom for a year-long "trial" where a pre-determined judgment could have been passed upon them? They had no need, however, to fear any such performance, but they were legally traitors to their sovereign King, and a legal tribunal with actual jurisdiction could have been constituted against them.

The American colonists were successful only because of aid from France and volunteer assistance from military men of high ability, like von Steuben, de Kalb, Lafayette, Pulaski. This foreign aid was decisive. England was involved elsewhere for bigger stakes, and was unable to devote sufficient military attention to the colonial uprising. Further contributing to the American effort was the internal English opposition which favored the colonies. The deliberate inactivity of General Howe is only one manifestation of this obstruction.

This long, hard, war marked the beginning of American political independence. The thirteen colonies stretched snake-like along the Atlantic seaboard. The hinterland was claimed by European powers whose days of empire were numbered in the Western Hemisphere: France and Spain. The political decline of Spain was reflected by the revolutionary figures of Hidalgo, Iturbide, Bolivar, who were bringing about the dissolution of the Spanish empire in the Western hemisphere. France was driven, under Napoleon's regime, to abandon the idea of a colonial empire which would replace the British empire overseas with a French one—Napoleon's original idea—and to adopt instead the idea of a European empire, the rebuilding of the Holy Roman Empire, but directed this time from Paris. To this end, the trifle of three million dollars was worth more to Napoleon than the vast Louisiana territory, and its *purchase* by the American union in 1803 was the most fantastic piece of luck any power has ever had. Frederick the Great had to fight seven heartbreaking years to gain tiny Silesia, and two more wars to hold it; Napoleon fought twenty years against six coalitions to control Western Europe; England paid a son for every square mile of its empire—and so on through the pages of imperial history. But America acquired an area the size of Western Europe for the price of a few ships-of-the-line. The latent Calvinism of the proto-American type regarded this, not as remarkable luck, but as a sign of predestination, of God's grace.

American boldness and Gothic instincts were shown by the Barbary War. This war demonstrated also that the human material in the colonies could produce the type demanded by successful imperialism: William Bainbridge, William Eaton, Edward Preble, Stephen Decatur.

The War of 1812 was another unbelievable piece of luck. Again Napoleon was fighting for American empire. England, involved to the hilt with the Colossus of the continent, was not even able to exploit its superior military position in America, and in spite of its military defeat, America was the political victor in the treaty of Ghent, 1814. The acquisition of Florida in 1819 was the result of negotiation and not of war. Already at this time, the Austrian maxim could have been paraphrased for America: *Bella gerant alii, tu, felix America, eme!*

The great Hamilton, at the very beginning of the union, had counselled the annexation of Cuba, and others demanded it during this decade, but it was not to become actual until 1900. But at this time, occurred an event that ranks with the great audacities of History: the manifesto to be known as the Monroe

Doctrine was delivered in the year 1823. This manifesto announced that America was pre-empting an entire half of the
globe for itself. This "Doctrine" was supported by the British
fleet, as a device to dissolve the Spanish colonial empire. If
England had opposed this doctrine, it would have been stillborn, but it served British policy, and enlisted America in the
service of England. This remained, however, unknown in
America, where it was thought that the bold pronouncement
had frightened all the powers of Europe, since none of them
challenged it. Furthermore, South America presented an in-
herently uninteresting field for further imperialistic ventures
by the powers, and it thus happened that a *tradition of success*
was slowly established in American foreign policy. The Cal-
vinistic feeling spread that America was predestined to rule
whatso it would. Almost a century elapsed before the "doctrine" was challenged, and by that time, the military force was
present in America which its maintenance presupposed.

Simultaneously with the outer events, the "inner" imperialism, so to speak, continued unrelentingly. The aboriginal inhabitants of the continent, whose wishes were never consulted
either by the European powers or by Americans, whether of the
colonies or of the union, resisted unceasingly the steady westward drive of American imperialism. The answer of the
Americans to this resistance by the Red Indians was the formula
"The only good Indian is a dead Indian." American merchants
supplied the Indians with arms, powder, and shot, and thus the
Indian wars continued down to the beginning of the 20th century. Despite the money-payments for which European powers
had given up vast claims, the Indians relinquished theirs only
to superior American force. At that time the American practice
and theory were the same: Might makes Right. Treaty after
treaty was made with Indian tribes laying down frontiers over

which Americans agreed not to pass. Each treaty was violated
by the American imperial instinct. Such treaty violations gave
rise to the Black Hawk War, the Seminole wars, and to a cen-
tury-long series of wars which only ended with the political
annihilation of the Indians.

During the 30's Americans had infiltrated into the Mexican
Empire, and by a successful revolt, they separated the vast
area of Texas from Mexico. Less than ten years had gone by
before this area was annexed by the union. An area larger than
any West-European power had been seized with only small-
scale fighting. In 1842, by treaty with England, the northwest
boundary was extended. Oregon was definitely incorporated in
1846.

But meantime the imperial instinct looked from Texas toward the Pacific, over Mexico. It was decided to deprive
Mexico of two-thirds of its territory, and since this could hardly
be done by purchase or treaty, a war was planned. Mexico
caused the war, by refusing to submit to American imperialistic
demands. A short war ended in the dictate of Guadalupe
Hidalgo, which stripped Mexico of its power.

The Clayton-Bulwer Treaty of 1850 with England specifically
referred to an American canal across Central America, and led
first of all to the completion of an American railroad there in
1855. Japan was "opened" in 1853, over its feeble military resistance, to the commercial side of American imperialism.

After the War of Secession, the American union smashed
the French attempt to add Mexico to its empire, and allowed
Maximilian to be shot by a revolutionary firing squad. Also
shortly after that War, Alaska was acquired by Yankee imperialism. This territory, of almost a million quadrate kilometers, was *purchased* by America from Russia for a trivial sum.
In the same decade the border with Mexico was again rounded

off, this time by a small money payment instead of a war, in the transaction known as the Gadsden Purchase.

American imperialism was everywhere active during the second half of the 19th century: Hawaii, Chile, Cuba, Colombia, China, Japan, Siam, Samoa. The American fleet bombarded foreign ports at will in the colonial areas of the world, and sent landing parties ashore when necessary to secure submission to American commercial-imperialistic or territorial demands.

In 1890 the last Sioux War was ended, and thereafter Indian resistance to American imperialism was scattered and local. Hawaii's turn had come, and soon a "revolt" prepared Hawaii for American annexation. This was mere preparation for an imperialistic venture on a larger scale than anything yet attempted. In 1898, Spain's possessions in the Carribean and Pacific were attacked. As a result of the Spanish-American War, most of Spain's colonial empire was transferred to America, including the valuable Phillipines and Cuba. In passing, the Pacific islands of Tutuila, Guam, Wake, Midway and Samoa had been annexed.

II

In all this, one thing must be noted: American imperialism was purely *instinctive*. It was neither intelligent nor intellectualized, like contemporary European imperialism. No public man ever advocated the building of an American empire, and few even recognized openly what was going on. It would in fact have been indignantly denied that America was an imperialistic power. It is true that the phrase "Manifest Destiny" as an apology for imperialism came into use around the turn of the 20th century, but there was no definite imperial policy or program. The colonies were acquired in a planless, purely instinctive fashion, without regard to position, significance, or economic value. William Jennings Bryan in his speech on Imperialism, August 8, 1900, did warn America against entering on a career of empire because it would destroy the American form of government, saying, "We cannot repudiate the principle of self-government in the Phillipines without weakening that principle here."

But he was not heard, and the tradition of confidence that had taken root during a century of successful imperialistic ventures without a setback was not to be undermined by a minatory speech. Nor was the opposite aspect of Bryan's warning heard. What he meant by "self-government" was the habit of class war, constitutionalized civil war, freedom for everyone to gouge and exploit everyone else within the limits of the criminal law. Thus his admonition meant: an imperial nation cannot have internal disorganization and formlessness.

There was no class however in America interested in anything else except self-enrichment, and so no one concerned himself with such questions except a few writers like Homer Lea. Imperial situations are everchanging, and one must be prepared for reverses. In that case, the home conditions must also be in order if the outer developments are to be mastered. In a country where even the word *politics* was completely misunderstood, and meant *corrupt economics,* it could not be expected that the political wisdom would be present that would inform the leadership that empire means war, and war presupposes internal order. In very fact, there was no leadership to tell. Every few years a new group of representatives of private economic interests were installed in the administration of the government, and there was no traditional policy, internal or external. There was no agreement on what was fundamental to America's interests, what would be *casus belli,* which powers were natural allies, which naturally inimical. The leaders at any one time were mainly self-interested, obsessed with the grand problem of perpetuating their tenure of office.

But American luck continued. Although isolated in its hemisphere, in the sense that no world power could afford to attack it, nevertheless America was not isolated in the sense that it could not send its gunboats and landing parties all over the colonial world on imperialistic adventures. Furthermore, as the Spanish War showed, America could easily defeat any European power in the Western Hemisphere.

The Spanish-American War marked, what the War of Secession had foreshadowed, the emergence of America as a world-power. This made seven world-powers at that time; the others being England, France, Germany, Austria, Russia, Japan. Among these, only Russia, Germany, and England were in the first rank. America was excluded solely by reason of its geographical isolation. It could act against a world power in the Eastern hemisphere only with allies, and in a subordinate role. This was the situation at the beginning of the 20th century, the Age of Annihilation-Wars.

For a full century—1800–1900—America had been engaged in imperialism, in the Caribbean, in South and Central America, all over the Pacific, and in the Far East. The sphere of American military influence was by 1900 larger than that of any other power except England. It had not in any way condensed or formed its empire, because of the purely instinctive nature of American imperialism. Thus Canada, for instance, although defenseless and contiguous to the base for power, had not been politically incorporated into the American Empire. Nor had Mexico. The American instinct was content merely to be stronger within a certain sphere than any other power, so that its economic ascendancy was assured there. Empire-building, in the European sense, was not known in America. The idea of a grand power structure was not understood. The American Empire merely grew, through lack of resistance to American imperial instinct.

For its empire, America had fought only one large-scale war. The first war, that of 1775, was for independence, and the War of 1812 is more accurately called the Second War for Independence. The War of Secession extended the Yankee empire southward, removing an emerging power from the North American continent, and this was the sole serious imperial war Yankee America had to undertake in its century of empire-building. For the landing parties all over Central America, the Mexican War, the fighting in Japan, China, and in the Pacific islands, the Spanish War, all had had slight casualties. Never before had an imperial power acquired so much territory and influence for such a trivial price in blood.

Yet this was not understood, either in Europe or in America. Americans were either embarrassed or smug about their empire. Europeans either did not know about it, or thought it was the result of wise and mature political-thinking. Neither Europeans nor Americans wrote or thought much about the new world-power, its potentialities, its soul, its imperial abilities.

Other parts of the world understood American imperialism better, and Japan in particular noted the lack of political thinking in America which made it capable of an entirely negative policy, one against its own interests.

Certainly no power in Europe, no government, no person, in 1900 thought that it was within the realm of possibility that within two decades an American army of two millions would be transported across the Atlantic to fight in an intra-European war.

Keen political thinking in America would have seen that

American imperialism was furthered by the mutual concern of all the other world-powers with the situation in the other hemisphere. This allowed America to proceed with imperialism in the Western hemisphere without the interference of any other world-power.

Every other power, even England, was helpless to frustrate American actions in the Western Hemisphere. But there was no American ruling class, no Idea, no Nation, no State. American imperialism was not a rationalized, planned effort, but a fortuitous agglomeration resulting from an imperialistic instinct at work against weak opposition, and with a background of luck.

Yankee financiers were not interested in creating a grand political structure which would stretch from Bering Straits to Cape Horn, nor in building any American empire whatever. Their personal interests were not only uppermost, but exclusive with them. The political leaders of America were dependent for their tenure of office on the financiers by 1900, for finance had by that time assumed dominance over industry and transportation. And the greatest financial coups were not to be made in South or Central American affairs, but in West-European affairs.

American Imperialism in the
Age of Annihilation-Wars

AT THIS PERIOD, the Western Civilization stood before the great turning-point of the First World War. This great epoch was to mark the demise of an historical phase, and the beginning of another. The Age of Rationalism, of Materialism, of Criticism, of Economics, of Democracy and Parliamentarism, in short the first phase of the Civilization Crisis, was coming to an end, and the Crisis was about to be dissolved in the new Age, that of Absolute Politics, of Authority, of Historicism. New currents had appeared in all spheres of Western life, manifesting themselves more in the decadence or collapse of the forms of the older age, than in the appearance of the new forms. Only one man, the Philosopher of the coming Age, formulated them in their entirety. While he was preparing his work on the coming Age of Annihilation Wars, and delineating the form of the Future in all spheres of Life, the materialists were, from one standpoint or another, denying the possibility of a large-scale war, and even as they spoke, the First World War broke out, in August, 1914.

The old Spanish traditions of cabinet-diplomacy gave their

last performance with the Austrian negotiations with Serbia in July, 1914, and then vanished forever from the Western Civilization.

The War was only the *political* aspect of the transition from one Age into the next, but since Action, and not Thought, is decisive for Life, the War took up into itself the entire significance of the world-epoch. The Cultural aspect of the War was the passing of the 19th century stage into the 20th century stage of the Western Civilization. That meant the demise of the English world-Idea, and the triumph of the Prussian world-Idea, for England had been the Nation inwardly imbued with the Idea of the first phase of the Western Civilization—Rationalism, Materialism, the spirit of economics, parliamentarism, nationalism—and Prussia was the Nation destined to give to the 20th century its appropriate form. This conflict on the cultural plane was independent of any conflict on the political plane. Only *one* of these Ideas could triumph—only *one* expressed the Spirit of the New Age. The alternative to the Prussian Idea is chaos. The Prussian Idea could have triumphed on the cultural plane without a war between Prussia and England, in fact they could have been and remained allies for *political* purposes. The higher development is purely spiritual, and it could only have the result of Prussian victory— or chaos in the entire Western Civilization.

The War was occasioned in a grotesque manner, by a Balkan assassination. Previous incidents, like that at Fashoda, could have occasioned the First World War, and in such case the distribution of powers would have been entirely different, and the results, both spiritual and political, would also. The form it did take—through no necessity whatever—was that of a coalition of all the powers in the world against Prussia-Germany, and its sole ally, Austria-Hungary.

Through connections formed before the War, the American financiers were committed to an English victory, and they were the real force in the American plutocracy. No public "politician" knew anything whatever of external affairs, since they could not relate them to their tenure of office, their sole concern.

It was a fate for America that at this time there was an adventurer at the head of the government. He not only failed to oppose the demands of the bankers for American participation in the War on the side of England, but he had private notions of using the war to further his own unlimited ambition. He and his entourage projected the idea of a "league of nations" of which he would be the head. The English government gladly acquiesced, being in desperate military straits.

Now emerges in full clarity the weakness of American Imperialism. The moment of a European War was obviously a time for American action in its own hemisphere. It was already at war with Mexico, and could have concluded this war without hearing a voice from any other world power. Or, on a higher plane, America could have offered its good offices to terminate a war that all Europe was obviously losing, to the benefit of Asia. America could even have brought the war to a close against the will of the belligerents, for it could have forced England to give up the war.

But America pursued neither self-interest nor the interest of the Western Civilization. Now the population of America was to reap the fruit of America's century of spiritual isolation, of insulation from History, from the sternness, harshness, cruelty and bitterness of History. Because America had fought only one hard war in its imperial history, because it had never been opposed by a great power, because it had acquired an enormous empire without any cost in blood, it had never developed any *political consciousness.* The word politics was not understood, nor was the fact of the power-struggle. There was no State, the focus of power. There was no ruling class, the custodian of the State. There was no Tradition, the guiding consciousness of the Nation. There *was* no Nation, no *Idea* in whose service the population-stream of the continent lived. There was no Genius in politics, since there was no politics, but only unclean personal struggles for offices and bribes. There was only the group of bankers, and the hapless opportunist Wilson, dreaming of world-rule.

The real, spiritual, significance of the War was known to no public person. Not even the superficial, purely political aspect of the War was understood. The closest thing to realism was found in Boise Penrose's public demand to enter the war because America had become financially tied to an English victory, which did not seem to be maturing.

If there had been a ruling class—a stratum dedicated by its existence to the actualization and service of the National Idea —America would either have remained out of the War, or have terminated it to save Europe. The atrocity-propaganda, the English monopoly of the news, the systematic efforts of private financial and social groups to bring about American intervention, would not have been allowed. A ruling-class tolerates no foreign propaganda or foreign political activity on the home soil.

II

The purely political aspect of the War was the struggle between two political powers, Germany and England. It wore this aspect for the first stage of the War. By 1916, the struggle had changed its nature, and a Pitt as Prime Minister would have seen it. By that time it was Western Europe against Asia, and in particular Russia. During the first two years, Russia, and the host of other powers against Germany, were serving English policy. After that, England had passed into the secondary role, having been surpassed in power by Asia and America. Every ship that England lost increased the strength of America and Japan. Every English soldier that was killed increased the strength of Russia, India, China and Japan. England had arrived at the point where military victory could no longer result in political victory. Its only hope for emerging unbroken from the War was to conclude peace in 1916.

Naturally the same was true of Germany. Every German ship that was sunk increased the strength of America and Japan, and every German battle-death increased Russian and Asiatic strength *vis-a-vis* the Western Civilization.

The white Western nations could not afford the losses that Asia and Russia could easily replace. The Western Civilization was outnumbered at that time already five to one by the outer forces. By engaging in an internal war—England *versus* Germany—Europe was fighting collectively only for the victory of Asia, Russia and America.

None of this was seen by responsible persons in America. A few thinkers and writers, like Frank Harris and John W. Burgess, saw more deeply into the real issues than any public man. Of these, only William Jennings Bryan opposed effectively for a time the trend toward intervention.

For what had the war to do with American imperialism? What could America gain from the war? Europe was not the enemy of America; both political realities, and the cultural bond prevented that. Asia—Japan and Russia—were not America's allies, that it was interested in their victory. There was nothing to be gained, from America's standpoint, by participation on either side of the European War.

This intervention did come about simply because there was

no such thing as *America*. There were only private groups, economically self-interested, a loose government representing the
strongest of these, and a prevalent total incomprehension of the
world of politics and of the unity and destiny of the West.

This was the weakness of American Imperialism: no plan,
no tradition, no policy, no design, no organization.

The English policy against Germany was the same it had
used against Napoleon: the "Balance of Power" policy, by
which the continent was to be kept divided into two groups of
equal power, so that in every war English power would be
decisive. Even by 1914, this policy was quite stupid and old-
fashioned, for the increase of Russian power had superseded it.
Those who had looked beneath the thin veneer of Western Culture, by virtue of which alone Russia belonged to the Western
State-system, and who had the discernment to assess rightly the
snarling Asiatic nihilism under that tenuous crust, knew that
the long-range interests of the nations of Western Europe were
identical, and that the continuance of petty-statism and intra-
European wars would be fatal to Europe's monopolistic power
position in the world, and to each European State.

This sort of thing was utterly unknown, unsuspected, un-
dreamed-of, in economically obsessed America. When the war
did come, the populace reacted with a carnival-spirit, as if to a
new type of public game or sport.

Nor did America learn anything about politics from the war.
Its losses were almost nothing—although, proportionate to the
length of front and length of time, they were greater than any
European power's losses—and its concluding idea was that it
had won the war. Actually, of course, the war was a defeat for
America, since it was not in any way involved in the War. The
American *situation* was neutral, regardless of any intervention
policy whatever.

After the war, America collaborated with the powers of

Europe, including Germany, in opposing Asiatic Bolshevism in Russia. America dispatched two expeditionary forces, one to Eastern Siberia and one to Northern Russia, to fight the Bolshevism that the European War had unchained against Europe.

Every bit of material, and every life, that America had given to the War was a complete loss from the American standpoint. True, it had emerged from the war with vastly more power than it had entered it, just as had Russia and Japan. But it proceeded to throw this power away at the Versailles Conference and the Washington Naval Conference. Not understanding power, it had remained unconscious of the new world-power distribution resulting from the war. It flung away its new power without knowing it. This ignorance was on a national scale, but was also individual. The ambitious ideal-monger Wilson, who set out to remap the world, had only the most general notions of European geography, ethnography, and history. The balance of Europe's economy was unknown to him, and he even had no idea of what belonged to the Western Civilization and what did not. He regarded Serbia and Poland, for instance, as Western "nations."

America learned nothing from the war because it had been, it thought, "victorious," and this pragmatic test proved the soundness of its policy. By throwing away its new political power, it showed that it did not grasp the fundamental that war is waged to increase power. If any other power had behaved as America did—i.e., fought against its own national interest in a World War—it would have been ruined, and probably partitioned by its neighbors. This could not happen to America because of its isolation in its hemisphere.

It is of secondary importance, but nevertheless must be noticed, that the official propaganda in America was nothing deeper than the slogan that "the world must be made safe for democracy." It was not found necessary to link up American policy with American interests. This is sufficient testimony to the primitivity of American political thinking. No mention of the crisis in the Western Civilization, of the form of the Future, of any issue whatever. War for war's sake. It was the same compulsion that Lincoln had had, to inject an ideological issue into wars. Every war must somehow involve "democracy." If necessary, Tsarist Russia, or Bolshevik Russia, figures as a "democracy." The only group in America—outside of the few brains who think independently, and who comprise America's hope for the Future—which was not subject to these idealistic slogans and catchwords was that of the financiers. To them, ideals are commodities which Money can buy. Had they not done it? America could not have lost the First World War in a military sense, just as it could not have won in a political sense. In one word, the American intervention in the First World War was a venture into *political Unreality*.

The American delegates at the Versailles Conference did not know what the nature of the gathering was. They regarded it as some sort of theologico-judicial tribunal where moral questions were being decided. This collective hallucination, which the European delegates did nothing to disturb, resulted in the strange moralistic terminology of the Versailles Dictate. The vocabulary of this Dictate was American, the provisions were English. The Americans were writing, as they thought, an epilogue to History, a sequel to the last of all wars forever. The English were preparing their initial positions for the next war.

III

The net result of the Versailles Conference was a complete failure for Europe. The petty-states retained their political sov-

ereignty *vis-a-vis* one another; the transfer of power to areas
outside of Europe was thus confirmed. The ground was laid for
a Second World War on the exact lines of the First. To make
more occasions for its outbreak, a host of microscopic "States"
were created. Small-space thinking was the order of the day.
Old-fashioned nationalism, which had brought the entire West
to a colossal defeat, was reaffirmed. The stupid ideology of
Wilson and his entourage was written into European political
documents. Questions of "guilt" were introduced into politics,
along with "international morality," "sanctity of treaties," and
similar asininities.

Yet towering over the whole landscape was the great fact:
all Europe, and particularly England, had lost the war.

In the new world-picture, there were four powers: Russia,
America, Japan, and England. The strongest power, if it had
only known it, was America, but, as we have seen, it relinquished most of its new power. The historical fact that had
been demonstrated, however—the certainty of complete American ascendancy in any Anglo-American alliance—was not to be
withdrawn, and remained there for the political instruction of
all Europe.

The result of the European debacle was a powerful negative
reaction throughout the American population. The soul of the
American people turned with disgust against the European
adventure, and no alert politician dared advocate America's
entry into the "league of nations," or any of its appurtenances.
The bankers had won the war, and had no interest in Wilson's
personal world-rule ambitions.

But this reaction was not to be taken as an abandonment of
American imperialism. That cannot be abandoned, coming
as it does from the instinct of the People-soul. The War was
detested precisely because it had been off the road of imperialism.

The American imperial march continued. American marines and naval forces continued to move about the coasts of the Carribean and the Pacific, bombarding, and landing troops, just as they had done for the previous century. Chinese ports were attacked, but no longer Japanese ports, for the First World War had made Japan into a Great Power, despite the fact that its war effort was *nil.*

Nicaragua was attacked and occupied for years by American forces in the 20's. Hardly had the troops in Nicaragua reached their objectives when America, allied with Japan, attacked China in 1927. The occasion of the war was Chinese resistance to Japanese and American commercial imperialism. Heavy reprisals were administered for the shelling of an American oil plant at Nanking.

While it was engaged in imperialistic fighting, America sponsored the Kellogg Pact. This famous treaty was supposed to do away with war. The mere fact that numerous Western governments signed this elaborate piece of nonsense was a grave sign of the sickness of the Western Civilization. Together with the political defeat of all Europe, a surface-victory had also been gained in the First World War by the 19th century Idea over that of the 20th century. The result was chaos in Western Europe after the First World War—complete disorganization, lack of public comprehension of the new economic, social, spiritual and political problems created by the forward development of the Civilization, and as a result of the debacle of the War.

American commercial imperialism was busy in South and Central America during all this time. For instance, revolutions were brought about in Panama, Peru, Chile, Paraguay, and Salvador, all in the year 1931. Another revolution was brought about in Chile the following year. In 1931, private American forces exerted strong influence on the Spanish situation, and helped create the situation which was to result in the Civil War of 1936–1939. Cuba was another country—nominally independent—which felt American imperialism.

American imperialism followed, after as before the First World War, the same double pattern: continual grasping after more power on further horizons on the one hand; complete inability to organize, plan, or intellectualize this conquest, on the other hand. As an example of the confusion, there was the ideology of "non-recognition," according to which America would not "recognize"—whatever that means—the acquisition by another power of territory by "force of arms." And yet the entire American empire, including its original base, was acquired as the result of American armed force. This includes the purchases, which were only sold to America because of American military preponderance in its part of the globe. But to touch upon this subject is to arrive at the American Revolution of 1933.

The American Revolution of 1933

THE AMERICAN WAR FOR INDEPENDENCE, 1775–1783, was regarded by two different types of participants in two different aspects. The creative leader-types, like Hamilton, Washington, Franklin, Rutledge, saw it as an *international* war, between an American nation, in the formative stage, and England. This American nation was to them a new Idea, and the various ideological slogans and ideals which were used as propaganda material were not the essence, but only the temporary clothing of the new national Idea. For under-types like Samuel Adams, Thomas Paine, and Thomas Jefferson, however, the war was a *class war,* and the Independence-Idea was only a technique for actualizing the equality ideals of Rationalistic literature. The implementation of these equality ideals has always taken the form of jealousy, hatred, and social destruction, in America and in Europe. The class-warriors regarded the war as a struggle for equality, not a fight for American national independence. They hated monarchy, leadership, discipline, quality, aristocracy, anything superior and creative.

But: a bunch of lawyers?
office stood aristocracy? &:

The Nation-Idea immanent in the minds of the creators, led by Hamilton, was the healthy and natural organic ranking of the population from the top down, with a monarch and aristocracy at the top, educated from birth to the idea of service of the National-Idea. They conceived, already at that early stage, the idea of a planned American Imperialism over the hinterland of the continent, and in the Carribean.

The two ideas continued through the history of America. Class-war is an autopathic Culture-disease which arises with the beginnings of the Civilization-crisis, and is only finally liquidated with the end of that crisis, and the beginning of the second phase of Civilization, the Resurgence of Authority. America's entire history up to now has been within the first organic phase of Civilization, which set in for the Western Culture about 1750, triumphed in 1800, and is now inwardly accomplished.

Class-war has thus always been looked upon as natural and normal in America, instead of as the expression of a great Culture-crisis with an origin, direction, and end.

The class-war forces, led by Jefferson at the time of the founding of the American union, in 1789, have been in the unique situation in which there was no ideology whatever opposed to them. Since the defeat of the Federalist Party, in 1828, there has been no spiritual, but only crude economic resistance to class-war in America. That it has proceeded to lengths of destruction in America to which it never could proceed in Europe is owing, however, not to this alone, but to the presence of extra-Western forces. These forces have intervened in the public life of America, and of necessity have distorted that life and warped it away from its Western origins.

The very nature of a Colony, as has been seen, not only generates centrifugal political tendencies, but also weakens the bond with the mother-soil of the Culture, whence the inner life of the Colony derives. This makes the Colonial area one of low Culture-sensitivity, and low resisting-power to extra-Cultural forces. It is this low resisting power to sub-Cultural and extra-Cultural forces that has brought about the obsession with economics, and has allowed the unparalleled influx of Cultural aliens to take place over the past half century.

At the Constitutional Convention, 1787, Benjamin Franklin sought to have included in the projected Constitution a provision forever excluding the Jews from America. The "humanity" and "equality" ideologists, knowing nothing whatever of what Franklin had in mind, unacquainted completely with the Jew—for there were almost no Jews in America until a century later—rejected Franklin's advice. His warning that if they did not, their descendants would be working for the Jews within two centuries was not heard. These ideologists only knew of "humanity," and wished to ignore the vast difference between those human beings within and those without a given world-feeling.

Immigration into America during the 19th century was from all parts of Western Europe, but principally from England, Germany, and Ireland. Toward the end of the century began the Jewish immigration, and shortly thereafter the influx of Balkan Slavs, Russians, and Eastern Mediterranean peoples. Feeble defensive measures were taken, like the Immigration Act of 1890, which put a quota on populations from each European country, calculated so as to favor Northern European immigrants over Slavs and Levantines. None of this, however, affected the Jew, for, stemming from a different Culture, his movements are invisible statistically to Western nations. He came in under the English quota, the German quota, the Irish quota, and every other.

In the outline of Culture-parasitism, the effect of the presence of vast numbers of Negroes, Asiatics, and Indians upon the American life was traced. Added to these numbers are those of the Eastern European populations—excluding the Jews—who, although assimilable, have not been assimilated. The world-feeling of Rationalism, which begets Materialism, Money-obsession, decline of authority, and political pluralism, worked against assimilation, and as Culture-distorters increased in social power and significance, assimilation was deliberately held up in order to keep America in a spiritually disarticulated, divided, and chaotic condition. Defensive efforts on the part of Americans of nationalistic feelings to restrict or abolish immigration were frustrated by Culture-distortion.

Between 1900 and 1915, fifteen million aliens immigrated into America. Few came from Western Europe. Nearly all were from South-eastern Europe, from Russia, Poland, and Asia Minor. Included in these masses were Jews, whose numbers are estimated in millions. The First World War interrupted the immigration-river, but it was resumed after the War, and was accelerated mightily by the European Revolution of 1933. The Jews who fled or were expelled from Europe went to America *en masse.*

It is worth noting that the lower Culture-exclusiveness in colonial areas had resulted in Jews being treated for civil purposes the same as Europeans from 1737 onwards in the American colonies, whereas a century had to elapse before this Rationalistic policy triumphed completely on the home-soil of the Western Culture. The only reason for it in the colonies was of course the fact that there were no Jews, as a group, but only a few scattered individuals, who were regarded as curiosities.

From 1890 on began the Jewish invasion of America. Within the next fifty years, the number of Jews in America increased from negligible proportions to a number estimated between 8

and 12 millions. New York City became in this period pre-
dominantly a Jewish capital. Of this Jewish immigration, approximately 80 per cent were Ashkenazic Jews. American reaction inevitably began against the phenomena which inevitably
accompanied the immigration of these vast numbers with their
own world-feeling, who immediately began to influence the
American life in every sphere and on every plane. A clever
propaganda making use of the American ideology to serve
Jewish purposes was the answer to this reaction. America became a "melting pot," after the phrase of the Jew Israel Zang-
will, and the purely quantitative American ideology lent this
picture convincingness in an America still in the money-obsession stage.

The word "American" was changed by this same propaganda
to mean an immigrant who had improved his personal circumstances by coming to America, and to exclude the native American who was displaced by the immigrant. If the latter showed
resentment, he was called "un-American." Thus native American movements like the second Ku-Klux-Klan, formed in 1915,
as an expression of the reaction of the American organism to
the presence of the foreign matter, were more or less successfully called "un-American" by the propaganda organs in
America, which even by that time had come under strong Culture-distorting influences.

The words "America" and "American" were stripped of all
spiritual-national significance, and were given a purely ideological significance. Anyone who came to America was *ipso
facto* an American, regardless of the facts that he retained his
own language, lived in his own racial-national group, nourished
his old connections with Russia, South-eastern Europe, or the
Eastern Mediterranean, and had a purely economic relationship
with America. Americans of native stock however, the repre-

sentatives before history of the new unit in the Western
Civilization called the American People, were not *ipso facto*
Americans. If they nourished any national feelings of exclusiveness whatever, they were "un-American." This transvaluation
of values is an invariable accompaniment of Culture-Distortion,
and represents a superpersonal life-necessity of the Culture-distorting element. The values of the host-Culture, or host-colony,
are hostile to the life of the Culture-distorter, and for him to
adopt them would be to disappear as a higher unit. Assimilation of the Jews would mean that there would no longer be a
Jewish Idea, a Jewish Culture-State-Nation-People-Religion-
Race. In fighting against nationalistic feelings in America, the
Jewish Idea is fighting for its continued existence against the
hostile Western Civilization. It is a tribute to the political skill
of the leaders of Jewry that they were able in the 20th century
to identify their Jewish Idea with America, and to label the
nationalism of America with the term "un-American."

II

For the inner history of America, four epochs had great significance: 1789, 1828, 1865, 1933. 1789 marked the formation
of the Union of the colonies, through the adoption of the
Constitution. 1828 marked the final defeat of the Federalist
Party, the sole authoritarian force in the Union. 1865 was the
complete financialization of the continent, but also the formation of the specific character of the American People. With
1865, however, the last barrier to economic obsession was removed, and the road was paved that was to eventuate in the
utter triumph of the Culture-distorter in 1933. Future Western
history will write down this date as the year of the American
Revolution—or more accurately as the first phase of the American Revolution—for in that year, Culture-distortion began to

penetrate the remaining spheres of American life, government, Army, administration, judiciary.

Yet this epoch passed unnoticed—not only by the great mass of Americans, for that is not surprising—but also by many of the custodians of the American national feeling.

On the surface, the profound meaning of events was not at once disclosed. To the population, and to the outer world, it looked as though there had been a mere change of administration, a substitution of one party-business for another. A gigantic revolution that in a European land would have brought about a war was slyly and invisibly put into effect in a politically-unconscious country.

Considerable opposition was aroused by the new regime from the very start, for it embarked, from inner necessity, on a program hostile to, and in every way destructive of, the American national feelings.

Keen political instincts in the Cultural-aliens had given them a complete mastery of the techniques of American party-contests, and they proceeded to monopolize the opposing party, so that thenceforward elections were mere pageantry, and no longer contained the possibility of a real change of government, but only the substitution of one Culture-distorting party for another.

Early in the Revolution foreign affairs were adapted to the policy of the distorter. Bolshevik Russia was accorded diplomatic recognition by the regime in 1934, and Litvinov-Finkelstein was sent from Russia to congratulate the successful regime in Washington. This was the first step in the formation of the American-Bolshevist coalition against Europe. The regime was still in the process of consolidating its hold on power, and had to proceed with caution, since the possibility still existed in 1936 of a national rebellion in the old, elective form.

Yielding to the popular concern with internal affairs, the

distorter conducted the "election" of 1936 on domestic issues. This was to be the last election in American history where even a remote possibility existed of a national revolution through the old voting technique. Thenceforward elections were to be managed in such a way that the Culture-distorting regime could perpetuate itself in power indefinitely by that means.

III

Culture-distortion in America, as elsewhere in the Western Civilization, was only able to twist, warp, and frustrate the soul of the host. It could neither kill it nor transform it. American autopathic tendencies, arising from the disintegratory influence of Rationalism and Materialism, are the source of the possibilities of which the Culture-distorter made use. His technique was to push them ever further in the direction of decadence, but at the same time he could always refer to Rationalistic doctrines, themselves products of the Civilization-crisis, as a semi-religious basis for his disintegratory work.

Thus the "equality" rhetoric of the Independence Declaration of 1775, and pious platitudes from Lincoln and other party-politicians, were used as the basis of the "tolerance" propaganda which teaches Americans that they must not in any way, not even in thought, discriminate against the Jew. This propaganda is spread from the highest official places down to the level of home, school, and church.

The Negro-movement is a powerful instrument of Culture-distortion, and was organized as such shortly after the advent to power in 1933. Similarly the numerous groups of recent alien provenance are artificially prevented from assimilating and becoming Americans, since every alien-thinking group in America is serviceable to Culture-distortion. Thus the Polish group, for instance, was very useful in war-agitation in the Fall of 1939. The usefulness of these alien groups is easily imaginable when it is realized that in 1947 only ¾ of the entire population of America consists of whites born in America, that only 55 per cent of the population had both parents American-born, while more than 20 per cent had one foreign-born parent, and almost 15 per cent of the population consisted of foreign-born persons. More than one thousand foreign language newspapers and periodicals appear in America, in forty different foreign languages.

The whole result has been to put the native American completely on the defensive, to confer a privileged position on the Culture-distorter, who embodies at the highest potential the idea of alienness, and to disintegrate progressively the American national feeling. Culture-distortion to this degree would not have been possible in Europe, because of the higher Culture-sensitivity and the higher exclusiveness of Europe, even under democratic-materialistic conditions.

It is necessary to observe precisely the spiritual products of Culture-distortion in America, in every sphere of life, for the America that intervenes in Europe is not the true America, which still existed in 1890, but an empire consisting of a master-stratum with its own culture, and a great mass of subjects, comprising the Americans, and the almost equally numerous alien-thinking groups. The lower strata supply the soldiers who invade Europe, but the brains who decide belong to non-Americans.

World-Outlook

THE TECHNIQUE for eliminating American resistance to Culture-distortion has been *uniformity*. Every American has been made to dress alike, live alike, talk alike, behave alike, and think alike. The principle of uniformity regards personality as a danger and also as a burden. This great principle has been applied to every sphere of life. Advertising of a kind and on a scale unknown to Europe is part of the method of stamping out individualism. Everywhere is seen the same empty, smiling, face. The principle has above all been applied to the American woman, and in her dress, cosmetics, and behavior, she has been deprived of all individuality.

A literature, vast and inclusive, has grown up on mechanizing and uniformizing all the problems and situations of life. Books are sold by the million to tell the American "How to Make Friends." Other books tell him how to write letters, how to behave in public, how to make love, how to play games, how to uniformize his inner life, how many children to have, how to dress, even how to think. The same principle has been extended to higher learning, and the viewpoint is nowhere disputed that every American boy and girl is entitled to a "college-education." Only in America would it have been possible for a journalist to denounce higher physics because it was creating a type of aristocracy.

A contest was recently held in America to find "Mr. Average Man." General statistics were employed to find the center of population, marital distribution of the population, family-numbers, rural and urban distribution, and so forth. Finally a man and wife with two children in a medium-sized town were chosen as the "Average Family." They were then given a trip to New York, were interviewed by the press, feted, solicited to endorse commercial products, and held up for the admiration of all those who fell short in any way of the desirable quality of averageness. Their habits at home, their life-adjustments generally were the subject of investigation, and then of generalizing. Having found the average man from the top down, his ideas and feelings were then generalized as the imperative-average thoughts and feelings.

In the American "universities" husbands and wives attend lecture courses on marriage adjustment. Individualism must not even be countenanced in anything so personal as marriage. In America, the Culture-distorter has laid down *one* way of doing everything. The men change from felt hats to straw hats on one certain day of the year and on another certain day discard the straw hats. The civilian uniform is as rigorous—for each type of occasion—as the strictest military or liturgical garb. Departures from it are the subject of sneers, or interrogation. The arts have been co-ordinated into the master-plan. There is in America, with its 140,000,000, not a single continuing opera company, or a single continuous theater. What theater there is produces only "revues," and journalistic propaganda plays.

For the rest, there is only the cinema, and it is, after all, the strongest single medium of the uniformizing of the American by the upper stratum of Culture-distorters.

In a land which produced West, Stuart, and Copley, there is to-day not a single painter of public note who continues in the Western tradition. "Abstractions," pictorial insanity, and preoccupation with ugliness monopolize the pictorial art.

Music is seldom heard in America, having been replaced by the cultureless drum-beating of the Negro. As an American "musicologist" put it, "Jazz rhythm, taken from wild tribes, is at the same time refined and elementary and corresponds to the disposition of our modern soul. It incites us without pause, like the primitive drum-beating of the prayer-dancer. But it does not stop there. It must at the same time take account of the excitability of the modern psyche. We thirst for quickly exciting, constantly changing, stimuli. Music has an excellent, time-honored means of excitation, syncopation."

American literature, which produced Irving, Emerson, Hawthorne, Melville, Thoreau and Poe, is today entirely represented by Culture-distorters who make Freudian and Marxist motives into plays and novels.

American family life has been thoroughly disintegrated by the Culture-distorting regime. In the usual American home, the parents actually have less authority than the children. The schools enforce no discipline, nor do the churches. The function of forming the minds of the young has been abdicated by all in favor of the cinema.

Marriage in America has been replaced by Divorce. This is said with no paradoxical intent. In the large cities, statistics show that one of every two marriages ends in divorce. Taking the country as a whole, the figure is one in three. This situation can no longer be described as Marriage, since the essence of

Marriage is its *permanence.* The divorce trade is a large business upon which lawyers, private detectives and other charlatans thrive, and from which the spiritual standards of the nation suffer, as reflected in the emotionally indifferent attitude of American children.

The Western erotic, grounded in the chivalry of Gothic times, with the concomitant honor-imperative of the centuries of Western history, has been driven out. The ideal of Wedekind, the Culture-distorter who preached compulsory Bohemianism in Europe around the turn of the 20th century, has been realized by the Culture-distorting regime in America. *Inverted Puritanism* has arisen. In this new feeling, the Puritan outlook is retained in sexual matters only to scoff at it in the cinema and in literature. Baudelaire's thesis "In evil only lies bliss" has been taken over by the distorter, and has resulted in the progressive disintegration of American morality in all spheres. In this effort, jazz music is a useful appurtenance, for this primitive beating is nothing but the expression of lust in the world of sound, a world which is capable of expressing all human emotions, both higher and lower.

A part of this general perversion is the physical-youth-mania that has been spread abroad in America. Both men and women, but especially the latter are inwardly obsessed with the idea of remaining physically young in appearance. Advertising plays upon these fears and commercializes them. The "girl" is the ideal feminine type. The mature woman aspires to be a girl, but not *vice versa.* A "girl" cult has come into existence, which, together with cinema, revue, jazz, divorce, disintegration of the family, and uniformity, serves the vast purpose of destroy ing the national feelings of the American.

Together with uniformity is the technique of *excitement.* The press presents every day new *sensations.* For the general purpose, it is quite immaterial whether the sensation is a murder, a kidnapping, a government scandal, or a war-scare. But for particular, political purposes, the latter sensations are the most effective, and during the years of preparing the Second World War, the distorter administered every day a new "crisis." The process increased until the population was ready to welcome the outbreak of war as a relief from the constantly mounting nervous tension. When the War did appear, the distorter immediately called it a "World War" despite the fact that only three political powers were engaged, and the strongest powers were not involved. It was, of course, intended to rule out the possibility in the American mind of any localizing of the War, and to prepare for American intervention.

The straining after excitement, pleasure, and constant motion has created a vast night-life, a crime underworld which staggers the imagination of Europeans, and a hurrying from one thing to another which excludes the possibility of contemplation, or individual culture. Almost one per cent of the entire population makes its living from professional crime. The art of reading has been taken away from the Americans, since the idea is to "do something." Individual culture is generally strangled under such conditions, and the prevailing mass-ideals impose limitations on the form of such personal culture as is attained. All history, all thought, all events, all examples, are used to prove the soundness of the ideal of mass-life, and of the American ideology.

II

In the Rationalistic and Materialistic atmosphere of 19th century America, there was only a very weak link with the sublime Western Gothic traditions of the spiritualized meaning of life, but under the Culture-distorting regime since 1933, America has been completely disenchanted. On every plane, the ultimate reality of the world and life is materialistic. The aim of life is "happiness." This must be so, since life itself is only a physico-chemical process, and articles appear which treat as imminent the discovery of a "formula" for life by "scientists."

The contractual side of the old Puritan religion, which regarded Man and God as keeping accounts with one another, has been pushed to its uttermost limits, and all living is simply changing legal relationships. Patriotism is simply a legal duty to the world-proposition called America, which has been equated with the mission of distorting the entire Western Civilization through a process of "educating" Europe. Heroism in the Western sense is unknown, and the hero whom the population admires is a capitalist *en grand* who has converted a great part of the public wealth into his private resources, or else a smiling film actor. Such a thing as a great spiritual movement or a national rising is not understood in America, first because it has had nothing of the kind in its history, and secondly, because the distorter has made all such things ridiculous. The American is taught that life is a process of cultivating friendly relations with all, joining as many clubs and secret societies as possible, and confining all his thought and effort to the personal plane.

The "happy-end" is the ideal of life and literature. There is no thought of bearing up under the bitterest and most crushing blows of Fate. These are overcome by avoiding one's glance. The *lucky* man, and not the man who has suffered in silence and become stronger, is the central figure in the happy-end literature.

The opposition between the Western idea of Destiny-fulfillment and the Culture-distorter's disintegrating substitute called "happy-end" is actually the focal idea of the world-outlook that he wishes to force upon the prostrate American nation and its parent Western Civilization. The irreconcilability between these two ideas extends from the personal plane upward through national economy, society, State, religion and ethics.

The great Western Life-feeling is the necessity of being ones self, of preserving that within one which cannot be compromised, which is synonymous with Soul, Destiny, Honor, Race. The distorter's idea of "happy-end" is opportunistic, weak, degenerate, and revolting to the Western honor-feeling. The empty, smiling, face, the uniform mind, the senseless chasing after noise, movement, and sensation, the obsession with money-making and money-spending, the rejection of all spiritual standards of attainment—all this merely reflects the basic interpretation of Life as a seeking for a happy-end. For happiness one will compromise anything, give anything, sell anything. Happiness becomes synonymous with pursuit of economic and sexual motives. It absolutely excludes any profitless struggle against odds, merely in order to be one's self. Understanding and respect for the tragedy of Life, the magic of Life, the power of the Idea, are precluded by the happy-end feeling.

Any idea of this kind is quite impossible for Europeans in the 20th century, even if they had not seen the horrible catastrophe of the Second World War, in which Europe succumbed to the double-invasion of barbarians and distorters. No great artist, no religionist, no deep thinker, has ever deluded himself that Life has the meaning of "happy-end." In miserable and crushing times, the Western man trains himself rather to bear whatever blows Fate may have in store for him. He does not talk of either happiness or unhappiness, and he does not try to avoid facts by looking away from them. Looking away is no solution, but only a postponement of a later reckoning. Happy-end has a purely negative significance. It is a denial of Life, an escape from Life. It is thus a deception, and an untruth.

The racial chaos in America, which, deliberately perpetuated by the distorter, delivers the American nation more securely into his hands, is only possible because of the de-nationalizing program for Americans. This program begins with propaganda in the schools to the effect that America was not colonized, cleared, conquered, or built by Americans, but by a great conglomeration of aliens. The contributions of the Jew and the Negro are taught as the decisive formative influences on the "American dream." In New York State, Shakespeare's *Merchant of Venice* is forbidden to be taught in the schools. The promoting of the anti-spiritual and anti-national "happy-end" idea, with its economic and sexual obsession, and its social atomism, is the prerequisite of continuing the whole program of degeneration.

Races and nations express themselves at their highest potential in strong *individuals,* who embody the prime national characteristics, and acquire immense historical symbolic significance. Therefore, the efforts of the Culture-distorter to strangle American nationalism take the form of an offensive against individualism, not against freakish, insane, individualism, but against the only kind that is historically effective—individualism which concentrates in itself a higher Idea, and is devoted to its service.

Thus the highest social value is "getting along with people." Strong characteristics of independence or strength must be put aside, and the ideal of mediocrity embraced. The *universal* spirituality, the same intellectual nourishment for all classes, replaces the natural, organic stratification of society. This nourishment again has only a *quantitative* measure of value. Just as the best product is the one most advertised, so the best book is the one that has the largest sale. The best newspaper or periodical is the one with the largest circulation. This equation of quantity with quality is the complete expression of the mass-idea, the denial of individuality.

A natural corollary of the happiness-sickness is *pacifism*. Only intellectual pacifism is meant, for the Culture-distorter knows how to make use of the fighting instincts of the native American type. Intellectual pacifism is war-propaganda. The enemy is identified with the idea of war itself, and to fight him is to fight war.

Naturally Hollywoodism is incapable of rousing a population to sternness, sacrifice, heroism, renunciation. Therefore American armies in the field in the Second World War had to be supplied with a vast, never-ending stream of picture-books, chocolate, soft-drinks, beer, juke-boxes, moving-pictures, and playthings of all sorts.

Fundamentals cannot be evaded, and so it was that despite eight years of preparation by the most intense bombardment of emotional artillery the world has ever seen, through film, press, stage, and radio, there was no war-enthusiasm whatever in the American population, and a negative feeling in the armies which were massed against Europe in the Second World War. Out of 16,000,000 men who were impressed into the armed forces from start to finish of America's brief military participation in the Second World War, less than 600,000 were volunteers. Almost twice this many volunteers out of half as many people were raised in *one year* in one European nation in the First World War. A large part of the American volunteers had already been notified of imminent conscription, and volunteered for appearance's sake.

The Western idea of destiny-fulfillment, with its inner imperative of honor and faithfulness to conviction, means that the vulgar are naturally the enemies of the upright. No higher idea is for everyone, and all creativeness comes from the few. Deeds with a high ethical content cannot be performed by all, and he who is capable of them has no reason to be ashamed, to renounce his spiritual values, and adopt the smiling face, the inner vacuum, and the ideal of "getting along with people," even at the cost of his soul.

Even destructiveness and distortion on the scale on which it has been successfully introduced into America is a task for a minority. The American and foreign masses are the mere object of the distortion. The organic unit which regards the disintegration of America as a part of its own life-mission is, at its very widest base, only ten per cent of the population of the American Union. And within this ten per cent, it is a comparatively few brains, and a reliable stratum of leaders who actualize the policy of the Jewish Culture-State-Nation-Religion-People-Race. To these leaders, the great mass of their own people are mere soldier-material in the non-military war against the Western Civilization all over the world. Nor need these brains be regarded as animated by any malice or evil motives. To them the Western Civilization is the repository of the collective evil and hatred of the world, the source of a thousand years of persecution, a cruel and unreasonable monstrosity, a sinister force working against the Jewish Messiah-idea.

5 Oct 95

The Negro in America

DEMOCRATIC-MATERIALISTIC CONDITIONS arise during the organically necessary Civilization-crisis, and are thus autopathic. Culture-distortion comes from the interference in the life of the host of a Culture-parasite, an organic unit which does not participate inwardly in the life of the Culture, but nevertheless lives in and on the body of the Culture. These two in conjunction increase the intensity of each other, and America is the clearest example of the multifarious effects these Culture-diseases can have on a people which cannot successfully resist them at the onset.

The population of America only consists now of a bare majority that is indisputably American racially, spiritually, nationally. The other half consists of Negroes, Jews, unassimilated South-eastern Europeans, Mexicans, Chinese, Japanese, Siamese, Levantines, Slavs and Indians. The Slavic groups are assimilable by the American race, but the process has been artificially held up by the intervention of Culture-distortion. The mass-ideals of noise, excitement, mental uniformity, and hurrying movement which the Americans share with these un-assimilated alien groups do not represent any kind of assimilation, because these traits themselves are anti-national, demoralizing, destructive of individuality, State, People, Race.

The Negro problem is one of the numerous racial disjunctions which press for solution in America. At the time when, as a result of the War of Secession, the Negroes were deprived of their security and delivered to financial slavery in an industrial civilization with whose problems they could in no way cope, they were a contended, primitive people. They had no dynamism, no mission to destroy. Their numbers at that time were about four and a half million, and they were nearly all in the Southern states, where the social life was adjusted to their presence, and kept the white and Negro races separate in every way. No desire existed on either side to disturb this natural formulation of the relationship.

To a finance-capitalist, however, a Negro merely represents "cheap labor," or a prospect for a small loan. The Master of Money knows nothing of Nation, People, Race, Culture. He is a "realist," which means, on the primitive-intellectual level, that he regards everything which *is* as the sum total of Reality. Actually, of course, that which *is* represents a stage already passed, an Idea already accomplished. True Reality is the Future at work, for this is the impetus of events. Thus no Money-thinker would ever think two or three generations into the future, for he regards larger conditions as stable, even though he seeks instability in immediate conditions.

After the War of Secession, progressively more Negroes went to the Northern States. This movement was vastly accelerated by the two World Wars, when millions of them went northward to replace conscripted white laborers in the Northern industrial districts. Reinforcing this proletarianizing process, Northern enterprises moved factories into the South to employ Negro "cheap" labor, and make large profits.

The converting of the Negro into a wage slave has demoralized him completely, made him into a discontented proletarian, and created in him a deep racial bitterness. The soul of the Negro remains primitive and childlike in comparison with the nervous and complicated soul of Western man, accustomed to thinking in terms of money and civilization. The result is that the Negro has become a charge of white society.

Marriage is almost unknown among the Negroes, and the women raise the large families. In the large cities, the Negro population supplies approximately ten times as many criminals as its numbers would indicate to be its proportion. Social diseases are general among this race, and the hospitals as well as the penitentiaries deal with highly disproportionate numbers of Negroes. Primitive violence is natural to the Negro, and the sense of social disgrace is lacking in him in connection with crimes. Negro sections of the Northern cities are dangerous to the life of white persons.

Bolshevism and Culture-distortion did not miss the potentialities of the Negro for purposes of inner disintegration and race war. Trials of Negroes for felony in the Southern states are made the object of wide-spread and intense Communist propaganda along the old lines of "equality" and "tolerance." The Communist party supplies counsel to Negroes accused of crime.

Like all primitive races, the Negro race is fertile, and possessed of strong instincts. His numbers to-day, including the mulattoes, are approximately 14,000,000. This ten per cent of the total population of America is an adjunct of the program of the Culture-distorter. Politically, this mass is organized as a unit, and supported the Roosevelt regime from the time of its seizure of power in 1933. The Negro has been the focus of much of the revolutionary activity of the Culture-distorting regime. From time to time, the distorter raises a racial issue publicly, in which the white Southerner is made the public enemy, and the Negro is the hero of "democracy." This results in increasingly serious race-war in the Northern and Southern cities.

The Negro has suffered more than anyone in being thrown into the slavery of finance-exploitation, and then into conscription for the race-war program of the distorter. From the happy, deeply and primitively religious, cotton-picking slave, with complete protection and insulation from the dynamism of Western industrialism, he has been made into a malcontented, diseased, fighter in race-war and class-war. His life has been made into a round of factories, hospitals, public relief offices, jails, and roaming of the streets. The new Negro is a dangerous potentiality, and he has been fitted out by the distorter with a program of demands, an ideology of his own within the Bolshevist framework, and dynamic leadership. A Negro writer has recently said: "Your land? How did it become yours? We were here before the Pilgrims landed. Hither we brought our three gifts and mixed them with yours: the gift of poetry and of song, tender and living melodies into a badly harmonized and unmelodious land; the gift of sweat and muscle-power, to defeat the wilderness and conquer the ground of this wide, rich, country, two hundred years before your weak white hands could have done it; the third gift, the gift of soul. Are these gifts worth nothing? Is this no work and striving? Could America have become America without its Negro folk?" This does not represent merely the thought of one mulatto, for these ideas have been drummed into the heads of the millions of the Negroes in the cities—not to mention the white element of weak instincts, the Liberal element which gives in to race-war and thus encourages it.

The Negro has a will strong enough to push his demands through, and today there are Negroes on all levels of the public life, officers, judges, administrators, labor-leaders, lawyers, doctors, professors.

For America there are two aspects to the Negro problem, the immediate, and the long-range. Immediately, the Negro movement is completely in the service of Culture-distortion, which controls all phases of domestic Bolshevism in America. An inner-crisis in which many issues of American public life will simultaneously present themselves, monstrous in their size and demands, will confront the American people in the near future. When, no one can tell, but it is inevitable, for America is no exception to five millennia of the history of High Cultures and their colonies. The position of the Negro *vis-a-vis* the organic existence of the American People is quite clear.

The long-range aspect of the problem is shown by the declining birthrate of the native American population, and the rising numbers of the Negro. The old white element is decreasing *absolutely* in numbers, and this process has been going on for two decades. The immediate relationship is spiritual-political; the more remote problem is spiritual-racial.

Culture-Retardation in America

IN ITS ESSENCE, as we have seen, Culture-Retardation is a mere negation of the Future. Destiny is not deceived, however, but only the minds of those who seek to maintain or restore dead conditions or ideologies. Only on the surface of History can Culture-retarders gain a victory, and then solely by virtue of their purely material preponderance. If they do gain such a temporary, surface, victory, it represents merely the defeat of quality by quantity.

America, being a colony, and therefore having lower organic resistance to Culture-disease, has succumbed more deeply to retarding influences than the home-soil of the Western Culture ever could have. In America, these retarding forces are managed and inspired by the larger Culture-illness, Culture-distortion, and they are heavily relied on in order to overcome the negative effect which would result from the open appearance of the alien distorter.

The popular world-picture which has been made compulsory for the uniformized American is simply the old, materialistic picture which Europe had already outgrown by the First

World War. Thus in the American universities, Darwinism is taught in biology, along with Mechanism.

In sociology, Mill and Spencer are the last word. In history, the naïve, linear, Ancient-Mediaeval-Modern scheme is retained, and Buckle and Gibbon represent the perfection of historical method. Carlyle, Lamprecht, Breysig, Meray, Eduard Meyer, Spengler, are entirely unknown. In psychology, the mass idea has triumphed, so that "genius" is equated with high intelligence, and the latter with "college education." Again—no qualitative differences among persons. The commercial maxim is "You can buy brains." For the rest, Freudianism is gospel. It is possible for the holder of high academic degrees in America to be entirely unacquainted with the history of the Western Culture, with the significance of Carlyle, Nietzsche, Spengler, of the revolt of the Western Civilization against Democracy and Materialism. His picture of events for the last 75 years in Europe is delineated by a few journalistic catchwords. The widening and deepening of the 20th century world-picture is unknown to him, and leads him to deny the very existence of facts and possibilities which are incommensurable with laboratory materialism.

Culture-retardation as a grotesque reality is illustrated by the fact that America is actually from 30 to 50 years behind the parent Western Civilization in the world of thought. No American university has heard of geopolitics, or anything resembling it. Mahan's sea-power theories are the last word on grand strategy, and the eventuation of the First and Second World Wars—which Americans are taught to regard as "victories"— only reinforce the sea-power idea, despite the fact that world-shaking events have fundamentally altered the relationship between continental power and sea power. This fundamental misconception in America will bear fruit in the Third World War.

In the theory of economics, the situation is similar. Adam Smith is the great foundation. Abstractions like "world economy" are regarded as concrete realities. List is unknown, although Marx is regarded as an economist. Sombart was put away after the American Revolution of 1933. The currency problem is handled on the basis of the gold-standard theory. The European departure from gold-thinking is regarded as morally wrong. The Classical economic theories of the Manchester school are the focus of *belief,* rather than historical curiosity. Departures from them are treated as downright wicked, or else as regrettable, temporary necessities. These 19th century doctrines are always described as "the laws of economics."

This retarded mentality has of course had serious effects in the sphere of *action,* that is of politics and economics.

Since America developed into a world-power in a part of the world where there was no opposition, it failed to develop a State, or true political consciousness. Consequently, in exception to all other Western powers, economics had always undisputed precedence over politics. Inner *politics* in the true sense did not exist in America—party-contests were understood by all to be mere business competition between the two party-trusts. True *political* events in America—disjunction of opposing groups into friend and enemy—have been only three: the War for Independence, 1775–83, the North-South hostility culminating in the War of Secession, 1861–65, and the Revolution of 1933, when Culture-distortion captured complete control of the American destiny.

This exclusive concern of all levels of the population with economics was responsible for the total ascendancy of the Master of Money over American life, the failure to develop a true Nation-consciousness, and the rise to power of Culture-distortion.

The larger cycles of financial fluctuations, with alternating "booms" and "depressions" ruined millions in each swing, and until recent decades these pauperized millions could always claim and settle new land in the West, and begin economic life anew. Political class war was never strong in America until recent years. The prevailing Puritan-Calvinistic sentiment of economic predestination militated against fundamental-political class-war, since each worker thought he might one day be chosen for wealth.

With the disappearance of the "frontier," however, the masses of industrial laborers, became material for the professional labor-leader to organize. From small beginnings, the labor-movement in America developed into a powerful political organization, which was able to make politicians in industrial areas dependent upon its votes for election. This point was reached by the 80's of the 19th century. This labor-movement embraced anarchists, Marxian Communists, nihilists, and liberal-capitalistic leaders. The political elements never dominated this movement, even after the Revolution of 1933, for the American laboring class thinks and feels economically and capitalistically, not politically and socialistically. "Socialism" in America means even *now* what it meant in Europe in the 19th century, *i.e.,* capitalism of the lower classes. Of true Socialism, nothing is known or understood in America, since Socialism is *not* primarily an economic organizing-principle, but a political-ethical-Idea, the Spirit of a Political Age, and politics is not yet understood in America.

II

Generally speaking, the economy of America is still in the capitalistic condition which Europe began to outgrow fifty years ago, and which was definitely ended for Europe for all time with the European Revolution of 1933.

Agriculture in America for instance is completely on a money basis. There is no policy of insulating it from the city-economy, or of safeguarding the farmers from financial exploitation. Thus during that part of the cycle when the finance-capitalists are contracting the volume of currency, the farmers are thrown into destitution, and their farms are foreclosed.

There is almost no peasantry in the European sense. The peasant has a spiritual connection with the soil, whereas the American farmer has only a financial relationship with it, and will leave at any time if better economic opportunity presents itself. This purely *economic* attitude has resulted in ruthless exploitation of the soil, with sharp decrease in its productivity, and even greater decrease in the nutritional value of its products. Farming is nearly all on an *extensive* basis, and the lack of care of the soil has resulted in devastating losses by erosion.

The exploitation of sub-surface mineral deposits is also on a purely financial basis, and a coal mine or oil well may be abandoned with 80 per cent of the mineral remaining in it. Opening of one well or shaft immediately causes an entire area to be opened up, since ownership of the surface includes ownership of the sub-surface in American law. The resultant waste can only be described as looting of the treasures of the soil, and is in the very sharpest contrast to the 20th century attitude of trusteeship toward the soil and its minerals.

Industrial production is merely a battleground for profits and control between the managers and the labor-leaders. The social damage and economic waste of strikes are regarded as normal in America, whereas the 20th century idea has no room for any inner strife in a political unit. Behind the struggle of the managers whom he appoints, and the laborers whom he hires, the

finance-capitalist dominates the economic scene. The outcome
of the strike cannot injure him, for he controls the motive forces
of the money economy.

This brings us to the currency of America. Since the War of
Secession, 1865, the entire country has, financially speaking,
been an empire of ignorant subjects, and the owners of the
large banks in New York have been the economic monarchs.
The codification of this situation took place in the year 1913,
when the Federal Reserve System was created by law. It provided for a system of twelve central banks upon which the central government would be dependent for financing. These banks
are privately owned, and issue money against government
bonds, which are sold through these banks. Thus the American
war effort in the Second World War earned approximately
$7,500,000,000 in interest for the owners of this system. The
only currency known in America is the private issue of these
central banks. This currency is spoken of as "secured by government bonds." These bonds however are payable only in this currency. The whole system of course is simply a device for private
control of the economic life of the country. The volume of currency may be increased or decreased at the will of finance-
capitalists, and in a country without a State, this is a technique
of domination.

To the 20th century soul of the Western Civilization, the
resting of public power in private hands is unthinkable. Equally
so is the domination of the economic life of a Nation-State by
money-thinking. Thrice abominable to the 20th century is the
conferring of any power whatever on the banker-mentality,
which regards human beings as a "cost of production," which
looks upon politics as a field for private trickery, and which
regards the heroism of soldiers as a useful device for conquering new financial domains abroad.

Finance-capitalism belongs to a past age, the Age of Money. Even in America, it has passed into the second place, and has become a mere *technique* of the absolute domination of the Culture-distorter. More important as a technique is the control of men's minds, and an understanding of America and its potentialities for Europe necessitates a knowledge of its propaganda system.

Propaganda

IF THE 18th century ideology of "equality" were actually believed in, there would be no such thing as propaganda, since every man would think quite independently, and would resent any attempt whatever to form his mind. This ideology however is shown precisely by the example of America, the country in which it was adopted with religious fervor, to have no correspondence to reality whatever. Spiritual equality may have more or less obtained in the salons of aristocrats and rationalist intellectuals, whether in France, Germany, England or America, in the 18th century, but by the middle of the 19th century, when the masses had been mobilized, there was no possibility of any equality, for these masses demanded leadership by their very existence. The more the mobilization of the masses proceeded, the greater was the feeling of need for strong leadership. As Nietzsche said: "Finally the insecurity becomes so great that men fall in the dust before a strong will-power."

There are two techniques of leadership, both of which are indispensable: discipline, and persuasion. The first is based on confidence, faith, loyalty, duty-sense, good instincts. The second is addressed to the intellectual side, and adjusts itself to the characteristics of the person or population to whom it is directed. Both techniques use sanctions, whether penal, moral, economic, or social. In a period when the reorganizing and forming of huge masses is the leading action-problem, persuasion, or propaganda, is correspondingly necessary, for only an elite is capable of the highest discipline, and masses must be continually re-convinced.

Thus, in America, the country where mass-thinking, mass-ideals, and mass-living dominate the collective life, propaganda is the prime form of dissemination of information. There are no publications in America addressed solely to the intellect; a Culture-distorting regime rests on its invisibility, and independent thinking by strong individuals is *ipso facto* hostile to such a regime. Nor are there any publications which purvey only *facts*. Any facts, and any viewpoints, are co-ordinated, with their presentation, into the ruling propaganda-picture.

The techniques of American propaganda is inclusive of every form of communication. The leading instrument is the cinema. Every week, some 80,000,000 people attend the cinema in America, there to absorb the propaganda message. During the period of war-preparation, 1933–1939, the cinemas produced an endless succession of hate pictures directed against the European Revolution of 1933, and its 20th century outlook and actualizations.

Second in effectiveness is the radio. Every American has in his home one or more wireless receivers, and through them, the mass-picture of events is brought to him again. He has already read the same compulsory viewpoint in the press, seen it in the cinema, and now he hears it. The press, both newspaper and periodical, is third in effectiveness. It should be said that in

America, effectiveness of propaganda is measured solely by the
numbers which it reaches, since the mass-thinking ideal has
triumphed over individuality, quality, and intellectual stratification of the population.

Fourth is the book press. Only such books may be printed as
represent or fit into the larger propaganda framework. Thus an
edition of the *Arabian Nights* for children was recently withdrawn in America because some of the contents were said to
have the possible effect of prejudicing readers against Jews, and
one objectionable illustration showed an unscrupulous merchant with the features of a Jew, in the story about Aladdin and
his lamp. During the years 1933–1939, the larger policy of the
distorter was entirely unquestioned in any paper, book, or
magazine of wide circulation.

Next are the universities and colleges. The mass-idea, as
applied to education means that "higher education" is generalized to an extent that the high academic standards of Europe
make impossible. America, with only half the population of the
Western homeland, has more than 10 times as many institutions
granting academic degrees. Actually what is disseminated in
these institutions is primarily a slightly more esoteric version of
the prevailing ideological and propaganda world-view of the
Culture-distorting regime.

Last is the stage. Outside of New York City, the spiritual
capital of the ruling regime, this hardly exists, but in New
York, the journalistic play is an important propaganda-tech-
nique. Particularly during the period 1933–1939 did the stage
play an important role. A constant stream of hate-plays was
produced directed against the world-outlook of the 20th century and its European representatives. Many of these plays were
in the Yiddish language, since the leaders in America require
uniformity also in their own people.

The propaganda-picture has two aspects, the domestic, and the foreign. The domestic propaganda is a revolutionary one, supporting the American Revolution of 1933. All ideological revolutions, from the French in 1789, through the 19th century ones in Europe, down to the Bolshevik Revolution in 1918, have the tendency to take on the form of a cult. In France Reason-worship was the focus of the religious frenzy; in Russia, it was machine-worship, according to the God Marx. The American Revolution of 1933 is no exception. The central-motive of the new cult is "democracy." In the propaganda-picture, this concept takes the place of God, as the center and ultimate reality. Thus, a Supreme Court Justice, speaking to the graduating class of a Jewish college, said in 1939: "In a larger sense there is something more important than religion, and that is the actualization of the ideals of democracy."

The word has been endowed with religious force, and has in fact attained to the status of a religion. It has become a numen, and cannot be the subject of critical treatment. Apostasy or heresy bring immediate response in the form of a criminal prosecution for sedition, treason, income tax evasion, or other allegation. The saints of this cult are the "Founding Fathers" of the War for Independence, particularly Jefferson—despite the fact that they uniformly detested the idea of democracy, and were nearly all slave-owners—and also Lincoln, Wilson, Roosevelt. Its prophets are journalists, propagandists, film stars, labor-leaders, and party-politicians. The fact that the word "democracy" cannot be defined is the surest evidence that it has ceased to be descriptive, and has become the object of a mass-faith. All other ideas and dogmas of the propaganda-picture are referred to "democracy" for their ultimate justification.

Immediately below "democracy" in importance is "tolerance." This is obviously fundamental to a Culturally-alien

regime. Tolerance means primarily tolerance of Jews and Negroes, but it can mean the cruelest persecution of Europeans or
other persons with a viewpoint differing fundamentally from
the prevailing mass-idea. This persecution is social, economic,
and, if necessary, legal.

To continue the atomizing of the host-people, class-war is a
basic tenet of the total view. It is preached as "labor's right to
organize," "the right to strike," and similar slogans. But
"capital" also has its rights, since neither side in any contest
must gain a decisive victory. *Division* is here, as always, the
technique of conquest.

Feminism is preached, pursuing the mass-uniformity idea into
the realm of the sexes. Instead of the polarity of the sexes, the
ideal of the merging of the sexes is promulgated. Women are
taught to be the "equal" of men, and the Western recognition
of sexual polarity is branded as the "holding down" and "persecution" of women.

Pacifism is preached as a part of the propaganda. This is of
course not true pacifism, for that supervenes without anyone
preaching it, and often without anyone knowing it, and always
without anyone being able to do anything about it. In practice,
doctrinaire pacifism is always a form of war-propaganda. Thus,
in America, Europe means war, and America means peace.
American imperialism is always a crusade for peace. A prominent member of the regime recently spoke of America's "duty
to wage peace around the world."

"Religious tolerance" is also a part of the propaganda, and it
is so interpreted as to mean religious indifference. Dogmas and
doctrines of religion are treated as quite secondary. Churches
are often merged or separated for purely economic considerations. When religion is not merely a compulsory weekly social
amusement, it is a political lecture. Co-operation between the

churches is constantly being organized, and always for some utilitarian aim, having nothing to do with religion. What this means is: the subservience of religion to the program of Culture-distortion.

11

Far more important to Europe than the propaganda about domestic affairs in America is that about foreign affairs.

The numen "democracy" is used also in this realm as the essence of reality. A foreign development sought to be brought about is called "spreading democracy"; a development sought to be hindered is "against democracy," or "fascistic." "Fascism" is the numen corresponding to *evil* in theology, and in fact they are directly equated in American propaganda.

The prime enemy in the propaganda picture was always Europe, and especially the Prussian-European spirit which rose with such self-evident force in the European Revolution of 1933 against the negative view of life, with its materialism, money-obsession, and democratic corruption. The more surely it appeared that this Revolution was not a superficial *political* phenomenon, a mere transfer of one party-regime for another, that it was a deep *spiritual, total revolution,* of a new, vital spirit against a dead spirit, the more violent became the hate propaganda directed against Europe. By 1938, this propaganda had reached an intensity, both in volume and in emotional frenzy, that could not be surpassed. Ceaselessly the American was bombarded with the message that Europe was attacking everything worth-while in the world, "God," "religion," "democracy," "freedom," "peace," "America."

This excessive use of abstractions was itself indicative that there was a lack of concrete realities to use. The failure to

arouse excitement, despite the propaganda bombardment, led
to the thesis that Europe was planning to invade the United
States with fleets and armies. Ideas like these indeed conquered
the intellectual side of the American mass-mind, but did not
penetrate to the emotional level of rousing genuine apprehen-
sion or effective hate.

"Aggressor" was another leading word in the intellectual
assault. Again, it did not relate to facts, and was only allowed
to work one way as a term of abuse. "International morality"
was invented and formulated so that the enemy of the Culture-
distorter became *ipso facto* immoral. If they could not find
political reasons for their politics, they were all the more re-
sourceful in creating moral, ideological, economic, and esthetic
reasons. Nations were divided into *good* and *bad*. Europe as a
whole was bad when it was united, and if Culture-distortion
was able to secure a foothold in any European land, such land
became thereby good. The American propaganda machine reacted with venomous hatred against the European partitioning
of Bohemia in 1938. Every European power which had participated in the negotiations was denounced as evil, aggressive,
immoral, anti-democratic, and the rest of it.

Fundamental in this political picture was the thesis that politics was a matter of "forms of government" struggling against
one another. Not nations or States, but abstractions like "democracy" and "fascism" were the content of the world-struggle.
This imposed the necessity of calling the opponent of the
momentary situation as "democratic" or "fascistic," and changing it from month to month, year to year. Serbia, Poland, Japan,
Russia, China, Hungary, Rumania, and many other units, have
been both "fascist" and "democratic," depending upon precisely what treaty they had made, and with what power.

The division into "democratic" and "fascistic" corresponded

exactly with that into *treaty-breaking* and *treaty-observing* powers. Supplementing it was the dichotomy: peace-loving nations, and—the other kind. The phrase "international law" was popularized, and it was used to describe something which has never existed, and cannot exist. It had no connection whatever with the real international law of 500 years of Western practice. It was popularized to mean that any change in the international territorial *status quo* was "forbidden" by "international law."

Any words whatever that had good connotations were linked with the leading catchwords of the picture. Thus *Western Civilization* was too impressive to treat as a hostile term, and it was used to describe parliamentarism, class-war, plutocracy, and finally—Bolshevik Russia. It was insisted by the propaganda machine during the time of the battle at Stalingrad in the Fall of 1942 between Europe and Asia that the Asiatic forces represented Western Civilization while the European armies were the enemies of Western Civilization. The fact that Siberian, Turkestani, and Kirghizian regiments were being used by the Bolshevik regime was adduced as proof that *Asia had saved Western Civilization.*

To Europeans, this sort of thing testifies to two great facts: the *total* lack of any political or cultural consciousness whatever in the masses of the American population, and the deep, total, and implacable enmity toward Europe of the Culture-distorting regime in America. Japan was also treated in the propaganda picture as an enemy, but not as an irreconcilable enemy, like Europe. The propaganda against Japan was never allowed to take a *racial* form, lest the racial instincts of the American population be awakened into a storm that would sweep away the distorter. The generally milder tone of the anti-Japanese propaganda was owing to the fact that Japan had not experienced, and could not possibly experience, anything like the great European Revolution of 1933.

Because of the primitive intellectuality in a country whose population had been mentally uniformized, this propaganda was able to adopt extremely crude expedients. Thus during the war-preparation, 1933–1939, the press, cinema, and radio were filled with stories of insults to the American flag abroad, of secret documents accidentally discovered, of conversations heard over tapped wires, of discoveries of arms caches in the possession of American nationalists groups, and the like. "Newsreels" purporting to have been filmed abroad, were actually made in some cases in Hollywood. So fantastic did it all become that when, a year before the Second World War, a wireless program carried an imaginative story of an invasion from Mars, there were symptoms of widespread panic among the propagandized masses.

Because America had never come strongly under the impression of the Spanish cabinet-politics usages which became engrafted on the European spirit, the Culture-distorting regime was able to engage in propaganda attacks of an extremely repulsive and vile kind directed against the private lives and characters of European leaders who represented the 20th century world-outlook. These leaders were represented as having been panders, homosexuals, dope-fiends, and sadists.

The propaganda was entirely free from any cultural basis, and was completely cynical with regard to facts. Precisely as the cinema-factories of Hollywood ground out lying plays and "newsreels," the propagandists of the press created what "facts" they needed. When the Japanese air forces attacked the American naval base at Pearl Harbor in December, 1941, the Culture-distorters did not know that Europe would take this occasion to retaliate against the undeclared war which the Culture-distorting regime in Washington had been waging against Europe. The regime therefore at once decided to exploit the Japanese attack as a European military measure. To this end, the propaganda organs at once spread the "news" that European planes with European pilots had participated in the attack, and had even led it. Although every capital ship in the base was sunk in this attack, the regime officially announced that only slight damage had been done. These fact-creations were as nothing, however, to the massive, post-war, "concentration-camp" propaganda of the Culture-distorting regime based in Washington.

This propaganda announced that 6,000,000 members of the Jewish Culture-Nation-State-Church-People-Race had been killed in European camps, as well as an indeterminate number of other people. The propaganda was on a world-wide scale, and was of a mendacity that was perhaps adapted to a uniformized mass, but was simply disgusting to discriminating Europeans. The propaganda was technically quite complete. "Photographs" were supplied in millions of copies. Thousands of the people who had been killed published accounts of their experiences in these camps. Hundreds of thousands more made fortunes in post-war black-markets. "Gas-chambers" that did not exist were photographed, and a "gasmobile" was invented to titillate the mechanically-minded.

We come now to the *purpose* of this propaganda which the regime gave to its mentally-enslaved masses. From the analysis in the 20th Century Political Outlook, the purpose is seen to be only one: it was designed to create a total war in the spiritual sense, transcending the limits of politics, against the Western Civilization. The American masses, both military and civilian, were given this mental poison in order to inflame them to the point where they would carry out without flinching the post-war annihilation-program. In particular: it *was designed to support a war after the Second World War, a war of looting, hanging, and starvation against defenseless Europe.*

Propaganda is merely an adjunct of policy, however, and we come now to the conduct of foreign affairs by the America-based regime from the time of its seizure of power in 1933.

12 Oct 95

The Conduct of
American Foreign Affairs from 1933

As WAS NOTED in the outline of the general thesis of Culture-distortion as a form of Culture-pathology, the Russian anti-semitic outbreaks after the Russo-Japanese War, 1904–1905, brought about a rupture of diplomatic relations with the United States. Since no other racial, cultural, national, or religious out-breaks of this kind directed against non-Jewish elements in Russia, or in any other country, had ever caused an American government to break relations, this can only be explained as an example of Culture-distortion. The actual inspiration for this startling international move came from certain elements in the entourage of the then President Theodore Roosevelt, which be-longed to the same Culture-State-Nation-People-Race as the vic-tims of the pogrom.

Historians will be able to trace the appearance of Culture-pathology through American foreign policy from about 1900. The immediate period under consideration however is that since 1933, a year of fate for both America and Europe.

The first positive act of a non-routine nature by the revolutionary regime, after its preliminary consolidation of power, was the diplomatic recognition of Bolshevist Russia. It was explained away to a loudly resentful American public as being merely a routine act, without ideological significance, and quite harmless politically. Actually it was the beginning of a cooperation between the two regimes which continued with only surface interruptions until the Russian and American armies met in the heart of the Western Civilization, and London and Berlin had been thrown into the dust.

In 1936, the Bolshevist revolution and the 20th century Western authoritarian spirit met on the battleground of Spain. The officials of the America-based regime privately expressed their sympathy with Red Spain. The unequivocal opposition of the Catholic Church to American aid for Bolshevist Spain prevented intervention. The Catholic Church in America has twenty million adherents, and the Culture-distorting regime had not sufficiently consolidated its power to engage in a domestic conflict of the type that would have resulted. It was about to contest its second national election, and large organized groups were still in the field against it. A blunder in foreign policy could have been fatal at that stage.

The perfection of its election technique continued the regime in office. In October, 1937, the open preparations for a Second World War were begun. It was officially announced that the American government was going "to quarantine aggressors." The propaganda organs had identified the word "aggressor" with Europe, and the custodians of the European Future. To satisfy nationalist elements, Japan was included in the term, but the regime continued to equip Japan with essential raw materials for its war-industry, while at the same time it refused to sell raw materials to Europe, and boycotted importation into America of European goods originating in areas not dominated by the Culture-distorting regime.

By the fall of 1938, the stage was set for a World War. The propaganda of almost half Europe had been brought under the control of Washington, and the governments of nearly half Europe were its puppets. The incorporation of Bohemia into Europe was the result of the mutual understanding of four European leaders, making their own decision, and the plans of Washington were completely frustrated, despite careful preparations. The American treasury had been made available to the regime as a "Stabilization Fund," and it could draw upon its billions without accounting to anyone. The subsidization of its representative propagandists in European countries was increased to such proportions that soon almost half Europe had been made to hate the leaders who had prevented an intra-European war.

But an Eastern border-state was needed for the next incident, since there was no direct possibility of a war in Western Europe, Poland was therefore coordinated into the plans of Washington. The Polish government, ostensibly the custodian of the national interests of Poland, brought about a hopeless war, and that precisely after Russia had publicly agreed to the partitioning of Poland. The government which had arranged the war's beginning disappeared promptly upon the outbreak of war, and was never heard of again. It had earned its pension. The American domestic propaganda at this time was to the effect that Poland could resist for years.

The war began in earnest in 1940. France and the Low Countries were detached from America in a few weeks. The American regime found its control of Europe severely limited, and a domestic population on its hands not only devoid of war enthusiasm, but hostile to any form of intervention in the war which the Washington dictature had itself created.

The non-intervention movement in America was then taken over by the Culture-distorter, and the propaganda was devised that sending war material abroad was a method of remaining out of the war. In other words, limited participation was non-intervention. American political unconsciousness being what it is in a country with no tradition, no State, and no higher History, this was convincing, and the overwhelming sentiment against intervention was thus brought into the service of the intervention plans of Washington.

The limited participation was ever less limited. A law which nationalist elements had passed long before the War, to prohibit this sort of involvement in wars, was cynically put aside. American expeditionary forces were sent abroad, American naval vessels were ordered to engage European vessels on the high seas, merchant ships of European origin were requisitioned —and all this from a government that had been giving pontifical lessons in International Law to the world.

The widening of the theater of war by the involvement of Bolshevist Russia against the Western Civilization led within a fortnight to the breaking of relations with Europe. But the domestic situation still prevented Washington from direct American involvement, and Europe had failed to react to the undeclared American war on the high seas. The sole remaining American bastion in Europe was the island, and it was only held by political and financial means which could at any moment give way. Direct intervention with the total military potential of America was essential if the war was not to terminate in a Western victory over Asiatic Russia and a general settlement of all old political problems in Western Europe, which would result in the creation of a Culture-Nation-State-People-Race unity of the West with an authoritarian political basis that would be impermeable to Culture-distortion, and would moreover, by its example, inevitably call forth an American nationalist revolution against the Culture-distorting regime.

Since efforts to antagonize Europe by undeclared war had not had the desired results, it was sought to create a Far Eastern war by which it was hoped involvement in the real war against the Western Civilization could also come about. To this end, an ultimatum was delivered to the Japanese Government in November, 1941. The ultimatum demanded Japanese evacuation of all its conquests since July, 1936. The answer of Japan was to sink the American battle fleet in Pearl Harbor in December, 1941. Public and official investigations carried out by nationalist elements after the war proved conclusively that *the Washington regime knew this attack was coming,* and even the day of it, since it had been reading Japanese diplomatic messages. *Nevertheless it took no military precautions,* and thus cynically threw away the lives of thousands of American soldiers and sailors. The propaganda machine was already geared to attribute this Japanese attack to the Western Civilization, but the Western war-declaration, following in a few days, made this propaganda pointless.

Thenceforward, 80 per cent of the American war-effort was devoted to the war against the hated Western Civilization. Australia and India were ignored except for weak efforts to contain a second Japanese attack-wave which never came. Had it come, the white population in colonial Australia would have passed into subjection to Japan, as a result of the presence in the Western Civilization of a pathological distortion. Europeans should note the significance of the statement of the American commander, precisely in this threatened quarter of the white world, made in the summer of 1942: "The future of civilization rests with the worthy banners of the Russian Army." From this, it is apparent that uniformity of mind is a prerequisite also to military rank.

11

The conduct of the American war effort, on the higher level, departed entirely from the principles of honor which have always governed the intercourse of Western nations and leaders. The prime attack against Europe was by bombing planes based on the European island which from 1942 was occupied by American troops. The air-bombardment was directed almost entirely against the civilian population of Europe, even though it was known that no decision could be achieved by this means. The American press spoke blood-thirstily of "block-busters" by which was meant a bomb which could wipe out a city-block of civilian homes, and kill several hundred civilians. Photographs were proudly displayed of the results of this dishonorable type of warfare against families and homes. A propaganda was developed that anyone opposing the armies or ideology of America was a criminal, and subject to a "trial" for his "crimes."

Europe was already familiar with atrocity propaganda stemming from America. Owing to the primitive intellectual level which Culture-distortion and Culture-Retardation have generalized in America, this sort of thing is taken literally, whereas the responsible minds of Europe recognize it for what it is, a mass-propaganda designed to reach marginal brains. Thus during the First World War, the American press circulated stories of atrocities committed—of course—by the opponents of American armies. Belgium was selected as the site of these stories, and it was said that Belgian civilians were crucified by occupying armies. There was much more of the same: hands cut off babies, and the like. So seriously was this taken in America that after the First World War a deputation of American journalists traveled in a group to Belgium to investigate the stories, and then reported to the American public that they had all been found to be untrue.

Thus the thesis that anyone opposing America was *ipso facto* a criminal was not taken seriously in Europe, but served as a preparation of the American mind for the post-war horrors to be committed in Europe.

A leadership that had been talking about "war crimes" for years, while waging its own warfare against homes and families, armed itself finally in 1945 with a projectile which could be used *only* against civilians, the "atomic" bomb. Under the tactical conditions then prevailing, this bomb could not be used against military forces, but only against cities, which in war are stripped of men of military age. This bomb was used without demonstration, and without warning, and obliterated hundreds of thousands of civilians in a few seconds.

In the period after the Second World War, American foreign policy retained its continuity. Occupied Europe was treated as an area to be devastated, factories were dismantled of machinery, which was given to Russia, and other installations were blown into the air as part of a deliberate policy of destroying the industrial-potential of Europe. The population was treated as sub-human, and a large-scale starvation policy was introduced, which continues in 1948. Although America was exporting food all over the world, not being under any obligation of honor or morality to do so, nevertheless it refused to send enough food to maintain human life into occupied Europe. Human rations were fixed far below qualitative and quantitative minima for health, and within a short time, malnutrition, skin-ailments, infections, and degenerative diseases began to kill millions. In the first wild exultation of its "victory," the American army forbade its personnel even to *speak* to the population. This continued until court-martials became too numerous, and it was discarded while in its place was substituted a violent hate propaganda among the American troops. The population of Europe was treated as totally and essentially inferior to the conquering Americans. It was officially referred to as "the indigenous population." In public buildings special sanitary facilities were set aside for them, while the superior Americans and Negroes used their own.

Requisitioning of homes was on a mass-scale: American soldiers and civilians were allowed to bring their families from America and to put them into undamaged houses, in which had been living perhaps fifteen or twenty members of "the indigenous population." The owners of these homes were allowed usually to take with them only their clothes and their food. No provisions were made for housing the dispossessed, for they were regarded and treated as sub-human.

This population was deprived of the physical right of self-defense against Americans. Europeans who struck Americans in reply to a blow were sentenced to imprisonment by American military courts. One European was sentenced to two years imprisonment for a hearsay reference to a Jewish member of the American forces as a "dirty Jew."

The ghastly *dishonor* attending the American occupation of Europe is sufficient to show the presence of Culture-alien elements, for no Western nation or colony could possibly proceed to this type of conduct. Its very inner constitution, its historical essence, a thousand-year honor tradition, would preclude the possibility. What Western nation would reduce the women of another to the legal status of concubines, and forbid marriage between its members and those of another Western nation? Yet this is what the American command did. It permitted concubinage, and forbade marriage. As a result of this policy, venereal disease assumed plague proportions in occupied Europe.

In the presence of this starving, disease-ridden European population, the American armies and their families, guarded by guns and barbed wire, live in the houses which their bombs did not damage, and eat an unrationed diet. The spiritual qualities developed by these conditions are not the highest. In the early phase of the occupation, waste food and clothing were actually burned in the physical presence of the starving and freezing "indigenous population."

When, in the summer of 1947, a food revolt threatened, one of the American governors announced officially that the American people had no duty in fact, in international law, or in morals, to feed its subject population in occupied Europe, and that if a revolt did occur, it would be put down with bayonet and machine gun. That which is here described is only partial, but the pattern of the facts is universal in American-occupied Europe. It continues today, and has a deep and wide influence on European thinking on the most important level.

III

As was revealed in the analysis of the motivation of politics, power-contests in our century derive their motivation from Cultural phenomena. In the early Western centuries, this motivation often came from the struggle between Emperor and Pope for universal rule; later it came from religious differences; later still from dynastic ambition; then from nation-units and from economic-commercial rivalry. Now the main fact in the world is the spiritual unity of the Western Civilization, just becoming conscious, and the awakened will-to-destroy of the outer world. In the realm of action it takes the form of a political struggle between the Western Civilization and its colonies on the one side, and the non-Western forces on the other. The enmity between America and Japan was therefore natural, and all nationalist elements in America so regarded it. The distorting elements in America however never regarded this enmity as important, for there was no anti-semitism in Japan. This throws the necessary light on the American policy in the occupation of Japan.

Upon the conquest of Japan, the utmost friendliness was at once put into effect as the policy of the army toward the Japanese population. The American army officially established brothels with Japanese women for its soldiers. Houses were not requisitioned for the troops, but barracks were built. The diet was adequate to maintain human health. The Emperor retained his rank and position, and his Godhead was not disturbed in the public mind. The Japanese self-respect was maintained by the dignified treatment generally accorded to Japanese civilians. The American policy was to restore the industrial potential of the country, and allow Japanese autonomy. The Japanese Diet, government and administration were maintained. Former political leaders were respectfully told to report for trial for war crimes, for this pettifogging nonsense has become a compulsion wherever American armies penetrate. The only exaction made of the population was the adoption of the American religion of "democracy"-worship. For a population whose national religion already consisted of Confucianism, Buddhism, Shintoism, and Emperor-worship, this was no great sacrifice.

The leaders over whom the protracted ritual of war-crime exorcism was practiced were not abused either in the Japanese press or in the American press. They were not photographed endlessly, subjected to Freudian inquisitions, tormented, forced to pick up the cigarette-ends of American soldiers, or systematically degraded as had been the case with the victims of American armies in Europe. Above all, the "war-crime" process was not extended throughout the entire organization of Japanese life, both civilian and military, as was done in Europe, and as continues to be done in 1948.

The difference in policy between these two occupations is quite sufficient to explain by itself the entire formative influence of American foreign policy. The dominating impulse of the occupation-policy in occupied Europe is *revenge*. As the analysis of politics showed, however, revenge is not a part of politics, but transcends politics. Politics is not carried on for the purpose of humiliating the enemy, nor of exterminating the population of the enemy-unit if it is defeated. Politics has the aim of increasing power, and the American regime has not consulted power-realities at any point in forming and executing its policy in occupied Europe. In an area with an enormous war-potential which it controls and could use for its own power purposes, it systematically destroys plant and machinery. Among a population which could furnish it with millions of the best soldiers in the world, the Americans conduct themselves with a ferocity and an affected superiority calculated to alienate the "indigenous population" forever. Finding themselves captors of the best military leaders in the Western Civilization, to whom they should go to school, they proceed to hang them for the crime of opposing American armies in the field.

In short, instead of increasing American power, the occupation-policy has decreased American power in every way. This shows conclusively that the motivation of this conduct is outside politics. Its motivation is derived from the complete, deep, and total organic irreconcilability between a High Culture and a parasitic organism within it. This relationship is one transcending ordinary international politics. It is somewhat similar to the relationship between the Roman legions and the barbarians of Mithridates and Jugurtha, or to that between the

Crusaders and the Saracens, or between Europe and the Turk in the 16th century. It is deeper even than these, because of the revenge-twist introduced into the soul of the parasite through centuries of silent sufferance of the unassailable superiority of the host. When defeated Europe—and in particular, the most vital part of it, the bearer of the grand European Idea of the 20th century—lay at the feet of this totally alien conqueror from a Culture of the past, no feelings of magnanimity, chivalry, generosity, mercy, were in his exultant soul. There was only there the gall which he had been drinking for a thousand years while he had bided his time under the arrogance of the alien Western peoples whom he had always considered, and still considers, barbarians, *goyim.* Seen from this standpoint, the American armies were just as completely defeated as the armies from the mother-soil of the Culture. The real victor was the Cultural alien, whose triumph here over the entire Western Civilization marked the highest refulgence of his destiny.

I V

The ultimate significance of American policy since the American Revolution of 1933 has been negative as far as America is concerned. America's natural, geopolitical, national interests lie in Central and South America, and in the Far East. In a world-struggle for control of the planet between the Western Civilization and the outer forces, the natural policy of Europe is directed toward Africa, the Near East, and the vastness of Asiatic Russia. America, being a colony of the Civilization, deriving all its spiritual nourishment from it, naturally complements this interest, and in no way conflicts with it. What interest has a nationalist America in Russia, Africa, the Near East? Correspondingly, what political interest has Europe in

Central or South America? Europe and America have no natural, organic, power-convergence. America and Japan have.

American foreign policy violates every feature of this natural disposition. It allied America to Russia—not against Japan, which could have been understood, but against Europe, which was madness for true American interests. It fought Japan, and proceeded after the conquest to rehabilitate Japan instead of reorganizing it into a permanent part of the American empire. It fought its main ally, Europe, not a mere political ally, but its spiritual parent and total, Cultural ally.

When the fortunes of war gave military victory to American arms it could have redeemed its previous mistakes. Japan could have been incorporated into the American overseas empire. Europe could have been rehabilitated. The exact opposite was done. Europe was looted, starved, and despoiled, while Japan, the natural enemy, was rebuilt for its next war against America.

In short, the foreign policy of America *was not American*. From its objective acts alone, this appears in a conclusive fashion.

Culture-distortion has exercised in America, since 1933, the supreme power of deciding the issue of war or peace for Americans. From the victorious dispersal of American arms, America gained no power. Japan has been an expense—much of its machinery has been given to Russia, and the burden of making up its food-deficit has been laid on the American people. While Russia has gained enormously in industrial strength by the machinery it has taken from Europe, and from what America has given it from its half of Europe, America has only incurred more expenses. So thoroughly has it devastated its area of occupied Europe that many material needs of its armies have to be brought from America.

American armies have evacuated China and India, North

Africa and Persia, giving up the largest empire in the world's history. At the close of the Second World War, Washington was the capital of a military empire embracing 18/20ths of the surface of the earth, including all the seas as subject to American control.

The policy of the Culture-distorter was thus not at all, as some people said, directed toward world-control. This grandiose idea could only arise in a Western stratum. An alien organism in the body of the Western Civilization can only *distort* the life of the West. The parasite cannot become Western, and world-domination is a Western idea. Nor is it an idea for everyone, but like all formative Western ideas it excludes persons without depth or intensity. This is why America could not hold the great empire it had gathered together. America has not yet had sufficient historical experience, it has not the consciousness of *politics,* to administer or create an empire. In the mass-mind of the American, the entire Second World War had the one negative aim: destroy the European Idea.

Thus Culture-distortion in America neither followed America's national interest, nor did it aim at world-conquest, either for itself or for America. As a result, it led America to a political defeat in the Second World War.

This fact is quite patent to Europe. More important is the question of how far this is realized in America. This involves the problems of the form of the Future in America, American nationalism, the prospect of continued Culture-pathology, and the spiritual possibilities of America.

The Future of America

THE ORIGIN of America contains its Future. As Leibnitz said, "The Present is loaded with the Past, and pregnant with the Future." America originated as a colony of the Western Culture. The organic unity called a High Culture is tied to its landscape of birth. Here it is born, and here it solves its last and mightiest problems. In its present stage, the Western Civilization dominates the spiritual orientation of the whole world. Units like Japan and Russia exist merely as active revolts against the Western Civilization, as denials of its world-outlook. The Western Civilization has created even its own opponents; its dynamism has mobilized the outer forces into their present activity. The colonies which this Culture planted around the world during the period 1600–1800 have maintained their spiritual relationship with the mother-organism. The leading souls of Argentina, South Africa, Australia, America, Canada, and the other scattered smaller colonies, reside spiritually in Europe, and from the fructifying and wider-working creations of the parent Western Civilization, they derive their world-outlook, their plans, ideas, and inner imperative. These colonies remain the spiritual allies of the Western Civilization. Their political interests cannot possibly be hostile to those of the West, for they will share with it a common fate.

In this Age, the motivation of politics is derived from Culture. The world divides into the Western Civilization, and that outside. A victory of Europe over Russia or India is a victory for America, and a victory of America over Japan or China is also one for Europe. *America and Europe together constitute a spiritual unit.* The possibility thus is real and organic that America and Europe will once again be politically united. That which shares a common Destiny is actually a political unit, and the continuance of political disunity is artificial and hostile to the Life-interests of the organism. The prime aim of Life is the actualizing of the possible. This is Life. Owing to the frightfully dangerous world-position of the Western Civilization, a condition which will not vanish even with a successful war, the organic tendencies to Reunion of Europe and America are inevitably going to express themselves by impressing the best brains of America and Europe with the necessity of Reunion. The time-span involved in the beginnings of this tendency is not longer than one generation. Whether the tendency will be actualized is unforeseeable, just as the fate of Karnak was unforeseeable to the Ramessids. But its Life-necessity will dictate that this tendency will become the focus of action.

But the organic Idea of Reunion is impossible of realization while the West is suffering from inner Culture-diseases. This poses the question of reaction to Culture-pathology in America.

The original stirrings of the soul of the American People were manifested by the early types of the independent colonial, the pioneer, the militiaman, the explorer, the frontiersman. The characteristics of this type were resourcefulness, fearlessness, *good use of Gothic rather than "Faustian"*

technical competence. It was simply the old Gothic urge into the distance once more, and the will to conquer that which lies between. The early American people had a powerful instinct of racial superiority coupled with its spirit of self-reliance. This human material was the basis of the Yankee type created by the War of Secession. That war had the result of engrafting onto this human material the form of the Age of Economics, Money and Materialism. It was a natural result, for the entire Western Civilization was at that time in the grip of the Civilization-Crisis. The soul of the American People was formed in that upheaval. It is a late people, by which is meant, technical, hard, externalized, but devoid of possibilities in the field of culture in the narrower sense. This hardness and externalization, this technical competence will always remain in the American soul, for they are of its essence. The ideological trappings were mere clothing, and they belonged to the Spirit of the Age. The 19th century spirit is quite dead, and America cannot perpetuate its charnel ideas any more than an organism can develop backwards, from age to youth.

The American ideology and world-outlook have no Future; the soul of the American people however has, for this people is an organism. The beating of this people into a thing of mass-ideals, mass-thinking, mass-conduct, mass-living, was a distortion and an exaggeration of the tendencies of the American soul, and of the possibilities of the Age of Materialism. This twisting and warping of the American Destiny was only possible because of the diseases of Culture-Retardation and Culture-distortion. Culture-Retardation in America was a reflex of the presence of the same disease in Europe: the Age of Materialism had been fortuitously victorious, on the surface of History, in the First World War, and the actualizing of the Idea of the 20th century in both America and Europe was thereby de-

layed. Culture-distortion in America was the result of the presence in huge masses of a Culturally alien group. The immediate
future of America is therefore bound up with Culture-distortion
and the American reaction against it. The distribution of power,
spiritual and material, must be assessed which will be called
into play. First the Culture-distorting group.

The numbers of the Jewish Culture-Nation-State-Race in
America are estimated between eight and twelve millions. The
numbers are however not of the first importance, for this organic unity has strong racial instincts and a powerful sense of a
mission. The numbers do indeed play a part, both in the extent
of Culture-distortion and the form and extent of the reaction
against it, but the public power of the Culture-distorting group
is based on its control of highly focused central organizations.

In propaganda, its control is *absolute.* This covers the cinema,
the radio, the press—newspaper, periodical, book—the universities, and the stage. The radio is controlled by means of the
few large nation-wide networks, which control the programs of
the member stations, even though these may be privately owned.
The newspaper press is dominated by its ownership of the few
great news-gathering associations, which control the presentation of the news of the member-newspapers, who are dependent on the associations, even though they may be privately
owned, and who may not change anything given them by the
associations. Periodicals and books are controlled by means of
ownership, in most cases, of the magazines, publishing houses,
and printing presses, and social, economic, moral, and legal
compulsion for the other cases. The stage is controlled by
ownership of the theaters, and the other compulsory means.
The universities are dominated by the disproportionate numbers of the Culture-distorting group, both in teaching and stu-
dent personnel, as well as the organized and aggressive activity
of these numbers.

Both political parties are controlled by the Culture-distorting group, forcing all the accepted kind of inner-political activity in America into its service. The technique of political control is through a vast bureaucracy, created since 1933, which is dominated and disproportionately staffed with members of the group. This administrative control is extended also over the armed forces.

In the financial world—which completely owns and controls the industrial—the power of this group is heavily disproportionate to its population-percentage. Its hold in this realm goes back to the War of Secession, when a few of the precursors of the invasion of 1890–1950 engaged in the arms traffic between the Confederate and Federal armies.

The result of all this is a powerful *spiritual* influence on the American people. This people reads the books which aliens write or edit for it. It sees the plays and cinemas it is allowed to. It thinks the thoughts that are put into its head. It is thrown into wars against American interests, which it can only lose. The issue of war and peace, life and death, is decided for America by the Cultural alien. America has been given a semitic countenance. Americans who hold power hold it in deference to the alien. To oppose him dare no public men. Americans were told that they must be concerned with the partitioning of Arabia, and no national channel existed through which an American could deny fundamentally the world-picture which supported such a policy.

But he who has looked into the essence of History knows that the alien and the proper *cannot* merge, they can *only* oppose one another. Disguise, terror, threats, dictatorship, pressure, propaganda—none of these can reach the essence of the relationship. The American people—not yet a nation—has its own soul, and it is only its lack of historical experience, and the stage of development of the Culture which created this people,

strong
confidence but "danger"?

which have made possible the wide and critical diffusion of Culture pathology throughout this people.

The very fact of Culture-distortion presupposes the existence, in its inner purity, of the soul of the host-people. Distortion cannot destroy the host, but can only direct the energy of the host onto false problems, and into the direction of the interests of the parasite.

II

As Europe now knows, the Second World War was a phenomenon of Culture-illness. It was created in America, skillfully prepared during the years 1933–1939, and it was cleverly cast into the superficial form of a contest between two European powers of yesterday, although the real world-issue was the uniting of the West against the threat to its life from the gathering outer forces—Russia, China, India, Islam, Africa. The true form of the war was disclosed to everyone in 1945, when the victors emerged as the Culture-distorting regime in America, and the Mongols in the Kremlin. For the first time in world history, the world was divided between two powers. Europe had lost the war, and achieved the unity in defeat which it had not entirely reached in its victories. Europe passed temporarily into the same status that China and India formerly occupied—spoils for powers from without.

The result of this war was also a defeat for America, first because the issue was false, and secondly because the exploitation of its military successes was false.

Facts of this magnitude cannot be concealed.

A knowledge of the organic nature of History would tell one that a reaction exists in America, even though he knew none of the facts concerning it. The facts of the American nationalist

reaction are precisely what we would expect. History works
through minorities, and the size of these minorities is a direct
reflex of the necessity of the historical phenomenon. The nationalist minority in America has at least ten million members. This
minority is almost completely unorganized. There are approximately a thousand resistance organizations, but they are in-
effectual politically, even though they are strongly symptomatic
spiritually.

In 1915 began the nationalist reaction to the invasion of Culturally alien elements, with the founding of the second Ku
Klux Klan. This year will be marked in retrospect as the beginning of the second phase of the American Revolution. The
figure of ten millions as the strength of these elements is of
course an estimate, but it refers to persons whose souls are
strongly influenced by the immanent Nation-Idea in America.
At less intensity, this feeling is general in the American population. Thus, no one denied ever that the overwhelming desire of
the population was to stay out of the Second World War which
the Culture-distorting regime in Washington had created in
Europe. This was despite the heaviest propaganda barrage ever
leveled at any population anywhere.

It is not traceable to true pacifism, for this does not exist in
America. It reflects the fact that the soul of this people instinctively distrusted and hated the whole attempt. In 1940, it was
given no chance to express its feeling in the "election," since
both candidates for power were committed to intervention. The
management of elections has so far frustrated expression of
the true American soul.

This nationalism is increasingly radical, even though it has
not yet assumed political proportions. Certain American nationalists were held in gaol for having said in 1941 that a military
defeat was to be desired for the welfare of America, since a

defeat would destroy the hold of the Culture-distorting group. The American nationalist element generally hoped for a defeat of the conscript armies which had been massed out of the un-enthusiastic and unwilling American youth. At the same time, it supported the war against Japan, the natural, geopolitical enemy of America.

The principle of individuality, of continuity of soul and character, applies to Peoples as well as to persons, and thus it is known that the Spirit still lives which was effective in such men as Nathaniel Green, Mad Anthony Wayne, Ethan Allen, Nathan Hale, Richard Henry Lee, John Adams, Daniel Morgan, Davy Crockett, the men of the Alamo and San Jacinto, Stonewall Jackson, Robert E. Lee, William Walker, and Homer Lea. The century of materialism and money-obsession naturally called forth no heroism, but the 20th century will change the spiritual aspect of America as it has changed Europe. The latent heroism of the American People will again be summoned forth by the stern creativeness of the Age of Absolute Politics.

Despite the extent of Culture-distortion and its attempts to render a People permanently into a feckless, uniformized mass, there are millions who have held themselves instinctively aloof. These people are the focus of great historical forces. They fight against gigantic odds, and they fight under enormous handicaps.

American nationalism has no connection with a grand tradition of life, thought, and action. It finds itself charged with a politically revolutionary mission, but the American people is not revolutionary. Its reaction to a Cultural disease is in a crude racial form. It faces a mighty political task, but is unconscious of the necessities of power-thinking. Its intellect is not free from the superannuated ideology of "equality," born in 1775, and still used by the distorting element for its own purpose.

The hammering of the mass-mind into the American people was at bottom merely a *technique,* an artifice. Strong individuality was *submerged,* it is true, but strong individuality cannot be *annihilated.* The Age of Absolute Politics will wake once more what there is of Genius in the American stock, and a powerful reaction may be expected from the mass-veneer over the American soul in the form of individual leaders upon whom absolute power will be conferred.

America is not a country with creative possibilities in the field of philosophy, and its higher understanding of the great realities of our time will come from its deep, determining connection with the mother-soil of the West.

The elements which will enter into the coming struggle between American nationalism and the Culture-pathological element will be numerous. It is probably no longer possible for the American Revolution to take a constitutional form. The perfected parliamentary-electoral techniques of late democratic conditions seem to exclude that possibility. There is left only civil war. In such a war, the race-war between the Negro and the white, the class-war of the unions against the managers, the financial-war of the money-dictators against the coming authoritarian nationalism, and the war for survival of the Culture-distorter against the American people, will all step forth for resolution.

Whether this crisis will be sharp and critical in nature, like the Secession-War, or in the form of an uncertain and long-drawn out evolution, like the Thirty-Years' War, or the struggle between the Spirit of Cromwell and the Restoration, cannot be foreseen. In any case, the struggle is one which is demanded by organic necessity, and only its occurrence can be foretold, but neither the form thereof, nor the date thereof.

These are Imponderables. When the American National

Revolution takes political form, its inspiration will come from the same ultimate source as the European Revolution of 1933. Therefore what is written here is also for the true America, even though the effective America of the moment, and of the immediate future is a hostile America, an America of willing, mass-mind tools in the service of the Culture-distorting political and total enemy of the Western Civilization.

13 x 95

THE WORLD SITUATION

"Imagination rules the world."

—NAPOLEON

"For the tasks of the next century, the methods of popular representation are the most inappropriate imaginable. The condition of Europe in the next century will once again lead to the breeding of manly virtues, because men will live in continual danger. I see over and beyond all these national wars, new Empires, and whatever else lies in the foreground. What I am concerned with—for I see it preparing itself slowly and hesitatingly—is the United Europe. The nations which *got to be* worth anything never attained to that condition under liberal institutions: *great danger* made out of them something which deserves reverence, that danger which alone can make us aware of our resources, our virtues, our means of defense, our weapons, our *genius*—which *compels* us to be strong."

—NIETZSCHE

"Pacifism will remain an ideal, war a fact, and if the white race decides to wage it no longer, the colored will, and will become the rulers of the world."

—SPENGLER

The Political World

POLITICS IS related to war, and war uses strategy. Strategy immediately involves the fundamental realities of physical and human geography. And so an examination of the facts and possibilities of world-politics begins with geography.

In this Age of Absolute Politics, the entire earth-ball is the object of the power-instincts of both the Western Civilization, and, by a process of outer negation that is just as total as the Western Imperialistic affirmation, also the extra-Western forces. Therefore the general geographic picture of the planet is the point of departure.

Dividing the world into two longitudinal hemispheres along the 20th meridian, it is seen that in the Eastern Hemisphere is the land-mass Asia-Africa, the outlying islands Australia and Oceania, and most of Antarctica. The total land-mass is more than 100,000,000 quadrate kilometers. In the Western Hemisphere are the two connected islands North and South America, and part of Antarctica. These areas are 47,000,000 quadrate kilometers, less than half the land-mass in the Eastern Hemisphere. More important than area is population, for power means control over *people,* and they can only be controlled politically where they *are.* The population of the Eastern Hemisphere is approximately 1,700,000,000 persons, while that of the Western is only 300,000,000.

This means that the world—politically speaking—is in the Eastern Hemisphere. The planet can also be divided into a Northern and Southern Hemisphere, along the Equator. In this division, more than 9/10ths of both land-area and population lie in the Northern Hemisphere. If the planet be divided into quadrants, it is seen that more than half of the population of the great land-mass Asia-Africa, or approximately half the total population of the planet, is in the North-East quadrant. This includes Europe, most of Russia, India, Asia Minor, and most of Africa. This entire land-mass is contiguous except for indentation by the narrow seas, the Mediterranean, the Arabian Gulf, the Persian Gulf, the Baltic. The whole area is controllable by land-power, including the narrow seas, whose entrances are commanded by the land.

It is thus quite obvious that world-control means in the first instance control of this north-east earth-quadrant. In the second instance, world-control means domination of the land-mass Asia-Africa. Thirdly, it means control of the Northern Hemisphere, and lastly, control of all the waters and land of the planet. The north-east quadrant, being the most important area, is the focus of all 20th century Imperialism.

These fundamental geographical facts are the basis of all large-scale political thinking. The *basis,* but not the *source,* for the origin of grand thinking of any kind whatever is a High Culture, making itself effective through a Culture-bearing stratum of human beings. The science of geopolitics was itself a knowledge-system created by a High Culture which had arrived at the stage of unlimited Imperialism, the Age of Absolute Politics. It bore however within it a remnant of materialistic thinking which led to the error of placing the origin, determination, or motivation, of politics in physical facts. This was an absolute error, since all Materialism, as a description of facts, is an absolute error. The origin of ideas, impulses, experience, is the soul. The origin of politics itself is the human soul. The origin of grand creative politics is the soul of a High Culture. The origin of destructive politics is in the negation, by the souls of outer populations, of the political imperative of a High Culture.

In the present stage of the Western Civilization, the motivation of politics is in Culture, and no longer in nationalism or economics, as was often the case in the 19th century. The spiritual unity of the Western Civilization and its colonies is a fact, and this prime fact is the source of the great political contest in this century. The unlimited Imperialism of the West has created in the outer populations an equally strong will to destroy Western Imperialism. The only way it can do this is by its own Imperialism. Thus the Idea of Imperium dominates the form of the world-struggle of this century and the next. Whether one is in its service or opposing it, he is coerced by its universality.

The error of geopolitics was in thinking that the outer could determine the inner. But the soul is always primary, and the use made of material, or of geographic position, is a mere reflex of the type of soul. The American Indians had far more resources than the American Colonials, yet their primitivity in techniques left them helpless. Total technical superiority however is not material superiority, but spiritual superiority.

Geopolitics, as developed before this time, was not founded on the 20th century view of history and politics, but on tacit materialistic ideas left over from the 19th century. The re-

searches of this science have, however, permanent value, and its
assertion of large-space thinking was an historically essential
development. The name of Haushofer will remain honored in
Western thought. The future of geopolitics will be readapta-
tion of the whole structure to the fundamental spiritual orientation of the world—the division between the West and its
colonies on the one hand, and the outer forces on the other.

13 X 95

The First World War

AFTER THE successful conclusion by England of the Boer War in 1901, and the Western crushing of the Boxer Rebellion in China, the entire world, with the exception of a few small areas, was under the direct rule of the West and its colonies. In the Far East, only Japan and Siam were excluded; in the Near East, only Turkey, Persia, Afghanistan; in Africa, only Abyssinia and Liberia; in the other hemisphere, only Haiti and Mexico. Of these, Western control was indirect in Turkey, Mexico, and Afghanistan. In Islam and in China, Westerners were under the exterritorial jurisdiction of their national representatives, and not under local tribunals. The conduct of the outer peoples to the Westerners was respectful and deferential. In one word: the entire outer world was *politically passive*.

This passivity alone made possible the grotesque disproportion between numbers and control. In India, for instance, England maintained its rule over 350,000,000 subjects with a garrison of less than 100,000 white soldiers. In the Indian Mutiny of 1857, England found its control of India restricted in a few days to parts of the coast and a few points in the interior. So swiftly can white rule of non-Western territory vanish when the subject populations become *active* politically.

With the political passivity of the outer subjects went another important fact in the world-wide power-monopoly of the West before 1914. This was the *comity* of the Western peoples. Paul Kruger was a symbol of this comity. In the Boer War, fighting against crushing odds though he was, he nevertheless resolutely forbade the employment of Negro barbarians against white Englishmen. The political genius his conduct showed was not appreciated.

Two great historical developments were on foot in the world in the period of preparation of the First World War: the emerging within the Western soul, of the superpersonal Idea of Ethical Socialism as the form of the next Western Age; and the growth, in the outer forces, of a world-wide revolt against Western domination.

These two developments on the planet were the actual problems of the First World War. They were the world-historical tendencies which would form the inner content of the coming World War, the inexorable approach of which was seen by all the leading brains of Europe. This great development was seen and described by many men of action and thinkers; among them Rudolf Kjellen, Werner Sombart, Paul Rohrbach, Bernhardi, Lord Kitchener, Homer Lea.

The Age of Capitalism was drawing to its close. England, the power which had been created by this Idea, and which had been in its service, had actualized completely this phase of the organic development of the Western Soul. Prussia-Germany was the power embodying the next phase, the actualization of Ethical Socialism. Thus the inner development of the West tended to take the form of a contest between these two powers.

Prussia-Germany was in the nation-style of the Age of Capitalism. It too was parliamentary-democratic, and was engaging in commercial imperialism. It was differentiated from England by the presence within it of the new superpersonal Idea of Ethical Socialism.

England had conquered, with its historically magnificent Inner Imperative, the largest empire in history up to that time. The Western world-monopoly of power was based primarily on the British Empire. To the outer forces which were waking into anti-Western political activity—in Africa, China, Japan, the East Indies, Russia—there was no difference between the Western nations. The great fact of Western nationalism was already by that time a great illusion, from which, however, only the Western peoples were suffering. The outer world knew better than the West that the West was historically a *unit*, not a collection of spiritually sovereign "nations."

The superficial form of the First World War was a nationalistic contest between two 19th century style Western nations. Superficially, it was England v. Prussia-Germany; *actually it was Capitalism v. Socialism.* Superficially it was a war between two nationalistic coalitions; *actually it was a war of the outer forces against the entire Western Civilization.*

By 1916, it was quite clear that the military contest between Germany and England was a draw, and that continuance of the war between them would only result in a defeat for *both*. The longer the war continued, the more clear this became. Japan's famous Twenty-One Demands were a test of Western strength in the Far East, and the West yielded in the middle of its suicidal war. Japan was obviously winning the war by remaining out of it; America was obviously winning; the Revolution in Russia showed that the entire West was losing. The power that had resided in Europe was steadily transferred, as the First World War continued, to the outer forces, Japan, Russia, America. From the old-fashioned, nationalistic, standpoint, England was losing, and from the new viewpoint, the whole

West was losing. If senile, uncreative brains had not dominated events, a European peace would have been concluded in 1916 to salvage Europe's world power-position. But weak heads, finance-capitalistic thinking, and mental rigidity, prevailed. Not only was the suicidal war continued to its bitter end, but the outer forces were mobilized to take part in the actual fighting.

England and France scraped their colonial empires for colored forces to use against the entire Western Civilization—including themselves, for the outer forces had always regarded the West as a unity. The genius of Paul Kruger had not been understood. If the only way to defeat an opponent is through suicide, the war has lost its meaning, and should be terminated. But the realizing of simple propositions like these takes genius, and that was nowhere present at the helm of European affairs.

For more than a century England had been arbiter of Europe: it had been able to prevent any power taking first place. During this period, it had controlled all the seas of the world: it had been able to deny them to any power it wished, and over them it had maintained uninterrupted communications with its overseas empire. Therewith, it had also been commercially supreme in the world, and could gain any foreign market it wished or needed.

In 1918, with the "victory" of England in the First World War, it found that it now had to share the seas with America and Japan. Its commercial supremacy was gone, and its military-political power was steadily declining in relation to the outer forces. Germany had lost in a military sense, but still had lost far less than England, for it had less to lose. The true, *political*, victors were Japan, Russia and—in a purely external sense—America. The great loser was the Western Civilization.

This brings us to the large-scale political results of the War. The world-problems of 1914 were two, the inner one of the rising Ethical Socialism, and the outer one of the growing world-revolt against the West. How were they resolved? The inner problem was resolved in the only way such an organic development can be resolved: Socialism triumphed over Capitalism, and the further behind the World War was left, the more obvious this became. The parliamentary-capitalistic-materialistic method of thought and action could not cope with the new world-situation and its organization-problems. Sickness spread over the life of the West—spiritual, political, social, economic. This sickness could only be cured by the new attitude of Ethical Socialism toward all these problems. The great, outer problem of the War was resolved against the West. All over the world, the subject populations stirred threateningly. Foundations of the empires of the old-style Western nations were shaking, cracking.

Where yesterday the Westerner had commanded, he now had to cajole and to promise. Where formerly he could move freely and proudly, he had now to be circumspect, and fearful, as official, of revolt, and as individual, of sudden death. The saddling of barbarian occupation troops on a Western nation after the First World War confirmed and strengthened the outer revolt against the West. The barbarians were given the feeling they could lord it over the white man. Anti-Western activity flamed all over the world: in South America, Mexico, the East Indies, Islam, Japan, China, *Russia.* What did this mean?

The indispensable basis of the Western domination of the entire outer world had been the political *passivity* of the subject peoples. After the First World War all over the Asiatic-African land-mass, the subjects became *active;* they began to stir, revolt, oppose, boycott, sabotage, demand, hope, and hate. *The War had undermined the very basis of the Western world-system.*

The third result of the First World War was on the same scale: an old spiritual world was swept away, the entire spiritual foundation of the 19th century vanished. Economic individualism, parliamentarism, capitalism, materialism, democracy, money-thinking, trade-Imperialism, nationalism and petty-statism. The end of capitalism and nationalism was symbolized by the creation and the genius of Benito Mussolini, who pro¬ claimed in the teeth of the apparent world-victory of 19th century ideas, the organization-will and Inner Imperative of the 20th century, the Resurgence of Authority, and Ethical Socialism. Precisely when the materialistic ideologists were playing logical exercises with international politics, and creating a stupid and useless "league of nations," this herald of the Future defied the stillborn nonsense of Geneva, and re-embodied the will-to-power and heroism of Western man. Over the paeans of "democracy," Mussolini spoke of the corpse of democracy.

The word *nationalism* changed its meaning after the First World War. From having meant frontier-squabbling, and jingo-patriotism, it meant henceforth the idea of Western unity. The "nationalists" in every country sought the welfare of their own countries in Western unity, through the doing away with intra-Western wars, which would automatically create a new political organism.

The old petty-statism of the West was in fact destroyed by the First World War, although this was not historically visible at the time. Not one of the former Western "nations" had sufficient political strength to engage the outer political forces. In other words, each one had ceased to be a political unit fit for the great world-struggle. But they had not yet realized their own unity, and hence the outer world was able to continue along the same lines of growing anti-Western activity which the War had begun.

The Second World War

THE FIRST WORLD WAR was a failure as far as solving the two great problems which formed the true, historical issues of that war. It resolved the issue of Capitalism v. Socialism by giving the apparent and material victory to Capitalism, which represented the Past, and could not possibly form the Future. In other words the result of the War was a mere political negation of the coming Spirit of Ethical Socialism. It resolved the issue of the world-revolt in favor of the outer forces, and against the Western Civilization. This result was historically, completely false, for such an outcome did not reflect the great spiritual realities. In reality, the Spirit of the West was then only entering upon its grandest Imperialistic stage, possessed of the necessary material power to actualize its Inner Imperative of unlimited, authoritarian, *political* Imperialism. The historically false eventuation of the War had not corresponded to these great spiritual realities, but had made it appear superficially as though the West was tired, and in retreat from its world-position, and that the outer world had sufficient vigor to dethrone the Western master of yesterday.

In its third great result—the complete sweeping away of the spiritual foundations of the 19th century—the War was also a failure to the extent that it only accomplished this great transformation in the depths, but on the surface of History the ideals and slogans of the dead Past were still the object of the lip-service of the uniformly stupid leaders whom the War had tossed up. These ideals were even carried to limits of comedy which would have been out of the question for the 19th century. For, apart from its tragic significance as a symbol of the victory of the barbarian over the West, the League of Nations was simply a huge world-historical joke.

But Destiny is irreversible, and the Spirit of Socialism, with its latent Resurgence of Authority and its youthful will-to-power moved steadily forward. The Spirit of the Age caught up the former powers of Europe, one after another. Only the intervention of two extra-European regimes, those in Moscow and Washington, prevented the complete inner pacification of Europe. This inner pacification would have meant, as the analysis of politics showed, the automatic creation of a new world-political unit—Europe—the Civilization of the West organized as a politico-economic-spiritual-cultural-national-military unit.

The powers that had existed in the 19th century had become in the last analysis mere spectators in the world-struggle. Russia, America, and Japan were the new arbiters of the world situation during the 20's and 30's of the 20th century. This was the legacy of the First World War and of the blindness that had continued it to the point where England's allies had triumphed over England as well as over Prussia-Germany.

The rise to absolute dictature of the Culture-distorting group in America enabled American power to frustrate the pacification of Europe as the prelude to European reconquest of its lost world-position of 1900—the status of power-monopolist of the world. By parliamentary-financial-propaganda means, Culture-distortion brought part of Europe under the control of Washington, and determined the form of the Second World War.

The European Revolution of 1933 let loose the most tremendous spiritual force that History knows—Destiny, the advancing Spirit of the Age. It was this same force that had given to the armies of France their victories on hundreds of fields all over Europe during the wars from 1790 to 1815. Against this Destiny, no inner forces of the Culture could prevail. To defeat Napoleon, it was necessary to call in Russia, and even then the "victory" was only on the surface, for Napoleon had been the symbol of destruction of the foundations of the 18th century. These foundations could not be rebuilt, even though the gentlemen of the Vienna-Congress thought it could be done.

In form, the Second World War started along the same lines as had the First. Superficially it appeared to be a petty-state contest between two European powers of yesterday. In its depths, the war was no such thing. Even the struggle between Socialism and Capitalism, which was an apparent issue of the War, was not real, for the issue had been settled in favor of Socialism. The alternative to Socialism was not Capitalism, but chaos.

This brings us to the real problems of the Second World War. During the years 1918–1939, the 20th century idea had triumphed all over the West, and only the intervention of the outer forces based in Moscow and Washington had frustrated the foundation of general European unity. In the outer world, the revolt against the West had increased to frightful dimension: in India, China, Japan, Islam, Africa, Mexico, Central and South America, the Caribbean, the East Indies, and above all in *Bolshevist Russia*. This outer development had been *accelerated* by the First World War, instead of being denied and put down as the true distribution of military force would have brought about. As a consequence, this gigantic outer revolt dominated the world-picture. The reversing of this outer revolt, and the reassertion of the Imperialistic vigor of the West, was the great problem of the world-situation in 1939. In its shade stood the problem of completing the unity of the West by driving out extra-European influence from the home-soil of the West.

Nevertheless, owing to the American Revolution of 1933, and the conquest of American power by Culture-distortion, the War started in a disastrous form, that of a struggle between two former European powers. The Culture-distorting group had not only its old mission of revenge against the West for a millennium of insult and persecution, but it was flaming with the unparalleled injury that was done to it by the renewal of Western exclusiveness in the European Revolution of 1933. For the first time, anti-semitism was as total as semitism. Mere social anti-semitism was welcome to the Culture-distorter, for it unified his followers. But *Cultural* anti-semitism meant the end of the sway of power within the West of the distorter. Against this threat, the Culture-distorter armed for a War which he was willing to continue if necessary to the physical extinction of the Western world. He developed a senseless formula, entirely new in European history—"Unconditional Surrender." This formula transcends politics. Politics aims at *political* surrender, not personal humiliation, deprivation of life, of honor, of rank, of humanity and decency.

In the form in which it started, its grand problem was doomed. The revolt of the outer forces against the West was temporarily overshadowed by the suicidal struggle between white Western troops against white Western troops, all of whom were slaughtered for the defeat of the West and the triumph of outer forces.

Who won the Second World War? First of all, in the military sense: America and Russia—for at the conclusion of the War, the world presented the picture of being divided between them. Russia dominated half of the political world—most of the northeast quadrant of the planet—and America dominated the other half. But, as we have seen, America threw away the greater part of its military victory, since the force governing American policy was not American, and hence could not pursue a Western policy of Empire-building, but could only exercise a distorting influence on American policy.

Second, in the political sense: Russia, and, probably, Japan. America cannot be said to be a political winner, since it has steadily lost power since the end of the War. A country in the custody of total, Cultural, aliens cannot gain a political victory, since whatever military victories it may achieve will be used only for the benefit of the alien, and not for the benefit of the subject nation. This lies in the nature of the host-parasite relationship, and America is an instance of it. Russia, however, gained enormously in strength in every way through its "victory," which was won for it by American forces. Russia's power is ascendant everywhere as the result of the War, and it is the only power which can definitely be said to have won the War. After two decades, however, it is probable that Japan also will be seen to have won the War, although naturally such a view is put forward with reservation as to intervening events. But the benevolent and protective occupation by American forces to rebuild the Japanese economy and political power might reach a certain point at which the occupier will find that a new power-relationship exists.

Third, in the spiritual sense: the great collective victor is the world-revolt against the West. Leading them is the Architect of the War, the Culture-distorter. From the top of a mountain of Western dead, he can regard his mission of revenge as having been apparently completely accomplished. Behind him is the spirit of Asiatic Bolshevism, which now lords it over "the rotten West," as 19th century Russian litterateurs named the Europe they hated so much. Then, everywhere, stand the outer forces, renewed in hope and success by the retreat of the West they have forced and continued to force daily. In India, Egypt, China, the East Indies, they stride forward, and the white man retreats steadily.

Those are the victors. Who are the vanquished?

First of all—Europe, the home-soil of the West. The organism of Western Civilization lost the War just as definitely as Russia won. The millions who died in battle, the hundreds of thousands slaughtered in their homes by American warfare against civilians, the millions who have been starved and frozen to death by the American-Russian occupation, the millions who are still starving and freezing—all these died and are dying for the victory of Asiatic Russia, Culture-distortion, and the world-revolt against the West.

The awful reality of the defeat of the West raises another aspect of the Second World War, the economic.

As already seen, the *political* basis of the Western power-monopoly in the world before the First World War, 1914, was the political *passivity* of the subject peoples. Its *economic* basis was the technical-industrial monopoly of the Western Civilization. The hundreds of millions who live in the tiny area of Europe are there because this economic monopoly permitted them to live from food-imports. The food-imports, and the fabulously high Western living-standard, were maintained by Western production of manufactured goods for the outer markers. The many hundreds of millions of Asia and Africa had to meet all their requirements for manufactured goods in the Western Civilization.

The first two World Wars undermined this situation completely. Giant industrial areas have been built up all over the outer world; the revolt against the West is *economic* as well as *political*. What does this mean?

It means this: that not only the power of the West is undermined, but *the livelihood of the West has also been cut off*. The great problem of the Second World War, the restoration of Western world-power, had thus also an *economic* aspect. *It was a struggle for the biological existence of more than one hundred million Westerners.*

The world-situation of the moment thus wears the aspect not only of a struggle for power—what is usual and universal in Nature—but of that which is extremely rare, but hideous and unheroic—*a struggle for physiological existence.*

Not only Europe, but also the American People, lost the War. Since the Revolution of 1933, this People has been working, producing, and exporting. It has given its treasures and the lives of hundreds of thousands of its sons; it has blindly obeyed Culturally alien leaders not of its choosing, and in obedience to them it has curtailed its standard of life and parted with its soul—and in return it has received nothing of any kind, spiritual or material. Nor is its time of sacrifices over. It will continue to pay for the Second World War, which it lost, for many a year. In America's cup of "victory," there was poison for the soul of America.

Russia

THE PARTICIPATION of Russia as a political unit in Western History begins with Peter the Great. Before that Russia had only engaged in political competition with Slavic States bordering on the Western Culture-area. During the centuries before Peter, there had always been two ways of thinking in Russia: the one was the feeling in the broad masses of peasants and men of strong instincts; the other was the more intellectual desire to adopt Western forms of thought and action and force them on the Slavic population. This latter was confined to a small stratum, the physical descendants of the Varangians, who had invaded Russia from Scandinavia during Charlemagne's time, and was recruited from time to time with new blood from Sweden and Germany. With this stratum, Peter overcame the "Old-Russian" faction, and dragged an unwilling Russia into the comity of Western nations.

Never did he succeed, nor did his Romanov dynasty after him, in implanting Western ideas below the surface of the Russian soul. Russia, the true, spiritual, Russia, is *primitive* and *religious.* It detests Western Culture, Civilization, nations, arts, State-forms, Ideas, religions, cities, technology. This hatred is natural, and organic, for this population lies outside the Western organism, and everything Western is therefore hostile and deadly to the Russian soul.

The true Russia is the one which Petrinism tried to coerce. It is the Russia of Illya Muromyets, Minin, Ivan Grosny, Pozharsky, Theophilus of Pskov, Avakkum, Boris Godunov, Arakcheyev, Dostoievski, the Skoptski and Vassili Shuiski. It is the Russia of Moscow, "the Third Rome," the mystical successor to Rome and Byzantium. "A fourth there cannot be," wrote the monk Theophilus. This Russia identifies itself with humanity, and despises the "rotten West."

Being primitive, Russia's spiritual center of gravity is in instinct, and thus it was that even during the Rationalistic-equalitarian 19th century, Russia was a land of pogroms. The Russian felt the complete alienness of the Culture-State-Nation-Church-Race of the Jew, and the Tsarist regime marked out a Pale of Settlement in which alone Jews could reside.

The upper Russia, the Westernized stratum which played with Western materialistic philosophy, spoke German and French, traveled to the spas of Europe, and concerned itself with European cabinet-politics, was the object of the fierce hatred of the pure Russians, the Nihilists, who embodied the wordless idea of complete destruction of the West, and the Russification of the world. Whether this great destructive Idea was expressed in the religious form of the assertion of the sole truth of Eastern Orthodox Christianity, or of the later political form of Slavophilism and Pan-Slavism, or of the present-day Marxist-Bolshevism, it continues to have the same inner imperative of destroying everything Western, which it feels is stifling its Russian soul.

The Bolshevik Revolution of November, 1917, was a political epoch both for Russia, and for Europe. The possibility of such a revolution had, of course, always been there, as shown by Pugachev's insurrection during Catherine the Great's reign, by the numerous assassinations in the 19th and 20th centuries, by the huge underworld shown in the writings of Dostoievski, by the huge secret police and spy network. The actual form of the Revolution when it did occur was dual: there was a revolt of the primitive Russian soul against the Western Romanov regime and all that it represented, and there was a simultaneous assumption of the leadership of this revolt by the Jewish Culture-Nation-State-Race. The necessary financing was procured in New York from members of the Culture-distorting group in America.

The influence of Culture-distortion on Russian policy has not been of the same degree as its influence in America, at least in foreign policy, for the world-aim of Russia is the same as the aim of the Culture-distorting group—destruction of the Western enemy. Nevertheless it is present, and is responsible in a great measure for Russian policy. With means both skilful and brutal, it maintained its power in Russia.

The duality of the Bolshevik Revolution meant that the one side of it was a failure, the primitive, Asiatic, instinctive, side. The aim of the Russian side of the rising was to sweep away *all* Western institutions, ideas, forms, and realities. Thus it wished to extirpate the Western technology and economic forms as well as the other aspects of the Westernization of Russia. In this it did not succeed, for the Bolshevist minority set itself to Western-industrialize Russia to the highest possible degree in preparation for a series of wars against hated Europe.

During the period 1918–1939, Russian policy abroad was actualized through its international organization, the Comintern, comprising all the Communist parties in the Western Civilization. The policy of the distorting group and the true Russia coincide in undermining the West from within by making use of the remnants of the outworn 19th century outlook in their most degenerate forms: class-war, trade-unionism, financial-manipulations, pacifism, parliamentarism, democracy, corruption of art and letters, social-traditional decay.

Such inner undermining was to be, of course, simply the prelude to complete domination. If necessary the last, military stage was to be applied at the time when the inner rottenness had made resistance hopeless. But the European Revolution of 1933 completely destroyed the value of this technique. By its positive and vigorous reassertion of the primal instincts of the West, and of the world-mission of the West, it made any undermining attempts hopeless, for the exclusiveness of the 20th century West is organically inaccessible to anything Culturally alien.

The outbreak of the Second World War in 1939 was brought about by Culture-distortion within the West, in co-operation with the Bolshevik regime in Moscow. The Bolshevik assessment of the possibilities was that the intra-European war would bleed the West to the point where Russian armies could occupy the entire West with a comparatively small military effort, and establish the world rule of "The Third Rome" on a foundation of the ruin of the West.

Things did not work this way at once, and the Bolshevik regime almost found itself in New York at one point in the Second World War. But the total intervention of America was finally brought about by the Culture-distorting group in America, and as a result, Russia was not only saved, but given a military victory which made it master of the largest contiguous empire ever to exist in the history of the world, and an empire

situated moreover in a commanding position in the center of the
political world, the Northeast quadrant of the planet.

II

Thus, there are two Russias: the Bolshevik regime, and the
true Russia underneath. Bolshevism, with its worship of Western technology, and of a silly foreign theory of class-war, does
not express the soul of the true Russia. This broke out in the
insurrection of the Streltse against Peter the Great, and of
Pugachev against Catherine the Great. In his rebellion, Pugachev and his peasants massacred every officer, official, and nobleman that fell into their hands. Everything having any connection with the West was burned or destroyed. Whole tribes
joined in the mass-movement. For three years, 1772–1775, it
continued, and the Moscow court itself was at one time in
danger. When arraigned after his capture, Pugachev explained
that it was God's will that he should chastise Russia. This spirit
is still there, since it is organic, and cannot be killed, but must
express itself. This is the spirit of Asiatic Bolshevism, which is
at present harnessed to the Bolshevism of the Moscow regime,
with its economic-technical obsession.

This brings us to the part that Bolshevist ideology plays in
the present world-situation. The equating, in the Western
Civilization, of Russia with a class-war theory is itself a triumph
of Russian propaganda. Theories in politics are *techniques*.
Politics is power-activity, not reasoning or arguing or proving.
For any Westerner to believe that Russia represents some sort
of desire to reform society or economics along the lines of
favoring this class or that class is to show himself utterly incapable of political-thinking. Nor is it any more correct to
think that Russia wishes to organize the whole world along the

same economico-socio-political lines as present-day Russia. The Russian mission is to destroy the West, and any inner agitation within the West promotes this mission. Class-war, race-war, social degeneration, crazy art, decadent films, wild theories and philosophies of all kinds, serve this vast Russian program. Communism is just one of these, but if another were more effective tomorrow, it would replace it.

The ideal of Communism, as a theoretical program for the reorganization of society, does not exist in the world of facts, either in Russia, or America. The communism that the West has to fear is of two varieties, neither of them in the least bit theoretical: first, class-war, and second the Communist organization. The first is an entirely native thing which can only be liquidated by the 20th century Idea of Ethical Socialism; pending this liquidation, it serves the Russian purpose of weakening and disintegrating the West from within. The second is simply the direct enforcing agent within the West of the political commands from Moscow.

At the moment, 1948, Russia's sole remaining enemy in the field is America. Towards America it occupies a position superior in every way except the technical. Its weapon against America is inner undermining through propaganda and social degeneration. These methods are efficacious against America because of the great spiritual split in that country between the true soul of the American People and the upper Culture-distorting stratum. Culture-Retardation in America makes 19th century materialistic propaganda and ultra-crazy social ideals effective in that country.

The presence of the distorter in Russia is shown by the fact that the ruling personnel are disproportionately drawn from this group, by the fact that anti-semitism is a crime, and more than anything else by Russian policy in regard to Palestine. For the four years, 1944 to 1948, Russian policy was the negation, at every point, of American policy. Nonetheless in the question of partitioning of Palestine, a part of the world of Islam, the Moscow regime was divided on the supporting of world-policy of the Jewish Culture-State-Nation-Race, even though it was in the imperialistic interests of Russian policy to oppose America on this issue.

But the nature of Culture-distortion as a mere illness is shown again by the situation of the moment. Despite their parallel inner situations, Russia and America are moving to war against one another. This period is one of preparation of and for the Third World War. The nature of politics, of the political side of human nature, impels this war, and the presence of active alien groups in the two existing political powers plays only a subordinate role in this great fact. Its role is to manage the war so that its own world-position is not damaged by the outcome. Russia's strategic position *vis-a-vis* America is vastly superior. First the great fundamental fact of Russia's position on the planet confers an inestimable advantage. The Northeast quadrant, as already seen, is the prime focus of world-control in the Age of Absolute Politics. Russia is situated within this quadrant, whereas America is not even in the *political* world, which lies in the Eastern Hemisphere, the ultimate source of six times as much power as the Western Hemisphere.

The Northeast quadrant, in a military sense, is controlled partly by Russian arms, and partly by American arms. The Russian holdings are contiguous and integrated. The Russian diplomatic method is that of terror, military occupation, kidnapping, and assassination. The American method is degenerative propaganda, puppet regimes which conduct their own terror, and financial conquest. Of these two methods, Russia's is entirely superior. Wars are fought with soldiers, and not with money, and diplomacy is simply war-preparation and war-exploitation. Financial means therefore are subsidiary to military means, a mere adjunct to them.

The American holdings in the Northeast quadrant are bought, but they can never be finally paid for. They are dependent upon the maintenance of puppet governments consisting of the least valuable stratum in Europe, the party-politicians who will sell themselves for money. Thus revolts, in the American spheres in Europe, of the more vigorous and honorable stratum, would automatically terminate America's ascendancy, whereas revolts in Russia's sphere under present conditions would be drowned in blood. Of course, in the last analysis, America's financial diplomacy is backed by American bayonets, but the dangerous illusion in the American mind as to the value of financial means is nevertheless there.

Russian diplomacy increases Russian prestige, while American diplomacy rouses hopes of material gain in its subject populations, and panders to the lowest instincts of greed and laziness. America conducts a gigantic hanging holiday called "war crimes," which is aimed at settling old semitic-vengeance scores. Russia values subject individuals according to their *present* and *future* value to Russian plans, and is not interested in their past actions. However, if Russia did choose to institute a "war crimes" slaughter, it could instruct the Americans in technique. The precedent of the Florinsky "trial" during the Red Terror in Kiew in the summer of 1919 is illustrative. Professor Florinsky of Kiew University was suspected of anti-semitism. Irritated by his lack of humility, one of his judges, Rosa Schwartz, drew a revolver and shot him dead at his "trial."

Russia's situation in the Northeast quadrant bestows upon Russia the possibility of a high degree of application of the strategic principles of Concentration, and Economy of Force. America's remoteness on the other hand compels it to support an enormous naval and marine establishment before it can put a soldier into the theatre of war. Russia has the advantages of the inner line against America.

And now the concluding remarks can be made about Russia, its mission, and its potentialities.

Russia is outside the West; its Imperialism is a mere negative of Western unlimited organizatory Imperialism. Russia's mission is thus purely destructive as far as the West is concerned. Russia is the bearer of no Utopian hopes for the West, and anyone who believes it is a Cultural idiot. Russia is internally split; the ruling regime does not represent the true, Asiatic, religious, primitive, soul, but is a technological caricature of Petrinism, and the possibility is inherent in this relationship that one day this regime will go the way of the Romanov. This split can be used against Russia, just as it tries to use inner-revolutionary tactics against its political enemies. Such a tactic was used with success against the Romanov regime in 1917 by the West. By virtue of its physical situation, on the border of the West, Russia will, and must always, remain the enemy of the West, as long as these populations are organized as a political unit.

Japan

THE CREATION of the world-power Japan was one of the results
of American commercial Imperialism of the 19th century style.
It was "opened"—the hypocritical terminology that always accompanies the spirit of Trade!—in 1853 by a cannonade from
an American fleet. Not having technological equality, the Japanese Emperor surrendered at once. From then on, the development of Japan was the history of Japanese imitation of the
material technique of the West and the methods of Western
diplomacy. Its development was a course of high political
achievement: it studied the art of the possible, and practiced it
with invariable success. In less than a generation after the
"opening," Japan secured its foothold on the Asiatic mainland,
for its leaders knew that world-political power cannot be based
on overcrowded islands, but must be based on control of land
masses and the populations thereon, like the British Empire was
based on India. By the last decade of the 19th century it was
ready for war. In the Sino-Japanese War, it was successful, and
extended the mainland base. By 1904, it judged the situation

favorable for a war against the greatest Western land power—
for at that time, Russia figured in the world as a member of the
Western State-system. In this second great war, it was victorious
both from the military and political standpoints. Its capable
political tradition knew how to exploit a military victory. In
1914, it cleverly attacked the weakest of the national garrisons
in the Far East, and acquired all the German Far Eastern Empire for no military cost whatever. Its mainland position was
constantly expanded. After the First World War, it suffered a
diplomatic defeat at the hands of England and America, and
retired to wait.

In more than three-quarters of a century, from 1853 until
1941, Japan did not make a political mistake. This is a remarkable achievement in world-history, and it built up a strong tradition of confidence in the national tradition and leadership. This
tradition was reinforced by the primitive religiousness of Japan,
which believes in the humanity of God, the divinity of the
Emperor, and the divine mission of Dai Nippon.

In 1941, the Japanese government was faced with a new
political situation. In the war between the West and Russia, its
purely political interests lay in a Western victory. This would
have extended Japan's mainland position to vast limits—to the
borders of India, to Tibet, to Sinkiang. But another Western
power, America, was in the possession of part of the mainland,
thousands of islands in Japan's expansion-sphere, a mighty
Pacific fleet, and the will to annihilate Japan. Leaving Europe
to fight its battle against Russia, it decided to devote all of its
military energy to the war against America. Only in a limited
sense can this be called a mistake, for there is no certainty
America would not have attacked if Japan had engaged Russia
instead of America. But on fundamental grounds, it is better
to attack a power already battling for its life than to engage a

fresh one. Any possible attack from the new quarter can then be sought to be contained while the embattled power is disposed of.

In any case, the Second World War was ended by a negotiated peace between Japan and America. The Japanese Nation, State, Emperor, and institutions were to be maintained, the Japanese Army was to be honorably disbanded, and American troops were to be permitted to occupy Japan. This decision was carried out with religious discipline. It involved no loss of Oriental face to the leaders, the Nation, or the individuals, for it was the command of the God-Emperor to adopt new conditions. The technological American superiority that had brought about the disciplined transformation from enmity to the teacher-pupil relationship within a few days had put Japan back into the spiritual situation of 1853. A period of learning was required. Once more America would teach it the techniques necessary to world-power. The American troops were seen as the Emperor's servants to instruct his people.

Does any Westerner think that the tradition of the Samurai dissolved in a week? In a nation with the Japanese spiritual integration and firmness, a nation which produced an endless succession of Kamikaze pilots, whose generals surrendered to save the lives of their troops and then committed hara-kiri? So to think is to fail to understand History and its silent, irresistible force, Destiny. The soul of the Japanese People has a Destiny. Its mission, like the Russian, and the other non-Western forces, is simply denial and destruction of the West.

Even coordinated and intelligent American policy in Japan cannot wipe out this soul, but can only hope to monopolize the means of its politico-military expression. But the American policy, springing from Culture-distortion in America, of rebuilding and aiding Japanese tradition, of asserting and solidifying Japanese spirituality, strengthens Japan enormously, and makes its Future more hopeful. What this Future may be, no one can tell. An American Revolution could sharply reverse the direction of affairs. The Third World War could affect it one way or the other. When a power is submerged, as Japan is, its own will counts for little.

Japan is, and will remain the enemy of the West, because it belongs to the outer forces, and the motive force of world-politics in this Age of Absolute Politics is in Culture. In the great spiritual division of the world, Japan belongs with the non-Western forces. Japan's threat to Europe is mitigated by geographical distance, but its threat to Australia makes the American-Japanese enmity more real, for America has the Cultural duty of protecting Australia since stupid Western diplomacy has lost all European influence in this area.

Japan is not in a class with India and China, for it is integrated. Politics is a struggle of will against will. India and China have, as such, no will. They are not organic units, but mere collections of areas and populations brought under one name for convenience. Their negative will is diffused throughout all the individuals, whereas the will of Japan is concentrated and articulated into a nation-bearing stratum. Japan is thus the potentiality of a power of the Future, while India and China will always remain mere spoils for powers from without.

More important than the outer forces to Europe and to its Future is America. The external situation, plans, and possibilities of America must be examined.

America

THE ARMED FORCES under the command of the Washington regime control Northern and Western Europe, part of Southeastern Europe, the entire Mediterranean, part of the Near East, Middle East, and Far East, as well as all of Central America, and most of South America. In addition, this regime controls all the seas of the world. The vastness of this empire is attenuated by its looseness. The physical remoteness of America from the political world is the first weakness of this empire. The second is the lack of Imperial thinking in its rulers. The third is the old-fashioned financial-diplomacy which is the sole link holding large areas of the empire. The fourth is the terrible inner tension created by the split between the true soul of the American People and the Culturally-alien regime.

The first weakness dictates that America's war effort against Russia for control of the world must be much greater than Russia's. This weakness of the American empire is not realized in America, where complete ignorance of present-day power relationships perpetuates the 19th century belief of the supremacy of sea-power over land-power. There was perhaps some-

thing to support this belief when the entire hinterland of Asia
—the world—was politically passive, and the control of a few
bridgeheads and strong-points along the coast automatically
gave access to and control over the hinterland. But in the new
conditions of outer revolt, the reflex of the stage of development of the Western Civilization, when all the formerly subject populations of the world are politically restless or active,
land-power emerges as the only power, and sea-power is a mere
auxiliary. It is simply communication and transportation, but
it is *fighting* that decides power-struggles. This means *armies,*
and whereas Russia can put its entire effort into land-power,
America must have gigantic sea-power as a mere *prerequisite* to
engaging in the battle for control of the world. In addition, the
most reliable populations in the Russian empire, for military
purposes, are half again as numerous as the most reliable in the
American empire, and the Russian birth rate is primitively high,
while that of America's fighting elements is in a severe decline.

Another aspect of the same weakness of the American empire
is its reliance on technical superiority. This is another form of
the sea-power fallacy, in that it thinks that power can have
another basis than armies. Weapons are mere adjuncts in a
fight: primary is, and always has been, the spirit. Against this
fundamental life-fact, no weapon can prevail. Technical superiority is helpless in the last analysis unless it is accompanied
by superiority of will-power, of the will-to-conquer. The same
weapon that could give a military victory might be helpless
afterwards against a country occupied by soldiers of the "victorious" power, which might find itself politically defeated.

The second weakness of the American empire is the fact that
the Culture-disease of Retardation in America has prevented
the arising of true Imperial thinking. Imperial thinking cannot develop in a land saturated with pacifist propaganda, with

pleasure-madness as the content of life, and intellectual average-ness as the spiritual ideal. Imperial thinking cannot be built on "league of nations" dawdling, nor on drooling idealism of any kind, and much less on blind hatred as the cornerstone of a foreign policy. Yet, for foreign-political purposes, this is all there is in America. There is no level of the populace, no American group, which feels any higher task than self-enrich-ment. There is no Samurai, no Comintern, no Black Dragon Society, no nobility, no Idea, no Nation, no State.

Nor will Imperial thinking begin to develop merely because an inner Culturally-alien group wants to use the supine Ameri-can populations as biological units to carry out its revenge-imperative against the Western Civilization. It must arise spon-taneously in the higher strata. Precisely because these higher strata are lacking as a guiding elite in America no true Imperial thinking can arise in America in the near Future.

The third weakness, that of reliance on puppet-regimes secured primarily by financial means, and only secondarily by military means, is simply one more effect of Culture-Retarda-tion. The financial method of conquest is outmoded. This is the Age of Absolute Politics, and power is not to be bought, nor is it secured as a means of enrichment. Whoever does not realize this Spirit of the Age will find himself suddenly de-feated by gigantic events which he could not foresee.

Financial-diplomacy is in this Age simply stupidity.

The fourth weakness is the inner tension in America itself. The Future of American Nationalism is quite definite spiritu-ally: it will participate in the struggle for American control of the American Destiny. This struggle arises out of the organic nature of things. The host and the parasite are hostile, and the hostility cannot be abolished. How, when, with what initial success—these are Imponderables.

In any case: Europe must know, and realize deeply, that both of the occupying powers, America and Russia, are inwardly split horizontally. In both of them the ruling stratum is inwardly spiritually alien to the great mass of dominated peoples. This is a primary, elemental, fact. It is essential to a long-range view of world-possibilities, a view which puts aside both optimism and pessimism, cowardice and bravado, exultation and despair. These powers differ for Europe's purposes in that the true America belongs to the Western Civilization, and the true Russia can never possibly belong thereto. But in the *immediate,* short-range view, extending over only the next quarter of a century, one of them is more dangerous than the other.

Russia's total alienness is realized all through Europe, horizontally and vertically. Under a Russian occupation of Europe, even the very European Communists would soon be in the great, never-ending revolt against the Barbarian. The European Michel element, with its weak urge toward parliamentary babbling and money-loving, and its detestation of the firm, strong, Prussian-European will-power, would find itself cleansed of its spiritual sickness under the lash of the Mongolian. It would become European. Nor could a Russian occupation hope forever to hold Europe down. First, the European will and intelligence are stronger than the will and intelligence of the Barbarian. Secondly, the Barbarian has not sufficient human resources to enslave the Western Civilization at this stage of its development, when its Inner Imperative is cast in the form of will-to-power, and the urge to unlimited authoritarian Imperialism.

America, on the other hand, is not generally understood in Europe. Even in the Culture-bearing stratum of the West there is no clarity that America under Culture-distorting leadership is Europe's total enemy. Only the development of historical thinking has enabled Europe to understand the organic nature of

Culture, and of Culture-Pathology. For the first time, Europe can now see America in its duality: underneath, the America of Alexander Hamilton, George Washington, John Adams, of the frontiersman, the explorer, the men of the Alamo; above, the America of Culture-distortion with its monopoly of cinema, press, radio, mind and soul, and with its revenge-imperative directed against the body and soul of the Western Civilization. By making use of Culture-Retardation in Europe, the distorter in America is able to split Westerners and divide them against one another on old, outgrown, 19th century nationalistic lines. The spiritual splitting and Balkanizing of Europe serves his purpose. For those who oppose this purpose, he is now demonstrating the sanctions he will employ against them, in his "war crimes" slaughter.

The differing relationship between Russia and America to Europe is thus simply that Russia, even though it try to split Europe, can only unite it. The effect of American occupation however is to split, for it appeals to the sub-Europeans, the Retarders, the Michel element, the money-worshipers, the lazy and the stupid, and to the worst instincts in every European. The material destruction accompanying a Russian occupation is considerable; so is that accompanying an American devastation. What difference does it make to Europe whether the Russians move a factory to Turkestan, or the Americans blow it into the air? The difference between the spiritual effect of the two occupations makes the Russian less harmful. Russian arrests in the night, assassinations, deportations to Siberia, convince no one. American "war-crimes" slaughters are another technique for splitting Europe while simultaneously actualizing the revenge-imperative of the Culture-distorter.

The Terror

"It is a weakness, in fact stinginess of heart, not to speak well of one's enemies, and not to pay them the honor they deserve."

—FREDERICK THE GREAT
Preface to his *History of the Seven Years War,* 1764

WITHIN EACH High Culture, the universally prevailing feeling has been the same as the quoted sentiment of Frederick II. The onset of the Civilization-Crisis itself has not served completely to destroy this wordless honor-feeling. However fierce the battles, or prolonged the war, every victor over an opponent within the same Culture has always shown generosity and respect to his former foe. It inheres in the very nature of politics within a High Culture that it is carried on solely for power, and not for the massacre of individuals after the war, whether by hanging or starvation. Once the power is gained, the objective is reached, and the individuals of the former enemy are seen no longer as enemies, but simply as human beings. In the thousand years of Western History, there have naturally been a few exceptions; dishonor has always existed. But the exercise of malice against a defeated opponent was never countenanced on a large scale, or over a long period, and it simply could not have occurred between two groups both belonging to the Western Culture.

In very late times this organic imperative has been well illustrated. For example, when Lee surrendered at Appomattox in 1865, the fierce warrior Grant, so ruthless in the field, showed himself a magnanimous and kindly victor. The case of Napoleon shows the same organic imperative at work in his captors, both after Leipzig, and even after Waterloo. Earlier, the English government, even when at war with him, had notified him of a plot against his life. Similarly, after the capture of Napoleon III, Bismarck saw to his honorable treatment and safety.

But between a power belonging to a High Culture and one belonging to a different Culture, these honor-usages have never been generalized, either in the conduct of warfare or in the treatment of a conquered foe. Thus in Gothic times, the Church forbade the use of the crossbow against members of the Western Culture, but sanctioned its employment against the barbarian. In such cases, the opposing group has not been looked upon as a mere opponent, but as a true *enemy,* as the 20th century once more uses that word to describe elements outside the Western Civilization. The Spanish court-martial which "tried" the last Inca, and sentenced him to death, did not feel bound by the same honor-obligation toward him that they would have felt to any Western leader of his status. *A fortiori,* the community of honor which arises within a Culture does not extend to the outsider belonging to no Culture whatever—the barbarian. Thus Jugurtha, Mithridates, Sertorius, and Vercingetorix were all hunted down to their personal deaths by the Romans. The barbarian understands the relationship in the same way, as the massacres of Mithridates, Juba, the Goths, Arminius, and Attila all show. It is not people, nor race, but the great fact of belonging, or not belonging, to a High Culture, which is decisive in this connection, as is shown by the slaughters of Genghis Khan's Mongolians and the present-day Russians, both outside a High Culture.

Thus when, after the Second World War, a huge and inclusive program of physical extermination and politico-legal-socio-economic persecution was instituted against the defenseless body of Europe, it was quite clear that this was no intra-Cultural phenomenon, but one more, and the most transparent and admonitory, manifestation of Culture-distortion. That which was here distorted was, specifically, the politico-military honor-usages of a millennium of high Western traditions. These usages were still observed by Europe during the Second World War, and a whole group of heads and high officials of petty States survived European imprisonment throughout the Second World War, for it had occurred to no European mind that they could be subjected to mock-trials and hanged. These usages were even extended to protect the life of the son of the barbarian leader Stalin, who was a captive in Europe during the War, and were even observed in some cases by barbarian Japan, which spared the lives of high-ranking American officers, when it could have killed them either with or without mock-trial. But the unconditional obligation of the honor of war, hitherto absolute throughout the Western Civilization, was twisted away by Culture-distortion after the Second World War.

Since Culture-disease can never influence the Culture-soul in its inmost depths, it can never permanently change that soul, but must wage an endless fight against it. In this fight, there can be no peace, no truce. The Culture-instincts will always resist disease elements, whether parasitical, retarding, or distorting. Since this is so, Culture-distortion proceeded to wage a European Terror after the War, when there was no longer any political struggle whatever going on in the Western Civilization.

The history of the "war crimes" program shows its nature. Its foundations were laid in the anti-European propaganda with which America was deluged from 1933 onward. The propaganda itself showed that extra-Cultural influences were at work, since it rejected the comity of nations and political honor. The leaders of Europe were represented as common criminals and sexual perverts, and through this vile propaganda, the idea was spread that these leaders could and should be killed. Gradually, the thesis was widened and the 20th century Idea of Ethical Socialism was equated with evil itself, and the populations in its service were described as suffering from mass-insanity, and in need of "re-education" by America.

Culture-distortion must always use the prevailing means, and established ideas and customs, in order to work its effects. Thus in America, it appealed to American patriotism and American legalism. During the Second World War, the propaganda explicitly began to demand "trials" of European leaders and of the Culture-bearing stratum of the West. A mass "treason trial" was ordered in America during the war of American elements hostile to Culture-distortion and friendly to Western Empire. In order to overcome, at least temporarily, the native Western honor-instincts, the war was represented as *unique,* as a war of "humanity" against "immorality," of "peace" against "war," a war which should therefore be followed by *unique* measures against the enemy in case of victory, a war in which the enemy should not only be defeated, but should be physically exterminated as "punishment" for "crimes." Law was brought in, as usual, to prop up the structrue, and the lawyers were instructed to prepare new "crimes," to devise new tribunals, procedures, jurisdictions, penalties. Not only the leaders, but the armies and even the populations must be brought into new "crimes."

On the lower intellectual plane, this operation was represented frankly as revenge, but this necessitated the creation of new facts, since nothing like this program had ever occurred

before in five millennia of the history of High Cultures. Therefore the infamous "concentration camp" propaganda was devised, in order to inflame the public imagination. Fantasy became fact, lie became truth, suspicion turned into proof, per-
secution-mania transformed itself into blood-thirst. Since Europe had conducted no mock-trials for which there could be revenge, the propaganda said that it would have if it had won the
War, and this demonstrable lie took rank as a fact.

The natural affinity of disease-elements in a Culture was
shown by the fact that the leaders of Culture-retarding groups
in the West, particularly in America, supported the program.
Without the Culture-retarding forces in America, the whole
operation of "trials" and "crimes" had been impossible. As
would be expected, the best minds of the Western Civilization,
both in America and Europe, rejected the entire scheme, but the
power to carry it through lay with the exotic victor.

The "crimes" scheme had three great facets: first the mass-
trial of the highest European leaders, the authors of the European Revolution of 1933; second, the mass-trials of soldiers of
all grades who had distinguished themselves in the War, of the
military personnel who had served as guards of the prison-
camp, and of civilians who had taken part in air-raid defense;
third, the individual trials of millions of small civilian members of mass political organizations.

Although these proceedings were called trials, they were
not actually that at all, for there was no legal system in existence which authorized any such action. Western International
Law excluded the possibility that the leaders of an enemy State
could be tried and hanged as a part of the exploitation of victory, for its basic principle was that of sovereignty of States.
International Law thus rested purely on comity, and not on
force. A genuine trial presupposes, on the purely *legal* side, a

pre-existing legal system, a pre-existing judiciary empowered to enforce the law, jurisdiction of the subject matter, and jurisdiction of the person. Without a pre-existing law, there can be no offense, no tribunal, no jurisdiction of subject matter or person. Mere custody is not jurisdiction, or else a kidnapper could be said to have jurisdiction of his victim.

Mock-trials are nothing new in Cultural history, but as between members of the same Culture, they are simply dishonor, and dishonor reflects on its author, and on him only, and never on the victim. They are dishonor, merely because they are deceit and subterfuge; they are an attempt to do by form of law, that which instinct and conscience forbid. Thus the preliminaries to the killing of Louis XVI and of Charles of England were not trials even though they were so named by those who participated in them, for under the existing law in both France and England at these times the monarch was sovereign and thus answerable to no tribunal.

Entirely apart from strictly legal grounds, and considerations of the intra-Cultural honor-community, there is an independent source of reasons why the "war crimes" processes could not be described as trials, and that is human psychology. A true trial presupposes *impartiality* in the court—actual mental impartiality, apart from mere legalistic presumption of innocence. But the actions in question were openly and avowedly against *enemies*. The victims were legally formulated as enemies, and the War was declared to be in legal continuance. Enmity excludes impartiality, and this was nowhere present in the "crimes" program. In an earlier age, the "trials" by which Phillip the Fair eliminated the Knights Templar as a power, the "trials" of Joan of Arc, of Lady Alice Lisle, and of the Duc D'Enghien, were not true trials because of partiality in the court. *A fortiori*, where the "trials" are the result of the impact

of two different Cultures upon one another, there can be no
question of an actual and fair trial, as the "trial" of the Christ
by the Roman Procurator and the "trial" of Atahualpa by a
Spanish court-martial are there to show. The Nuremberg spectacle was one more, and the most conclusive, instance of the
complete irreconcilability of two Culture-souls, and of the
abysmal depth to which Culture-disease can descend. Even
while the "trial" was going on, its organizers ordered their
press to speculate for the public on what method of execution
would be used against the victims.

It is, of course, impossible to deceive the entire population of
a Culture forever. There is a certain stratum which sees through
devices to the reality, and in this stratum, the "crimes" propaganda and "trials" had precisely the opposite of the intended
effect. Every one who has oriented himself historically knows
that the epithet "criminal" can be placed, with superficial and
temporary success, on any one in the power of another. During
the millennium of Western History, hundreds of creative men
or persons in high places have been either charged with crime,
or imprisoned. The Holy Roman Emperor Conradin Hohenstaufen was beheaded even though he was the most highly
placed secular person in Christendom. A few others either
gaoled or charged with crime were: Coeur de Lion, Roger
Bacon, Arnold of Brescia, Giordano Bruno, Columbus, Savonarola, Joan of Arc, Galileo, Cervantes, Charles of England,
Shakespeare, Oldenbarneveldt, Louis XVI, Lavoisier, Voltaire,
Napoleon, Emperor Maximilian of Mexico, Thoreau, Wagner,
Charles XII, Frederick the Great, Edgar Poe, Napoleon III,
Garibaldi.

The French Reign of Terror, beginning in 1793, lasted little
more than a year, even though it grew out of prolonged and
continuing conditions of inner and outer political activity

heightened to a degree thitherto unknown in Europe. The new French Republic was carrying on in the field a struggle for its life, and fighting simultaneously against the majority in its own population. Under these conditions of struggle for power, the horrors of the Terror can be seen historically to fit into the political scene. The dramatic qualities of the Terror cannot obscure the fact that it only put to the guillotine a number calculated by its opponents at between two and four thousand.

Quite different was the Terror after the Second World War. Its entire motivation was beyond politics, as that word is used in intra-Cultural power-activity. It was not a phase of a struggle for power. Defeated Europe was completely occupied by armies serviceable to Culture-distortion. No physical resistance was present. Thus, from pure revenge-imperative, it embarked on a program of persecution and mass-killing.

The elaborate pretense of legalism is another sign of Culture-disease. So prolonged an orgy of self-deception to attempt to cover up patent dishonor would be impossible to any group belonging to a High Culture against an intra-Cultural opponent. Suffice it to say that there is no record of any such proceeding in five millennia of higher history.

Culture-distortion is also evinced by the *indefinite prolongation* of the killing-program. The organizers of the scheme had no honor-community with the people they tried to death, and could have continued it forever. Three years after it began, the enterprise was on a larger scale than when it started. No development of self-disgust takes place in a Culture-alien, the way it finally did even in the intransigent Jacobins and the *canaille* of Paris.

The ridiculous legalistic equipment, which was used purely *pro forma,* and which was in no case allowed to interfere with "conviction" and "sentence," is a further sign of extra-Cultural origin. Western law-thinking has never been extended to the annihilation of Western honor, even though it has often been put to political, economic, or religious use in the disguise of "pure" legal-thinking. But to the Cultural alien, the fine sense of limitation is lacking, and he continues to wear the disguise even after he is recognized.

Nor is the "crimes" program a manifestation of barbarism, for barbarism is far more hostile to the polysyllabic legerdemain of the lawyers than is even the honor-feeling of the upper strata of a High Culture. Thus, in its occupation of Europe, the Russians carried on no "crimes" killings, but simply slew when they wished, without mock-trials.

The French Terror had also a positive idea for the nation, and the killing and destruction was for the purpose of imposing a new regime through intimidation and destruction of the old. When it had attained its political objective, the Terror was spent. The Terror after the Second World War, however, started with the political objective already gained, and had thus no Cultural-political raison d'etre. Its motive was *existential hatred,* and the aim was simply total, apocalyptic, revenge— but revenge is no part of Culture-politics.

Groups within a Culture, in previous history, have always extended generosity to a conquered foe within the same Culture, even in the stage of annihilation-wars. It is only the enemy *State* that is sought to be destroyed, not the sum total of individuals. The very length of the "trials" themselves shows Culture-disease. The French Terror tried to death even such an important person as the Queen of France in two days, but the infamous "concentration camp" mock-trials were dragged out to many months, and the Nuremberg torture was prolonged to a year.

The cruelest aspect of the larger scheme was undoubtedly

that directed against the small people, since it aimed at *millions* of persons. Puppet regimes, set up by the American regime, instituted "denationalization" courts to implement the grand program of mass-persecution. The victims were completely deprived of their property in every form. Professional men were forced to become manual laborers. Young men were forbidden to attend universities. Lower food-rations were issued, this technique having been learnt from Lenin's program of exterminating the "bourgeoisie" in Russia. Opponents of Culture-distortion were sent to gaol for years. The families of the victim were treated similarly so that they could not help him.

The entire program, in all its aspects, was of course contrary to the documented international conventions binding all Western States to a common code of Cultural-international community of politico-military honor. These conventions represented Western feelings, or they would not have been concluded, and thus their total disregard by America in its post-war occupation of Europe is the final proof of the Culture-pathological nature of the vast Terror-program. No Western force could ever have engaged in the prolonged and fraudulent attempt to present Western International Law as a *penal* code, for it never had any penal provision whatever. But Culturally alien elements, in the last analysis, never penetrate to the feeling behind Western ideas and institutions, any more than Westerners could ever grasp the subtleties of the Kabbalah or the Maimonidean philosophy.

Last, and spiritually most important, is the desperate attempt which the Terror made at a transvaluation of all Western values. The life and health of the host are the death of the parasite, and the flourishing of the parasite is the sickness and distortion of the host. Therefore any natural and normal attempt by Culture-bearing elements within the West to oppose

Culture-pathological phenomena in the Western Civilization were represented as criminal and morally reprehensible. Opposition to Culture-distortion and its instruments was declared as a "crime," and support of the European Revolution of 1933 was declared subject to the penalty of death. In the attempt at transvaluation of values, an official of the American Forces, himself not a member of the Western Civilization, went so far as to say officially that if Bismarck were alive, he would be "tried" as a criminal by the American forces. Finally the notorious "Control Council Law No. 10" actually defined as "criminals" the leaders in the political, military, industrial, and financial life of Europe and its Eastern associated States, in those very words.

This Terror shows the significance of an American occupation of Europe. The nature of America, as a colony, separated by great distance from the mother-soil of the Western Culture, explains fully why Culture-disease has been able to play such a dominating role there. Western honor-usages, extant also in America, have never taken such deep root in that country, and thus the Cultural alien was able to engraft his revenge-imperative onto the American organism. Such a process is organic and therefore has a direction. It cannot go on forever without a deep and powerful challenge by the national instincts of America, but in this decisive age, the meaning of America to Europe is symbolized in the Terror program of Culture-distortion which it let loose in the former States of Europe, now become its colonies, after the Second World War.

The Abyss

EUROPE is in a spiritual-political abyss. The history of the West since 1914 is exacting now its price of shame and horror. Frontier-obsession has developed to the point where there are no longer any European frontiers, and the frontiers of extra-European powers meet in Europe. Universal poverty, disease, starvation, looting, cold and deliberate killing of members of the Culture-bearing stratum of the West—these are the legacy of nationalism and yesterday-patriotism. They thought about the Rhine, and not about the Amur, the Ob, the Yangtse, the Ganges, the Nile, the Niger. As a consequence, Europe has become spoils, and marauding powers from without dispose of its lives and treasures, even of the works of art which express its inmost soul.

Have we seen in the past nine years events which spell the end of the Western Civilization? The sacred soil of our Culture is occupied by armies of Barbarians and distorters of our Cultural instincts and heritage. Once Rollo, William of Normandy, the Hohenstaufen, Coeur de Lion, de Bouillon, the Teutonic

Knights, Rainald van Dassel, Gustav Adolf, Wallenstein, Alba, Cromwell, Richelieu, Turenne, de Saxe, Frederick the Great, Pitt, Napoleon, Bismarck, trod this soil. Today, as I write, it is occupied by Kirghizians, Mongolians, Armenians, Turkestani, Sengalese, Negroes, Americans, Jews. These Culturally alien armies rule through traitor governments, whose members have sprung up from between the cracks in the pavement, and who deal in hatred of the Spirit of the Age.

Since 1900, Europe has been declining steadily in world-power. The First World War accelerated vastly the outer Revolt against the West, and the Second World War eliminated Europe entirely from the combinations of world-power. The European Revolution of 1933 was a ray of hope for Europe. It seemed that Europe also would be able to engage in the struggle for world-dominion, and could reconquer the world-position which is the basis of the physical life of Europe's millions, instead of being the mere spoil for Barbarians from without.

What resources can Europe muster in the struggle for its spiritual and physical survival? This is another way of asking, what are the inner possibilities of Europe?

II

The false and distorted form of the Second World War may perhaps lead some to think that Culture is not the motive force of politics in this Age of Absolute Politics. But in actuality the Second World War is the proof of it. In reality, *three* separate wars were going on within the phenomenon called the Second World War. First there was the war of the Culture-distorting group against the Western Civilization. Secondly, there was the war of the Western Civilization against Russia. Third was the war between America, as colony of the Western Civilization, against Japan. All three of these wars were Culturally motivated.

The conflicts now going on in the world also are based on Culture-contrasts. Throughout the entire Western Civilization there is a horizontal struggle: underneath, the vigorous and heroic Idea of the 20th century, Ethical Socialism; above, the disease-phenomena of parasitism, retardation, and distortion. Added to this are the struggle of Japan against America, also a Cultural struggle, and the conflict between America and Russia.

The present situation in Europe is dominated by the fact that in the depths the 20th century idea triumphed in the Second World War, and only on the surface did the 19th century ideas of Capitalism, Materialism, nationalism, and yesterday-patriotism prevail. All over Europe, and not alone in Prussia-Germany, the birthplace of the 20th century Idea of Ethical Socialism, the Spirit of the Age is present. There are attempts to confuse it, to distort it, to direct its energy onto false issues. In particular is the technique employed of trying to rouse 19th century national hatred and old-fashioned patriotism, the suicide of Europe. In the first phase of annihilation-wars, all the nations of Europe were the victim of annihilation, and the outer forces were the victor over the whole Civilization. This process cannot be undone. Whatever has once become a fact remains, and forces adaptation to it.

Thus it is, that both for material and spiritual reasons, *nationalism of the 19th century type is dead.* It is dead spiritually for the reason that Europe has reached in its Cultural development the stage of Imperium. Even if there were no such frightful outer threat as exists, this would still govern. But, in addition, the basis of the power of every one of the old Western nations has been destroyed. No single one has sufficient resources, spiritual or material, to engage in world-politics independently. Their only choice is to be vassals collectively, or to form a unity of Culture-State-Nation-Race-People. This creates automatically an economic-political-military unit.

On the other hand Europe can resist the 20th century Prussian-German Idea of Ethical Socialism, and continue the present chaos. The result of this will be the political elimination of the Western Civilization *forever* from the world-struggle. Russia, Japan, or other powers not now in existence, will fight one another for control of the ruins of the West, as the barbarian outsiders waged endless wars for the control of the Egyptian, Babylonian, Chinese, Roman, and Islamic Empires. The purely spiritual and intellectual tasks remaining to our Culture can fulfill themselves under a barbarian domination, but the grandest inward task of all, and the sternest Imperative of the strongest will-power ever known to History, will remain unaccomplished: the creation of the Western Empire.

In every stratum of Europe it must be realized that the unity of the West is something that can only be accomplished on *one* basis. From 1940 to 1944, nearly all Europe was united, and the eventuation of the Second World War showed to the entire world the unity of Europe, for all Europe was defeated, despite the tricky attempt to make some parts of the West feel "victorious." European unity can only be brought about by force, since that is the sole weapon History knows. The way the outer forces defeated Europe is the same way it can be liberated and reunited. Whether this takes the form of civil or international wars is unimportant: the two fronts are the same. On the one side, the Barbarian and the distorter, Chaos and Death, on the other the Spirit of the Age, the Prussian-European Idea.

This Idea is not "national" in the old 19th century sense— this was the propaganda of parasitic elements, and convinced only the sub-Europeans. This Idea cuts straight across the old "national" divisions of the West. It is itself simply the soul, the mission, the ethical form, of a new Nation, a nation whose population and home territory are coterminous with those of the older "nation" formations of the West: Spain, France, Italy, England and Germany. It is no federation, no "customs union," no economic device to maintain Europe at a marginal level of existence sufficient to keep it from revolting against the Barbarian and distorter. It is a *spiritual* unity, and naturally as a result an economic unity. But this spiritual unity would have to occur even though it were economically injurious, for economics no longer motivates History.

Imperium

THE HISTORY of nations in the Western Culture follows a great Triadic development. The Thesis was Western unity, the unity of the Crusades and the period of Empire and Papacy. This continued, in the great essential of preserving this unity *vis-a-vis* the Barbarian, down to the middle of the 18th century. The Antithesis was the period of political nationalism, which accompanied Materialism, and which exercised such a powerful sway that at one time men thought the nations produced Culture, instead of the reverse. Finally the insistence upon nationalism became so great, that some leaders were willing to betray their nations into bondage to extra-Western forces rather than join a united Western organism. The Synthesis is the period of the Future. It exists everywhere in the minds of the Culture-bearing stratum of the West, and for a while it was actualized, in its first crude, provisional, form during the Second World War. It returns to the Thesis, but retains the creations of the Antithesis, for this great Synthesis is not a mere negative. No European "nation" of the older type can any longer, under this new Idea, be the object of any forcible attempt to change or abolish its local characteristics. Considered as a spiritual reality, the Synthesis cannot be spread by physical force.

Not only in the sphere of nations, but in the totality of the life-manifestations of the Western Civilization, the Synthesis penetrates with its new values, its higher imagination, and its new creative powers.

During the progressively radical disuniting of the West, the antagonism of the various Ideas for one another sharpened itself into mania. Trade contested against Authority, the Third Estate against Society, Protestant against Catholic, North against South, England against Spain, France against Spain, England against Prussia, Science against Religion, Rationalism against the Soul, class-war against Authority and Property. The nationalist fever, the worst of all, was spread everywhere by the armies of France under the great Napoleon. The same nationalistic fervor of his troops which gave him his victories on 150 fields communicated itself, since it was the content of the Spirit of the Age. This Spirit infected the entire West, and informed the Spanish resistance and the Prussian rising which finally brought him down.

There was no inner necessity for the horrible denouement of the Age of nationalism, of annihilation-wars. It was not Destiny, but Culture-pathology, that the entire West went down, and that outsiders came in to fight their wars over its soil, and with its blood. Nevertheless it happened, and the gruesome result of the Second World War imposes a new way of thinking upon the entire Culture-bearing stratum of the West. On the contrary, however, there *is* inner necessity in the final passing of the Age of nationalism and annihilation-wars. The great Synthesis, Imperium, replaces it. The Synthesis contains within it the older components of Thesis and Antithesis. The primal

Gothic instincts of the Western Culture are still present in the Imperium-Idea. It cannot be otherwise. Also present are the various Ideas which these instincts, within the framework of this Culture, shaped for itself, the religions, the nations, the philosophies, languages, arts and sciences. But they are present no longer as contrasts, but as mere differences.

Gone—forever gone—is any notion that one of these Ideas—national, linguistic, religious, social—has the mission of wiping out another Idea. The adherents of Empire are still distinct from the adherents of Papacy—but this distinction does not rule their minds, for uppermost now is the Idea of Imperium, the return to superpersonal origins, and both of these mighty Ideas have the same spiritual source. The difference between Protestant and Catholic—once excited into a *casus belli*—has gone the same way. Both continue to exist, but it is inconceivable that this difference could again rend the Western Civilization in twain. There have been also the racial and temperamental differences of Teuton and Latin, of North and South. Once these may have contributed to the furnishing of motives to History—this can they no longer do. Again, both are part of the West, even though different, and the Imperium-Idea monopolizes the motivation of History.

The former nations, the religions, the races, the classes—these are now the building-blocks of the great Imperial structure which is founding itself. Local cultural, social, linguistic, differences remain—it is no necessity of the Imperium-Idea that it annihilate its component Ideas, the collective products of a thousand years of Western history. On the contrary, it affirms them all, in a higher sense it perpetuates them all, but they are in its service, and no longer in the center of History.

Nor is the Idea of Imperium to be confused with any stupid rationalistic doctrine or system, any cowardly millennium. It is not a program, it is no set of demands, no scheme for justice, no juristic quibbling with the concept of national sovereignty. Just as the Future has had always to fight against the entrenched forces of the Past, so must this powerful, universal Idea. Its first phase is the spiritual conquest of the minds and souls of the Culture-bearing stratum of the West. This is entirely inevitable. The next phase is the external actualizing, in a new State-form and Nation-form, of the Idea. In this phase there may be civil wars, perhaps belated "international" wars between former Western nations, possibly Wars of Liberation against the outer forces.

The first phase has already begun, with slow, irresistible rhythm. The other phases must succeed it, whether the last perfection of the Idea in Actuality is reached or not. The Treaty of Fontainebleau, 1763, concluded before his birth, had fateful consequences for Napoleon, against which he struggled, as it developed, in vain. The West has to fight against the legacy of two World Wars, which dethroned Europe, and made it vassal to barbarians and colonials. It must reconquer the world-supremacy which the jealous little opponents of the Hero flung to the winds.

The sole hope of success lies in the intensity and thoroughness of the accomplishment of the first stage, the victory, in the significant minds, of the Imperium-Idea. No force within the Civilization can then resist the Cultural Reunion which will unite North and South, Teuton and Latin, Protestant and Catholic, Prussia, England, Spain, Italy and France, in the tasks now waiting.

II

The employment of military force is for the purpose of combating the Outer, for it is not subject to the Destiny of the West. Every non-Western political organism, by its very existence, denies the West, its Destiny, its Imperative, and its right to physical existence. This struggle for power cannot be evaded.

As already seen, the present situation of the West imposes upon it not only a struggle for power, a fight to keep from passing into slavery to the Barbarian, but also—*a struggle for the continued biological existence of the population of Europe.* There are 100,000,000 too many Europeans for the territory of Europe. These millions are there to carry out the tremendous life-task of the Western organism. Before this, their lives were maintained by the Western monopoly of industry and technics. Two disastrous and stupid World Wars have destroyed this monopoly. The labor of these millions is not wanted. They are facing dispersal, starvation, and slavery. If the present situation continues, this result cannot be evaded. The Persepolis of Europe is beginning to take shape.

Within a century, Berlin, London, Rome, Paris, Madrid can occupy the status of Tenochtitlan, Luxor, Samarra, and Tel-el-Amarna, if the present Conquest of Europe can be maintained. Shall this be?

The spiritual preconditions for the contest have been shown. This entire work has been devoted to setting forth the sole world-outlook and single Inner Imperative which can enter this contest for the liberation of the West. How can the liberated West solve this great task of saving one hundred million Western lives? There is only one solution, and it is the nearest one. The agricultural territory of Russia provides the means of preserving the population of the West, and the necessary base for world-dominion of this Civilization, which alone can save the West from the threat of annihilation by the outer forces. It is thus a military solution—and there is no other. Our commercial-industrial-technical monopoly is gone. Our military technical superiority remains, as does our superior will-power, organization talent, and discipline. The glorious days of 1941 and 1942 show what the West can do against the Barbarian, however superior his numbers. Like Russia, the Western Civilization is situated in the Northeast quadrant. Against the West, therefore, Russia enjoys none of the military advantages it has against America. The common land-frontier enables the West to dispense with a gigantic assemblage of sea-power as a prerequisite to the land-fight. The West will be able to deploy all of its forces on to the plains where the battle for the Future of the West will be fought.

This military solution presupposes a liberated and united Western Culture. Its precondition is the setting free of the Western soul from the domination of traitors and parasites. I set forth here then the two great action-tasks of the Inner Imperative of the West:

First, the liquidation of the tyranny of 19th century ideas. This means the complete cleansing of the Western soul from every form of Materialism, from Rationalism, Equality, social chaos, Communism, Bolshevism, liberalism, Leftism of every variety, Money-worship, democracy, finance-capitalism, the domination of Trade, nationalism, parliamentarism, feminism, race-sterility, weak ideals of "happiness" and the like, of every form of class war. Replacing these ideals is the strong and manly Idea of the Age of Absolute Politics: Authority, Discipline, Faith, Responsibility, Duty, Ethical Socialism, Fertility, Order, State, Hierarchy—the creation of the Empire of the West.

Second, the solution of the immediate Life-problem of the West by conquest on the eastern plains of a base for the further existence and fulfillment of the world-mission of the Western Civilization.

III

Does the situation of the year 1948 allow us even to dream that this grand Imperative can be fulfilled? Millions are starving in Europe as I write, and no one in the outer world concerns himself with it. Other millions are living in a sub-human condition in gaols, concentration-camps, or as an Untouchable caste, devoid of human status. Not only has the West no Army, but its former leaders are in gaol, those who have not yet been hanged. The power in Europe to-day is held by two kinds of men: Cultural aliens, and traitors. Can a Civilization die thus? Will two formless powers be able to strangle a Culture, starve and disperse its population? This work is an expression of my belief that they cannot, that the inscrutable force of Destiny will prevail over outer forces as well as against the inner obstacle of the Past. Precisely at the moment when their victory seems full-blown and permanently secured, Europe begins to stir. Widened and chastened by tragedy, defeat, and catastrophe the Western soul is emerging from the ruins, unbroken in its will, and purer in its spiritual unity than ever before. The great dream and aim of Leibnitz, the uniting of all the States of Europe, is closer by virtue of Europe's defeat, for in that defeat, it perceives its unity. The mission of this generation is the most difficult that has ever faced a Western generation. It must break the terror by which it is held in silence, it must look ahead, it must believe when there is apparently no hope, it must obey even if it means death, it must fight to the end rather than submit. Fortifying it is the knowledge that against the Spirit of Heroism no materialistic force can prevail. Like the men of Aragon and Castile who fought the Moor, like the Teutonic Knights and Prussians who fought the Slav, the men of this generation must fight for the continued existence of the West. Ultimately nothing can defeat them except inner decadence.

The West has something to devote to the contest that neither the Barbarian nor the parasite has: the force of the mightiest superpersonal Destiny that has ever appeared on this earth-ball. This superpersonal Idea has such tremendous force that no number of scaffold-trials or massacres, no heaps of starved or pyramids of skulls, can touch it.

The West has two centuries and tens of millions of lives of the coming generations to give to the war against the Barbarian and the distorter. It has a will which has not only emerged un-broken from the Second World War, but is now more articu-late all over Europe, and is gaining in strength with every year, every decade. Merely material superiority will do them little good in a war whose duration will be measured, if necessary, in centuries. Napoleon knew, and the West still knows, the primacy of the spiritual in warfare. The soil of Europe, ren-dered sacred by the streams of blood which have made it spiritu-ally fertile for a millennium, will once again stream with blood until the barbarians and distorters have been driven out and the Western banner waves on its home soil from Gibraltar to North Cape, and from the rocky promontories of Galway to the Urals.

This is promised, not by human resolves merely, but by a higher Destiny, which cares little whether it is 1950, 2000, or 2050. This Destiny does not tire, nor can it be broken, and its mantle of strength descends upon those in its service.

Was mich nicht umbringt, macht mich stärker.

(What does not destroy me makes me stronger.)

FINIS

Index*

A

Adams, John, 556
Adams, Samuel, 447, 493
Adolf, Gustav, 608
Adrian VI, 341
Agassiz, 70
Alba, 608
Albert, 34
Alembert, 370
Alexander the Great, 60, 269
Alexander VI, 34
Allen, Ethan, 556
American Civil Liberties Union, xvi
Anselm, 35, 262, 410
Aquinas, 34, 147, 262
Aristotle, 34
Arminius, 597
Armstrong, Newton, xvii
Arnold of Brescia, 602
Atahualpa, 602
Attila, 597
Augustine, 34

B

Bach, xxvi, 386, 439, 436
Bacon, 13, 340, 370, 602
Bainbridge, William, 474
Ball, John, 260
Bates, 68
Baudelaire, 308
Bayazid, 410
Beethoven, 254, 366
Bellamy, 81, 240
Bentham, 13
Berkeley, 427
Bernhardi, 566
Bibby, Geoffrey, xxxvii
Biel, Gabriel, 262
Bismarck, 174, 608
Bolivar, 227, 473
Bouillon, 607
Boussuet, 219
Breysig, 32, 36, 245, 518
Bruno, 29, 602
Brutus, 19, 28

* For Subjects treated, see Table of Contents.